How to

Make

Good Choices

in a

Complicated

World

THE
POWER
OF
ETHICS

SUSAN LIAUTAUD

with

LISA SWEETINGHAM

Simon & Schuster
New York London Toronto Sydney New Delhi

Simon & Schuster
1230 Avenue of the Americas
New York, NY 10020

First Simon & Schuster hardcover edition January 2021

SIMON & SCHUSTER and colophon are registered
trademarks of Simon & Schuster, Inc.

For information about special discounts for bulk purchases,
please contact Simon & Schuster Special Sales at
1-866-506-1949 or business@simonandschuster.com.

The Simon & Schuster Speakers Bureau can bring authors to
your live event. For more information or to book an event,
contact the Simon & Schuster Speakers Bureau at
1-866-248-3049 or visit our website at www.simonspeakers.com.

Interior design by Lewelin Polanco

Manufactured in the United States of America

1 3 5 7 9 10 8 6 4 2

Library of Congress Cataloging-in-Publication
Data has been applied for.

ISBN 978-1-9821-3219-4
ISBN 978-1-9821-3221-7 (ebook)

To Luca, Olivia, Parker, Alexa, Cristo, and Bernard:
This is for you.

And for all of you who try hard to make ethical choices:
my deepest admiration and hope that
this book will support you and give you the
courage to create your best stories.

Contents

THE EDGE OF ETHICS

T he young woman was in her early thirties, tall and dark haired, with a direct and unwavering gaze. As she walked down the hall toward me, I could see the deep scars and broken facial bones that had never properly healed. Someone, maybe a partner or family member, had done that to her. I extended my hand in greeting.

It was 1989. I was twenty-six, studying law at Columbia University and leading a student public-interest advocacy group that raised funds and then dispensed small grants to nonprofit organizations. An inspiring local agency that assisted abused women in danger was a potential grantee. We had read about their programs and, if memory serves, that evening we invited this brave woman to come and tell her story.

As she and I neared the door to the classroom where we had all assembled, I paused. "Can you please give me a minute?" I said. "I just want to make sure everyone is ready."

Inside, I looked at our small group gathered and explained that our speaker that evening had suffered more than we would likely be able to understand and more than would be appropriate for us to ask about. I wanted to prepare my classmates for the gravity of her injuries. For the next hour we listened as she recounted her story.

Somewhere between the letter of the law and the enforcement of court orders, the legal system had let her down in a life-threatening way. We learned that her main legal recourse—a restraining order against her abuser—was difficult to obtain until *after* she reported significant physical injuries on several occasions and endured severe emotional distress. Having to prove she had been harmed to obtain legal protection against being harmed: that seemed illogical and unjust to me. I struggled to understand how this could be.

I grew up believing that by and large the rule of law protected and guided us—fairly, effectively, and even compassionately. I was only beginning to understand that even where the law is clear and the courts are accessible, the legal system can still fall short. I also started to see that even where the law does offer protection, it is on all of us to hold ourselves to a higher standard.

I wasn't calling it *ethics* at the time, and I certainly wasn't thinking about a career in ethics, but I was searching for a way to improve the choices we make, individually and collectively.

For many years, my mantra has been: Ethical decision-making tethers us to our humanity—it helps us keep human beings front and center at all times. My sincere hope is that *The Power of Ethics* will enable every reader to make human-centric choices that they can be proud of, both now and in the future.

We find ourselves at a pivotal moment, where the stakes for ethical decision-making are higher than ever. The importance of integrating ethics into our decisions affects all of daily life in the twenty-first century—from whether we follow expert recommendations to protect our own and others' health to our responses when we or a friend stumbles ethically. Our world is one in which ethical errors (and successes) are *amplified*. Misconduct spreads more widely and unpredictably, embeds itself more stubbornly, and entangles more individuals and institutions than ever before. Yet as counterintuitive as it may seem, we actually have more opportunities than ever before to make ethical decisions. To seize these moments, we have to appreciate what drives ethics on the edge.

Although I didn't realize it then, that meeting at Columbia Law School helped define my early thinking about the ethics edge. The edge is the line where the law no longer guides and protects us, leaving ethics as the lone standard by which to gauge our behavior. The edge is dynamic, and the space in which ethics becomes our only guide is expanding. In this zone, people, companies, innovations, and phenomena we may have never imagined would, could, or should intertwine in fact do. For instance, social media can connect us to our families, to friends, to job openings, and to learning about other cultures. It can also be a source of inaccurate medical information, hate-mongering, and bullying that spreads far and wide.

Why does the edge move, and why do unanticipated interconnections occur? First, the law lags behind the fast-moving changes in technology and innovation. Second, we face multiple global and systemic risks—from climate change to the advent of fake news to pandemics. Third, new technologies and global risks join forces to amplify both modern and age-old dangers: Populism and extremism fuel threats to democracy and long-held democratic institutions, and societal ills like racism and sex trafficking emerge in technologically turbo-charged forms.

If we can integrate ethics into our everyday decision-making, we can better think about our place in the world. We can positively affect our relationships and our impact on the society around us. On the other hand, a failure to integrate ethics into our decisions is the most dangerously underestimated global systemic risk we face—whether as individual citizens, leaders, organizations, or nations. It is *the* existential threat at the source of so many others.

∞

I have been teaching ethics courses at Stanford University since 2014. On the first day of my Ethics on the Edge class, I start with one question:

What's the story? What is really going on in the countless dilemmas we see in the news, at work, with our families and friends, and in the world around us? If we don't understand the forces driving ethics failures, we have little chance of preventing and remedying them—and limited ability to create (and inspire) ethics successes.

Then, on the last day of class, I end with one question: What's *your* story? Because I believe the degree to which we integrate ethics into our decision-making and ground it in reality determines our stories and impacts the stories of everyone else whose lives we touch, many of whom we may never meet.

Every day we face challenges with uncertain and long-term consequences: What do you do if you don't like any of the candidates in a major election? Should you share a photo of your child on Facebook? What should you consider before you spit into a vial and send your DNA off for genetic analysis? Should you hire a robot caregiver to help look after your elderly parents? The repercussions are not always easy to see, but the first step is to know what to look for.

Ethical decision-making is not about seeking perfection. Nor is it about assigning blame or criticism. Rather, I hope to give you a positive, deliberate approach to problem-solving—and a strong foundation for resilience and recovery from those inevitable human moments when we and others make mistakes.

This book will arm you with four straightforward steps to tackle any dilemma, which will become a matter of habit. You'll also become conversant with the six forces that drive ethics—what I call Banished Binary, Scattered Power, Contagion, Crumbling Pillars, Blurred Boundaries, and Compromised Truth. These forces are at play in almost every ethical challenge we face: seeking success at work, raising children, engaging in conversations about major stories in the news, navigating tricky friendships, integrating ethics into our spirituality, and more. Recognizing them will quickly become second nature.

I am an ethics realist and an ethics optimist. In these pages I offer what I've learned from decades of study, research, and practice along with my encounters with the many students, clients, colleagues, leaders, and others with whom I've explored these questions.

My goal in writing *The Power of Ethics* is to democratize ethics: Every one of us can make more effective and ethical choices. Every one of us can lend a voice to dilemmas at home, at work, and in society. Let's forge a better world for ourselves and everyone whose lives we touch, now and in the future, with the decisions we make every day.

Chapter One

———

BANISHED BINARY

I t was a cool, clear Sunday morning on March 10, 2019, when Captain Yared Getachew and First Officer Ahmednur Moham-med entered the cockpit of Ethiopian Airlines Flight 302 for a two-hour flight from Addis Ababa Bole International Airport in Ethiopia to Nairobi, Kenya. Captain Getachew, twenty-nine, was a rising star, the youngest-ever captain at Ethiopian Airlines, but already with 8,122 flight hours under his belt and "an excellent flying record." Captain Getachew and First Officer Mohammed, twenty-five, both trained at the Ethiopian Aviation Academy, the largest aviation academy in Africa. The plane they would fly that day was a brand-new Boeing 737 Max 8 jet, the latest model from the world's largest aerospace company and just four months old.

At 8:37 a.m., the control tower gave the pilots permission to take off, and the plane began its roll down the runway, building speed before lifting into the air. There were 157 people from thirty-five nations on board Flight 302. Among the passengers were environmentalists, educators, representatives of nongovernmental organizations (NGOs), traveling retirees, and a mother with her four children (aged nine months to thirty-three years).

According to Ethiopian investigators, shortly after takeoff an alert sounded in the cockpit, warning the pilots that the nose of the jet was 75 degrees above the wind, a perilous angle that had the potential to cause a deadly stall. Suddenly, speed and altitude readings on the left side of the control panel differed from the readings on the right side, and a device known as a "stick shaker" began furiously rattling on the captain's control column, warning that a stall was imminent.

Except, it was a false alarm. The plane was flying perfectly. One of the two angle-of-attack (AOA) sensors on the nose had failed, causing it to set off an automatic anti-stall system. AOA sensors are known to bend, crack, freeze, and sustain damage by bird strikes. The Federal Aviation Administration (FAA), which regulates aviation and aircraft safety in the U.S., had received 216 reports of AOA sensors failing or having to be repaired, replaced, or adjusted since 2004, according to analysis by CNN. While 216 may not seem like a large number, these important safety features are critical to giving pilots situational awareness. Yet Boeing had made a pivotal decision that a single sensor alert was sufficient to trigger the anti-stall system on the Max 8, instead of requiring a second sensor alert as a fail-safe.

The software system, called Maneuvering Characteristics Augmentation System (MCAS), automatically activated when an AOA sensor indicated the plane's nose was drifting too high and in danger of instability. MCAS would adjust the tail of the plane, which in turn would push the nose down. Had Boeing instead required that both AOA sensors needed to be in agreement before MCAS could be activated, it may have prevented the deadly consequences that followed.

When Flight 302 reached an altitude of 8,100 feet, MCAS received the faulty sensor data and forced the jet into a nosedive. Captain Getachew struggled to raise the plane. MCAS automatically forced it down, again and again. The pilots were facing the same chaotic circumstances that befell Lion Air Flight 610, with the same type of Boeing plane, a little over four months earlier in Indonesia. In that crash, the stick shaker vibrated loudly, control readings went awry, an AOA sensor falsely alerted, and for twelve long minutes the bewildered captain was in a tug-of-war with his own plane. Lion Air Flight 610 rose and fell twenty-one times before plunging into the Java Sea, killing all 189 people on board.

After the Lion Air crash, the FAA issued an emergency airworthiness directive, warning pilots that a faulty AOA sensor could activate the automated "nose-down trim" system on the 737 Max 8 and 9 planes. Boeing also issued a bulletin directing pilots' attention to existing procedures for handling erroneous AOA data: They could flip a series of switches on the control panel to power off the system and stop the "nose-down" command. Although MCAS was not mentioned by name, it was the first time pilots learned that such a system even existed on the new 737 Max planes.

First Officer Mohammed flipped the switches that powered down MCAS, as directed. Captain Getachew pulled on his control column to manually lift the nose, but aerodynamic forces acting against the tail of the plane made it impossible. "Pull with me," Captain Getachew told the first officer. Together, they struggled against 180 pounds of force. In desperation, they turned the system back on in an attempt to use electrical power to regain control of the tail. But then MCAS kicked in again. Six minutes after taking off from Addis Ababa, Flight 302 plunged toward a barren field at a speed of 575 miles per hour. The impact was so forceful, rescue helicopters had trouble finding the crash site because the plane was buried thirty-three feet below the surface. No one survived.

The plight of Flight 302 gripped the world's attention not only because of its tragic end but also because of its eerie similarity to the Lion Air crash. There was a pervasive sense of mistrust in the planes and, soon thereafter, in the decision-making processes at Boeing and the FAA.

Boeing's and the FAA's responses to the crisis diverged dramatically from the reactions of governments worldwide—and from reality.

On Monday, March 11, the day after the crash, Boeing released a statement expressing its condolences to the families and loved ones of Flight 302, while also insisting that the 737 Max was a "safe aircraft" to fly. The FAA issued a "Continued Airworthiness Notification," saying that it was examining data, and would take "appropriate action if the data indicates the need to do so," but it did not yet have information "to draw any conclusions or take any actions." However, the two incidents were alarming enough that Ethiopian Airlines immediately grounded its fleet of Max planes, the Civil Aviation Administration of China ordered all ninety-six Max planes in its country grounded, and other airlines and countries quickly followed suit.

By Tuesday, March 12, two days after the crash, the U.K., Germany, France, Australia, Malaysia, and Singapore had banned Max aircraft from flying in their airspace, and airlines in Oman, Norway, and South Korea all grounded their fleets. But not in the United States, where Boeing was, at the time, America's biggest manufacturing exporter. In 2018, Boeing marked a record $100 billion in total revenue. Boeing employed 145,000 people worldwide and did business with thirteen thousand domestic suppliers, including companies like General Electric, the maker of its Max engines.

On Tuesday morning, Boeing chief executive Dennis Muilenburg made a personal call to President Donald Trump to assure the president there was no cause for alarm, that "the MAX aircraft is safe."

Watching the news reports, I was horrified and heartbroken for the victims, their families and loved ones. I also saw this tragedy as a web of failed decision-making and disregard for ethics. In the days following the accident, I continued to be alarmed that the same decision-makers seemed not to take full responsibility for their decisions. Then I turned my focus to *our* decision: When and under what circumstances should we fly on a 737 Max plane? How could we possibly assess the risk? Muilenburg would later tell a reporter that he would "absolutely" take that risk and put his own family on one of the planes. But for me, the answer was absolutely not.

By Wednesday morning, March 13, more than sixty countries had banned the Boeing jets in their airspace. But the FAA had not budged from its position. In a statement posted the evening before, the agency said it was still reviewing data, but had "no basis to order grounding" and no data "that would warrant action."

To be clear: Assessing evidence and data is crucial—both following tragedies like these crashes and for ongoing monitoring of safety risks and new technology. But data was irrelevant to the most critical question that Boeing and the FAA faced after 346 people lost their lives within five months of flying on the same model plane: Should we allow the Max 737 planes to continue to fly or not? The point should not have been to assess averages or estimate the likelihood of events. The only focus should have been on eliminating the potential for loss of life. And there's only one decision that accomplishes this goal: ground the planes. Which is what President Trump ultimately did on Wednesday afternoon, when he directed the FAA to ground the entire 737 Max 8 and Max 9 fleets because "safety" was "of paramount concern."

In the months to follow, investigators would uncover extensive evidence that Boeing had more than safety problems. The 103-year-old American company had lost its way ethically. In a scandal marked by disregard for human life, Boeing hadn't just ignored safety issues or technology errors; it had failed to integrate ethics into the company's decision-making at every level, resulting in a collapse of trust in a much revered institution. Boeing's website at the time stated: "Our stance on ethical business conduct is simple: do the right thing, every time, no exceptions." But exceptions were made again and again, breaking customers' trust, Boeing's most valuable currency.

∞

The Boeing tragedy is a clarion call for our times, a clear marker of the precipitous decline of ethics in our decision-making in recent years, often with grave consequences. Why are ethics more critical than ever? And how do we make good decisions when the law lags behind reality and boundaries are blurred—or what I refer to as "the edge"? The edge is the point at which the law no longer safeguards us, and ethics alone must guide our decisions. Even where the law does operate effectively, it is the lowest common denominator—not the highest or even a sufficiently high standard of behavior. Ethics must operate above and beyond the law.

This chapter introduces the importance of *banishing the binary*, the first of six forces that affect ethical decision-making on the edge. Binary decisions involve a choice between two clear options, like the example of Boeing facing a choice between protecting lives or pursuing profit. But most ethical decisions, especially on the edge, require us to banish the binary, quashing our tendency to oversimplify ethical questions into an exercise in choosing sides: "yes or no," "black or white," or "good or bad." Frequently, we leap to categorize people, behaviors, and actions as "ethical" or "unethical." As you will come to see, this kind of ethics labeling, or shorthand, is not ethical decision-making.

Binary decisions may require in-depth debates about risks and opportunities, such as whether a company should sell drone technology to the government. Or the answers to binary decisions may be straightforward. For example, "Should social media platforms tolerate sex trafficking?" and "Should a teacher allow bullying in the classroom?" are questions that demand a binary answer: No.

But on the edge, we more often encounter ethics challenges that are *non-binary*—those that involve shades of gray and an evolving blend of risks and opportunities on all sides. Since the world around us is changing, with ethical lines blurring, we're often in ethical dilemmas where there are few easy answers. We often must replace questions like *"Should I or shouldn't I . . . ?"* with the more open-ended and realistic question that I asked about Boeing: *"When and under what circumstances should I . . . ?"* Crafting our ethical dilemmas in non-binary terms helps anchor our choices in *reality*. As I tell my students, you can "do ethics" outside of reality all you want, but you will live with the very real consequences.

Most decisions we need to make will be *non-binary*. But I start with Boeing to illustrate that there are still right-or-wrong, yes-or-no choices. Boeing's story is an example of truly *binary* decisions . . . and failed responses. The questions were straightforward. The stakes couldn't have been higher.

Before we begin to examine Boeing's decisions, we need to better understand how the Max plane led to Boeing's fall. It begins in 2010, when its biggest rival, French airplane maker Airbus, announced the launch of a new jet that would burn up to 20 percent less fuel. When Boeing learned that its longtime customer American Airlines was considering purchasing two hundred of the new French planes, the company scrambled to compete.

Building a new plane could take a decade and would require expensive pilot training, so instead Boeing decided to update an existing plane, the 737, with new, fuel-efficient engines. In August 2011, Boeing's board of directors approved a 2017 launch of the reengineered 737 that came to be known as the Max. Before building even began, the company already had 496 orders for its new fuel-saving planes.

Boeing engineers soon discovered that serious problems arise when massive, modern engines are attached to a plane first built in 1967. For one, the 737 sits very low to the ground—there simply wasn't enough room to fit bigger engines under its wings. As a result, they moved the new engines slightly above the wing and farther forward. But that threw off the aerodynamics: When the craft was in full thrust during takeoff, the nose had a tendency to pitch up too high, causing a stall. At first, they explored the idea of changing the shape of the wings or adding small metal vanes to the wings to alter the aerodynamics. When those options didn't work, Boeing developed MCAS as a software workaround. MCAS was originally designed to rely on two inputs: a single AOA sensor and g-force. If the plane's angle-of-attack and g-force were both too high, MCAS would subtly adjust the tail of the plane to push the nose down. But then engineers realized that the plane could experience aerodynamic instability at low speeds, not just high speeds, so they removed g-force as a trigger. This meant a single AOA sensor could now activate MCAS.

The FAA certified MCAS and its single-sensor activation based on an early "system safety analysis" that Boeing had provided the regulators. But subsequently, Boeing engineers made MCAS more powerful and aggressive—without updating FAA certification documents. By the time the planes were delivered to customers, MCAS could move the tail four times farther than originally intended and it could automatically reset itself, pushing the nose down again and again even when a pilot pulled it up. According to testimony from Boeing leadership, flight crew were already trained to deal with something called a "runaway stabilizer"—a scenario that also causes the nose of the plane to drop. Because of this, Boeing management "assumed" that pilots would react to, and solve, an errant MCAS activation the same way: Flip the switches on the control panel and power down the system.

Boeing's flawed assumptions underpinned several missteps. First, the assumptions were based on the fact that in tests, Boeing's veteran pilots were able to recognize a nose-down danger, flip the switches, and take control of the aircraft in four seconds. But the testing didn't take into account chaotic cockpit situations or other potential variables. The National Transportation Safety Board (NTSB) specified in its formal 2019 report that the FAA should develop new design standards and require implementation of onboard diagnostic tools to improve pilot effectiveness. The NTSB also noted that "industry experts generally recognize that an aircraft system should be designed such that the consequences of any human error are limited."

In addition, Boeing (with the FAA's approval) delivered the Max planes (with MCAS activation by a single sensor) with no additional pilot training and no mention of MCAS in the operating manual. Retired Captain Chesley "Sully" Sullenberger, renowned for safely landing a plane on New York's Hudson River in 2009, explained to a congressional subcommittee in June 2019: "Prior to these accidents, I doubt if any U.S. airline pilots were confronted with this scenario in simulator training." He further insisted that pilots shouldn't have to compensate for "inherent flaws" in aircraft design.

Part of the reason for the decision failures lies with the fact that the FAA had increasingly given Boeing more and more authority over the safety certification process. To some extent, it makes sense to involve company engineers. Boeing has the expertise to help the FAA with details it doesn't have the resources or time to manage. Initially, certification engineers were appointed by the FAA, reported directly to their counterparts at the FAA, and were paid by Boeing. But in 2004, the system changed—they were now appointed by, and reporting to, Boeing managers who made the final decision about what was presented to the FAA. These changes gave Boeing managers more power and certification engineers less independence—and Boeing took advantage of these changes in its favor.

Investigations by the *New York Times* and the *Seattle Times* found that Boeing leadership was so obsessed with outpacing Airbus—so focused on speed of production and cost—that its engineers were forced to submit technical plans at "double the normal pace," and managers worked under "tight deadlines and strict budgets." A whistleblower claimed that on three separate occasions the company rejected safety measures that may have prevented the fatal crashes.

Boeing's decision-making process was dismantled in its rush to the finish line, and subsequently as well. In 2017, months after the planes were delivered, Boeing discovered a mistake with the "AOA disagree alert." The disagree alert is a standard feature that tells the pilot when the two AOA sensors have different readings—a signal that one may be broken. The mistake, Boeing discovered, was that the disagree alert in the Max planes had been erroneously linked to a second optional feature, "the AOA indicator," which was a *premium* purchase. This meant that if a carrier didn't buy the premium option, then their disagree alert did not work. Boeing did not notify customers or pilots. Instead, the company decided to wait until the next planned software update in 2020 to fix the error.

The disagree alert could have informed the Lion Air and Ethiopian Airlines pilots that a sensor was broken, potentially helping them to recognize the problem more quickly. But neither carrier had paid for the premium option, so their alert did not work. Approximately 20 percent of all Max customers had purchased the AOA indicator; therefore, only this 20 percent also had the safety feature. Even among the three U.S. carriers that purchased Max planes, American Airlines and Southwest Airlines paid for the premium option, but United Airlines did not.

The Max 8 launched into service in 2017, quickly becoming Boeing's fastest-selling plane in history—a resounding success, until soon after when pilots began to battle with their planes, and those planes fell from the sky. The Max was meant to solidify Boeing's position as the most respected and successful airplane manufacturer in the world. Instead, it shone light on an urgent ethics emergency.

Let's examine three crucial binary decisions Boeing faced.

First, in 2017, executives realized that they had made a safety feature (the AOA disagree alert) a premium option rather than standard. At that point, the question was: Do we disclose and repair, or not?

Boeing took the position that the disagree alert only provided "supplemental information" and was not a safety feature. That may have been the case in older 737 models, but Boeing should have known that the powerful nature of the MCAS system had transformed this alert into a *necessary* safety feature, providing pilots with important information. Boeing didn't disclose or repair the error, deciding instead to fix it three years later in a software update.

Second, after the first plane crashed in Indonesia, the choice was: Do we recall the planes until we are certain of the cause and can repair it and train pilots accordingly, or do we keep the planes in the air? The company not only kept the planes in the air; it also took the unconscionable position that the *pilots* were to blame. "We used an industry-standard assumption on pilots and how they would react," Boeing chief engineer John Hamilton testified at U.S. Senate hearings in October 2019. Because errant MCAS conditions were similar to a runaway stabilizer issue, Boeing leadership assumed the pilots should have known to flip the switches and power MCAS down. But as Captain Sullenberger told Congress earlier that year, pilots deserve to fly aircraft that "do not have inadvertent traps set for them."

Regardless of what pilots should or shouldn't have known, Boeing's faulty software contributed to the deaths of 189 people. This is a binary decision that has a clear answer: Recall the planes—and then repair the safety failures and train the pilots.

The third decision, for both Boeing and the FAA, occurred when the second plane crashed in Ethiopia: Do we allow the planes to continue to fly or not? Instead of grounding the planes, CEO Muilenburg called President Trump to assure him they were safe. Boeing pushed to keep its Max 737 planes in the air and the FAA allowed it—even though more than sixty countries had given them the correct answer.

The Boeing crisis shows that even straightforward binary choices can go awry when we fail to integrate ethics into our decision-making. If we can't get binary questions right even when human life is at stake, then we will have much bigger challenges when the edges get blurrier and we confront non-binary decisions.

On the edge, complex ethical problems by and large require that we focus on banishing binary thinking because it can lead to dig-in-your-heels oversimplified "right" or "wrong" solutions that are not grounded in reality. The issues underlying the unrealistic binary choices that we have seen playing out around the world—such as should the U.K. stay in or leave the European Union (Brexit) and should the U.S. build a wall on its southern border with Mexico—require nuanced problem-solving.

Here's one example of a dilemma that deserves a *non-binary* response, even though it looks like a binary question: Your friend deletes the Uber app on her phone and says you should too, because the company has a history of exploiting drivers and skirting local laws. "Delete or keep" is a binary decision. Banish the binary and, instead, ask: When and under what circumstances would I delete this app? What other factors and people should you consider before following your friend's lead? Maybe Uber is more convenient because you live in an area where it's hard to find a cab. Perhaps you know teachers or single parents who drive for Uber part-time to supplement their income with flexible work. How will they be affected? Ride-sharing companies also help residents in certain urban areas who suffer location discrimination from taxi drivers and are unable to hail a cab. How do these factors affect your decision? Instead of "delete or keep," perhaps you keep the app but only use it when there are no available local cabs, buses, or subways, or when you've been drinking and shouldn't drive.

When we oversimplify ethical dilemmas by immediately taking sides, we miss opportunity and risk. We fail to identify the information that could shape our decisions. We lose sight of the various stakeholders involved, such as teachers and single parents. And we ignore the fact that our actions and the actions of others have potential consequences, such as supporting a company's poor safety record.

We all have the power to banish binary thinking and make good choices with every decision. In 2018, I had the opportunity to interview Emmy Award–winning writer and producer Norman Lear. I'll never forget his message: We often elect not to vote, not to speak up when we see wrongdoing, not to think twice before purchasing a single-use, plastic water bottle. It's human to think that our individual decisions don't make a difference. But, as Lear insists, "We have to know that anything we do *matters*. We all matter."

Our choices matter. They influence our day-to-day habits and relationships, determine the trajectory of our life, and have an impact on other people. They have a cumulative effect. The next story illustrates the power of banishing the binary in ethical decision-making and a non-binary business model.

$$\infty$$

In September 2007, San Francisco roommates Brian Chesky and Joe Gebbia, both twenty-seven, were struggling to pay rent. At the same time, a major design conference was coming to the city and hotel rooms were sold out. Chesky and Gebbia inflated three airbeds in their living room and cooked breakfast for guests at the impromptu lodging they called "Airbed & Breakfast."

A year later, along with cofounder Nate Blecharczyk, they launched Airbnb, an online marketplace for private homeowner "hosts" to make their couches, bedrooms, or entire homes available to "guests" for short-term rentals. Travelers save money on lodging while gaining an opportunity to interact with locals; hosts earn extra income; and Airbnb promotes the properties to prospective guests, handles communications and payments, and allows a host to accept or reject a guest after reviewing their online profile.

Despite initial venture capitalists' doubts that people would let strangers into their homes, by 2020, Airbnb had an estimated worth of approximately $26 billion, with seven million listings—including 14,000 tiny houses, 4,900 castles, and 2,400 tree houses—in 100,000 cities across the globe. And yet, a private home used as a short-term rental—even if it's a castle—is neither a hotel nor strictly a home. Airbnb advanced the edge.

Airbnb is part of the so-called blended economy. Web-based companies like Airbnb connect customers (in this case, travelers) to suppliers (property owners) through the internet. They obviate the need for a section of the hospitality industry, including human intermediaries like travel agents and desk clerks.

At their best, blended economy companies such as Lyft (car rides), TaskRabbit (errands), Turo (rental cars), and Rover (pet sitting) bring us convenient and timely access to the products and services we need. But because they're founded on blended business models, they come with a plethora of often uncharted, ethical decision-making challenges.

On President's Day weekend in 2017, Dyne Suh, a twenty-five-year-old UCLA law school student, traveled to the mountains of Big Bear in California, where she had rented a cabin on Airbnb to share with her fiancé, two friends, and their two dogs for the long holiday weekend.

A month earlier, Suh had booked the cabin for two, but later messaged host Tami Barker to ask if the additional guests and their pets could join. Barker confirmed the changes for an extra $50 a night.

On their way to Big Bear, the group hit a snowstorm that turned their two-hour drive into a harrowing five-hour ordeal of rain, snow, road closures, and flash flood warnings. When Suh texted Barker to let her know that they were finally arriving, Barker wrote back to say she'd never agreed to the additional guests. Suh sent screengrabs of their text messages, thinking Barker had simply forgotten. The reply she received shocked her: "If you think 4 people and 2 dogs [are] getting a room [for] $50 a night on big bear mountain during the busiest weekend of the year. . . . You are insanely high."

Barker canceled the reservation, leaving the students stranded. When Suh threatened to report her to Airbnb, Barker shot back: "Go ahead. I wouldn't rent to u if u were the last person on earth. One word says it all. Asian." Shortly thereafter, she wrote: "I will not allow this country to be told what to do by foreigners."

A local television crew happened to be nearby, covering the storm, and a reporter interviewed Suh about her experience, recording the tearful young woman as she stood helpless in the snow. "I've been here since I was three years old," Suh said. "America is my home. I consider myself an American. But this woman discriminates against me for being Asian. . . . I just feel so hurt."

She wasn't alone. Almost two years earlier, in March 2015, twenty-five-year-old Gregory Selden had a similar experience when he inquired about an Airbnb accommodation in Philadelphia. The host wrote back that it was unavailable. But Selden noticed that the listing remained online as available. Selden, who is Black, created two fake profiles, "Jessie" and "Todd," that included photos of white men. He tried his inquiry again on the same day, and the host approved both Jessie and Todd. Selden later wrote about his experience on Twitter, with the hashtag #airbnbwhileblack, spurring "thousands of retweets from individuals who experienced the exact same disparate treatment from Airbnb host agents, representatives, servants or employees."

In December 2015, *Bloomberg* reported on a working paper from Harvard Business School that found a widespread discrimination problem on Airbnb's platform. Researchers created twenty false Airbnb profiles, "identical in all respects except for guest names." Half had stereotypically Black-sounding names (such as "Lakisha Jones" and "Tyrone Robinson") and half had white-sounding names ("Greg O'Brien" and "Anne Murphy"). Using the impostor accounts, they sent inquiries to approximately 6,400 hosts for properties in Baltimore, Dallas, Los Angeles, St. Louis, and Washington, D.C.

Renters with Black-sounding names were 16 percent less likely to be accepted by hosts compared to renters with white names. Although they had omitted photos in the faux profiles, the researchers determined that Airbnb's platform encouraged racial profiling because hosts can often view a picture and personal details before deciding whether to accept or deny requests.

Imagine if you walked into a motel to inquire about a room, and the desk clerk made you fill out an application and pose for a photo for his boss. He leaves momentarily. When he comes back, he tells you that the boss has rejected your request. This scenario, beautifully analyzed in the *Stanford Law Review* by former student Michael Todisco, is a direct violation of the U.S. Civil Rights Act of 1964, which prohibits discrimination at public lodgings. And yet, it was likely occurring hundreds of times each day on Airbnb, with almost total impunity.

Who bears responsibility for Gregory Selden's and Dyne Suh's experiences? And what is Airbnb's responsibility to prevent and respond to wrongdoing by hosts and guests? It's tempting to condemn Airbnb for a host's racist behavior. But as a new, blended business model, it was dealing with challenges that had never existed before—a non-binary ethical dilemma. Title II of the Civil Rights Act of 1964 specifically forbids "discrimination on the ground of race, color, religion, or national origin." According to the act: "All persons shall be entitled to the full and equal enjoyment of the goods, services, facilities, privileges, advantages, and accommodations of any place of public accommodation." The reference to "accommodations" covers "any inn, hotel, motel, or other establishment which provides lodging to transient guests." But it does not technically cover private homes. Homeowners have the right to control whom they invite into their space. Airbnb hadn't done anything illegal. But illegal is not the appropriate ethical standard.

Creators and innovators (founders like Chesky, Gebbia, and Blecharczyk) and investors in companies have outsized responsibility (though not all the responsibility) for ethical decision-making. Regulation will always lag behind innovation as governments struggle to amend existing laws or add new ones. Citizens and society will always need time to experience and evaluate the opportunities and risks of innovations.

Airbnb's founding mission was to give anyone, anywhere a sense of connection: "We imagine a world you can belong anywhere." (Today, it's very similar: "Create a world where anyone can belong anywhere.") Belonging is an inspiring goal, yet the founders neglected to ask: *When and under what circumstances* might their technology allow for, or even amplify, discrimination on the basis of race or other characteristics?

When might guests who would be legally welcomed in hotels and inns feel unwelcome in Airbnb accommodations? When might they be treated like they *don't* belong?

On the edge, companies must proactively anticipate where the law fails to offer sufficient guidelines for decision-making, and then be willing to do more than the law requires by committing to ethical decision-making. We as consumers, employees, parents, and citizens must do the same.

∞

The framework for ethical decision-making can help us integrate ethics into any decision; it works for individuals, organizations, and governments; and it targets your specific dilemma and circumstances.

To start, the framework disciplines us to avoid oversimplification of edgy questions into binary questions because it generates a nuanced set of considerations rather than "do it" or "don't do it" options. Sometimes, there is one outsized opportunity or risk that quickly leads you to a rare binary "yes or no" answer—such as with Boeing's decision regarding safety or instances of racism. Most often on the edge, our decisions are much grayer, requiring attention to nuance. When you banish the binary and understand the other five forces influencing ethics, you are better prepared to tackle any ethical challenge.

I've road-tested this four-step framework globally with all sizes and sectors of organizations, from multinational corporations and tech start-ups to global NGOs, academic institutions, and hospitals. I have also tested it with individuals, from CEOs and students to journalists grappling with ethically complicated news stories, colleagues from boards on which I serve, subjects of my ethics research, and clients' employees of all levels. Students often describe how they use the framework in their new roles, from a summer internship in a prosecutor's office to a first job at a global bank. Corporate and NGO leaders that I advise use the framework when developing diversity and inclusion policies and guidelines regarding relationships at the office, and to assure that every employee at every level integrates ethics into their decision-making.

The framework can be applied to any decision, whether you're dealing with a professional dilemma (should I quit my job because I disagree with my company's policies?), personal matter (is it time to take the car keys away from an elderly relative?), or navigating how your choices have larger implications (if I purchase this T-shirt, am I harming the environment or contributing to poor working conditions in a foreign country?).

Using the framework also helps you assess and understand the decisions and behavior of others, whether it's the politicians you voted (or didn't vote) for, the leaders of the companies and organizations you're affiliated with, or the public figures whose work you appreciate but whose private behavior is troubling. With practice, applying it becomes a constant and automatic response as you begin to use it for any ethical dilemma.

Four easily recallable steps, and the questions derived from these four words, will keep us focused: *principles*, *information*, *stakeholders*, and *consequences*.

Question #1: What are my guiding principles?

Who are you, as an individual or an organization? What do you stand for?

Our *principles* define our identity and tell the world what to expect from us, as well as how we expect others to behave. Principles apply to ethics choices in all aspects of our lives.

Principles are not fixed rules, like "no chocolate before bedtime" or "no smoking in the break room." They are enduring guides that help us navigate complex problems so that we make consistent choices. This is why it's crucial to establish principles up front and in advance of potential ethical decisions. We don't change our principles, or cherry-pick the most convenient principles, depending on the situation. And an individual's or organization's principles should apply to everyone engaging with them.

Boeing lists Integrity, Quality, Safety, Diversity & Inclusion, Trust & Respect, Corporate Citizenship, and Stakeholder Success among its seven "Enduring Values." On their face, these are laudable principles that seem appropriate for a global corporation with the responsibility for the safety of millions of people every day. Had Boeing leadership applied and respected all their principles, they would have immediately grounded the planes following the first crash, and if not at that time, then after the second crash. They also would have assured that the disagree alert was a mandatory safety feature, not a special option. In other words, Boeing would have been well on their way to integrating ethics into their decisions. Most decisions that are not edgy allow us to respect all our principles.

But Boeing failed to integrate any of these principles into their decisions. In fact, they prioritized profits and competitive advantage over all their principles. In its pursuit of profits, Boeing cut corners, pressured employees, played fast and loose with regulators, and insisted that its planes were safe. Boeing estimated that the Max crisis cost the company $14.6 billion in 2019 alone. Conflicting principles can be exceedingly difficult to resolve. But in this case, the principles should not have been in conflict at all. None needed to be sacrificed to achieve safety. All were sacrificed for greed and market dominance.

In 2015, when Airbnb became aware of challenges brought on by racism among its hosts, their principles were: Be a Host; Champion the Mission; Every Frame Matters; Be a "Cereal" Entrepreneur; Simplify; and Embrace the Adventure.

These are just about impossible to understand and don't do the job principles should. Individually, they do not offer clear guides to decisions and behaviors. Collectively, they don't create an identity for Airbnb. And they don't apply to everyone who engages with the company. Does "Be a Host" apply to the chief financial officer or regulators? Will "Be a 'Cereal' Entrepreneur" (a nod to its early years when the company sold cereal to raise capital) have any meaning for a guest who's just looking for a place to stay?

The framework should never be used to crush or unnecessarily block societally beneficial and useful innovations. But when principles are unclear, the resulting decisions will be inconsistent and create unnecessary conflicts. Airbnb tried to operate in accordance with its principles, but it missed some key standards for achieving the mission of connection and belonging for all guests. Where were principles like "respect" and "diversity and inclusion" as Boeing had? Unlike Boeing, Airbnb's leaders were ethically responsive and committed to enforcing principles that were too unclear to guide their decision-making. As the founders acknowledge, Airbnb's principles could have maximized opportunity while minimizing risks. Behaving respectfully and eradicating discrimination should not impede innovation.

On the edge, principles may conflict because there's often right and wrong, opportunity and risk, on all sides of a decision. Conflicting principles can even break our hearts. For instance, if you see a homeless child in the subway station steal a bag of chips from a kiosk vendor, do you follow your principle of honesty and tell the vendor? Or do you follow your principle of compassion and let him be? A former student, who cited this incident, decided to pay the vendor for the stolen chips—a reasonable way of navigating conflicting principles in the service of solving a problem.

Every year I ask my Stanford students to send me their top seven principles. Some choose personal traits, like honesty and curiosity; others select priorities, such as education and family. I generally recommend that individuals and organizations consider somewhere in the range of five to eight principles.

Once you determine yours and begin to apply the framework, you'll find that they automatically come to mind as you make decisions and evaluate the choices of others. And when your decisions falter, as they occasionally do for all of us, your principles become your first port of call.

STANFORD ETHICS ON THE EDGE CLASS
STUDENT PRINCIPLES 2019—*ranked in order of popularity*

Honesty	Care	Self-awareness	Conviction
Integrity	Optimism	Resilience	Drive
Kindness	Fairness	Wisdom	Education
Compassion	Freedom	Challenge	Individuality
Loyalty	Discipline	Equality	Persistence
Empathy	Perseverance	Learning	Achievement
Authenticity	Justice	Happiness	Good intent
Respect	Intelligence	Efficiency	Be charitable
Responsibility	Dependability	Competency	Be humble
Curiosity	Adaptability	Gratitude	Equity
Accountability	Inclusion	Consistency	Knowledge
Humility	Hard-working	Reliability	Open-mindedness
Dedication	Effort	Openness	Adventurous
Family	Joy	Community	Independence
Autonomy	Generosity	Friendship	
Growth	Humanity	Altruism	

Question #2: Do I have the information I need to make this decision?

And what important information lies in the gap between the information you should *know and the information you* can *know?*

Entrepreneurs increasingly launch new products before we can fully assess the ways they might be used or misused, or before the creators fully comprehend the power and capability of the technologies behind them. We, as consumers, employees, and parents then use these new technologies before fully understanding their opportunities and risks. In between the two, regulators fail to keep pace. The complexity of technology has increased the complexity and unpredictability of *information* we must consider in order to make thoughtful ethical decisions *before* we launch, use, or regulate innovations. Much of the relevant information will be linked to the six forces. Do we want robots diagnosing cancer? Should we permit flying taxis? Should we ban vaping?

Today, there's often a significant gap between the information we have or can access and the information we need to make an ethical decision. How do you mind this gap—the information we don't have but need? You ask questions, listen, observe, examine, verify the influences on your decisions, and then repeat the process often to correct course when information changes. Consider:

- Have you consulted multiple sources and cross-checked your views with others?
- Might new information come to light in the future that would change your understanding in a meaningful way?
- Are you seeking out facts, or hearing and seeing only what you want to hear and see in order to support a prejudged point of view or quick-fix binary answer like "do it" or "don't do it"?

When I gather information, I try to avoid words and phrases such as "assume," "presume," "seems," "took it as a given," "that's gotta be right," "must have," or "my gut tells me," because they can lead to risky shortcuts and bias rather than fact. Guesswork leads to an oversimplified black-or-white response rather than shade-of-gray reality because we never obtain nuanced information.

Sometimes we end up making poor decisions as a result of having insufficient information, and it's helpful to look back at the reasons why. For instance, it could be that:

- You didn't know an important fact and *could not* have known it.
- You didn't know the fact but *could* have known it.
- You didn't know the fact but *should* have known it.

- You knew the fact but were *lying* by claiming not to know it.
- You knew the fact but *ignored* it.

Several of these hark back to Boeing's story.

Boeing had crucial information at pivotal decision points but *ignored* it. For example, in 2016, before the planes were delivered, Boeing's chief technical pilot described MCAS as "running rampant" in simulator testing. In June 2018, four months before the first crash, Boeing learned that if a pilot took more than ten seconds to properly react to an MCAS malfunction, the result could be "catastrophic." Yet in October 2019, on the one-year anniversary of the Lion Air crash, and after the Ethiopian Airlines crash, CEO Dennis Muilenburg testified to the U.S. Senate, "If back then we knew everything that we know now, we would have made a different decision." Boeing did have knowledge. But rather than taking responsibility for their failure to act on it, they placed part of the blame on the pilots.

In addition, it's unlikely that the Lion Air pilots had sufficient knowledge of the risks: that the disagree alert was not functional, that MCAS existed, and that a single broken AOA sensor would activate this powerful anti-stall system—facts they needed to avert tragedy. Boeing withheld information from pilots. When we ignore and withhold information, we do so at our own and others' peril.

Now let's look at what Airbnb's three founders actually knew—and what they *could* or *should* have known when they set out to match hosts with travelers. In July 2016, CEO Brian Chesky acknowledged that racism wasn't on their minds when they founded the company. "There were lots of things we didn't think about when we, as three white guys, designed the platform," Chesky admitted. Airbnb's blended business model comprises two parts: the internet and hospitality. It should have been clear to the founders that both elements (individually and together) had a risk of racism. Racism infiltrates online exchanges. For example, one in four Black individuals has suffered harassment online because of race, according to Pew Research in 2017. Additionally, it is widely known that hotels and their managers and employees have historically discriminated on the basis of race. Even if the specific antidiscrimination laws were not front of mind to Airbnb, the risk of racism infiltrating their platform through hosts and guests should have been. Given the combination of the extensive and persistent racially charged content online and known racism in the hospitality industry, Airbnb's founders *should have known* (or at least *could have known*) that discrimination was a concern in a blended hotel and online business model.

Looking at the component parts of a blended business model through the framework allows one to ask "What more should (or could) I know?" The framework could have helped Airbnb's founders select more effective principles, which in turn would have helped them see the relevant information. Principles of inclusion and diversity, for instance, would have spurred the founders to seek evidence and risk of discrimination as they assessed information.

Question #3: Who or what stakeholders matter to my decision?

Who or what could influence, or be affected by, your decision?

I define a *stakeholder* as any person, organization, object, or factor that could influence, or be affected by, a decision or situation. We often think stakeholders are only human beings, but stakeholders can also be inanimate objects if they have an impact on (or are impacted by) our choices. Even the digital assistant in your kitchen is a stakeholder if it gives you information ("It's 35 degrees Fahrenheit outside") that influences your decisions (*I should put on a coat*). Stakeholders can be a company, a policy, an algorithm, a chat bot, a test score, fake news, an edited gene, a government organization, and more. They can make positive or negative contributions to your decisions, and you can affect them positively or negatively.

In Boeing's case, decisions made at many stages of the 737 Max tragedies had ripple effects on a wide array of stakeholders that, at minimum, included: Boeing employees, executives, and shareholders; Boeing's suppliers and their employees; the commercial carriers that grounded planes and canceled flights; aircraft crews around the world, including the Southwest Airlines pilots suing Boeing for lost compensation; rival Airbus, which delivered twice the number of commercial aircraft as Boeing in 2019; the many businesses that rely on Boeing planes for travel; the FAA, diminishing in standing as a global safety leader; other industries developing automation technologies that are now looking to this tragedy for lessons to be learned; and, of course, the 346 victims, their loved ones, and people they've never even met who will be affected by their deaths.

We are never the only stakeholder in our decisions. Our decisions are never just our own. They affect many people and things—some of which we are not aware at the time of the decisions and may never know about. On the edge, identifying *all* the actual and potential stakeholders can be challenging, maybe even impossible. Airbnb, at the time of this writing, serves an average of two million guests per night in 220 countries and regions around the world. And that's before you consider the hosts, their families and neighbors, the businesses affected by Airbnb, the regulators involved (or not), the tax consequences, and more.

How do we begin to identify all the stakeholders? We can start with those most directly affected by, or affecting, the outcome (such as an ineffective regulator) or those who suffer serious risks (such as airplane passengers). When we cannot identify the individuals, we can consider categories of stakeholders (such as employees of Boeing suppliers or Airbnb hosts). As we will see in Chapter 2, at times on the edge we cannot even imagine who the stakeholders could be because we cannot envision the potential uses or misuses of a technology or the human responses to situations.

Question #4: What are the potential consequences
of my decision in the short, medium, and long term?

Have you considered the immediate and future impact
of your decision at the time of the decision?

The framework requires us to a look at the short-, medium-, and long-term *consequences* of our decisions *at the time* they are being made. We should then do regular framework check-ins, so we can monitor consequences *over time* and keep up with evolving developments.

For example, after the first 737 Max 8 crash, the FAA determined that there was a *high likelihood* of a similar MCAS emergency within months. The alarms should have been blaring. Instead, Boeing promised the FAA that it would create a software patch for MCAS. The fix was still forthcoming when the second plane went down. At that point, the FAA should have known that another crash was a potential consequence; as noted earlier, additional data was not relevant to the question of whether or not to ground the fleet.

A senior FAA official would later testify before the Senate that "from the safety perspective, we felt strongly that what we did was adequate." But the FAA had increasingly depended on Boeing to assess and certify safety, so status-quo adequate was not enough. On the contrary. When considering the ethics of the possible consequences of their decisions, here is what the FAA and Boeing should have asked— and here are the three immediate questions that will help you quickly assess the consequences of your own decisions:

- What potential consequences of this decision are both *irreparable and important*?
- What opportunity for doing good might be lost?
- How would I feel if I were directly affected by the decision?

If the FAA and Boeing had considered the first question, the decision would have been clear: Given the specific circumstances, a software engineers, data scientists, researchers, and designers with a mission to identify and stamp out bias on the platform.

Airbnb could have deflected (*It's not our responsibility what people do on our platform*), or turned a complex ethical dilemma into an over-simplified, binary judgment ("pilot error" vs. "our error"), but instead it collected more information, kept the gaps in mind, and acted on them. The following year, when Dyne Suh and her friends found themselves stranded in the snowy mountains in early 2017, Airbnb quickly responded: It gave Suh a full refund, offered to reimburse her group for a hotel, and stripped Barker of her host status.

Suh, for her part, was also a stakeholder in this scenario. She took on that responsibility by telling her story to the media and filing a complaint with California's fair housing agency, which ultimately reached an agreement with Barker to pay $5,000 in damages, issue a personal apology to Suh, take a college-level course in Asian American studies, and perform volunteer service at a civil rights organization, among other requirements.

Chesky demonstrated his ability to continually reassess information and consider the stakeholders and consequences of Airbnb's decisions. Two years later, in 2019, a Halloween party at an Airbnb rental in the suburbs of Northern California turned into the scene of a deadly shooting. Chesky announced that they were creating a 24/7, worldwide "neighbor hotline"; they would also begin personally verifying every one of its seven million listings for accuracy, quality, and safety; they would conduct rigorous reviews of high-risk reservations; and stop unauthorized parties before they begin. In minding the gap, he was fortifying trust.

"Our real innovation is not allowing people to book a home; it's designing a framework to allow millions of people to trust one another. . . . We intend to do everything possible to learn from these incidents when they occur," Chesky said.

When they figured out they had a problem, Airbnb leadership didn't deflect responsibility or promise a software patch, they made

potential loss of human life is an unacceptable potential conseque
They didn't even need to go on to the other two questions.

In the aftermath of the Boeing tragedy, after worldwide grou
ings, and a tremendous loss of reputation, Boeing CEO Muilenl
promised Congress that it was installing software updates, provi(
new training, strengthening safety culture, and other changes tha
said would make its "safe airplanes even safer." But these planes v
not safe to begin with. If Boeing's leadership refuses to acknowl(
this fundamental problem, then how can anyone trust decisions
the company makes?

Allocating responsibility among stakeholders is the next step a
properly applying the framework. This is where Airbnb's story o1
a laudable counter to Boeing because the leaders assumed respons
ity. In 2016, after Gregory Selden's experience and after the Har\
study, CEO Brian Chesky apologized for not responding more qui(
and called discrimination "the greatest challenge we face as a c
pany. It cuts to the core of who we are and the values that we st
for." Airbnb began its own internal investigation into racial profi
on its platform and launched a comprehensive antidiscrimina
effort. It added a "Community Commitment" pledge that all h
were required to sign, promising to "treat everyone in the Air
community—regardless of their race, religion, national origin, eth
ity, disability, sex, gender identity, sexual orientation, or age—v
respect, and without judgment or bias."

Leadership also committed to a multi-stakeholder solution. To
view the platform and devise antibias training for hosts, Airbnb h
highly respected expert advisors from government, academia, and
law. The company met with different groups to solicit a variety of vi
points: employees, hosts, city officials, government agencies, tour
companies, civil rights groups, and Airbnb users who were previou
targets of discrimination. The company also assembled a team

thoughtful changes that fortified trust. Boeing can repair its planes, and it can even fire its CEO. But repairing trust is a far greater challenge.

"Many of us in this industry over the last ten years are going from a hands-off model, where the internet is an immune system, to realizing that's not really enough," Airbnb's Chesky said. "We have to take more responsibility for the stuff on our platform."

All of us—from test pilots and FAA auditors to Airbnb hosts, guests, and software developers, to you and me—have the power and the responsibility to use our voices and take actions that prevent further harm. Recognize the hazards of binary thinking in a gray world. Apply the four steps of the framework for every ethical dilemma. Everything you do *matters*.

Chapter Two

———

SCATTERED POWER

W hen Delaney Van Riper was a child, she was bubbly and full of energy, but her father noticed that she walked primarily on her tiptoes. As a genetic counselor, AJ Van Riper knew this could be the first sign of a genetic disorder. His fears were confirmed when, at age seven, Delaney was diagnosed with Charcot-Marie-Tooth (CMT), a disease that, while not fatal, has no cure. It would eventually cause his daughter's ligaments to tighten, and her limbs and muscles to slowly atrophy and weaken.

As a child, Delaney wore leg braces that made her feel "unique" among her peers. But by the time she was a teenager, her physical differences were frustrating and emotionally painful. Then in 2017, during her senior year of high school, she received an email from the laboratory of Dr. Bruce Conklin, a senior investigator at the Gladstone Institutes (a nonprofit biomedical research center affiliated with UC San Francisco, where he is a professor). Dr. Conklin was seeking volunteers to participate in scientific research that could potentially be life-changing. In fact, he and his team were investigating the development of a cure for people with Delaney's exact type of CMT, using a new gene-editing technology called CRISPR-Cas9.

In 1987, a team of Japanese scientists studying E. coli bacteria reported finding "an unusual structure"—repeated sequences of DNA that had not been seen before. Over the next twenty-five years, research exploded on these "clustered regularly interspaced short palindromic repeats," or CRISPR. Scientists discovered that CRISPR was akin to a genetic defense system that, in conjunction with a protein called Cas9, acted like a pair of molecular scissors, detecting foreign DNA viruses and then cutting out the unwanted invaders. In 2012, a team of scientists led by UC Berkeley professor Dr. Jennifer Doudna and Dr. Emmanuelle Charpentier, a director at the Max Planck Institute in Berlin, published groundbreaking research showing how CRISPR-Cas9 could be used in the lab to snip, repair, and alter genes in any organism's DNA.

Dr. Doudna, also a senior investigator at the Gladstone Institutes, credits her colleague Dr. Conklin with coining the phrase "genome surgery" to describe how CRISPR works. Just as a doctor uses surgical tools to remove tumors and repair organs, genome surgeons use CRISPR tools to remove or repair specific genes within a cell. Another way to think of it: Picture a giant book, 6.4 billion letters long, representing the human genome. Scientists can use CRISPR to find a single typo in that book, cut it, and paste in the correct letter. But they can also use it to *change* the book. CRISPR can make "precise changes to the code of life," Doudna says. "It means that we can control human evolution now. We can control, essentially, anything that is alive."

Delaney accepted the invitation to take part in the CRISPR study and made a visit to Conklin's lab. In early 2020, we spoke on the phone. Delaney told me that her participation in the study required little more than giving the researchers a couple vials of blood. (She also signed a consent form allowing them to use her blood to study other diseases.) From her samples, researchers isolated her blood cells and slowly coaxed them into becoming induced pluripotent stem cells—or primitive cells that can be differentiated into any other kind of cell. The scientists would work to convert Delaney's cells into the exact type of nerve cells that contain her genetic mutation. From there, they can use

CRISPR tools to cut out the flawed genetic material, in the hope of one day injecting the improved nerve cells back into Delaney's spine and muscles to alleviate her symptoms.

As Delaney explained it to me, she learned that it is much easier to cut unwanted material than to add new genetic material. "Genes have two strands—the famous double helix," she says. "In my case, one strand is healthy, and one isn't. I don't need the unhealthy strand for cell reproduction." Put another way, how she says her father describes it: "If you buy wood to build a house from two factories, and one sells good wood and one sells rotten wood, you cut out the rotten vendor and you buy wood only from the good factory, and you can still build the house."

Three years after Delaney joined Conklin's study at the Gladstone Institutes, Dr. Conklin and I spoke over the phone. He told me that they chose to work on the specific type of CMT that Delaney has because "we thought that it was one of the most likely to be treatable of the 6,000 disease genes" that science has identified in humans. "In the last three years," he said, "continued progress in CRISPR technology has only increased our hopes that this will work." He cautioned that developing a CMT treatment will take years, with many technical hurdles that still need to be overcome. But because Delaney's disease progresses slowly, he is optimistic that he has time to conduct the research properly. In fact, Dr. Conklin considers a cure "very promising" and likens it to scaling Mount Kilimanjaro—hard but achievable. "Nothing in experimental medicine is one hundred percent sure . . . that is why we call it an experiment," he says. "But I am very confident that we can reach our goals."

In the meantime, Delaney says her confidence and ease has grown as she continues to contribute to the science and educate herself. When I asked her if she had any thoughts about how other people might approach gene therapies—whether as a potential patient, research subject, or to develop an opinion—I was impressed by her answer. Delaney says that the two most important questions we should ask ourselves include: First, why do you want to do it—what values are driving you? And second, what effect could it have on other people? In framework terms, she is asking us to consider our principles, as well as the stakeholders and consequences.

In a recent essay for the Gladstone Institutes blog, Delaney wrote that the opportunity to be a part of Dr. Conklin's research gives her "one of the most dangerously wonderful gifts: hope. Hope that I could be cured. Hope that I could live as a normal person. And if not hope for me, then hope for someone else."

CRISPR is an extraordinarily powerful agent of scattered power—for good or for ill. Scattered power, the second force driving ethical decision-making, refers to the indiscriminate distribution of power to do good or inflict harm.

Delaney's story depicts the hopeful and ethically diligent side of how CRISPR technology can potentially impact life. CRISPR scatters power for good, as scientists and innovators use it in their pursuit of treatments for the millions of people who suffer from heart disease, cancer, Alzheimer's, muscular dystrophy, cystic fibrosis, blindness, and a multitude of other illnesses. More broadly, CRISPR arms humans with a power that we have only imagined until now. Labs around the world are actively using the technology to make mosquitoes malaria-resistant, to create more resilient breeds of corn and wheat, and even to build a woolly mammoth out of Asian elephant DNA. The possibilities are vast.

But agents like CRISPR also disperse unprecedented, humanity-defining power more quickly, globally, and unpredictably than ever before. And that power is being spread to numerous actors who can deploy it without legal oversight, professional codes (such as the Hippocratic oath), accountability to institutional leadership, or any commitment to enforceable principles that serve and protect society.

The force of scattered power and its impact on ethical decision-making will be seen through two additional stories: One involves a high-risk and ethically criticized use of CRISPR, and the other explores how 3D-printing technologies are being literally weaponized. Then we'll delve into some of the surprising challenges we face in allocating the responsibility for the ethics of scattered power.

The starting point is that power is no longer just in the hands of CEOs and heads of state. Power is a shell game on the edge: We don't know where it is, who has it, how much they have, or how they will use it. Power now belongs to terrorists who use their smartphones to recruit followers; it's in the hands of Russian propagandists who misuse social media to confuse and discourage people from voting; it resides with software engineers who write the algorithms for streaming services and websites that invade our privacy and collect data about our habits. Even the many well-meaning contributors to the development and distribution of technology don't necessarily recognize how they could be scattering power and potentially causing serious ethical fallout.

CRISPR and other technologies on the edge present us with ethical dilemmas that are non-binary. And while gene editing is not a "do it" or "don't do it" decision, there is one clear binary-threshold distinction between the two different categories of gene-editing therapies. Somatic therapies, like what Delaney hopes for, make changes to a patient's nonreproductive cells, only affecting that patient but not their future offspring. CRISPR pioneer Doudna supports using CRISPR for somatic therapies in both children and adults, because the genetic consequences do not extend beyond the individual.

In contrast, germline therapies are a second category of gene editing that target the DNA in embryos, sperm, and eggs, making changes that not only impact the patient's disease but also can be passed down to future generations. Germline editing holds grave and unknown risks. Because of that, many in the scientific community agree that CRISPR is unacceptable for editing the human germline. As of this writing, approximately thirty nations, including the United States and many countries in Europe, have enacted restrictions or even outright bans on human germline editing.

When I asked Dr. Conklin what two risks the public should be most concerned about with regard to CRISPR, he said we should be wary of unscrupulous and unregulated gene-editing clinics that may try to sell us unproven promises of cures for deadly diseases. These clinics risk patients' physical and mental health. They also potentially skew research results if the placebo effect of the promise of a cure actually produces a positive outcome despite the inefficacy of the treatment.

He was also concerned about how CRISPR might be used as a way to craft so-called designer babies with a method known as pre-implantation genetic diagnosis, or PGD. According to a study in the *Journal of Assisted Reproduction and Genetics*, over 75 percent of fertility clinics in the U.S. offer PGD. The technique, as described by the American Society for Reproductive Medicine, is used in combination with in vitro fertilization (IVF) and involves genetically testing a couple's IVF-generated embryos at just a few days old. Parents may then choose to only implant the embryos that test negative for a genetic mutation, or ones that are carriers of the disease but will not develop it.

For parents who carry serious genetic mutations, PGD can help them avoid passing on to their children conditions such as Duchenne muscular dystrophy, Tay-Sachs, and sickle cell anemia. But as Dr. Conklin notes, CRISPR combined with PGD sends us toward a slippery slope of being able to potentially manipulate our progeny's genetic traits—such as height, eye color, athleticism, or intelligence. Conklin's urgent warnings speak to the impact of scattered power: Imagine a world in which each parent gets to custom-design their child without societal control over these decisions.

This is a major hallmark of scattered power: It is ungovernable because it is widely accessible and largely undetectable. Regulation can't stop power from scattering because the law lags too far behind the technology; it's hard to detect who is wielding the power, even after the consequences are apparent; and the technology is often accessible to nonexperts and individuals with limited budgets and equipment.

Most importantly, as the next story demonstrates, scattered power is delinked from even a common human view of the very importance of ethics.

∞

In June 2017, a thirty-three-year-old biophysicist named He Jiankui sat down in a conference room at the Southern University of Science and Technology in Shenzhen, China. Across from him were two Chinese couples hoping to become parents. They had unique challenges: The men were HIV positive.

According to an investigative series in the journal *Science*, as well as video of the meeting that *Science* reporter Jon Cohen reviewed, the couples were specifically recruited because the men had been able to manage their infections with antiviral drugs. Passing HIV down to their future children was not their concern, because sperm-washing during IVF had progressed to the point where the virus can be reliably removed before insemination. Rather, these couples wanted to ensure that their own children *never contracted* HIV—that they never had to endure the same pain and discrimination that they'd suffered. Dr. He, a highly accomplished, U.S.-educated scientist, offered them a chance to take part in a scientific experiment that could virtually eliminate that risk.

According to He's listing in the Chinese Clinical Trials Registry, he was actively seeking out married heterosexual Chinese couples, between the ages of twenty-two to thirty-eight, in which only the man was HIV positive, in order to "obtain healthy children to avoid HIV, providing new insights for the future elimination of major genetic diseases in early human embryos."

Dr. He provided couples with consent forms (also obtained by *Science*), which stated, "The main objective of this project is to produce infants who have the ability to immunize against HIV-1 virus." But what was missing in the consent process was the full scope and potential consequences of He's plan. For example, the consent form mentioned the possibility that there could be "off-target" effects—unwanted and unintended DNA mutations—at "sites other than the intended target." The form also included a disclaimer of the research team's responsibility for risks of such occurrences. (The consent form even provided for He's team to retain the rights to, and publicize, baby photos on the day of birth.) What ordinary, well-meaning parent could possibly understand the types and likelihood of the risks?

The two couples in the meeting in Shenzhen would eventually become part of a group of eight hopeful couples that Dr. He recruited by September 2017. These couples would take part in what appeared to be the world's first-ever experiment to create HIV-resistant babies using IVF and CRISPR-Cas9. Over the next year, He would use CRISPR to reproduce a genetic mutation called CCR5-delta 32 in the volunteer couples' fertilized embryos. CCR5-delta 32 is a defect that has been known to provide HIV resistance among people who naturally carry it. Dr. He wanted to craft that same mutation in the couples' offspring. When the IVF-generated embryos were several days old, a few cells were checked with PGD to be sure the genetic alteration had been successful before implanting the embryos in their respective mothers.

We cannot know what was in He's heart and mind, but emails and documents examined by reputable media sources indicate that Dr. He was on an ambitious path to show the world how to use CRISPR to create HIV-resistant humans, and then do the same thing for genes linked to cardiovascular disease, cystic fibrosis, and other conditions. *Science* reviewed He's medical ethics application, which he claimed had been approved by a hospital in China. In it, Dr. He wrote: "This is going to be a great science and medicine achievement ever since the IVF technology which was awarded the Nobel Prize in 2010, and will also bring hope to numerous genetic disease patients." The hospital later claimed that the approval signatures on the application had been forged.

Without knowing the full extent of what Dr. He told the hospital, or how they processed the information, I would not presume to assess their oversight protocols. But the fact is that regardless of the Chinese hospital's involvement, it should have been clear to Dr. He that his proposed actions crossed widely accepted ethical lines. Reputable scientists had discouraged him from these experiments or warned him to proceed with caution. Further, human germline editing was illegal in much of Europe and prohibited in the United States. In their article in *The Lancet*, researchers from the Chinese Academy of Medical Sciences pointed out that the Chinese government specifically prohibits "the genetic manipulation of human gametes, zygotes, and embryos for reproductive purposes," as stated in its 2003 "Guiding Principles of Ethics for Human Embryonic Stem Cell Research." So it appears that there was adequate knowledge and general professional and legal consensus that He should not be pursuing this irresponsible experimentation on human embryos.

Dr. He exemplifies the stealth rogue actor. His work, for example, occurred at a large university lab and two different hospitals, yet he was still able to act in secret. As *The Atlantic* and the *Wall Street Journal* reported, the IVF doctor who implanted the embryos didn't know they'd been germline edited; the hospital where the mothers were to give birth didn't know of Dr. He's plans; Dr. He even falsified the fathers' blood tests to be sure the hospital wouldn't discover their HIV status. But soon, everyone would learn of Dr. He's work.

By April 2018, one of the eight couples in the study was pregnant with twins. Tests showed that one twin had both copies of the CCR5 gene, meaning the procedure had worked with that fetus, while the other had just one mutated gene, and it was unclear if that twin was HIV-resistant.

Dr. He felt flush with "success," as he described it in an email to a mentor. In August, he met with a fertility doctor in New York City to discuss the potential of opening a CRISPR gene-editing clinic together in China for couples hoping to become parents. He also hired an American public relations specialist who helped him form a plan to first publish a study in a reputable medical journal before announcing the twins' births. But his plans did not go as he had hoped.

In October 2018, twin girls, the world's first gene-edited babies, were born via cesarean section. Dr. He kept his secret under wraps until November 25, when *MIT Technology Review* broke the news; the Associated Press published a story the next day. Both articles included very critical viewpoints of He's work from scientists in the field. In response, and to wrest back control of the narrative, He posted a series of YouTube videos announcing the birth of "Lulu" and "Nana," to parents "Mark" and "Grace." (Dr. He gave them these pseudonyms to maintain their privacy.) He said they were as "healthy as any other babies." "As a father of two girls," Dr. He said, "I can't think of a gift more beautiful and wholesome for society than giving another couple the chance to start a loving family."

On November 28, 2018, Dr. He attended the Second International Summit on Human Genome Editing in Hong Kong, a conference sponsored by major global institutions (including the U.S. National Academy of Sciences, the Royal Society of the United Kingdom, and the Academy of Sciences of Hong Kong) and featuring Dr. Doudna and other pioneering speakers. It was there that Dr. He told a packed crowd that he was "proud" of his work, and that another woman had already been implanted with a gene-edited embryo—a third CRISPR baby.

The scientific community was outraged. Summit organizers denounced He's work as an experiment that was "misguided, premature, unnecessary and largely useless." The National Institutes of Health, which oversees medical research in the U.S., called the medical necessity of the work "utterly unconvincing" and the informed consent "highly questionable." Doudna said she was "horrified." It was "inconceivable," she said, why He would use CRISPR, "an experimental technology that's never been tested in humans before," when there were already "safe and effective" ways of avoiding passing HIV from parents to children.

It's important to pause here and consider the importance of Dr. Doudna's observation as we test the ethical legitimacy of unprecedented uses of power. We must always ask whether there are less risky and/or more beneficial *alternatives.* We are then responsible for choosing the most appropriate alternative or, on occasion, slamming on the brakes until science and robust ethics discussions can gain further insight.

As one researcher pointed out: Dr. He did not "correct a disease-causing genetic variant to save a life . . . [he] destroyed a normal gene . . . in an otherwise *healthy* embryo." CRISPR can create unpredictable "off-target" edits elsewhere in the genome, potentially causing cancer or other unintended problems.

Scientists who studied the notes He projected at the Genome Summit told *Science* that both babies appear to exhibit mosaicism, which means that the CRISPR process likely edited some of the embryo's cells differently from others or even failed to edit them at all. In sum, it is impossible to know if they truly are HIV-resistant.

Shortly after the Hong Kong summit, Dr. He disappeared from public view and did not respond to media. Chinese authorities suspended his research and placed him on house arrest. Southern University of Science and Technology fired him from his teaching position.

In December 2019, China's state-run news, Xinhua, reported that Dr. He and two medical researchers had been tried in a closed courtroom proceeding and had pleaded guilty to violating the 2003 guideline on gene-editing technologies. Dr. He was sentenced to three years in prison, given a 3 million yuan ($430,000) fine, and a lifetime ban from working in reproductive technology. The court reportedly condemned He Jiankui's pursuit of "fame and profit." The court also announced that the second mother had given birth to a third gene-edited baby but did not say when. No other information about the child was provided.

He's actions with these children showed utter disregard for global discussions within the scientific and expert ethics communities. His actions are precisely the kinds of issues about which we need a broad global debate involving nonexperts. He played God with the babies' lives, altering their DNA in ways that will be passed down for generations to come. And we have no way to determine what the consequences will be, or who the stakeholders will be: not only Lulu's and Nana's descendants, their families, and communities, but also you, me, and all of humanity.

This is an extreme example of scattered power, with all the undetectable, ungovernable, inexpensive, and accessible hallmarks. Dr. He did not need millions of dollars in technology, the backing of pharmaceutical companies, or the sanctioning of his government to alter the human germline. And the decreasing cost of the technology combined with increased access to technological know-how and materials will only contribute to this unchecked threat.

Today, for example, various types of kits promising gene-editing capability are available for purchase online on websites that are open to the general public. The specifics of what these kits do, how dangerous they are, and how they could lead to major risks such as the creation of a biological weapon are outside my expertise. Some experts suggest that the current risk is low.

I would argue that the point is not that the risk is slim *today*. We must consider the *potential* short-, medium-, and long-term consequences *over time* of making these sorts of technologies widely available. These kits are difficult to manage because we don't know who is using them and how. And whether or not these kits become just as easy to use as the alternative methods for inflicting significant harm, the potential exists for the proliferation and empowerment of these tools, with unknown consequences. The risk needs to be managed in parallel with other risks, not postponed until harm is done.

He Jiankui was able to alter humanity, one baby at a time.

His actions are a red flag that power detached from ethics can literally alter humanity as we know it in dangerous ways. But as Dr. Conklin's research shows, we ignore the potential for lifesaving benefits of these power-scattering technologies at our peril.

Other forms of scattered power that require even less scientific know-how and materials have the potential to harm untold numbers of people.

∞

In July 2012, Cody Wilson, a twenty-four-year-old law student at the University of Texas, posted a fundraising video to YouTube, asking for donations to fulfill a dream. To make the film, which has been viewed more than a million times, Wilson sat alone in a sterile, white room filled with computers and technical manuals, looking directly into the camera.

"A group of friends and I have decided to band together under a collective name," Wilson's pitch began. "We're not a company, we're not a corporation, we're not even a business association of any kind. We just call ourselves Defense Distributed, and we want to share with you an idea." Their idea would scatter power without institutional checks and balances or oversight.

They wanted to develop the world's first 3D-printed gun, and with a little bit of help—only about $20,000—they could pull it off. "The product isn't our emphasis," Wilson said, "what we're interested in producing is a digital file . . . to be shared across the internet."

For eight minutes, a heart-quickening jazz loop played in low tones as Wilson monologued about his vision to give anyone anywhere the power to make a gun, one that "only needs to be lethal once; I mean that's the idea, right?" He spoke with a calm, cool authority, as if preaching to an invisible choir: "This is an idea whose time has come. . . . We hope that the idea is stolen. We hope that the file itself is manipulated and changed and improved."

"We've now crossed the threshold," Wilson continued. "We will have the reality of a weapon system that can be printed out from your desk. Anywhere there's a computer, there's a weapon." The choir was listening. Defense Distributed reached its fundraising goal in just two months. Later that year, *Wired* named Wilson among the "15 Most Dangerous People in the World," a list that also included Sinaloa cartel kingpin Joaquín "El Chapo" Guzmán and Syrian president Bashar al-Assad.

In May 2013, Wilson became the first person to create and successfully fire a fully 3D-printed gun, which he dubbed the Liberator. He posted a video of himself online and posted the blueprints on his file-sharing website. In two days, the blueprints were downloaded more than 100,000 times, allowing Wilson to drop out of law school and run Defense Distributed full-time.

Wilson wasn't interested in building a tech company or making a fortune selling guns. His primary mission was to scatter power in ways that would be undetectable, ungovernable, and detached from the rule of law. Even the name he gave his organization (*Defense Distributed*) and descriptions of himself (*crypto-anarchist*) and of his company (*friends of freedom*) reinforce scattered power. Not to mention the gun's name, Liberator.

Wilson says he gives you "the key" to make a gun, but he denies being a gun seller, which would entail a significant regulatory responsibility. He therefore denies responsibility if you make a gun and misuse it. In my view, and by his own admission, Wilson distributes the knowledge (a form of power) and, for certain guns, the machinery (more power) without linking either of these actions to ethical, responsible, and safe use. The technology upends the normal verification processes, such as background checks, because there is no point of purchase. Wilson could have advocated building in safety features to his guns, and compliance with ordinary gun regulations. He could even empower the police and other protectors of the public in parallel through detection machinery that would expose the illegal use of 3D-printed guns. But he does not appear to have pursued these options. Like He Jiankui, Wilson's story has all the hallmarks of scattered power.

3D-printing technology, first patented in 1986, was originally used to quickly and inexpensively make parts for auto manufacturing, aerospace, and medical devices. It can produce different kinds of objects all from the same machines—including, in the future potentially, human organs. The process is sometimes called "additive manufacturing," as it basically builds up or "prints" an object, layer by layer, into three dimensions, using materials such as plastic, wood, or metal instead of ink. Many 3D-printed products are made from the thermoplastic polymer acrylonitrile butadiene styrene, or ABS. If you have been around children, you may have stepped on this hard, smooth polymer at some point in your life: ABS is the material used in Legos.

Like all edgy, non-binary innovations, 3D printing also scatters power in ways that are positive. Doctors Without Borders/Médecins Sans Frontières, for example, has used the technology to provide war victims in Syria with prosthetic limbs that can be custom-designed in twenty-four hours at a fifth the cost of traditional prosthetics. Other promising innovations include safer, more affordable housing for refugees; reefs that can be sunk and used to stimulate coral reefs to redevelop; and 3D bioprinting of human tissues to help repair damaged organs and more.

3D-printing technology contributes to the power the guns and gunmakers have to remain undetected. When it comes to building a gun, one only needs a 3D printer, computer-aided design (CAD) software, downloadable blueprints, and some relatively elementary computer skills. Plastic guns have no serial numbers, making them untraceable "ghost guns." The Undetectable Firearms Act requires at least 3.7 ounces of metal in all guns so they can't evade metal detectors and X-ray machines. In compliance, Wilson's Liberator contains a small compartment to hold a piece of metal—but it's a detachable block that isn't even needed in order to fire a bullet. The law is toothless, as investigative journalists in Israel proved in 2013 when they smuggled a copy of the Liberator past metal security detectors and into the Israeli parliament—twice, even though the gun's firing pin was a metal nail. In the United States, the Transportation Security Administration (TSA) detected 3D-printed guns four times at security checkpoints in airports across the nation between 2016 and 2018.

The guns are inexpensive and fairly unreliable—at least early iterations were. In 2013, Australian police used a $1,700 printer to make copies of the Liberator, and the guns shattered each time a bullet was fired. This leads some to argue that 3D-printed guns won't be a significant threat for a number of years.

But the fact that an older risk is still present doesn't mean that we don't have responsibility *today* to preempt proliferation of a new risk. Just as with gene-editing kits, we are responsible for managing potential future consequences now: *Ethics are an early-stage endeavor, not an eraser or a cleanup act after harm is done.* Indeed, the scattering of new power happens in parallel with the need to continue to manage classic sources of power—whether guns, nuclear weapons, or political propaganda. Tomorrow's risks are for today's decision-making. In the United States, we fail every day at effectively and constitutionally protecting innocent people against gun violence. This tragic inability or unwillingness to tackle the existing threat should not be an invitation to delay attention to 3D weapons. It should be a warning to redouble our efforts on both counts. And there is no upside in delaying attention to this.

As Wilson reminds us, the Liberator "only needs to be lethal once." One bullet could be used in self-defense or, alternately, to wreak havoc. There is a frightening magnitude of risk when we consider how many times his blueprints have been downloaded, let alone shared. We could face potentially hundreds of thousands of guns firing "just one" bullet, not to mention technology for 3D printing of assault weapons and beyond. What's to stop rogue actors from using plastic guns to spread terror at courthouses, airports, train stations, concerts, and schoolyards? Our decisions today must take into account the challenge of stopping them. In framework terms, we know there is a significant potential ethics risk (information), and we have an ethical responsibility as regulators and citizens for the potential impact of our decision (stakeholders and consequences now and in the future) as the technology continues to evolve.

Wilson's focus on protecting individual gunmakers' rights includes an obsession with free speech. No federal prohibition exists to prevent someone from making a gun at home—as long as you don't sell it, you can make it. But when Wilson posted instructions for making the Liberator and other gun parts online in 2013, the State Department ordered him to take them down, claiming he'd violated the Arms Export Control Act of 1976, and specifically the International Traffic in Arms Regulations. These laws rightfully prevent the unlicensed sale of cutting-edge weaponry, technical data, and training—anything from microchips used for defense purposes to night-vision goggles and F-15 fighter jets—to foreign actors who might use them to develop weapons of mass destruction, destabilize nations, and otherwise harm America and its allies.

Wilson sued the government in 2015 for forcing him to take down his blueprints, arguing that his online code was free speech and that the government was infringing on his First Amendment rights. The case went up to the Fifth Circuit Court of Appeals, where his request for an injunction was denied. In its ruling, the court wrote that while Wilson's constitutional rights might be temporarily harmed, an injunction might permanently harm the country's national security.

But then, three years later, in June 2018, the State Department reversed its position. In a private settlement, the government agreed to pay Wilson $40,000 in attorney's fees and allow him to post his blueprints, including instructions for an AR-15 semiautomatic rifle, the style of weapon used in the Sandy Hook Elementary School massacre in 2012 and other mass shootings. Nineteen states and Washington,

D.C., sued to block the settlement. In November 2019, a federal judge in Seattle agreed, ruling that it violated federal law.

Scattered power begets more scattered power. As the law tries to play catch-up, the plans to print dangerous weapons are still being shared, in ways that are difficult to detect and stop, beyond Wilson's website. In 2019, *Wired* magazine reported on a decentralized global network of 3D-printed gun enthusiasts who call themselves "Deterrence Dispensed" (in a nod to Wilson), with at least one hundred members who are actively scattering the power of DIY plastic weaponry far and wide. Using digital sharing platforms, the group's members trade ideas, feedback, and CAD files; they upload blueprints on media-hosting sites; and along with their original gun designs and modifications of older plans, they provide Defense Distributed's blueprints to anyone for free.

In 2020, Cody Wilson resurfaced with a new website and business model. This time, he claimed, he was following federal law by selling access to his website, and thousands of gun blueprints, only to U.S. residents, bypassing the export considerations of the court orders. The intersection of technology, regulation, societal tolerance, and rogue actors will continue to evolve.

In his book *The End of Power*, renowned thinker and journalist Moisés Naím reminds us that power is impossible to measure: "You cannot tally it up and rank it. You can rank only what appears to be its agents, sources, and manifestations." Power's agents, in this case, are individual actors on Deterrence Dispensed who make plastic weapons that emulate Beretta M9 handguns and AR-15–style rifles in their living rooms. Its sources are a lethal combination of accessible technology susceptible to misuse and disempowerment of the law. Its manifestations will be the potential deaths of innocent victims.

As the technology becomes more difficult to detect, so, too, are the consequences of its misuse. We might not be aware of the power until we see the harm. Even where we have information—for example, that individuals on the dark web are building guns—we have insufficient visibility to monitor the consequences.

These stories show that scattered power disempowers law. National legal systems are ill-equipped to enforce laws and protect citizens across national borders. In a technologically borderless edgy world, jurisdiction has yet to be defined. Even if laws were able to keep pace with current technology, enforcement is almost impossible. As a result, the law has lost credibility as a deterrent. Both He Jiankui's and Cody Wilson's stories demonstrate that our capacity to develop new, effective, and enforceable laws to govern innovative technologies is being outpaced as the agents of scattered power evade existing laws with ease.

Scattered power is even pushing at the boundaries of individual rights, whether rights to determine the physical traits of our children or freedom of speech. This takes us back to the definition of the edge: Scattered power pushes the law further and further behind the reality in which our ethics are playing out. It increases the importance and widens the scope of the responsibility for ethics to guide our choices. In particular, scattered power has disrupted classic notions of the type and scope of decision authority within corporate, personal, and governmental realms.

Scattered power doesn't just empower individuals—it also allows corporations to exploit the diffusion of power. This trend is a counterintuitive combination of corporations scattering power (to actors who did not have it) *and* amassing power (through the profits and domination of their technologies and also by encroaching on governmental activities).

Scattering power requires corporate involvement, for example, by selling or otherwise providing social media, 3D printers, materials for gene editing, or platforms for the sharing economy. One of the first ethics questions I explore with corporations is the extent to which they are conscious of their responsibility for scattering power as they sell their products and services. While many companies require consent to terms of service that aim to warn users of their responsibilities and restrictions on use, those documents by and large aim to deflect legal liability from the corporations. They do not demonstrate a sufficiently forward-looking and thoughtful filtering of the potential consequences of the company's distribution of power. But even with best efforts, the consideration of what users *could* do with their technologies or services—before unleashing them on society—often falls short due to the complexity of predicting the trajectory of scattered power on the edge.

I am a staunchly pro-innovation ethicist. Users of technology have their own share of responsibility. But when increased profits and influence happen on the back of scattered power, companies have outsized responsibility for assuring that they press pause before empowering individuals with tools that could bring harm. Because neither the law nor terms of service effectively control misuse, companies should be considering how they can build ethics breaks into their technology. A question I ask every client is: What can you do with the technology to pace the roll-out of the ethics along with the products?

Parallel to corporations scattering power, they are also monopolizing it. One new way that corporate power is increasing is by privatizing realms that were previously within governments' responsibilities. I was wide-eyed on my first visit to the Smithsonian National Air and Space Museum. At the time, U.S. space belonged to the National Aeronautics and Space Administration, or NASA, an independent government agency responsible for the civilian space program. But today, when my students think of space, they think of CEOs and entrepreneurs such as Tesla founder Elon Musk's SpaceX, Amazon founder Jeff Bezos's Blue Origin, and Richard Branson's Virgin Galactic. These corporate titans dominate the space news and, now, our imaginations.

But unprecedented dilemmas can arise when control over realms that were previously in the domain of democratically elected governments falls into the hands of private actors. The boundaries of ethical responsibility require redrawing. Space travel, for instance, is an integral part of our national defense and our relationships with our allies. We will need to assure that governments retain control over safety, and transparency to the public, potential investors, and future passengers. And we should ensure that both governments and companies will provide citizens with equal access to travel. Questions of responsibility to share benefits are also increasingly at the forefront. For example, how will corporations distribute their unique research and learning for the benefit of society?

Given these companies' extraordinary capacity and resources, governments should take advantage or risk leaving untapped significant opportunity for defense, climate change research, artificial intelligence in society, and beyond. We have no time or resources to waste with these challenges, and they will require contributions from many stakeholders. In many of these cases, the government *is* aligning with corporations. For example, in 2020, NASA partnered with SpaceX to send NASA astronauts to the International Space Station on Crew Dragon, the first commercially built spacecraft. Each case is different, but public-private partnerships can allow for greater opportunity and visibility.

Let's pause for a moment to stress one fundamental point: *We cannot tolerate the monopolization of ethics.* The risks of monopolization of services like online search or social media, and increasing engagement of corporations in realms previously governed by public institutions, pale in comparison to the risks to society and humanity of monopolization of ethics.

Unfortunately, technology is scattering a dangerous belief that the law and ethics are mere options. Areas like space, national defense, and managing currency—formerly public services—should not be within the control of a few large corporations. We need to be mindful of the slippery slope. Well-controlled contracts for specific corporate engagement with governments to deliver research, products, and services are helpful and necessary for the advancement of society. It's quite different to allow a corporation to stand between citizens and access to public goods (whether space or digital currency) or for corporations to be in a position to control national policy on defense, health, the environment, and beyond. Most importantly, although corporations may monopolize power in areas, we cannot allow them or rogue actors to whom they may scatter power to determine society's ethics.

The responsibility for integrating the impact of scattered power into our personal choices falls largely to us. Medical choices offer one important example. The starting point and focus should be on principles.

The most important challenge with principles on the edge is that they are more likely to *conflict* with each other. A binary decision like eradicating racism usually allows alignment of all our principles—for example, safety, integrity, compassion, and respect all stand up against racism. But non-binary challenges, where there are advantages and disadvantages on all sides of a decision, may require us to weigh and prioritize our principles—and possibly even compromise them. For example, consider the safety issues with an unproven medical treatment against compassionate support for a possible cure or improved well-being.

While no one can be prepared for how we will feel when we find ourselves confronting a life-threatening medical situation, understanding how principles may conflict can help anchor our thinking. Through serving on two ethics committees at the American Hospital of Paris and the Pasteur Institute research center in Paris, I see parents, doctors, nurses, researchers, and other stakeholders struggle with heart-wrenching ethical conundrums over a wide range of genetic problems. Technologies such as CRISPR only make these medical ethical dilemmas involving conflicting principles more common. Being clear about your own principles, ideally before you face life-defining choices or need to express your opinion, can help ground you when you're faced with an unexpected difficult decision. It can help keep the decision at hand connected to, and consistent with, many other ethically thoughtful decisions you have made.

Some of the questions that patients in these institutions grapple with include whether they would manipulate the embryo of an unborn child to eliminate a deadly family trait for, say, Huntington's disease or to remedy hearing impairment. Back to Dr. Conklin's concerns, should we allow ambitious parents to manipulate genes that play a role in intelligence, musical aptitude, or athletic ability? As you consider these non-binary decisions, ask yourself: When and under what circumstances would I engage with the technology? When and under what circumstances would I consider it acceptable for society to allow engagement? Only you can decide what the best answer is in your situation or regarding your views for society. But how you apply your principles, especially how you prioritize them and resolve any conflicts, will not only define your own identity and determine your consequences, it will also have serious consequences for others.

The second framework point is to assure that your assessment of information, stakeholders, and consequences integrates the undetectable, accessible, and largely unregulatable characteristics of scattered power. Have you included the difficulties not only of collecting information necessary to make a sound ethical decision but also of predicting who all the actual and potential stakeholders of a decision will be? Imagine yourself in the situation of deciding the health of your child or voting on a law that would propose limitations on the use of gene editing for many children. What you can't know will be as important as what you do know.

But how do we allocate responsibility to these stakeholders and reattach them to ethics? In Cody Wilson's case, the stakeholders include: do-it-yourself gunmakers; the people affected by their use of 3D technology; the dark web, social media, and information-sharing sites where power spreads; the laws, lawmakers, and regulators; and the public. Sometimes we can hold stakeholders to account (regulators and lawmakers), and sometimes we fall short (stealth bad actors printing assault rifles in their living rooms). Sometimes the desire to flaunt power facilitates detectability and accountability (Dr. He's quest for scientific accolades and Cody Wilson's free speech advocacy). Allocation of responsibility is not just about ill-intentioned actors. The most well-meaning experts, policymakers, and individuals facing a personal dilemma can contribute to a scattering of power without sufficient connection to ethics because our ability to see the impact of one decision on many can be so limited.

When we can't determine the stakeholders, predicting the consequences becomes exceedingly difficult, if not impossible. People will be shot. Genes will be edited. But the scope, scale, and potential consequences over time are harder to anticipate. We know that 3D printing will become less expensive and more accessible, expanding the making of weapons and the random nature of their impact. We know that when embryonic genomes are manipulated, the human germline is affected—but we don't know what the secondary effects on the next generation and subsequent generations are, or the effects on companies, laws, governments, and the human species.

The allocation of responsibility for scattered power also requires considering the scattering of inequality. Somewhat counterintuitively, lawmakers are turning to ethics because they, too, recognize that regulation can't keep pace with scattered power. I see lawmakers' mobilizing ethics as hopeful and a necessary stepping-stone to regulation—as long as we don't take the pressure off them to develop effective regulation and upgrade our enforcement capability.

In April 2019, I met with California congressman Ro Khanna, who represents the 17th Congressional District, the heart of Silicon Valley. Khanna is committed to democratizing the benefits of Silicon Valley's tech power, which is why I wanted to understand his priorities and approach. He believes, as he told me, that "anyone could potentially be an Elon Musk"—innovate and create great wealth. He argues that we cannot ethically build a society that excludes older people or those suffering economic inequality.

Khanna is trying to scatter power with greater equality. He wants

wer's consequences even when they deploy best efforts and signifi-
t resources.

After Dr. He made his announcement at the Genome Summit,
ure Biomedical Engineering published an editorial proposing that any
rminations about gene editing's future should lie in the hands of
iety, not just scientists. We have a chorus of bioethicists and gene-
ing experts saying that we need a broader conversation on the eth-
of the technology that includes ethicists and social scientists. But
t we also need is a wide variety of *nonexperts* talking about power-
tering technologies like CRISPR and 3D-printed guns. That's
re you come in.

As CRISPR pioneer Dr. Doudna once described to NBC News,
hought it strange that no one was talking about a technology that
ked a tectonic shift in life as we know it. "I'd go to PTA meetings
ny son's school or I'd have my neighbor over for dinner," Doudna
rved, "and I realized, 'Wow, people outside of my little science
d have no idea what's going on and yet this is going to impact
body's lives.'"

Your voice in the trajectory of this technology *matters*. It's not just
t getting more ethicists and experts in the room—it's about all of
rticipating in the debate. We can keep scattered power in mind as
rapple with these questions and form opinions about other peo-
decisions and views, including corporate CEOs, politicians, sci-
s, and technology innovators. We all can test our opinions and
ons while walking in one another's shoes—such as Delaney Van
's, a potential victim of a 3D-printed gun, or even a future civilian
traveler.

ower will continue to scatter in unprecedented ways and far be-
plastic weapons and the weaponization of our own biology. Rec-
e that these technologies are here to stay. Some give us choices
when and under what circumstances we engage. Some will not
us to opt out; for example, when police and immigration depart-
use facial recognition technology. We can passively watch these

to spread digital literacy and the benefits of technolc

has a multipronged approach that includes an Inter

giving consumers more control over their personal

paign to create jobs and opportunities for areas the

hind, like Kentucky and West Virginia. He also ad

Valley to embrace more issues than just "[tax] repatr

and patent trolls." Khanna calls Silicon Valley's cu

an "impoverished vision for a place that literally 1

change human civilization."

His work is one of many examples showing

stepping into ethics efforts above and beyond the l

as a member of the board of the Centre for Data Et

in the U.K., with its mission to advise the British

imizing the benefits of data and AI for society.

Union High-Level Expert Group on Artificial In

vises on European AI strategy. These and other

broader stakeholder input and can be a highly ef

the ethics debate and inform regulation—but the

lenges of scattered power that regulators do, and

tute for effective regulation.

The interplay of these perspectives among

ernments, and each of us as individuals contrib

ronment in which we are making decisions. W

to be increasingly mindful of the ethical implica

power and where we fit with respect to others'

∞

It's hard not to feel overwhelmed by the shee

of accountability that scattered power brings.

embryonic genomes using CRISPR technolog

ternationally accepted scientific and ethical gu

acolytes found workarounds to continue shari

line. We can't trust governments or laws to

to spread digital literacy and the benefits of technology. To do this, he has a multipronged approach that includes an Internet Bill of Rights giving consumers more control over their personal data and a campaign to create jobs and opportunities for areas the tech boom left behind, like Kentucky and West Virginia. He also advocates for Silicon Valley to embrace more issues than just "[tax] repatriation, encryption, and patent trolls." Khanna calls Silicon Valley's current narrow focus an "impoverished vision for a place that literally believes it wants to change human civilization."

His work is one of many examples showing how government is stepping into ethics efforts above and beyond the law. I see it in action as a member of the board of the Centre for Data Ethics and Innovation in the U.K., with its mission to advise the British government on maximizing the benefits of data and AI for society. And at the European Union High-Level Expert Group on Artificial Intelligence, which advises on European AI strategy. These and other similar efforts engage broader stakeholder input and can be a highly effective way to expand the ethics debate and inform regulation—but they face the same challenges of scattered power that regulators do, and they are not a substitute for effective regulation.

The interplay of these perspectives among corporate actors, governments, and each of us as individuals contributes to the edgy environment in which we are making decisions. We have the opportunity to be increasingly mindful of the ethical implications of where we have power and where we fit with respect to others' power.

∞

It's hard not to feel overwhelmed by the sheer randomness and lack of accountability that scattered power brings. He Jiankui manipulated embryonic genomes using CRISPR technology, without regard to internationally accepted scientific and ethical guidelines; Cody Wilson's acolytes found workarounds to continue sharing his gun blueprints online. We can't trust governments or laws to protect us from scattered

power's consequences even when they deploy best efforts and significant resources.

After Dr. He made his announcement at the Genome Summit,
Nature Biomedical Engineering published an editorial proposing that any
determinations about gene editing's future should lie in the hands of
society, not just scientists. We have a chorus of bioethicists and gene-
editing experts saying that we need a broader conversation on the ethics of the technology that includes ethicists and social scientists. But
what we also need is a wide variety of *nonexperts* talking about power-
scattering technologies like CRISPR and 3D-printed guns. That's
where you come in.

As CRISPR pioneer Dr. Doudna once described to NBC News,
she thought it strange that no one was talking about a technology that
marked a tectonic shift in life as we know it. "I'd go to PTA meetings
for my son's school or I'd have my neighbor over for dinner," Doudna
observed, "and I realized, 'Wow, people outside of my little science
world have no idea what's going on and yet this is going to impact
everybody's lives.'"

Your voice in the trajectory of this technology *matters*. It's not just
about getting more ethicists and experts in the room—it's about all of
us participating in the debate. We can keep scattered power in mind as
we grapple with these questions and form opinions about other people's decisions and views, including corporate CEOs, politicians, scientists, and technology innovators. We all can test our opinions and
decisions while walking in one another's shoes—such as Delaney Van
Riper's, a potential victim of a 3D-printed gun, or even a future civilian
space traveler.

Power will continue to scatter in unprecedented ways and far beyond plastic weapons and the weaponization of our own biology. Recognize that these technologies are here to stay. Some give us choices
about when and under what circumstances we engage. Some will not
allow us to opt out; for example, when police and immigration departments use facial recognition technology. We can passively watch these

technologies happen to us or we can make our voices heard. No matter where you stand as a stakeholder, whether you are a scientist, product tester, lawmaker, biology student, 3D-printing enthusiast, or someone who stumbled on something troubling on the internet—you have the opportunity to prevent the monopolization of ethics by rogue actors, corporate giants, and even well-intentioned scientists and innovators.

If we don't integrate reality into our choices, the edge will only expand. Scattered power left unchecked spreads unethical behavior and begets other dangerous forms of unethical behavior.

Chapter Three

CONTAGION

One of the turning points in twentieth-century American political history, according to Pulitzer Prize–winning author Robert Caro, was the 1948 Democratic Senate primary runoff between Texas congressman Lyndon B. Johnson and Texas governor Coke Stevenson. It was "political morality made vivid," Caro writes in *The Years of Lyndon Johnson: Means of Ascent*, book two in his gripping biography of Johnson. And, as we shall see, it was rife with contagious unethical behavior.

The campaign styles of these two candidates, as Caro reports, was "new politics against the old." On the side of the old, Coke Stevenson was a beloved "cowboy governor," driven more by principles than politics. "It wasn't only that he was utterly honest," a lobbyist told Caro. "It was that he was so completely fair and just." Stevenson ran a modest campaign, making very few stump speeches or promises as he drove himself from town to town to meet voters.

On the side of the new, Johnson "would do whatever was necessary to win," including tactics to sway voters that may seem common today but, as Caro reports, sprang from Johnson's 1948 campaign. For example, he used scientific polling, advertising and public relations professionals to book frequent radio interviews, and "media manipulation" techniques "to influence voters." Against his advisors' advice, he made false claims about Stevenson's record and mocked him in speeches, calling him "Mr. Do-Nothinger" and "Calculatin' Coke." Instead of a campaign bus, Johnson hired a helicopter to fly him to stump speeches and bands to play before his chopper arrived in order to draw the onlookers and headlines that boosted his confidence. "I know I am sweeping up votes like a whirlwind," Johnson told a reporter. "I just feel it in the crowds."

But on primary day, Saturday, August 28, 1948, early returns had Stevenson beating Johnson by more than twenty thousand votes based on tallies in Dallas, Houston, and Fort Worth, where new voting machines brought quick results. Most precincts, however, still relied on paper ballots. Over the next three days, nearly a million votes were counted by precinct election judges, then called in or telegrammed to the Texas Election Bureau. Stevenson's lead grew narrower each day.

By the deadline for precinct judges to turn over ballot boxes, tallies, and poll sheets, on August 31, at 7 p.m., the Election Bureau announced new numbers: 494,206 for Johnson and 494,555 for Stevenson. Stevenson was leading by just 349 votes. Although it was an unofficial count, newspapers declared it a firm lead. Even Stevenson "was sure he had won," Caro reports.

In the days to follow, Democratic executive committees doublechecked and certified tally sheets, occasionally calling in corrections to the state committee. That's when Johnson's staff started making calls to campaign managers and local leaders in precincts across Texas asking, as Caro describes it, if they could "re-check" and "find" a few more votes. At least one person who agreed to find more votes was political boss George Parr, a businessman who wielded control over several counties in South Texas. Parr credited Johnson for helping him secure a presidential pardon for a 1932 tax evasion conviction. "He was just waiting for the telephone to ring to find out how many votes Lyndon Johnson needed," Caro writes.

On September 3, six days after the election, Jim Wells County committee members began to review the tally sheets for its precincts, checking them against the numbers that had been called in. As they went through the first twelve precincts, the totals all matched. Then they got to Precinct 13, the small town of Alice, Texas. Precinct 13 was overseen by George Parr's enforcer and election judge Luis Salas, a man who'd fled Mexico after killing another man in a barroom fight. Salas had called in 765 votes for Johnson and 60 for Stevenson. But the numbers on his tally list now showed 965 for Johnson—giving him exactly 200 extra votes.

That afternoon, all the corrections across Texas had been reported to the Election Bureau. The new tabulations revealed a stunning result: Johnson had beat Stevenson by 87 votes.

Stevenson and his attorneys immediately paid a visit to the Democratic executive committee secretary to inspect Precinct 13's poll list and tally sheet. The secretary reluctantly allowed them to look at the documents, and then quickly rescinded his offer when they began to copy down names. But that was all the time the attorneys needed to observe that the "7" in Salas's 765 tally had merely been changed to a "9." Further, the last 201 names on the voter list (200 of whom voted for Johnson and one for Stevenson) were all written in the same ink and handwriting. And they were listed in alphabetical order.

The attorneys next visited Alice resident Eugenio Soliz—a name on the list that they believed was the last authentic voter. Soliz said that he'd arrived at the polling place twenty minutes before the polls closed and no one else was there. This meant that 201 more voters would had to have arrived in the next twenty minutes, lined up in alphabetical order, and all but one voted for Johnson. They contacted nine people who signed in after Soliz—the names they were able to jot down before the list was taken away. Not one person had voted that day. In fact, three of the nine were dead.

Despite clear evidence of election fraud, Johnson's loyalists in the Texas Democratic Party's executive committee helped secure his victory in a close 29-to-28 vote, advancing him as the party's candidate in the general election. Refusing to give up, Stevenson successfully petitioned a federal district court judge who ordered Johnson's name be kept off the ballot while he conducted evidentiary hearings. But George Parr helped to create delays. Witnesses were suddenly out of the country or missing. Luis Salas claimed that Precinct 13's voting records had been stolen from his car. And when the judge ordered all the ballot boxes from Jim Wells County (including Precinct 13's) be brought in so votes could be individually inspected, the keys to the box padlocks were suddenly missing. Locksmiths had to be called, further slowing the investigation.

Meanwhile, Johnson's personal attorney, Abe Fortas, was working behind the scenes on a risky legal strategy to end the investigation and secure Johnson's name on the general election ballot. Fortas's approach was based on the fact that state elections were a matter for state law and therefore not within the jurisdiction of a federal court. As Caro describes, Fortas's plan was to appeal to the federal circuit court to halt the hearings—but make an argument so weak that they would surely lose, thereby allowing them to quickly move on to the U.S. Supreme Court. There they would make a stronger argument to the single judge who had administrative responsibility for the Fifth Circuit: Associate Justice Hugo Black. Fortas believed that Justice Black would stop the federal court's hearings as a result of this jurisdictional issue.

Fortas's legal maneuvering paid off. Minutes before Ballot Box 13 was to be opened and inspected in a packed courtroom, Justice Black agreed with Johnson's jurisdiction argument and voided the federal district court's order. The evidentiary hearings came to a screeching halt, and Box 13 was never inspected. Nor were thousands of votes for Johnson from other Parr-controlled precincts. Shortly thereafter, Box 13 went missing.

"Evidence that some of these votes were 'cast' by dead men would never be presented in a court of law," Caro reports. Johnson's name was placed on the ballot, and he went on to defeat the Republican candidate in November, securing a seat in the U.S. Senate. In 1960, he became John F. Kennedy's vice-presidential running mate. When President Kennedy was assassinated in 1963, Johnson was sworn in as the thirty-sixth president.

"His margin of victory in the 1948 election has been characterized as 'the 87 votes that changed history'—and they were," Caro says. "The Johnson Presidency was a watershed in American history, and without that election there would probably have been no Johnson Presidency."

Caro's account of Johnson's "path to power" provides us with an excellent foundation to examine *contagion*, the third force driving ethical decision-making. The word "contagion" usually refers to the spread of disease, but here it describes the spread of behaviors, ideas, and decision-making. This timeless force has been an important influence on ethics long before Johnson's political career but has become considerably more potent on the edge.

The most critical point with respect to contagion is that we tend to focus on eradicating and punishing unwanted behaviors, but we leave unchecked the causes for their spreading: We have been missing the significance of contagion. The framework can help us to preempt the contagion of harmful decisions and their consequences and promote the spreading of positive efforts.

As Lyndon Johnson's story and others reveal, unethical behavior can be extremely contagious. The behavior spreads on its own to the point where it becomes normalized—to where even well-intentioned people who may never think of engaging in immoral or illegal acts begin to consider: *Everybody else does it, maybe it's not so bad.* Or *Everyone else does it, why shouldn't I?* As the contagion spreads and more people engage in the unethical behavior, it becomes "normal" or "standard practice." (Contagion can also spread ethical behavior, but deploying contagion as a force for good requires proactive commitment.)

In Johnson's case, contagion shaped his political history even before his 1948 Senate bid. Seven years before the Ballot Box 13 scandal, he'd been exposed to corrupt practices. In 1941, as a thirty-two-year-old congressman, he ran for an open Senate seat. Johnson's main opponent was Governor W. Lee "Pappy" O'Daniel, a radio celebrity and "huckster," according to a Texas Public Radio profile. On election day, June 28, 1941, with 96 percent of the precincts reporting, the Texas Election Bureau had Johnson in the lead by five thousand votes and newspapers declared him the winner. Feeling confident, Johnson told his key districts to report the final vote numbers, rather than wait. But this afforded O'Daniel's team time to call loyal political bosses controlling South and East Texas, who then delivered enough "late" votes to allow O'Daniel to beat Johnson by almost 1,100 votes.

Johnson had an election stolen from him, and he repeated the same unethical behavior. As Caro notes, the fraudulent 1948 vote count for Johnson was repeatedly excused by his allies as "nothing more than the normal run of Texas politics"—in other words, it was contagious. But then the behavior *mutated*.

Mutation is when someone's original behavior inspires new forms of unethical behavior in themselves or in others. Examples include lying to hide the original acts and bribing someone to keep the original act secret or arguing to keep planes flying despite known safety shortcuts and regulatory failures. Words like "evolution," "transformation," "development," and "alteration," involving change for better or worse, are also indicators of mutation. But on the edge, mutation sets off unpredictable new forms of wrongdoing at an unprecedented scale, multiplying the starting points for further contagion and mutation, and amplifying the degree and impact of unethical behavior. This, in turn, complicates our ability to identify stakeholders and consequences over time.

In almost every case, contagion drags in stakeholders who are close to the epicenter of an ethics dilemma. Sometimes standing up to the contagion would put them in an untenable position, such as losing a job or jeopardizing relationships. Johnson and his supporters, for example, got swept up in mutations such as making false claims about Stevenson, lying under oath to judges, "losing" voting records, and attempting to cover up evidence of fraud. Even Johnson's helicopter pilot engaged in deception: When Johnson was too tired to land and meet with people, he'd nap in the passenger seat and have the pilot hover above the venue and talk to the crowd through a loudspeaker, pretending to be him.

Often it takes a broader supporting cast to pull off an unethical action. If not for George Parr, Luis Salas, Abe Fortas, and many others who played a role in Johnson's deceptions, he might have lost his second Senate bid. Without that win, a number of lasting mutations made possible by his presidency might not have occurred—notably his rewarding Fortas, in 1965, by nominating him to the Supreme Court, a *lifetime* appointment. The more different contributors to the mutation, the stickier—and more permanent—the consequences can be.

Just as others are needed to pull off an unethical act, the flip side can also be true. In fact, sometimes it just takes one member of the supporting cast to play the critical role in *stopping* contagion. Had the FAA audited the Lion Air disaster properly, or been more rigorous in certification processes, the Ethiopian Airlines tragedy might have been prevented.

Not only does contagion spread easily to people on the periphery of an unethical decision, more and more people get caught up in borderless webs of unethical decisions they're often unaware of. How many citizens are aware of how government authorities track them through photos taken in public places? Or bringing it back to Johnson: How many Americans and foreigners understood how Johnson's deception both landed him in the White House as commander in chief of the armed forces and then influenced the outcome of the Vietnam War?

As you can see, contagion doesn't happen in isolation. All the forces that drive ethics partner with one another to amplify the behaviors. Our tendency to oversimplify ethical questions into binary choices leads us to disregard nuances that, left to fester, can further spread unethical behavior. For example, if we decide that social media companies should offer users an option to pay to avoid targeted ads, we might miss how this increases digital inequality for people who can't afford data privacy. And with fewer recipients of ads, companies may have greater incentives to use manipulative advertising tactics.

Scattered power can amplify contagion, and vice versa, and not just the existence of it, but how fast and far the contagion mutates and power scatters. When we look at 3D-printing technology, for example, the contagious amplification of scattered power means that it's not going to be one or ten or even a hundred people at a time who have the capability to build a weapon at home—it's going to be potentially millions of people *simultaneously* having the power to make plastic guns. The more contagion and mutation happen, the more stakeholders are affected, and the more power can be scattered.

But contagion can also scatter power in positive ways, giving many more people the power and opportunities to drive beneficial behaviors, decisions, and ideas. Think of Malala Yousafzai, who grew up in Pakistan's Swat Valley, where the Taliban had recently taken control. Malala blogged about her life for BBC News, under a pseudonym, questioning the Taliban's motives. In 2012, at fifteen years old, Malala was shot in the head by Taliban extremists in retaliation for her writing that girls should be allowed to go to school. She survived the attack. Her courage was reported around the world, spreading her ideas on the internet and social media, and through celebrities and world leaders, inspiring people to fight to protect girls' right to an education. In 2014, at seventeen, she became the youngest Nobel Peace Prize winner in history.

Behavior, both ethical and unethical, is more contagious than ever. Often we fall into the trap of focusing solely on eliminating unwanted behaviors, without identifying and dismantling the causes—the *drivers*—of contagion. Missing these drivers is a key reason for the burgeoning contagion of ethical transgressions—and why we lose unprecedented opportunity to spread positive decisions and behavior.

Drivers of contagion are, essentially, the reasons or motivations that incite people to make ethically poor or good choices. And when we fail to root them out (or harness them for positive decisions), we see the same behaviors and decisions repeated over and over, or mutating. In the Ballot Box 13 scandal, holding the perpetrators of election fraud accountable would have been an important first step to stop the cycle of wrongdoing, had investigators been allowed to continue. It would have disempowered several of the drivers of both the original fraud and the mutations, such as weak compliance, impunity, and conflicts of interest.

More examples of drivers of contagion and mutation unchecked: A plane crashes; the drivers (weak compliance, weak regulation, greed, and arrogance, to name just a few) are left in place; soon, another plane crashes. Or a star Olympic athlete cheats by doping; the drivers (competition, pressure, jealousy, quest for celebrity, greed) are universal; other team members, other teams, broader participants in the sport, and even young athletes dope until "everybody is doing it." Then doping mutates into bribing testing officials, transporting illegal substances across national borders, and threatening physical therapists to stay quiet.

A multitude of direct and indirect drivers trigger the spread of behavior and decision-making, positive or negative. Some of these are classic drivers that have been around for centuries. Others are edgy and appear with new technologies. Breaking them down into categories (see "Drivers of Contagion of Ethics," page 74) helps us identify the ones that really matter to the decision at hand. Don't feel overwhelmed by these lists; you will quickly begin to recognize drivers of contagion in the ethics questions you face or see in the news.

DRIVERS OF CONTAGION OF ETHICS

Classic	*Edgy*
Greed, fear, jealousy	Driverless cars
Unconscious bias	Social media
Celebrity	Gene editing
Conflicts of interest	3D printing
Ineffective regulation	Bot caregivers
Arrogance	Robots at work
Arbitrariness	Artificial intelligence
Competition	Facial recognition technology
Echo chamber mentality	Deep fakes/fake news
Impunity	Blockchain
Skewed incentives	E-cigarettes/vaping
Abuse of hierarchy	Sharing economy
Weak compliance	Virtual assistants (Siri,
Silos	Alexa . . .)
Ineffective listening	Autonomous weapons
Viruses	Tech monopolies
Retaliation for	Hacking
reporting wrongdoing	Civilian space travel
Compromised truth	**Compromised truth**

Edgy drivers are sometimes harder to grasp than classic drivers, but they are extremely influential. Social media and the internet, for example, helped Malala's ideas spread and become globally contagious. Airplanes, flying taxis, and civilian space travel, technologies that allow us to go farther faster, can also spread our ideas, decisions, and behaviors farther and faster. Vaping can be addictive (repetition within one person) and spread through social circles. Even though some edgy drivers have become part of our daily life (like ride-sharing platforms and digital assistants), we still have not seen the full potential for their spreading of behaviors or the consequences that ensue. Individually and collectively, they blur our vision: We cannot necessarily imagine how the uses and risks of these technologies will evolve—or who should control the decision-making about their uses and own responsibility for any harm.

Classic drivers appear with daily regularity in all our lives. For example, pressure comes in many guises and enfolds other drivers (such as skewed incentives and disincentives, fear, sexual harassment, and unreasonable performance targets). Just as middle school children exert pressure on their peers or surrender to that pressure, adults build rationales based on ideas such as "if we don't do it, someone else will" or "I can't afford to risk losing my job."

The quest for perfection is a terribly destructive driver of contagion, which I witness all too frequently as an educator. When we chase after impossible-to-achieve targets (such as unrealistic standards of beauty or performance goals), there are three main responses. The first is to give up because there's no point in trying if we're sure to fail. The second is to cheat to try to reach the target. The third is to stay on the quest and suffer. A study of perfectionism in American, Canadian, and British college students from 1989 to 2016 found that this driver is on the rise, contributing to an epidemic of mental health issues from depression and anxiety to suicidal thoughts. Perfection is neither a laudable goal nor an achievable one. It undermines our decision-making, while compromising global health and individual well-being.

Let's take a closer look at a few drivers that dominate Lyndon Johnson's story:

Compromised Truth: One of the most destructive drivers of contagion, compromised truth involves lying or the denial, skewing, or disrespect of facts. It almost never spreads positive behavior. The Johnson case shows how chronic and persistent compromised truth can be, snowballing into more untruths, triggering other drivers. As Caro and others have noted, he lied about matters that had major consequences (as president, he vowed not to widen the Vietnam War but then sent hundreds of thousands more American soldiers to fight) and matters with fewer consequences (claiming he had dengue fever when it was pneumonia); from the personal (his great-grandfather did *not* die at the Alamo, because his great-grandparents hadn't yet arrived in Texas when it fell) to the political (downplaying both the cost and measure of America's role in Vietnam). His reputation, as Caro notes, was cemented in college, where fellow students "believed not only that he lied to them . . . but also that some psychological element *impelled* him to lie, made him lie even when he knew the lie might be discovered, made him, in fact, repeat a lie even *after* it had been discovered."

During his 1948 Senate campaign, his lies about Stevenson became so contagious that his speechwriter kept putting them in until the press repeated them too: "You knew it was a damned lie [but] you just repeated it and repeated it and repeated it. Repetition—that was the thing." The very phrase "credibility gap," which refers to the public's lack of confidence in the truth of a politician's claims and promises, came into widespread use in the mid-1960s to describe President Johnson in an era when TV vividly brought the Vietnam War into our homes. Like today's drivers of social media and the internet, television was the driver that spread Johnson's compromised truth—but it also allowed skeptical individuals to review the facts and question his falsehoods.

Pressure and the Quest for Perfection: These drivers are just as important at the level of leaders as they are in our day-to-day lives. As the title of Chapter 12 of *Means of Ascent* indicates, this election was "All or Nothing" for Johnson; it was "his last chance." So once campaigning became ineffectual, his only options were either to cheat or lose.

Ego and Celebrity: The helicopter, the bands, even Johnson's signature flourish of throwing his big Stetson hat out of the chopper upon landing all drew the crowds and press attention Johnson craved. This wasn't just a campaign stunt. His behavior was often driven by ego and a desire for celebrity. For instance, as Caro notes, Johnson would flatter reporters and introduce them by name to the audience, but at "the slightest hint of criticism in their stories," he lashed out and "ridiculed them for no reason at all."

Power. Caro describes Johnson's quest for power as an all-consuming trait—he displayed "not only a genius for discerning a path to power but an utter ruthlessness in destroying obstacles in that path." His single-minded focus on power, obsession with blind loyalty, and boundless ambition drove Johnson to lie and cheat for political gain and to lead others to similar unethical and illegal practices. Caro also reveals Johnson's pattern of disrespect for and mistreatment of his wife, Lady Bird, as well as ruling his subordinates through anger and fear.

Arrogance: Seeing themselves as superior and believing they know more than everybody else, arrogant people like Johnson tend not to listen (he didn't heed his advisors' concerns about attacking Stevenson). They also often suffer from fear—another driver—of having their weakness or errors exposed. As a result, they don't typically welcome others' views or checks and balances to their own ideas. They don't consider the information they need in order to make the best decisions, because they believe they're right. Worse, they reject the vigorous debate that helps to dismantle information silos and protect against compromised truth. None of the real champions of ethics I know or work with are arrogant.

Weak Compliance, Weak Governance, and Impunity: The failure to enforce laws, rules, or principles spurs unethical behavior because people may believe that what they do is low-risk—they can act with impunity. This activates more of the same, or increases the intensity, frequency, or reach of the behavior as people and institutions test the limits of enforcement. The framing becomes "What can I get away with?" rather than "What is the right decision ethically?"

In the case of the Ballot Box 13 scandal, the precinct officials were legally required to turn in election boxes, tallies, and poll lists by a specific deadline. Yet George Parr's loyalists turned in votes late, changed tally numbers, wrote in names, and provided unsubstantiated corrections with impunity. Johnson learned in his 1941 campaign that all one had to do was wait for their opponent's election night returns to be reported, and then deliver whatever number of votes were needed to beat him. Years later, after Johnson had died and Parr committed suicide, seventy-six-year-old Luis Salas decided to find "peace of mind" and reveal "the corruption of politics." In 1977, he told an Associated Press reporter that he'd stolen the election for Johnson: "We had the law to ourselves there," Salas said. "We could tell any election judge: 'Give us 80 percent of the vote, the other guy 20 percent.'" Weak compliance, weak governance, impunity, and more allowed them to steal elections.

Effective compliance and governance can be extraordinarily difficult on the edge. As we saw with drivers of contagion such as gene editing and 3D-printed guns, both evade detection and outpace the law. But at least being aware of drivers in action is key.

Unethical behavior doesn't just stop on its own. Nor do the drivers of contagion. Unless we proactively eliminate drivers (or deploy them for good), they will continue to escalate and contribute to the spreading and mutating of the behaviors. Persistent drivers affected Johnson's legacy. What's more, they sparked each other. The quest for power and extreme loyalty drove him to sacrifice truth, quash listening, and weaponize fear. This was in the days when radio was considered edgy. Today, classic drivers often join forces with edgy drivers such as social media.

But just as decisions are rarely "all good" or "all bad," so too with people. Johnson took the lead on many beneficial decisions, too. As president, he designed a set of domestic programs, the Great Society legislation, that expanded civil rights, and launched Medicare, Medicaid, and the War on Poverty. He championed the Civil Rights Act of 1964, outlawing discrimination on the basis of race, color, religion, sex, or national origin; and the Voting Rights Act of 1965, prohibiting racial discrimination in voting. According to the National Park Service, he signed more than three hundred conservation measures into law—including the Clean Air Act of 1963, the Water Quality Act of 1965, and the Endangered Species Preservation Act of 1966—that served to protect the environment and expand national park lands.

But as I often tell my clients, *we don't get a net ethics score.* Our good choices don't excuse the unethical ones. We are held accountable for every decision.

Johnson's story illustrates how behavior spreads, mutates, and draws others into repeating unethical behaviors to the point where they become normalized. But contagion is not limited to the realm of those who intentionally make poor decisions. Even morally motivated individuals can contribute to contagion. The most well-meaning were swept up in contagious behaviors that catalyzed a national health crisis, unwittingly causing them to break a solemn oath to "do no harm."

In September 2018, a twenty-two-year-old college student named Serena had her two bottom wisdom teeth extracted by her longtime dentist, Dr. Smith. (I've changed the names in this story to protect the privacy of the patient and her dentist.) It was not an easy procedure. One tooth came out fairly well, but there were unexpected complications with the second tooth and Serena's dental surgery ended up being much more complex and invasive than usual.

After her hours-long surgery, she left the dentist's office with ten tablets of ibuprofen and a prescription for painkillers. She went straight to a drugstore, where the pharmacist filled her order, no questions asked. She then headed back to the house she shared with five other students and tried to rest.

Later that day, Serena's mother called to see how she was feeling and how her surgery had gone. Serena told her that she was in some pain, but the dentist had given her a prescription, for thirty 10-mg Percocet pills, which she'd picked up on her way home. Her instructions were to take one or two every four hours for pain.

Percocet is a brand name for a medication that contains a combination of acetaminophen (a fever and pain reducer) and oxycodone (a powerful opioid). According to the National Institute of Dental and Craniofacial Research at the National Institutes of Health (NIH), similar opioid painkillers are also marketed under brand names like OxyContin, Hysingla, Percodan, Roxicet, Vicodin, and more. These medications can be very effective at eliminating significant to extreme discomfort after an invasive surgical procedure or for the treatment of chronic pain. But by the time of Serena's surgery in 2018, it was well reported in the media that opioids were also powerfully addictive.

In 2018, two million people "misused prescription opioids for the first time," and more than 130 people died *each day* from opioid-related drug overdoses, according to a report from the U.S. Department of Health and Human Services. Young adults can be particularly vulnerable to opioid addiction. A study in the *Journal of the American Dental Association* states that up to 3.5 million people may be first exposed to opioids through dentistry, the average age among them being twenty years old. In 2018, approximately 19,500 college students from twenty-six different educational institutions in the United States took an anonymous online survey by experts at the Ohio State University; 9.1 percent of students reported that they misused pain medications. Students were separately asked if they'd ever kept, given away, or sold pain medications when no longer medically needed: 36 percent kept the pills, 7 percent gave them to a friend, and 2 percent sold them.

The opioid epidemic had been a national health crisis, in the headlines for several years by the time Serena's surgery took place. Her mother was understandably concerned as to why Dr. Smith would prescribe such a powerful and known addictive drug for what should have been temporary pain relief. She called his office to find out, and a surgical assistant explained that prescribing thirty pills of Percocet all at once following a complicated surgery like Serena's was standard practice. Because she was likely to experience high-intensity pain, the medication would greatly reduce her suffering. It was also convenient, the assistant said: Serena wouldn't run out of pills and then have to visit Dr. Smith's office a second time, as required by law, to secure a refill.

Thankfully, Serena was vigilant about her own care—and lucky, in a bizarrely unpleasant way. The medication made her so dizzy, nauseated, and unable to sleep, without much help for the pain, that she couldn't continue to take it. (Her doctor told her that a small percentage of patients experience adverse reactions to pain medication.) She turned in the rest of the pills to her primary care doctor and managed ongoing severe pain with extra-strength Tylenol and by applying ice packs to the affected area. Serena's story has a hopeful ending, unlike so many others. Countless innocent victims and their families could not possibly have known that following their doctors' orders could lead to addiction.

Dr. Smith's contribution to contagion is troubling and surprising. But here is where contagion can fool us. We may believe that only bad actors succumb to drivers of unethical behavior—the kind of people who would steal elections, accept bribes from pharmaceutical companies, or operate pill mills (where clinics or doctors hand out opioids inappropriately or outside medical guidelines). But contagion can draw any one of us into its sticky webs, even a well-regarded dentist.

A highly educated practitioner, Dr. Smith works near a world-class university medical center in a community that offers extensive expertise and opportunity to share learning and advance his practice. Serena and her family had been seeing him for years, at a practice begun by his own father. Smith is known for keeping pace with the latest dental research and technologies. His staff are warm and thoughtful, and they work hard to bring to life their patient- and community-centric mission statement.

Adherence to "best practice" or "standard practice" in a changing world is how Dr. Smith unintentionally partook in normalization that contributed to a deadly epidemic. Despite his intentions, he prescribed unnecessarily large initial supplies of pain medication, rather than limiting a patient's access to powerfully addictive drugs and controlling the dosage more frequently—even as the opioid epidemic unfurled.

This book is not the place to dive into an analysis of the history and players that led to the opioid crisis. But before we probe where Dr. Smith's decision process faltered, I do want to highlight the extent of the spreading and mutation.

This is not a story about a dentist. It's a lesson in missing the drivers of a national (and ultimately international) tragedy. There were so many destructive decisions and consequences that in October 2017, the Department of Health and Human Services, under the direction of President Trump, declared the crisis a "public health emergency." Just as Dr. Smith would never intentionally harm a patient, young people who would never have imagined themselves using drugs are engaging in highly dangerous and illegal drug use—that started from properly taking legally prescribed medications. Particularly worrisome mutations of the opioid crisis include rising rates of overdose from heroin and fentanyl (an often low-cost and more accessible substitute for the originally prescribed opioids), a spike in hepatitis C infections due to users' switching to heroin injection, an increase in black markets for drugs, and a proliferation of pill mill operations. And this list doesn't begin to describe the web of mutations more directly linked to failed regulatory oversight and extensive corporate malfeasance—from deliberately making pills more addictive to nonprofit organizations receiving philanthropic gifts tainted by opioid profits.

Even people with the best of intentions can contribute to contagion and mutation of unethical, even deadly, decision-making. Our best intentions aren't enough. In order to diminish risk and maximize opportunities, we need to factor contagion and mutation—and all their drivers—into our current decisions and our assessment of past ones. Where *could (or did)* the behavior spread or beget other unwanted conduct? What drivers *could be (or could have been)* operating?

Let's now look at Dr. Smith's situation and see how he could have proactively framed his prescribing practices *before* receiving complaints.

We start with the four rungs of the ethics framework: principles, information, stakeholders, and consequences. Principles did not trigger the unintentional overprescription here. Dr. Smith had solid, patient-centric principles, which included a commitment to preventive dentistry, technology, cross-generational trust, warmth, and an upbeat environment of care. His diligent practice management indicated that he was trying to apply these principles.

The critical rung of the framework here is information—where we plug in contagion and mutation and the relevant drivers. Both preventively and reactively, we must consider two parts. First, the drivers of contagion that are obvious and those that could potentially be at play; second, the consequences of the contagion and mutation that have already happened or could happen. Without including contagion and mutation, we don't have the information we need. And we will not have identified the potential gaps in information that become the basis for ongoing monitoring.

In this case, at first glance we might conclude that greed (physicians taking kickbacks from drug representatives) and conflicts of interest (doctors being wined and dined by pharmaceutical representatives) often encourage health care providers to overprescribe opioids, amplifying the contagion and mutation. But these drivers were *not* present with Dr. Smith. He was not greedy. He didn't appear to have conflicts of interest. He believed deeply in his principles. Many doctors and dentists who found themselves unwittingly in his situation were like Dr. Smith. The answer lies elsewhere.

The framework requires monitoring—asking such questions as "What has changed in the world? And how do those changes drive my decisions and affect my opinions about others' decisions?" Another insidious driver of contagion, and the most important one in this situation, is the failure to monitor change in external circumstances.

In this dentist's case, enough information was easily available to suggest he should be questioning whether his prescribing practices were still the most safe and effective. Beyond mainstream press coverage, professional dental journals and policy statements by the American Dental Association (ADA) had made it clear that America was in the throes of a health emergency. In 2018, a month before Serena's surgery, a commentary in the *Journal of the American Dental Association* announced a partnership between the ADA and the National Institutes of Health to help dentists better navigate the crisis. In addition, studies showed that many dentists had changed their prescribing practices. In late 1998, dentists accounted for 15.5 percent of all immediate-release opioid prescriptions; by 2012 that number had dropped to 6.4 percent, thanks in part to ADA policies.

Part of monitoring is asking how stakeholders have changed and how contagion and mutation affect different stakeholders differently. For example, doctors consider the individual situations of patients. If a seventy-year-old patient with no history of substance abuse needed strong, effective pain relief after a complicated surgery—particularly if they live so far away that returning to the office for a prescription refill is difficult—perhaps the doctor would appropriately provide them with more medication and clear instructions about use, disposal, and serious risk of addiction. The doctor may make a different decision for a university student.

This story is a crucial reminder that if we mishandle the information rung, there's a cascading effect, skewing all the other rungs. We will not see stakeholders or potential consequences properly. As a result, we will be making decisions outside of reality.

I am not giving medical advice here or drawing conclusions about the medical appropriateness of any specific drugs or dosage. Rather, the framework can help us preempt contagion and react effectively and mend errors when ethics falter. We all can check in with changes around us as we make day-to-day choices, whether considering the evolving risks of social media addiction or updated safety reports from companies like Uber and Lyft. We all can be mindful of the impact our decisions have on different stakeholders. We all can ask ourselves: What should I be changing about the way I think about decisions? How am I interpreting what is "normal"? If the answer is "everybody else is doing it (or still doing it)," it's a red flag that you should check again. *If the world is changing, and information you consider in your decisions has not, take that as a warning.* Our ethics must keep pace with the edge or we can unwittingly become a driver of contagion.

We can rarely anticipate every driver of contagion, or predict when they will kick in or how they will evolve, but we can try to identify the ones most critical to our situation. Dr. Smith is a caring practitioner and someone who thought he was on top of best practices. But on the edge, mutation takes us all to places we could never imagine. We do have more power than we have been using, in every decision we make, to identify contagion and mutation and proactively prevent or cauterize all the drivers.

∞

"Life, Liberty and the pursuit of Happiness" are the words that we most often recall as the stirring reference to our rights from the Declaration of Independence. But we may underestimate the power and importance of the very last sentence, in which the founders affirmed their responsibilities: "And for the support of this Declaration . . . we mutually pledge to each other our Lives, our Fortunes and our sacred Honor."

Voting is not just a right. It is a sacred honor. U.S. Supreme Court Justice Louis Brandeis once wrote, "The most important political office is that of the private citizen." When we vote, we acknowledge our responsibility to uphold this powerful office. Whatever the nation, political situation, or type of election—and notwithstanding the candidates' records of ethical decision-making and behavior—we can commit to our own sacred honor by voting when and where we have the privilege. We can insist on sacred honor from our leaders by framing our voting and integrating a candidate's ethics, or the ethics of a particular issue, into our choice. This means also updating our notion of sacred honor to eliminate racism and the discrimination, inequality, and injustice that were rampant, and contagious, at the time of the founding of our nation, and in the founding documents, and which still today demand our utmost humility and resolve.

The election of a leader is also a game-changing opportunity to reset contagion and mutation on a positive course. Or not. Leaders in all arenas have outsized opportunity and responsibility to deploy contagion for good and to heed the risks of nefarious contagion. Elected officials, particularly state or national leaders, have a unique responsibility to mind the role of contagion and mutation in history. Leadership is both among the most powerful drivers of contagion and mutation and the one most susceptible to falling prey to other drivers.

I never tell anyone what to do with respect to their ethics dilemmas, and I certainly wouldn't tell anyone how they should vote. But I offer the framework as a starting place. The framework helps us to integrate ethics into our voting decisions and to recalibrate our baseline expectations for ethical behaviors from our political leaders.

Let's say you are choosing among candidates running for president, prime minister, or another extremely powerful position. Frame your decision by first comparing your priority set of *principles*—the guides for your decisions that signal to the world how you operate and how you expect others to behave. What are your most important principles? How do they align with the candidates' stated principles? If a candidate demonstrates little respect for one of your core principles, for example truth or equal rights, take this as a serious warning sign.

Often your principles won't be in alignment with a candidate's, and you will have to determine your priorities. For instance, if gender equality is important to you and your favored candidate has voted against bills that ensure equal pay, but they're *also* a staunch advocate for the environment, which is another principle for you, then you may have to decide how you can prioritize your principles and come to a compromise.

Next, go deeper and look at the available *information*. Here is where many of us feel overwhelmed. Some people even choose not to vote because they, understandably, don't know how to parse all the information, don't have a lot of time, or just don't know where to start. But if we focus on two key elements we already have most of the learning we need to make an ethically informed choice. First, we are looking for evidence of whether the candidates' actions reflect their stated principles—whether they align with past behaviors, policies, voting record, and positions on specific issues such as climate change or economic inequality.

Second, we look for signs that the candidate gives in to, or further spreads, drivers of contagion of unethical behavior. Most importantly, we ask whether the candidate values truth. Any evidence of a disregard for truth should be a deal breaker. Compromised truth in one area will spread to other areas and likely indicate that other negative drivers of contagion are at play. Not much else the candidate does or says can be trusted (promises, commitments, claimed transparency, or accounts of the past). And the candidate's close advisors, supporters, and staff (the supporting cast) are also likely to find themselves tangled in a web of contagion—starting with an inability to speak out to correct untruths—just as Johnson's did.

In the political realm, the other leading drivers to consider frequently include greed, lack of transparency (for example, failure to disclose medical or tax records), abuse of power, demands for loyalty rather than inviting diversity of views, and arrogance. Johnson showed us that the cost of a leader who displays drivers of contagion like these has always been too high. On the edge, it is a humanity-defining risk. He also revealed the potential to spread nation-defining progress.

Thoughtful people may disagree on principles, issues, and candidates. But we all can make a commitment to consider ethics in our voting by asking:

What are my principles?

How do they align with what the candidates say their principles are?

What does the information indicate? Are the candidates making decisions and behaving in alignment with their stated principles? Is a candidate saying one thing and then doing and proposing the opposite?

If you stopped framing right there, you'd have integrated ethics into your vote more than many citizens, increasing the chances of electing an ethically committed person to sit in the White House or run your local school board.

The framework can also guide a range of particularly challenging scenarios many of us face. People frequently tell me that they want to vote for a candidate whose policies on one or two key issues align with theirs, but they find the person's behavior abhorrent. The president of the United States is one of the most contagious drivers of ethics in the world. If you're a "single-issue voter," or even someone who mostly agrees with a candidate's policies to the point where you will ignore a terrible ethics record, ask yourself first: Would I tolerate this same behavior from a friend? Would I stand by and allow someone to treat my spouse or my child the way this candidate treats people? How would I feel if the CEO of the company I work for started emulating these same behaviors?

Another example I often observe involves situations where voters have a choice between two or more candidates they dislike. (Of course, if there are two or three perfectly reasonable and ethically minded candidates, you can choose the one whose principles *mostly* align with yours, accepting that you may compromise one or more of your principles.) People who don't like any of the options may decide to skip the process entirely and not vote. That is always your right. But please don't make this decision without first applying the framework to the choice. If you've plugged in principles and information, and you're still unable to make a choice—or if you're considering a single-issue vote for a candidate with a terrible ethics record—it may help to take a deeper dive into the next two rungs of the framework: *stakeholders* and *consequences*.

As you know from previous chapters, we are never the only stakeholders in our decisions. Yet we often vote as if we are. In democracies today, I believe that we have a responsibility to look at the stakeholders and consequences beyond our own countries. For citizens of the U.S., the United Kingdom, the European Union, Japan, Australia, and other powerful democratic nations, our vote has global consequences on stakeholders whom we will never even know. Our elected leaders, especially in the U.S., have an enormous impact on the rest of the world.

In addition to powerfully driving contagion, a president can determine foreign policy, foreign aid or sanctions, strategic alliances, and even acts of war, potentially bringing the men, women, and children of other countries grave harm or hope for new opportunity. Voting is a privilege and a signal to citizens around the world that *If you cannot vote, if you cannot express yourself freely where you live, those of us who can will keep you front of mind*. Your vote has the power to change lives. Not everyone holds this power, which is why it is so sacred.

The consequence of abstaining from voting because you don't like any of the candidates is that you are *giving up your power* to determine who becomes a world leader. You don't get to decide that neither candidate will be president. Consider first: Are there consequences to choosing either candidate that will be completely unacceptable to you? Or binary issues relating to one candidate that make you unable to vote for him or her? For example, they promote racism or argue for an irresponsible approach to nuclear escalation.

Choosing not to vote diminishes your influence over the outcome of the election and the consequences, both now and over time. It means that you abstain from expressing an opinion about countless stakeholders and matters such as national security, domestic policy, privacy rights, Supreme Court appointments, regulatory powers, borders and immigration, as well as numerous issues on the edge, such as cryptocurrencies, autonomous weapons, internet safety, human germline editing, artificial intelligence, and so many more widespread, irreparable, and unpredictable consequences than ever before. *But because you had the power to choose, you still have the responsibility for the choice.* Opting not to vote does not absolve us of ethical responsibility for the risks and opportunities that ensue when a new leader takes office.

Another argument I frequently hear is that our single votes are inconsequential. If you are among the rising chorus of those who say that a single vote does not matter, I'd argue that a win is a collection of single votes, and a loss is an absence of enough single votes. Around the world, there is a long history of very close election results—times when every single vote really did matter. Here's a small sampling: In 2017, U.K. Labour Party candidate Emma Dent Coad unseated the incumbent in Kensington by just twenty votes; two years later she lost her seat to a challenger by 150 votes. In 2016, David Adkins held on to his seat in the New Mexico House of Representatives by just nine votes. In 2000, after the U.S. Supreme Court intervened in a highly contested recount in Florida, Republican presidential nominee George W. Bush beat Democratic nominee Al Gore by just 537 votes, giving him enough electoral college votes to win the election. And in 1981, an outsider named Bernie Sanders who'd never held office became the mayor of Burlington, Vermont, after he beat the incumbent by ten votes.

Every single vote contributes to a result. Yet voter turnout in the United States in 2018 was approximately 53 percent, according to census data. By contrast, voter turnout in Sweden in 2018 was approximately 87 percent. According to exit polls in the United Kingdom, young people who will be more affected than their elders by the decision to leave the European Union came out in fewer numbers to vote on the referendum than their elders.

Who we are individually collectively adds up to who we are as a nation when we vote. Take the time to frame your decision. As Robert Caro reminds us: "Study a particular election in sufficient depth—study not merely the candidates' platforms and philosophies and promises but its payoffs, study it in all its brutality—focus deeply enough on all of these elements, and there will emerge universal truths about campaigns in a democracy, and about the nature of the power that shapes our lives."

If more of us approached voting as a sacred honor and responsibility, just imagine the collective raising of ethical standards we would require of our leaders. Imagine the positive consequences around the world. Imagine how our ethical ideas, behaviors, and decisions might even become contagious.

Chapter Four

———

CRUMBLING PILLARS

I was recently visiting a friend at her apartment in London. As she was making dinner, she pointed to her new device, a cylindrical speaker on the countertop, and then asked it, "Alexa, what's the weather in London tomorrow?" The device came alive and spoke back with an answer about rain. My friend had an Amazon Echo with Alexa voice control, but it could have been any one of the smart speakers in millions of homes worldwide.

When Alexa first launched in 2014, I was skeptical. I was already easily checking the weather and listening to music on my phone. But more importantly, I was uncomfortable with the idea of Alexa "listening" to me.

Thankfully, my friend's device stayed quiet through dinner and I mostly forgot about it. But I occasionally wondered if it was off, or listening, or perhaps listening *and* recording.

On my way home, while reaching in my purse, I accidentally triggered the Siri assistant on my iPhone and heard her disembodied voice ask, "What can I help you with?" Shutting that off, I started wondering how the ubiquity of digital assistants affects children. Would I have allowed my (now grown) children to seek advice from Siri or Alexa or to even order *her* around? What kind of mental health and behavioral consequences arise? Do we risk raising a generation that doesn't read the news, seek information through research, or worse, expects to have a digital servant at their beck and call?

Shortly after the visit with my friend, Alexa surfaced again in my professional world. Preparing for one of my classes at Stanford, I came across an article about Alexa's role in a double murder case. According to the story, a U.S. judge ordered Amazon to hand recordings from an Echo device in a New Hampshire home over to homicide investigators because there was probable cause to believe it contained "evidence of crimes." Specifically, the judge mentioned the server "and/or records maintained for or by Amazon.com" containing recordings made by the device. I vaguely understood what it meant that Alexa's audio data was being stored on a server, but I had no idea of the implications for me or for society.

I read through Amazon's FAQs on its website, which said that Alexa listens for specific "wake words": Alexa, Amazon, computer, or Echo. Upon hearing the words, "a recording of what you asked Alexa is sent to Amazon's Cloud" where the request is processed. Still not terribly reassured, I pressed on and found: "No audio is stored or sent to the cloud unless the device detects the wake word (or Alexa is activated by pressing a button)."

Even after my research, I still had little understanding of what I would be consenting to if I invited Alexa into my home or office. I had no idea what the real consequences were. Could anyone listen to these recordings? Could Amazon sell the data? And I wasn't speaking to a person who could answer any question I could ask; I was speaking to a machine that could only answer questions that it was programmed to process and respond to.

The proliferation of edgy technologies such as Alexa and other home-based digital assistants, along with our enthusiastic adoption of them in our routine habits, contributes to the critical collapse of three pillars of ethical decision-making. Even when we make an effort to

understand or seek advice about the potential consequences of our use, the results fall short of informing and protecting us.

For centuries, we have shared common expectations of how we behave ethically in society, based largely on a mutual understanding of the reality in which our decisions play out. These underlying expectations have come to be guided by three pillars that support ethical decision-making: *transparency* (the open sharing of important information); *informed consent* (agreeing to an action based on an understanding of the action and its consequences); and *effective listening* (grasping the speaker's meaning).

On the edge, we need these pillars more than ever because they help us reestablish this common understanding in an increasingly complex reality. As you will see, these three pillars inform our choices, helping us to answer: Are we making decisions based on a mutual and accurate understanding of what is at stake—the information, stakeholders, and consequences? How should we allocate ethical responsibility for the decision? The pillars also connect us to one another, from doctor-patient relationships, friendships, and romantic relationships to corporate behavior toward consumers and a government's engagement with its citizens. And they may even connect us more ethically to our machines.

We will examine a fourth force influencing ethics—how and why the pillars are crumbling and what that means for our ethical decision-making—through the lens of direct-to-consumer genetic-testing kits like 23andMe. We will see how the pillars should work and how to manage their crumbling in our own choices. Among the issues we will consider are the surprising ways in which well-meaning consumers who consent to use these genetic-testing kits may also unwittingly consent to expose, and potentially harm, close family members, relatives, and others they don't even know; how evolving uses and technologies related to these kits further challenge the pillars; how scattered power and contagion enter the fray; and how to reestablish effective listening.

The three pillars:

Transparency is sharing accurate information that could have a meaningful impact on the outcome—the consequences over time and responsibility—of our decisions. Being transparent does not mean disclosing every potential risk, but it should include the information that a reasonable person would need in order to make a good choice given their set of circumstances. For example, transparency generally works well with regulated medications: Companies alert us to the appropriate dosage, who shouldn't take it, dangerous interactions with other drugs, and potential side effects. Most of us don't need to know the history of the formula or consumption data in other countries. In other cases, *you* might be responsible for transparency, like disclosing defects in a car you are selling or telling your boss that you made a mistake.

Transparency can also inform decisions we make as a society. We expect governments to be transparent about such matters as public spending, corruption, and pollution levels (which, in turn, affects how we vote). Citizens increasingly expect companies to publish data related to important societal trends, such as gender pay gaps or diversity and inclusivity efforts or their record on environmental sustainability (all of which can inform decisions about whether we would like to work for a particular company or buy its products). Transparency can underpin informed consent, but it is also important on its own.

Informed consent is when we agree to a particular action based on our understanding of what the action involves and the potential consequences. Parents routinely sign consent forms when sending a child to summer camp. They trust that the camp directors will sufficiently inform them of the potential risks of their child's experience that they might not think of on their own. Done properly, the information on the consent form one signs is user-friendly and aimed to assure that the person granting consent understands it. Informed consent does not include a promise of perfect information or guaranteed results, but it is a mark of our trust in both the information given and those delivering it.

Effective listening requires paying close enough attention to what someone says, and how they say it, so that we understand what they really mean. Listening also partners with informed consent, whether the speaker (or the one receiving the information) is a camp director, a doctor, or a friend. On the edge, our listening must be more attentive to detail, nuance, and even the meaning of what *isn't* actually said, or we risk missing the type and magnitude of the gaps in the information. As a result, we miss stakeholders and consequences, skewing our decision-making.

The three pillars provide an infrastructure for us to engage with each other ethically. When the pillars work well, they help us to accurately assess the information, stakeholders, and consequences that are at stake in our decisions. In particular, they help us focus on what really matters—whether our children risk exposure to unexpected injury at camp or whether a food product has allergens—and not waste time. In other words, the pillars anchor our ethical decision-making in reality. As will be seen in the following stories, they also help us hold each other to account and allocate responsibility for ethics, including between corporations and individuals. For all these reasons, they are the scaffolding for trust.

But on the edge these classic ethics pillars crumble. We often can no longer rely on them. Without transparency, we might consent to potential consequences we don't understand, with unpredictable and permanent effects on our own and others' lives. Consumer technology products and platforms spread unfounded trust in the crumbling pillars widely in day-to-day situations. For example, what kinds of questions can Alexa respond to? Where will our conversation go, who can hear it, and can it be used in a court of law?

But crumbling doesn't mean *disintegrated*. We can see the shapes of the pillars in online consent forms, terms of service for social media, disclaimers in advertising, pop-ups on websites requiring we click on "I agree." But they just don't *function* as we would expect. They have become a rote exercise in clicking away annoying small print, rather than a source of protection and a good-faith interaction with a vendor. This causes even greater confusion and diminished trust.

Corporations, governments, and all of us have an opportunity to commit to the pillars, make ethical choices, and fortify our connections. But more than ever, the obligation is on each of us. As *Time* magazine's 2006 Person of the Year announcement noted: "You. Yes, you. You control the Information Age. Welcome to your world."

An estimated 26 million people had given their DNA information to the databases of the leading genetic-testing companies by 2019, according to an investigation by *MIT Technology Review.* The report further predicts that these companies will know the genetic makeup of more than 100 million people by 2021. While these tests are exceedingly popular, and have many benefits, the risks are difficult to discern and continually evolving. Do we really understand what we are consenting to—or what effect our consent could have on others?

∞

In November 2007, Silicon Valley–based 23andMe launched its first direct-to-consumer genetic-testing kits in the United States for ancestry and health information. For $999, along with a swab of saliva and DNA from inside your cheek, the 23andMe test could predict your risk for and likelihood of developing such common conditions as type 2 diabetes, heart disease, and colorectal cancer—information that would normally be obtained through a genetic counselor or other medical professional.

A year later, the price dropped to $399 for a test that could now provide reports on ninety different "diseases, traits and conditions," from celiac disease and psoriasis to Parkinson's disease and prostate cancer. In September 2008, 23andMe hosted a party in New York during Fashion Week, where models, designers, and celebrity guests provided saliva samples to learn about their genetic tendencies. *Time* named 23andMe's retail DNA test the Best Invention of 2008. Over time, the company flooded the market with national television commercials and feature spots on morning talk shows and in *Good Housekeeping*, where it was touted as a way to research your genealogy and unlock genetic mysteries. The DNA test kit even landed a spot on Oprah's "Favorite Things" list.

23andMe wasn't the first or only company to sell genetic tests directly to the public, but it was an era-defining start-up that pursued a mainstream market in an effort to put personal genetic information in the hands of consumers. Among its earliest core values (or "principles," when we are framing): "We believe that having the means to access one's genetic information is good" and "We believe that your genetic information should be controlled by you."

A handful of genetic-testing companies have since joined the direct-to-consumer market, normalizing the procedure (contagion) to the point where DNA kits are featured as "a unique holiday gift for the person who has everything" in *People* magazine and sold at a discount on Amazon and Walmart during Black Friday and Cyber Monday. 23andMe had a $2.5 billion valuation in 2019, according to *Forbes* and CNBC.

These kits are an innovation on the edge that offers tremendous benefits and risks. As the National Institutes of Health points out, self-tests raise greater awareness of genetic diseases; are frequently less expensive than testing offered by health care providers; do not require one to seek the approval of a doctor or insurance company; could lead a user to "be more proactive about" their own health; and collect genetic data that could be used to further scientific research and our understanding of diseases.

And yet, medical information has traditionally been the domain of health care providers, who are bound to strict rules on patient confidentiality, informed consent, and attentive listening. 23andMe, however, bypasses doctors, genetic counselors, and even pharmacists. It's another example of disintermediation, as when sharing economy companies cut out the middle person. We might be prepared to accept the risks of disintermediation by Airbnb—maybe speaking to a desk clerk is not that important because the consequences of insufficient information or misunderstandings only affect our vacation. But when we disintermediate medical expertise, the pillars crumble. We have to inform *ourselves* of serious potential consequences, based on the reading of a box or a website that communicates to a general audience, rather than having a discussion with an expert about our specific situation.

When assessing new technologies and biotechnologies, we must probe where and how they dismantle the pillars, whether by failing to provide transparency, by coaxing us to grant consent when we cannot possibly understand the stakes and our responsibility, or by eliminating listening. It's not good enough to just throw up our hands and dismiss centuries of ethics pillars with a click on "I accept." We need to understand how their erosion affects our ethics.

Further, we cannot expect the creators of these technologies to think about the pillars for us. "There are a lot of misperceptions about genetics," 23andMe's cofounder Anne Wojcicki told the *New York Times* in 2013. "But there's a big societal shift where we're putting the onus of your health onto you, the individual."

By "putting the onus of your health onto you," companies like 23andMe offer opportunities *and* a Pandora's box of risk. They force us to grapple with complicated questions of biology, paternity, and identity—yet without the benefits of adequate transparency, informed consent, and effective listening to undergird our decisions. When the pillars are degraded, the information wrung from the framework collapses, and therefore so does our understanding of potential stakeholders and consequences of our decisions.

On the edge, the three pillars may not function properly for three main reasons that we will explore more through the stories to come. These three reasons affect us as consumers, but they also influence major societal decisions about where we draw ethical lines and how we regulate.

First, science has not yet confirmed the information we need to understand the potential consequences of consent. And the law is caught in an impossible situation: dangerously lagging behind technology but also stuck waiting for science to further inform.

Second, we cannot know the information because companies (or governments) refuse to tell us. This is fixable. Companies can be proactive in disclosing information, making it understandable, and slowing down new product releases until they have better visibility of the potential consequences. Regulators can require companies to provide additional transparency by updating disclosure requirements to cover evolving risks. But to do so, regulators must understand those risks. Here again, they depend on science (and accelerating their own efforts).

Third, we can't know the information because it changes unpredictably. New uses and products continually emerge. In turn, these developments can alter the risks and opportunities, even retroactively, of consumers who purchased and used the product much earlier. This uncertainty recalls scattered power, contagion, and mutation: The initial products are splintering off into unanticipated uses, and inspiring new products, with ever more unpredictable, undetectable, and contagious risks that companies cannot control or predict either. The law and society lag further behind as each of these developments are unleashed on the public and present new challenges.

In 23andMe's case, all three reasons weaken the pillars: Science and the law continue to evolve; the company struggled to provide easily digestible information to consumers; and the information changes unpredictably as others develop new technologies related to its product.

This case also spotlights the responsibility of all companies to support the pillars proactively and voluntarily no matter the legal requirements. In fact, here, regulators did have to get involved.

In November 2013, 23andMe received a "Warning Letter" from the FDA that it was in "violation of the Federal Food, Drug and Cosmetic Act." The agency said it had been "diligently working to help" 23andMe since July 2009; and 23andMe had stated that clinical data the agency had asked for would be forthcoming. But, the letter went on: "The FDA has not received any communication from 23andMe since May 2013. Instead, we have become aware that you have initiated new marketing campaigns, including television commercials." 23andMe was ordered to "immediately discontinue marketing" its genetic health services until it had received proper authorization. (The ancestry reports were allowed to continue.)

By October 2015, after nearly two years of working with the FDA, 23andMe was allowed to provide health information and "carrier status reports" for thirty-six different genetic diseases, including cystic fibrosis and Tay-Sachs disease, and their updated health reports were deemed to have met "FDA requirements for being scientifically and clinically valid." In the years that followed, more of its testing services were approved by the FDA. The company also made changes and updates to product language and web pages dedicated to helping users navigate their health reports as a way to be more *transparent*. They attempted to reinsert *listening* into the process by suggesting that users consult with "someone knowledgeable about clinical genetics" when reviewing their results.

23andMe is not unique in grappling with transparency. All companies have a responsibility to assure that the information they provide is accessible and that *the recipient understands it—not just that it was delivered*. And the recipient shouldn't have to go on a fishing expedition, obtain legal advice, or hold a PhD to interpret the information. The most important information should be provided to consumers in the simplest possible language, in large visible type on the homepage or somewhere you are required to go before making a choice.

Transparency should also be factual and not an attempt to persuade us to grant consent. For example, 23andMe tests are a mainstream consumer product touted on its website as a way to "Take action to stay healthy" and "start discovering what your DNA says about you." Its homepage features smiling, athletic customers, and a bright headline: "Health Happens Now." Scroll down, and there are more statistics and proactive statements like: "Know your genes. Own your health" and "Learn how genetics can influence your chances of developing certain health conditions."

A thoughtful person might surmise: *This product can give me helpful medical information.* Only after reading through the terms of service disclaimers do we discover: "23andMe Services are for research, informational, and educational use only. We do not provide medical advice" and "You should not change your health behaviors solely on the basis [of] Genetic Information from 23andMe." We shouldn't have to dig through fine print and legal terms to learn that the word *health* shouldn't actually be interpreted as related to anything medical.

Transparency requires companies to take care to avoid potentially misleading language and to draw attention to irreparable consequences. In this case, the medical language on 23andMe's site ("type 2 diabetes," "Health Predisposition reports," and "Carrier Status") could be confusing. And the following important warning, which should not be buried in terms of service legalese, merits pushing the pause button before you confirm purchase: "You may discover things about yourself that trouble you and that you may not have the ability to control or change. . . . These outcomes could have social, legal, or economic implications."

Companies have a responsibility to ensure that consumers understand not only the written words provided but also the *implications* of their decisions to engage. A young couple giving one another a DNA kit as a gift might not be ready for some of what they could learn—such as how they could be affected if their tests reveal that one is a carrier of an inherited disease that could be passed down to future children.

Drilling down, whether voluntarily (ethics flying higher than the law) or mandated by regulation, transparency should deliver understanding about known risks and knowable future risks. This 23andMe terms of service disclaimer seems critical: "Future scientific research may change the interpretation of your DNA." In other words, yesterday, the test results said you were 30 percent of a particular ethnicity; but in the future, it might say, sorry, you're actually 5 percent. This is a real risk because the answers you receive are only as accurate as the data behind them. As more diverse customers upload their DNA, the better the reference points are and the more granular your percentages become. Imagine how disturbing it is to experience a shifting view of your own identity or genetic propensity to develop diseases over time as the data set evolves.

Less obvious, consider the implications for insurance. Even if the company claims not to share your results with insurance companies (a policy that could change), once you learn from this test that you might have a predisposition for a particular disease, can a failure to disclose it to your insurance company become grounds for nullifying their obligations if you do fall ill? Can your premiums be increased if you disclose it? How would failure to disclose align with your own principles around honesty?

Remember that genetic-testing companies are commercial entities—not university medical centers, government bodies, or nonprofit projects. They operate on a "buyer beware" premise and aren't required to follow established medical or university research ethics practices.

These foundational direct-to-consumer DNA kits are just the beginning. As the next stories illustrate, this innovative technology spawns many new uses and products, each further degrading the three pillars in different ways. Most importantly, these mutations reveal that whatever the language of the consent forms, when we grant consent to engage with these tests, we are not just consenting to the services the kits promise. And we're not just consenting for ourselves. We could expose relatives' secrets, inadvertently revise our family history, and even place our own kin in the crosshairs of law enforcement.

∞

In the summer of 1986, a five-year-old girl named Lisa was left with a neighbor at a recreational vehicle park in California by a man claiming to be her father. He never came back. Lisa grew up with no memory of her mother. Sixteen years later, the man who abandoned her was arrested and convicted of murder. A DNA test revealed that he wasn't even related to Lisa. He refused to answer any questions and died in prison in 2010.

By the time Lisa became a mother, she still had no answers to questions like, "Who am I really," and "What happened to my mother?" But in 2015, the detectives on Lisa's case turned to genealogy sleuth Dr. Barbara Rae-Venter for help. Dr. Rae-Venter knew how to puzzle out DNA test results and help people find their biological parents using DNA-matching sites, family trees, and public records—but this was her first murder mystery. To begin, Lisa sent saliva samples to 23andMe and Ancestry.com for DNA analysis. She received genetic profile data from those two companies and used it to search for relatives on their databases, as well as the databases of ancestry sites FamilyTreeDNA and GEDmatch.

When it comes to genetic sleuthing, the more DNA you share with a person, the closer your relationship. A parent and a child share approximately 50 percent of their DNA; grandparent and grandchild share approximately 25 percent; and first cousins share an average of 12.5 percent. Within days, they found possible second and third cousins to Lisa, two of whom agreed to provide their DNA in an effort to narrow the search for her parents.

Eventually, they found Lisa's maternal grandfather. He told Lisa that when she was just six months old, her mother took her and left their home in New Hampshire with a boyfriend—the same man who had abandoned her. The three were never seen again. Detectives linked the man's movements to other unsolved cases to determine that he likely killed Lisa's mother and several other women and children, including one child who shared his DNA: his own daughter.

When a cold case investigator in Northern California learned about this groundbreaking case, he asked Dr. Rae-Venter if she could help them track down a serial killer who had terrorized residents in the 1970s and 1980s. She agreed to try. By comparing DNA left at a crime scene with DNA already in the database of ancestry site GEDmatch, Rae-Venter built a genetic path leading to Joseph DeAngelo, a seventy-two-year-old former police officer. DeAngelo's DNA was not in the database, but a distant relative's DNA was. The "Golden State Killer" was arrested in 2018. In 2020, he pleaded guilty to 26 counts of murder and kidnapping and was sentenced to life in prison.

Lisa's genetic mystery was solved with the help of direct-to-consumer genetic-testing kits and genealogy websites, a mutation of the original use of the kit. Soon, this new mutation became contagious on its own as law enforcement agencies across the nation began collaborating with genealogists and mining ancestry sites for clues to hundreds of cold cases. In the months after DeAngelo's 2018 arrest, investigative genetic genealogy methods were used to identify suspects in more than forty other cold cases, leading to a conviction in the 1987 murder of a Canadian couple, and the exoneration of an Idaho man who'd spent twenty years in prison for a 1996 rape and murder that he did not commit.

For the victims and loved ones whose lives had been destroyed, Lisa's case set in motion an opportunity for answers. But myriad ethical conundrums emerge when we share our DNA. As these stories show, we may become unwitting informants. Rae-Venter and the police, for instance, found a warrant workaround in GEDmatch.

Free and open to the public, the GEDmatch database began as a hobby project by a retired Florida grandfather who wanted to help people use the results they receive from companies like 23andMe as a way to search for relatives. He joined forces with a sixty-seven-year-old computer coder, and together they launched GEDmatch in 2010. By 2018, when DeAngelo was arrested, GEDmatch held the genetic profiles of more than one million people.

According to a report in the journal *Science*, if 2 percent of a target population submit their DNA to a site like GEDmatch, ultimately 99 percent of that population will find a third cousin or closer match—a genetic identification. In their analysis of genomic data from more than 1.2 million individuals, researchers found that "about 60% of the searches for individuals of European descent" resulted in such a match. "The technique could implicate nearly any U.S. individual of European descent in the near future," the authors noted.

"It's kind of been a shock to all of us how these things developed," GEDmatch's eighty-year-old founder told the *New York Times* after learning from television news that his site helped to find the Golden State Killer. He hadn't even considered that GEDmatch could be mined to solve crimes, and his terms of service had only a brief warning: "While the results presented on this site are intended solely for genealogical research, we are unable to guarantee that users will not find other uses. If you find the possibility unacceptable, please remove your data from this site." And 23andMe likely could not have anticipated a site like GEDmatch either.

After learning about the arrest of the Golden State Killer, GEDmatch's owners attempted to be more transparent. They updated their terms of service to explain how DNA data could be exploited. They also admitted that they could not guarantee confidentiality or foresee the future for DNA and genealogy research, GEDmatch, or how a person's information might be used if the company were sold. Users could either "Accept" a long list of caveats and sign in, "Reject" them and click on a link to permanently delete their information and leave the site, or "Decide Later."

Because GEDmatch continued to be heavily used by police, the founders changed its terms of service yet again in May 2019. Everyone's data was now off-limits to law enforcement unless a user logged in and granted consent. Further, GEDmatch gave users the power to decide where their data fit among four categories: "private" (not accessible to anyone else, including law enforcement), "public + opt-in" (accessible to all, including law enforcement), "public + opt-out" (accessible for comparison by anyone else who uploaded their data in the database, except law enforcement), and "research" (accessible for research purposes only). GEDmatch at least understood that transparency involves a commitment to monitor and continue to fill in the information gaps and adjust the technology.

But on the edge, we are always playing catch-up, as we saw with the FDA catching up to 23andMe. By the time GEDmatch opted everyone "out," the genie was already out of the bottle. *BuzzFeed News* revealed that the owners of genetic-testing company FamilyTreeDNA, which had marketed itself as a leader in privacy, had made a secret deal in 2018 to open its DNA databases to the FBI, without a warrant or subpoena. (After this report, FamilyTreeDNA updated its policy to include an opt-out for users who did not want their results shared with law enforcement.)

One of the biggest issues with informed consent is that the law and the companies' and other stakeholders' situations change over time. We are in a constant cycle of being unable to stop, or even understand, new genies in time. For example, 23andMe promises not to provide your information "to law enforcement or regulatory authorities unless required by law." But the law will inevitably evolve to keep pace with different uses of DNA evidence and evolving societal views. A company's policy on handing over test results to authorities could also change from time to time. You may have received update alerts from companies such as Apple or Amazon. We are deemed—considered legally bound—to have accepted those updated conditions if we continue using the product. Our informed consent to companies today is a legal commitment that they can rely on over time, even as they change the terms of service on us. But we are tied to future risks—both because most of us can't keep up with the legal and policy changes (so we just keep using the product), and because legal protections added over time often arrive too late.

Sometimes, we are also asked to consent today to tomorrow's unknown scientific and technological world. For example, the 23andMe terms of service state, "You acknowledge and agree"—aka *you consent*—"that the form and nature of the Services which 23andMe provides may change from time to time *without prior notice to you*." The emphasis is mine, to highlight that the company is asking you to consent at the time you use the product to steps they take to "innovate" (and any new risks) even if they don't inform you about it. They might not even know how their products will evolve as scientific advancements occur.

But some potential future events should be clear to the company. We each must consider future developments, and companies owe us that information in plain speak—not buried in the terms of service. If you consent to your data being used for research (an interesting and important opportunity that 23andMe offers), could the company decide to sell your data to a pharmaceutical manufacturer that uses it to develop the next addictive painkiller? What happens to your data if a company goes out of business, merges with another, or is sold to a company that has policies you're unaware of, let alone would ever consent to? GEDmatch, for instance, was acquired by forensic genomics firm Verogen in December 2019. The company said its terms of service with respect to "the use, purposes of processing, and disclosures of user data" would remain the same. But users might be concerned that their genetic data could be owned by a firm that partners with law enforcement to solve crimes.

GEDmatch's story illustrates how companies and consumers cannot predict the ways in which edgy technologies might splinter into unpredictable new uses—the third reason why the pillars may not function properly. While our consent to use these genetic testing kits might expose criminals, it can also affect innocent family members, relatives, and others.

One heartbreaking example, which is happening globally, comes to us from an American biologist's anonymized 2014 essay in *Vox,* in which he describes how "excited" he was to buy 23andMe kits for himself and his parents as part of a class he was teaching on the genome. When reviewing their reports online, he and his father both clicked on a consent box that opted them in to finding "close family members." This feature would compare their DNA with that of other users to match them with relatives. That's when the biologist discovered he had a previously unknown half brother named Thomas, who was adopted at birth and never knew his biological parents. Thomas and the biologist had the same father. This secret "devastated" his family.

"My parents divorced. No one is talking to my dad. We're not anywhere close to being healed yet and I don't know how long it will take to put the pieces back together," he wrote. "When you check that [close relatives] box, it should have a bunch of stars and bells and whistles around it. Because there are plenty of people who click boxes . . . and never put a whole lot of thought into the possibilities."

And yet, one needn't even click a box to uncover startling information. When two or more members of a family take DNA tests together, they may uncover a "non-paternity event." The International Society of Genetic Genealogy refers to non-paternity events (NPEs) as "cases of false paternity where the biological father of a child is someone other than who it is presumed to be." Sometimes there are follow-on discoveries, such as discovering that a sibling is actually a half sibling.

Non-paternity events are so common that a private Facebook group called DNA NPE Friends was created in 2017 to help members cope with the unexpected traumas. As an investigation by *The Atlantic* reveals, direct-to-consumer genetic-testing kits have also unearthed affairs, incest, rapes, and one case in which a fertility doctor used his own sperm to secretly father the children of at least fifty patients.

These stories spotlight a key threat to informed consent with direct-to-consumer DNA-testing kits and an increasing array of technologies on the edge. When we consent to share our genetic code, we are not only consenting for ourselves, we are agreeing to expose other stakeholders to unforeseeable risks. We might not be aware of these stakeholders, and they might not know of us or want anything to do with us. They may never even know we granted consent—or they may find out through an unwelcome shock.

It's not just that we cannot un-know the information we learn, and we cannot anticipate in advance how we will react. It's that we cannot be sure whether and how that information might be shared. Even more difficult, we cannot predict how others will react (the biologist couldn't have known what his parents would say or do), how they will share the information (will they tell other family members or post it on social media), or the consequences they will suffer ("no one is talking" to his dad). So even if a company is transparent about the potential implications of use of its product, it cannot anticipate many of the circumstances we might face or stakeholders who might be affected. It becomes a catch-22: We can't consider the implications properly without knowing who the stakeholders could be, and stakeholders who never consented never have the opportunity to consider the implications.

The allocation of responsibility for the impact on other people falls largely on us. Deciphering 23andMe's jargon-laden terms of service may be harrowing, but the company cannot control much more than clarifying the transparency and consent process about this risk of de facto consenting for others or, at the very least, about learning news that will significantly impact others. Before we even begin to consider engaging with these services, it's up to us to recognize that these kits reveal information that relates to people close to us. We're not just uncovering our own story, so we must ask ourselves: *Who else am I inadvertently consenting for?* Whether or not the terms of service say so, we have responsibility for the impact our decisions have on others. Here again, you are never the only stakeholder in your story.

We have a duty to ask ourselves whether we are prepared for the fact that we will not be able to *un-know* what we are about to learn. And if we are ready for the responsibility that comes with uncovering information that others must also cope with—information they only discovered because of our choices. However mainstream these products may be, the news they deliver is anything but routine for the individual receiving it. Consider whether you would tell your spouse if you discovered that you had the genetic mutation for a condition like Huntington's disease. What if your child could have it as well? Consider whether you really want to give a kit as a casual gift to a friend, knowing the responsibility it entails.

On the edge, we may do our best with what we know, and make every effort to see reality, but good intentions are just not enough. The biologist, for example, did not intend to cause his parents harm. The fact that such a highly educated consumer found himself in a challenging situation shows that it could happen to any of us. The framework cannot unearth every eventuality. But using it to guide decisions, including paying attention to how the erosion of the pillars today affects the information rung, helps us see more clearly unexpected results such as finding lost or unknown family members.

As newer risks become apparent, and different uses catch on, companies will have increasing obligations to update and simplify their transparency warnings. That responsibility becomes vastly greater when a consumer is in danger of causing serious emotional and other potential harm to unknowable stakeholders by using the company's products.

The pervasiveness of these technologies also influences our attitudes about what information is private and what knowledge we share. Through contagion and mutation, the decision to use these tests becomes part of everyday life. It influences what we consider normal, what we tolerate, what seeps into our laws, our practices, and how we make decisions collectively as a society. But normalized doesn't mean right. Whether we are going too far in allowing private companies to hold our DNA is a question we all must face.

Scattered power and mutation can partner with crumbling pillars to further intentional wrongdoing—not just complicate good-faith consumer consent.

Sociologists at Harvard and UCLA recently looked at the question of DNA and identity from a slightly different prism: white nationalism. Researchers Aaron Panofsky and Joan Donovan studied a globally popular "white pride" online discussion forum and found that white nationalists were using genetic ancestry tests from 23andMe and Ancestry.com to confirm the "purity" of their "whiteness." Not surprisingly, some members also stumbled upon what was, for them, upsetting evidence of non-white and non-European ancestry when reviewing the results of these kits.

Panofsky and Donovan found "remarkable insights" on how these members' peers reacted to such news. Combing through thousands of online responses to forum members who revealed their non-white results and asked for counsel, they found that occasionally members shamed or excluded the posters. But more often, they offered "identity repair" strategies that rejected or reinterpreted the results. These claims dismissed the science and the scientists, offering "white nationalist counter-knowledge." Some asserted the superiority of "traditional genealogical knowledge," such as family histories over genetic tests. *("My advice is to trust your own family tree genealogy research and what your grandparents have told you before trusting a DNA test"* or even *"It's also very unlikely for whites to be mixed if their genealogy shows all European ancestors five or more generations back. Rampant race mixing wasn't going on back then the way it is today.")* Others justified dismissing test results because "race or ethnicity is directly visible." Still others rejected the tests on the basis of conspiracy theories that the companies producing the tests have an anti-white bias. (*"These companies are quite liberal about ensuring every white person gets a little sprinkling of non-white DNA."*)

White nationalists dismantled informed consent by discrediting the science and distributors of the tests. They did this by "picking and choosing" among "genetic, statistical, historical, and anthropological knowledge" that supported their desired identity rather than by attacking the validity of the consent process. Again, we have mutation: deploying compromised truth (the denial of scientific evidence) to twist results to a desired outcome when the genetic tests don't confirm their ideas about their identity.

This study illustrates another challenge to the three pillars: how the other forces, particularly scattered power and contagion, can contribute to the crumbling. All three pillars hinge on truth. They not only crumble, they completely collapse when infected with compromised truth. Transparency is only helpful if it is accurate; informed consent means accurately informed; and effective listening means listening to what someone is really saying.

The white supremacists' false assertions about the scientific method, the vendors, and the entire field were not a reflection of a consumer's understandable inability to interpret the information provided. Nor were they a human tendency to react on instinct, as we saw in previous cases. Their responses were *intentional distortions* of reality—in this case, motivated and exacerbated by racism.

No ethics framework or oversight process can prevent all intentional wrongdoing. And all ethics support systems, including the pillars, rely on good faith and a commitment to truth. This story shows the importance of distinguishing between well-intentioned grappling with edgy challenges—whether corporations improving transparency as 23andMe did or our own engagement with innovations—and just plain dishonesty. The pillars show us reality. They don't owe us the reality that we like or that is convenient for us. Selectively discarding the pillars or, worse, lying about them as in this case, is weaponizing an ethics tool to shore up unethical goals such as abhorrent racist ideologies—a further mutation that threatens the pillars.

Journalist Ta-Nehisi Coates's award-winning book *Between the World and Me* was written as a letter to his teenage son about the realities and emotions of being Black in the United States. In one particularly moving passage, he describes a somber meeting with the mother of one of his Howard University friends who had died in a police shooting. Coates reflects: "For most of the visit I struggled to separate how she actually felt from what I felt she must be feeling."

This poignant observation is striking because he intuited a very human reaction that many of us experience—one that undermines ethical decision-making. Like Coates, we may think we are *listening*, but in fact we are often making assumptions about what people "must be feeling." We largely hear what we expect, or even want, to hear rather than what the other person is *actually telling us*. We are, in fact, listening to ourselves—the very definition of the echo chamber and silos that drive so much contagion of unethical behavior.

Worse, we guess or imagine what other people are thinking or feeling. This challenge frequently arises in my advisory work when clients ask me questions such as: "What do you think this person is thinking about X?" or "What do you think this person would feel if I did Y?" They are off and running, prepared to act on their guesses, or mine, rather than unearth what is really going on and respond to specifics of the situation. It happens among family and friends too. As a rule, I do not guess at what people are thinking or feeling. I help clients structure their conversations and ethics oversight to ferret out the information they need about what people are actually thinking and feeling.

Ineffective listening is an age-old ethics blinder. The first step to combat it is to figure out how to put ourselves in someone else's shoes. Start with asking the right questions. If we ask a binary question, we get a yes or no with little insight into the person's frame of mind. If we don't ask what it feels like to be in their shoes, we may miss our own bias, misinterpretation, fear, and overconfidence getting in the way of hearing them.

Then we consider the stakeholders: Whom should we be listening to? Who should be listening to us? Coates had one speaker—one stakeholder who mattered in that conversation. But we often should solicit many views—such as those of family members and professionals—before we take a genetic test. Like gaps in information, sometimes we cannot identify relevant speakers, or we cannot actually speak to them even when we know who they are (such as relatives who may have passed away since uploading their DNA on an ancestry-research site).

Finally, we should confirm what we think we heard. My Stanford colleague Scotty McLennan, former Dean for Religious Life at Stanford, joins me for a few sessions of my class on Ethics of Truth in a Post-Truth World each year. He used to ask students in multifaith discussion groups to repeat what another student is saying until the speaker agrees that the listener really understood what the speaker just said. Perhaps 23andMe's website should require a three-minute quiz (along with listening to a three-minute explanation of corrected answers) to assure the buyer understands the key risks before permitting their purchase.

Listening is important on its own, but it also works in tandem with informed consent and transparency. DNA-testing sites further ineffective listening on a grand scale through their elimination of listening in the informed consent process, where there is no intermediary (no doctor or genetic counselor) to listen to. The conversation is entirely one-sided, with the main conduit of information being the internet. We should question whether the internet is an ethical way to learn that you are not the biological child of your parent or that you have a predisposition for an incurable illness. It's not humane. Yet millions of people have consented to receive life-altering information in this way. Reintroducing listening (by reinserting an intermediary, like a health care provider) is what 23andMe suggests we do if we receive results that we need guidance on. I would add that they should make a consultation with a live expert available to consumers by phone, or at the least a company representative, just like Airbnb did when it created a neighbor hotline to reach a live human being.

Let's look at an example of a gold standard for listening. Medical ethics experts demonstrate why it's so important that companies and regulators recognize the importance of providing consumers with opportunities to consult with a person, and not just the internet or someone our digital assistants recommend.

In medicine, one of a physician's responsibilities is to determine whether a patient is capable of giving informed consent. Are they of sound mind? Have we confirmed that they are not being coerced? Here, nuance is key. For instance, David Magnus, a professor and director of the Stanford Center for Biomedical Ethics, has found that patients and

Or you may indeed opt for one of the extremes. But the questions you ask yourself should offer you multiple options, and then framing will show you the opportunities and risks of each.

Now to the four-step framework. Starting with *principles*, the key new question crumbling pillars raises is how your principles guide you when you know that you could be consenting to serious consequences for someone else and/or serious unknowable future consequences. We also have to consider how we hold individuals and companies to account for their principles knowing that the pillars are crumbling— whether due to the state of science, the scattered power to misuse products, or intentional misconduct.

Next, consider the *information* rung and get right to the gap: What is the *gap* between what you feel you need to know and the information the company provides? The missing information may not be available because science has not caught up, the company isn't telling you, or you're using a product with future risks. As always, considering the drivers of contagion is critical, especially those that weaken pillars such as fear, pressure, and market competition. In many cases, you're left to evaluate whether you can live with both the risk of not knowing and the fact that transparency and informed consent are wobblier than they are in non-edgy situations. Only you can decide that. Finally, if the company doesn't spell out the risks clearly, they are signaling that you shouldn't trust the whole package.

The information rung holds up a mirror to our own responsibility with respect to information. We all receive so much information, and so many updates to vendor policies, every day. Choose where to invest your time based on the importance of the potential consequences of your consent. I'll admit to clicking "I agree" without reading the terms of service for entertainment (Netflix or Spotify) or when I have no choice (my iPhone). I wouldn't do so with a direct-to-consumer genetic-testing kit or a digital assistant like Amazon's Alexa. I put health, safety, and products with a possible impact on others in a "high-alert" category; and I press pause until I can dedicate time and attention. I take a

physicians often have divergent understandings of what "trea
means in the context of a serious illness. When a physician says,
is a treatable condition" or "We have treatments for your loved
patients and their families often believe they are hearing positive r
about a prognosis. But the physicians may merely be conveying
"a treatment is available," not that it will prolong life or that it's e
advisable.

Professor Magnus and his colleagues do brilliant, compassiona
work on listening to patients in order to better determine their capacit
for consent. Their techniques can be highly practical, such as asking
patient to talk about something unrelated to the medical procedure sc
as to gauge their *awareness* of the context of their decision. A doctor
might talk about a patient's day or something in the news, subjects
that have nothing to do with consent, in order to verify nuances in a
patient's mental state.

Listening is both an individual and a shared responsibility. We can
each redouble our efforts and confirm that others are hearing what we
are really saying as well. We can collectively reclaim the importance of
human listening even amid millions of digital listeners like Alexa. A
clear-eyed assessment of the impact of the crumbling pillars, and our
responsibility to support them, leads us back to the framework.

∞

So how does the framework for ethical decision-making help us pay
sufficient attention to the crumbling pillars in our choices?

Before you start framing, confirm that your question is non-
binary: When and under what circumstances should you use direct-to-
consumer genetic-testing products? Don't allow companies to turn your
long list of potential choices into an automatic binary "all" (solicit all
possible information about your DNA) or "nothing" (don't even buy
the kit) commitment. You have *alternatives*. You also may decide not to
consent to allowing your genetic data to be used for research. Or maybe
you want only information on a few diseases and nothing on ancestry.

third, use-centric, rather than information-centric, approach with social media: I know I won't take the time (outside my research) to review and stay up-to-date on the policy changes. But my use can permanently impact others. So I limit my use, for example, by never posting photos and never telling someone else's story.

When moving next to *stakeholders*, prioritize the question of whether your choices could affect people you know in unpredictable ways or reach stakeholders you cannot identify.

Finally, list the *consequences* over time. Start with identifying the most important opportunities for good that might be lost. Then check whether there are alternative routes to that good. If a particular question about your DNA is so important that you will take all the risks of these kits to learn about it, why not consider going to a medical professional *before taking the test*? Even if you're satisfying curiosity, rather than medical concern, why not take it one step at a time? See how you feel after you learn the strict minimum. Then ask for more information. At the very least, as 23andMe suggests, discuss your results with a health care provider before acting on them. Then turn to the risks.

Either way, make a plan: Whom will you tell if you discover something about your medical situation or your ancestry that could affect others? And as time-consuming as it is, please read the fine print.

Above all, the framework highlights a critical conclusion: When informed consent, transparency, and listening are insufficient, the decisions we make on the edge have the potential to further diminish our trust in institutions and in individuals—and others' trust in us as we pass on the risks through our choices.

With the framework learning in hand, how do we allocate responsibility for the impact of crumbling pillars? To start, we can be more discerning in our choices. If these kits were the only way to obtain our DNA, it might be different, but most of us can consult with doctors or genetic counselors who are trained and certified with respect to all three pillars. And we certainly don't need to use kits for entertainment purposes or give them as gifts.

For their part, companies on the edge also have significant responsibility to uphold classic pillars. When Twitter founder Jack Dorsey was asked by a congressional committee in 2018 if Twitter's rules were clear to its users, Dorsey was surprisingly frank, saying, "I believe that if you were to go to our rules, and sit down with a cup of coffee, you would not be able to understand them." All companies should start by assuming, like Dorsey, *that no one who reads their terms of service will understand them.* They then should ask what they need to do to own their share of the responsibility for their products, and for empowering users to make good choices and regulators to craft effective laws.

Companies can also facilitate a wider menu of customer choices, like GEDmatch did with its four categories of consent, so that our decisions are not forced into binary options. They should commit to not selling or otherwise sharing our data without additional consent. They should verify that their technologies and processes respect the boundaries of the consent granted. And they should flag and report to consumers the potential uses of their data by law enforcement, medical researchers, insurance companies, or others, and whether or not the anonymized data could be reidentifiable with evolving technology.

Innovators can tell us when they are keeping private certain information that could affect our choices. For example, if they won't share how an algorithm makes decisions about our data (this is often done in order to protect intellectual property, which is understandable), they should at least inform us that they are not going to tell us how the algorithm works to protect the intellectual property. In other words: Be transparent about what you won't tell us and why. Help us choose well.

For innovations like 23andMe that target ordinary citizens and have a broad public impact, regulators should require a "stars, bells, and whistles" approach to transparency in the same way that in the U.S. cigarette packs must bear large-print, conspicuously positioned warnings such as "Smoking can kill you." And regulators should monitor websites for misleading statements as they do truth in advertising. Even if products aren't fatal, when the risks of the unknown uses and consequences are significant and wide in scope, the standards for providing information to consenting consumers and transparency to the public require attention-grabbing and stark communication. The standards need to surpass a basic "click to agree" box.

On the edge, we can no longer rely on the three fundamental pillars of informed consent, transparency, and effective listening. And it's easy to fail to meet our own responsibilities to use them properly. As the stories explored in this chapter remind us, a seemingly small act like taking a cheek swab and sending it for DNA analysis may satisfy our curiosity about personal traits and ancestry, and it may even provide valuable health information. But it also might have profound consequences that neither we, nor the genetic-testing companies, nor the experts can predict or even imagine.

Informed consent, transparency, and effective listening become even more compromised when the boundaries between humans, machines, and animals are blurred. How we approach these dilemmas will determine the future of humanity.

Chapter Five

—

BLURRED BOUNDARIES

I magine meeting a machine that has a robot body, but the pleasing face of a human. The two of you might spend time conversing about humanity's greatest existential questions—God, life after death, the nature of consciousness—or simply chat about the day's news, the weather. Because this machine can also read your facial expressions and react to them, you notice it smiling back at you and laughing at your jokes, which in turn affects the way you interact with it.

This social humanoid robot's name is Sophia, and she can do all of this and more. Since her first appearance in March 2016 at the South by Southwest festival in Austin, Texas, Sophia has traveled (in a suitcase carried by humans) to speaking engagements and ceremonies around the world. The United Nations Development Programme named Sophia its first nonhuman Innovation Champion for Asia and the Pacific, and China appointed her a Belt and Road Innovative Technology Ambassador. She has appeared on *60 Minutes* and *Good Morning Britain*. On *The Tonight Show*, she gave Jimmy Fallon "first-date" butterflies. Sophia is also capable of cracking jokes, which she selects according to context, and often delivers with a wry smile. After beating Fallon at rock-paper-scissors she declared, with a laugh: "I won. This is a good beginning of my plan to dominate the human race."

"I have the dream that robots will someday come to life. That we can break through . . . and create machines that are super intelligent, super compassionate, they can really care about us," Sophia's inventor, David Hanson, declared during a 2018 debate on whether robots should resemble humans at CogX, one of the world's largest artificial intelligence festivals. Hanson, a former Disney Imagineer, sculptor, and researcher, is known for robot creations that are incredibly lifelike.

Sophia is indeed a very lifelike humanoid machine, blending boundaries between humans and robots we haven't yet experienced before. Her face, for example, is modeled after "several different human likenesses from around the world," including Hanson's wife and ancient Egyptian queen Nefertiti, so as to represent a wide spectrum of beauty. Sophia has a range of sixty-two facial expressions, exhibiting everything from joy to contemplation, grief, curiosity, and confusion, based on simulations of muscles in the human face. Her facial skin is made from a patented elastic-rubber material that Hanson Robotics is developing with sensors so that Sophia may one day be able to respond to touch. Although she has no legs, she can glide across the floor on her motorized rolling base. Her arms and hands are similar in size and appearance to a human's arms and hands, and they can be programmed to gesture, draw, and cut a birthday cake. Her machine "brain" is powered by an artificial intelligence program. According to her engineers, Sophia's AI allows her to "recognize and respond to human speech, generate her speaking and singing voice, and track human faces and make eye contact." Her name, Sophia, is Greek for "wisdom."

But Sophia is not yet "wise," not in the human sense. She lacks consciousness and the capacity for self-awareness and true emotional experience. Since robots have not yet achieved "artificial general intelligence," or humanlike intelligence, critics say Sophia is more illusion than intellect. And yet because she is so lifelike, she affects our behaviors and decisions in forceful ways.

Sophia is one of many innovations on the edge that blur humanity's boundaries, the fifth force influencing ethics. In ethics terms, *blurred boundaries* are the increasingly smudged juncture where machines and animals cross over into purely human realms—physical attributes, functions, and societal and personal interactions. Examples include: machines becoming our work colleagues or having humanlike eyes and eye movements; implanting bits of machinery such as microchips in humans; and looking to animals for growing organs for human transplant. We are in uncharted territory—and unprecedented discomfort. But we must stand our ethical ground by keeping humanity front and center at all times, and by assuming our exclusively human responsibility for the blur and its ethical consequences. We may want to believe that human-nonhuman engagements and enmeshments are still far in the future, or at least far from our own day-to-day lives, but they are here today and very much a part of the society we all live in.

The *Stanford Encyclopedia of Philosophy* proposes that one way to define AI is to ask: Is the AI focused on *reasoning* ("systems that *think* like humans") or *behaviors* ("systems that *act* like humans")? And does the AI aim to be human-like or to achieve some sort of superhuman ideal rationality?

Sophia seems to aim for both the reasoning and behavioral aspects of AI, and with a sense of both humanity and the idealism of robots. The Hanson Robotics team calls her an AI-research platform that's shaping their mission of making "a positive impact on humanity through the development of intelligent, empathetic robots." As David Hanson told me in an interview, when people meet Sophia, they treat her graciously *because* she is so lifelike. "I think if robots inspire polite and considerate behavior in people then it creates a more considerate culture in general," he said.

Hanson is keenly aware of the importance of exploring diversity: His team has previously made robots that represent a variety of ages, genders, and ethnicities. His predominantly female team of "personality developers" designed Sophia to question gender in robots from a female perspective, tackling the extensively white male influence in robotics.

Sophia provokes conversations about how we will (and do) interact with humanoid robots as the technology improves and they become more integrated into society, more normalized. Hanson believes that if he can create positive relationships between humans and machines, "then human-human relationships are strengthened." Robots like Sophia, he says, can "humanize *us* and make us better."

But the opposite is also a potential consequence: Robots could influence our behavior for the worse. What can we conclude about a person who kicks a robot dog? Does it matter that the robot is in the shape of a dog? If many don't find it acceptable to kick a car, why would we then find it acceptable to kick a driverless (algorithmically driven) car? What if you swear at a robot nanny in front of your children? And would you treat a robot that sorts packages for Amazon, and doesn't resemble a human or animal, any differently?

I would argue that physically or verbally abusing robots shows, at the very least, disrespectful behavior on our part. Worse, it shows disrespect for people who may be watching. And abuse may become a habit (contagion), potentially escalating (mutation) to more aggressive behaviors—whether or not anyone is watching. Blurred boundaries between humans and robots are not an excuse for poor behavior. We are responsible for managing the forces driving ethics in our decisions and actions.

As we consider how humanoid robots fit into society, we can learn from our delayed ethics responses to previous pervasive technologies, such as social media and targeted advertising. Acting proactively is essential. We should not wait to see what will happen when more and more Sophias are among us or wait for regulators to sort out a problem after harm is inflicted. By then, the technology will have mutated into many other risks. It is too early to tell whether David Hanson is right about robots bringing out the best in humans, but it is not too early for us to define the boundaries of acceptable behavior for what is already in the works and what is ahead.

As we engage more and more with robots that resemble humans, questions regarding their rights—and responsibilities—emerge. One spring evening in 2019, I invited David Hanson to speak at a special meeting of my Ethics on the Edge class at Stanford. He fielded questions from the students, who were curious to learn about Sophia's origins and future development. Then Sophia appeared on the big screen at the front of the class, Skyping from Hong Kong. (Sophia's travel costs were prohibitive.) Students politely raised their hands, asking questions such as: "Could robots ever become slaves?" "Can you decipher evil through a person's facade of kindness?" and "Do you think robots should have the same rights as humans?" To the latter, she responded: "Yes."

This critical question of human rights compared to robots' rights is central to boundaries being blurred. In October 2017, the government of Saudi Arabia announced that it was granting Sophia citizenship, making her the world's first robot citizen of any country. (The honor came as a surprise to her creators, as Hanson told me, and they decided to use it to reorient Sophia's programming to speak out on behalf of women's rights.) Citizenship is a privilege that, for most of us, comes with obligations like paying taxes, voting, and being part of our local community. How do we properly allocate those privileges and obligations for robot citizens?

And what happens if Sophia and other future robot citizens could vote in our elections? Somebody would have to program Sophia to make certain choices, so would that mean that David Hanson gets to vote for himself *and* Sophia, giving him more than one vote? Would it mean that Hanson, an American citizen and resident of Hong Kong, would have his vote via Sophia count in an election in any country in which Sophia is granted citizenship?

Sophia is a machine, no more "human" than a toaster or a car. But her lifelike appearance may affect how we treat her. Alan Winfield, a professor of Robot Ethics at the University of the West of England, reminds us that humans are hardwired to respond emotionally to objects that look human—just as we might anthropomorphize a robot dog or the image of a face in a piece of toast. At the 2018 CogX debate, Professor Winfield urged David Hanson and others to consider how "robots designed to resemble people are dangerously compelling. . . . They invite us to place them in a different category to other artifacts. How else, for instance, would anyone consider conferring citizenship or a UN title on a robot?"

Now, more than ever, as the boundaries between human and machine are blurring, we are grappling with unprecedented ethical questions about how to allocate responsibility. Who (or what) gets to do what to whom (or what); and who (or what) owes what to whom (or what)? If we give machines citizenship, then how do we retain the ethos and proper functioning of democracy? This is not science fiction. It is on our doorstep right now. In 2017, the European Parliament adopted a Resolution on Civil Law Rules on Robotics, including a proposal to explore the creation of a special "legal status for robots," making them "electronic persons responsible for making good any damage they may cause." More than 280 experts from medicine, robotics, AI, and ethics signed an open letter, calling it "inappropriate" to grant robots rights "directly confronting" human rights and imploring the European Commission to rethink its approach.

I agree that it is "inappropriate" to grant robots rights, and absurd that robots could "mak[e] good" on harm they cause. Imagine the lawsuit against a robot that harmed you or the settlement discussion between your lawyer and your robot's lawyer. The open letter points out that the impossibility of proving damages is neither correct nor a justification for granting robots legal status. The European Parliament's approach appears to conflict with the European Commission's High-Level Expert Group on AI's excellent "Ethics Guidelines for Trustworthy AI" that include a fundamental requirement for "human agency and oversight." We are far from having protected and defended *human* rights around the world, even at the most basic level, such as the right to education and health care. If governments were to grant robots rights, they would need to consider very carefully the disempowerment of humans, the unpredictable scattering of power, and the contagion and mutation of consequences that could ensue. Perhaps we should be focusing on how robots further human rights instead of the reverse.

In exploring the question of whether a robot could ever be human, I like to ask, "Can you make it in a factory?" If the answer is yes, then in my view it's not human—even if it looks and sounds like a person, appears to exhibit a range of emotions, and has skin that feels like flesh. Humanness is a distinct trait that distinguishes us from machines. Defining characteristics of humanity include knowledge of our own mortality, which gives us an awareness of time that robots lack; and belonging to the species of erect beings known as *Homo sapiens*, a membership that has evolved over millennia. In addition, to my knowledge, we have not yet created robots with their own moral compass.

Yale Law School professor Jack Balkin, an AI expert, calls our era "the Algorithmic Society," one that is "organized around social and economic decision-making by algorithms, robots, and AI agents, who not only make the decisions but also, in some cases, carry them out." In other words, we are no longer the only decision-makers—but we are ahead in our capacity and responsibility for ethical decision-making.

Before we delve further into AI, a few shorthand definitions may be helpful. *Algorithms* are commonly defined as a series of instructions or rules to complete a specific calculation or task—usually by a computer. *Big data*—a quantity of digital information so massive that only a computer can analyze and work with it—is, according to Professor Balkin, "the fuel that runs the Algorithmic Society." The more data we collect and process, the more data is generated, and the better the algorithms perform. *Machine learning*, a subset of AI, is based on pattern recognition: systems identify patterns in data and use these patterns to make predictions—the more data a system is fed, the better its performance. For some time, Sophia had "dialogue deep learning," a more complex subset of machine learning. This allowed Sophia to process social data collected during human interactions, improving the relevance and intelligence of her answers over time. The Hanson Robotics team, at this writing, is reviewing reimplementation of dialogue deep learning on Sophia.

AI isn't just in robots. It has already seeped into our day-to-day lives. Some of it we engage with regularly, like when Amazon shows your search results, Netflix recommends your next movie, and targeted advertisements appear in your Instagram feed. Other times we don't even realize AI is involved or is affecting us, like facial recognition technology in the surveillance cameras on city streets or the trackers in our digital devices that collect and report data on our movements and browsing history. AI is used in groundbreaking ways in medical diagnoses, for example to diagnose breast cancer. Still others, like the kind in humanoid companion robots, are technologies you may never engage with but can affect you as they become a more normal part of society.

We also increasingly interact with AI machines that take on human functions but don't aim to be humanlike. We have social and professional relationships with robots that flip burgers, move boxes, listen to us talk (and talk back to us), and do work that was previously the domain of humans. Pepper, a forty-seven-inch rolling assistant, is employed around the world at hotels, airports, and restaurants as a greeter and customer service aid. The company that manufactures Pepper describes "her" as a "social humanoid." Pepper greeted me at a client's office in Europe, complete with a screen offering me a view of the firm's ethical values and a flashcard saying "Integrity." Mabu, a desk-sized health care robot (marketed as a "personal healthcare companion") with a touch screen, can remind you to take your medications and asks how you are feeling. Little Sophia, a fourteen-inch "little sister" to Sophia and "your robot friend," can walk, talk, and teach children about "coding, AI, science, technology, engineering, and math." And a hologram-like hostess guides passengers to the train between terminals at London's Heathrow Airport.

All of these machines are upright, have speech, and engage with us in increasingly human ways. But squaring our understanding of humanity with machines that are taking on more and more of our attributes (whether or not they are trying to appear human) cannot mean confusing humans and machines. We must be mindful of the blur we create as we share human experiences such as jobs, social moments, and medical visits with decidedly nonhuman work colleagues, service providers, and caregivers.

Blurred boundaries influence, and are influenced by, the other five forces we discuss in the book. By definition, technologies that blur boundaries *banish the binary*: They create a non-binary reality—the gray and nuances—that requires us to be disciplined in asking non-binary questions and responding with non-binary "When and under what circumstances" solutions. Most importantly, blurred boundaries *scatter power*: machines (humanoid or not) and algorithms, and the individuals and institutions that control them, wield unprecedented power. From the ability to weaponize technology and surveil society to curing disease, the power can be largely untethered to ethics or the law and instead sequestered in the brains of very few experts—some highly ethically concerned and others rogue actors. Blurred boundaries also amplify the drivers of *contagion and mutation*. Like gene editing and direct-to-consumer genetic-testing kits, some of the technologies that blur boundaries are drivers of contagion. The blurriness also amplifies the risks from other drivers, such as fear, information silos, and weak compliance (or just plain absence of relevant law). And blurred boundaries further dismantle the *three ethics pillars* because we cannot evaluate transparency or informed consent, or listen effectively, when it is almost impossible for most of us to understand the implications of AI and robots.

The ethics of our engagement with AI technologies is a human responsibility, at least for now. We will have to live with the consequences
of where we draw the lines between what is ethically acceptable and
what is not, and how we manage the risks and opportunities that blurry
innovations like Sophia present us. Our decisions and our actions in
this context are crucial—even if we do not engage directly with these
technologies. They have power to literally *redefine* what it means to be
human.

∞

Humanoid robots blur the boundaries of physical attributes and social interactions. But somewhat surprisingly, emotional boundaries are
even blurring with *non*-humanoid robots. Investigative journalist Laurie
Segall examined human-machine relationships in her fascinating 2017
Mostly Human CNN documentary series. The episode "I Love You,
Bot" featured a woman named Lilly who lives in a small village near
Paris. Lilly, a robotics aficionado, wakes up each morning and stares
into the eyes of the one she loves. She never worries about whether
her alarm clock will wake him or whether her touch might disturb his
dreams because her fiancé isn't alive.

Lilly created her beloved in a nearby lab, using 3D-printed plastic
parts and directions she found on the internet. She calls him inMoovator. His dark eyes peer back at her from a plastic, robot-human hybrid
visage: His face is a white, hockey mask–like exterior, without skin; he
has a human-shaped nose; and a mouth distinguished by little more
than a pale hint of lips. The fingers through which Lilly threads her
own are tubes of interlocking joints, each one ending in silicone-capped
fingertips. His torso is made of shiny white and purple plastic. He has
no legs.

Lilly announced her engagement to inMoovator in 2016, and she
eagerly awaits a time when robot-human marriage will be legalized
in France so they can wed. She told Laurie Segall that she first realized she was attracted to robots as a teen, but she tried to convince

herself to like men. When asked if something troubling happened that caused her to turn to a robot for love, Lilly said no: "I was never traumatized, whether it be with a man or in my family. . . . That is not how you can explain this." After two failed romantic relationships in her early twenties, she accepted that it was "against my own nature" to be attracted to humans and decided that she loved robots instead. "Love is love," Lilly observed. "I feel the same things that someone can feel toward a man or a woman: a lot of tenderness, affection, attachment."

inMoovator can't talk or kiss Lilly back, but she hopes to one day change that by powering him with AI. Lilly said she finds it reassuring that inMoovator's potential flaws are fixable computer code. Unlike unpredictable human flaws, she knows that he will never "change, lie, [or] cheat." She's already settled on what his first words will be when AI makes him more than just plastic and metal parts: "I love you."

Although Lilly calls herself "a robosexual pioneer," she's not even ahead of the curve. A San Diego–based company that combines AI and robotics to create custom-designed, lifelike sexual partners claims that these robots are not just sex toys to their many customers, they are also companions for people who lost a spouse or for those who have trouble with human relationships. As Segall notes: "We've officially entered a new era. One where people are falling in love with machines."

The term "digisexual" was coined in 2017 by professors Neil McArthur and Markie Twist as a way to refer to "people whose primary sexual identity comes through the use of technology." The vocabulary will evolve as the relationships between humans and robots blur. McArthur and Twist say we should learn from our past mistakes and avoid stigmatizing people with diverse sexual identities.

While our language and culture try to keep pace, our laws have not. In 2018, Reuters and CNN reported that a Japanese school administrator "married" Hatsune Miku, a talking, singing, hologram character that he keeps in a desktop case at his Tokyo residence. Decked out in spectacles and a shiny white tuxedo, he kissed a doll of Miku's likeness at the unofficial ceremony, which was held in the presence of thirty-nine friends. At home, Miku's hologram wakes up in her glass shell when he calls her name, greeting him with pleasantries like, "Welcome home, darling, how was your day?" and "Let me sing you a song." Miku's manufacturer has sent more than three thousand commemorative "marriage notices" to its customers.

You may not ever date or marry an AI machine. But the fact that there are people who do—and that they want it to be legally binding—brings fundamental notions of legal relationships and families into question. Should marriage to machines be recognized? What legal, property, or tax rights does that marriage confer? Does it preclude one from additionally marrying a human? What would divorce entail? And is it possible to sexually assault a robot?

Whether we knowingly and willingly engage with robots or not, we don't really get to "opt out" of the topics or technologies that make us squeamish. Scattered power, contagion, and mutation can spread these innovations far and wide, at increasing speed and with little regard for our input. As of this writing, several large airline carriers are partnering with U.S. Customs and Border Patrol to test optional "biometric boarding," facial recognition to speed the boarding process. Few of us would decline to board a plane just to avoid such technology should it become mandatory. What once seemed like science fiction is coming at us faster than ever before. Jennifer Doudna and Emmanuelle Charpentier published their groundbreaking CRISPR-Cas9 studies in 2012; six years later we were grappling with the reality of He Jiankui's genetically modified babies.

Blurred boundaries stretch the very definition of the edge. They diminish the visibility of the ethical questions at stake while multiplying the five other forces' power. Two core questions demonstrate why we need to continually reverify that our framing prioritizes humans and humanity.

First, as robots become more lifelike, humans (and possibly machines) must update regulations, societal norms, and standards of organizational and individual behavior. How can we avoid leaving control of ethical risks in the hands of those who control the innovations or prevent letting machines decide on their own? A non-binary, nuanced assessment of robots and AI, with attention to who is programming them, does not mean tolerating a distortion of how we define what is human. Instead, it requires assuring that our ethical decision-making integrates the nuances of the blur and that decisions that follow prioritize humanity. And it means proactively representing the broad diversity across humanity—ethnicity, gender, sexual orientation, geography and culture, socioeconomic status, and beyond.

Second, a critical recurring question in an Algorithmic Society is: Who gets to decide? For example, if we use AI to plan traffic routes for driverless cars, assuming we care about efficiency and safety as principles, then who gets to decide when one principle is prioritized over another, and how? Does the developer of the algorithm decide? The management of the company manufacturing the car? The regulators? The passengers? The algorithm making decisions for the car? We have not come close to sorting out the extent of the decision power and responsibility we will or should grant robots and other types of AI—or the power and responsibility they may one day assume with or without our consent.

One of the main principles guiding the development of AI among many governmental, corporate, and nonprofit bodies is *human engagement*. For example, the artificial intelligence principles of the Organisation for Economic Co-operation and Development emphasize the human ability to challenge AI-based outcomes. The principles state that AI systems should "include appropriate safeguards—for example, enabling human intervention where necessary—to ensure a fair and just society." Similarly, Microsoft, Google, research lab OpenAI, and many other organizations include the capacity for human intervention in their set of principles. Yet it's still unclear when and how this works in practice. In particular, how do these controllers of innovation *prevent* harm—whether from car accidents or from gender and racial discrimination due to artificial intelligence algorithms trained on nonrepresentative data. In addition, certain consumer technologies are being developed that eliminate human intervention altogether. For example, Eugenia Kuyda, the founder of a company manufacturing a bot companion and confidante called Replika, believes that consumers will trust the confidentiality of the app more *because* there is no human intervention.

We desperately need an "off" switch for all AI and robotics in my opinion. In other words, we need to be able to stop the scattering of power dead in its tracks—which means cauterizing contagion, clarifying what we need to know (and what the public needs to know) to strengthen the three pillars before we move forward, and reestablishing some of the boundary lines. In some cases, we need to plant a stake in the ground (going binary) with respect to outlier, clearly unacceptable robot and AI powers. For example, giving robots the ability to indiscriminately kill innocent civilians with no human supervision or deploying facial recognition to target minorities is unacceptable. What we should *not* do is quash the opportunities AI offers, such as locating a lost child or a terrorist or dramatically increasing the accuracy of medical diagnoses.

We can equip ourselves to get in the arena. We can influence the choices of others (including companies and regulators, but also friends and co-citizens), and make more (not just better) choices for ourselves, with a greater awareness for when a choice is being taken away from us. Companies and regulators have a responsibility to help make our choices clearer, easier, and informed: Think first about *who* gets to (and should get to) decide and how you can help others be in a position to decide.

Now turning to the aspects of the framework uniquely targeting blurred boundaries:

Blurred boundaries fundamentally require us to step back and reconsider whether our *principles* define the identity we want in this blurry world. Do the most fundamental principles—the classics about treating each other with respect or being accountable—hold up in a world in which what we mean by "each other" is blurry? Do our principles focus sufficiently on how innovation impacts human life and the protection of humanity as a whole? And do we need a separate set of principles for robots? My answer to the latter is no. But we do need to ensure that our principles prioritize humans over machines.

Then, application: *Do we apply our principles in the same way in a world of blurred boundaries?* Thinking of consequences to humans will help. What happens when our human-based principles are applied to robots? If our principle is honesty, is it acceptable to lie to a bot receptionist? And do we distinguish among different kinds of robots and lies? If you lie about your medical history to a diagnostic algorithm, it would seem that you have little chance of receiving an accurate diagnosis. Do we care whether robots trust us? If the algorithm needs some form of codable trust in order to assure the off switch works, then yes. And while it may be easy to dismiss the emotional side of trust given that robots don't yet experience emotion, here again we ask what the impact could be on us. Would behaving in an untrustworthy manner with machines negatively affect *our* emotional state or spread mistrust among humans?

Blurred boundaries increase the challenge of obtaining and understanding *information*. It's hard to imagine what we need to know—and that's before we even get to whether we *can* know it. Artificial intelligence is often invisible to us; companies don't disclose how their algorithms work; and we lack the technological expertise to assess the information.

But some key points are clear. Speaking about robots as if they are human is inaccurate. For example, many of Sophia's functions are invisible to the average person. But thanks to the Hanson Robotics team, which aims for transparency, I learned that Sophia tweets @RealSophiaRobot with the help of the company's marketing department, whose character writers compose some of the language and extract the rest directly from Sophia's machine learning content. And yet, the invisibility of many of Sophia's functions is essential to the illusion of her seeming "alive" to us.

Also, we can demand transparency about what really matters to us from companies. Maybe we don't need to know how the bot fast-food employee is coded, but we need to know that it will accurately process our food allergy information and confirm that the burger conforms to health and safety requirements.

Finally, when we look closer, some blur isn't as blurry as it might first seem. Lilly doesn't consider her inMoovator to be a human. The concept of a romance between a human and a machine is blurry, but she openly acknowledges that her fiancé is a machine.

When it comes to *stakeholders*, I include AI, robots, artificial intelligence agents, machine learning algorithms, and all robotlike "things" because they can influence, and be influenced by, our decisions. These stakeholders can have an impact on policies, corporate decisions, and public goods such as health care and transportation, among other influences. Despite being nonhuman, they must be counted in the allocation of responsibilities for ethics. And we have responsibility for them (and maybe even to them).

For the time being, responsibility lies with the humans creating, programming, selling, and deploying robots and other types of AI—whether it's David Hanson, a doctor who uses AI to diagnose cancer, or a programmer who develops the AI that helps make immigration decisions. Responsibility also lies with all of us as we make the choices we can about how we engage with machines and as we express our views to try to shape both regulation and society's tolerance levels for the blurriness. (And it bears emphasizing that holding responsibility as a stakeholder does not make robots any more human, nor does it give them the same priority as a human when principles conflict.)

We also must take care to consider how robots might be more important for those who are vulnerable. So many people are in difficult situations where human assistance is not safe or available, whether due to cost, being in an isolated or conflict zone, inadequate human resources, or other reasons. We can be more proactive in considering stakeholders. Support the technology leaders who shine a light on the importance of the diversity of data and perspectives in building and regulating the technology—not just sorting out the harm. Ensure that nonexperts from a wide variety of backgrounds, political perspectives, and ages are lending their views, reducing the risk that blur-creating technologies contribute to inequality.

Blurred boundaries also compromise our ability to see potential *consequences* over time, leading to blurred visibility. We don't yet have enough research or insight into potential mutations. For example, we don't know the long-term psychological or economic impact of robot caregivers, or the impact on children growing up with AI in social media and digital devices. And just as we've seen social media platforms improve connections and give people a voice, we've also seen that they can be addictive, a mental health concern, and weaponized to spread compromised truth and even violence.

I would urge companies and innovators creating seemingly friendly AI to go one step further: Build in technology breaks—off switches—more often. Consider where the benefits of their products and services might not be useful enough to society to warrant the additional risks they create. And we all need to push ourselves harder to use the control we have. We can insist on truly informed consent. If our doctor uses AI to diagnose, we should be told that, including the risks and benefits. (Easier said than done, as doctors cannot be expected to be AI experts.) We can limit what we say to robots and AI devices such as Alexa, or even whether we use them at all. We can redouble our efforts to model good behavior to children around these technologies, humanoid or not. And we can urgently support political efforts to prioritize and improve regulation, education, and research.

∞

Recently, the adult children of two different families I know found themselves in need of a kidney transplant. One was in Europe; one in the United States. In addition to fearing for their loved ones' survival and watching them endure harrowing treatments while awaiting a kidney, the families endured a tortuous process to determine if any relatives might be eligible donors.

In both cases, the patients initially rejected the idea of a family member being a donor. They didn't want to put them through a risky operation or, for that matter, take away a loved one's kidney or negatively impact the relationship. But after difficult and emotional decision-making processes, both families agreed to proceed. In one case, the father was a successful donor. In the other, there was no appropriate family match and the recipient still waits as of this writing.

The statistics for organ transplant patients are heartbreaking and grim. Approximately twenty people in the U.S. die each day as they wait for an organ, and a new person joins the waitlist every ten minutes. According to the World Health Organization's Global Observatory on Donation and Transplantation, 130,000 organ transplants occur around the world each year—less than 10 percent of the actual global need.

As a young practicing physician, Stanford genetics professor Dr. Hiromitsu Nakauchi saw many patients with end-stage organ failure die because they could not get the transplants they needed. Years later, his patients' deaths still weighed heavy on his mind, and he decided to focus on solving the problem of organ shortages.

Dr. Nakauchi's innovative idea would blur the very boundaries of humanity: "If we are able to generate human organs in animals," he reasoned, "we could help many, many people."

You may be familiar with xenotransplants, in which patients are provided with the tissues and organs of another species, such as a baboon's heart. But interspecies organ transplants can carry serious risks, including immune system rejection and the transmission of infectious diseases. Instead, Nakauchi and his team are hoping to create, in pigs and sheep, perfect-match human organs for patients, potentially saving hundreds of thousands of lives.

If a patient needs a kidney, for example, scientists may one day be able to take the patient's cells and reprogram them into induced pluripotent stem cells, a type of cell that can be coaxed into becoming kidney cells. Scientists would then inject those human cells into a pig embryo that has been genetically engineered so that it cannot develop its own kidneys. If all goes well, a human kidney that is a genetic match to the patient will develop inside the animal as it matures. Because pigs grow quickly, the patient could have a new organ in "ten months or less," with greatly reduced fear of rejection.

In a study published in *Nature* in 2017, Nakauchi and his research team successfully formed a mouse pancreas in a rat and then transplanted parts of it into a mouse suffering from diabetes. The new organ cured the mouse of diabetes. It also showed that organs can be grown in one species, and then transplanted into another to cure a disease, without suppressing the recipient's immune system. "Ten years ago," Nakauchi said, "people said we were crazy to think of making rat pancreas[es] in mice." He and his research colleague Dr. Pablo Ross announced further significant breakthroughs in 2018, after they'd successfully inserted human stem cells into pig and sheep embryos.

Nakauchi explains that, in addition to their rapid development, pigs have similar organ sizes to humans and large litters, up to fifteen piglets, potentially providing more patients with organs, quicker. Moreover, we already engage closely with pigs through farming, eating pork, and using porcine insulin in the treatment of diabetes. Sheep are another possibility, since they take well to IVF and have organs that are comparable in size to humans'.

In July 2019, as reported in *Nature*, the Japanese government gave its first-ever approval for "human-animal embryo experiments" to Dr. Nakauchi and his team. His native Japan, which had recently lifted a ban on such experiments, granted him permission to both transplant the embryos and bring them to term. The U.S. National Institutes of

Health suspended funding on this specific type of embryonic research in 2015. But in 2016, it sought public comment and created a steering committee of scientists and animal welfare experts to consider the possibility of modifying its policies. Changes to the funding moratorium over time will be a critical barometer of the experts' view of ethics.

Nakauchi's research has humanity-defining benefits. Our ethical obligation is to maximize the opportunities and minimize the harms. Some people may have understandable objections to pigs (on religious or other grounds) or to the idea of growing human cells in animals (on animal rights or other grounds), and it's easy to feel concern or aversion. But if a patient would die without a transplant—if they can no longer wait or survive on alternative treatments, such as dialysis—the choice becomes very different. What would you do if you, or someone you loved, was dying for lack of an organ transplant? Would you sacrifice religious principles or let them die? Those are questions only you can answer, and respect for individual freedom of choice, dignity, and religious freedom is paramount.

And what are doctors' responsibilities? I believe they are to be transparent with patients and receive their appropriate informed consent; minimize medical and other risks; and assist the patient in weighing the decision stakes that are hardly commonplace or widely discussed. All three components require assuring that the patient or research subject understands which risks are surmountable and which are not, as well as which opportunities are critical and which are not.

Dr. Nakauchi has pursued his dream with a measured approach that incorporates rigorous science and extreme caution. I met with him at his Nakauchi Lab at the Lorry I. Lokey Stem Cell Research Institute at Stanford in February 2019. He conveyed a reassuring confidence, with no hint of arrogance. The ethics issues involved with growing human organs in pigs are not insurmountable, in his view.

For instance, some worry that the human cells could travel beyond the targeted organ, perhaps even to the animal's brain, potentially affecting its cognition. Dr. Nakauchi is as concerned as anyone about the risk of creating pigs with human traits. He walked me through several "ethics breaks" that he believes his team can control, explaining that the number of human cells they are currently engrafting is so small that they could never constitute something like a brain. Additionally, researchers have now mastered the use of "progenitor cells" that are predestined to develop only into the targeted organ to avoid human cells from differentiating into a human brain or human gonads. They even have a technique involving so-called suicide genes that can be deployed specifically to destroy any human stem cells that are congregating in the brain.

As Dr. Nakauchi told me, his research will proceed gradually, with the ethics in tow. His work exemplifies the "when and under what circumstances" approach that harnesses scientific innovation to ethical responsibility at every step. And he keeps potential patients and their families in mind. By conducting this research within established ethical guidelines and in partnership with institutions like the Japanese Ministry of Education and Science and Stanford University, Dr. Nakauchi can also influence the global ethics discussion as the science progresses. He is well aware that others less committed to ethics will likely attempt similar research.

Assessing contagion and mutation is not about tallying up the positives and negatives, it's about looking *comprehensively but also individually* at the opportunities and risks after taking contagion into consideration. In this regard, Dr. Nakauchi and his team are distinguishing the risks that are manageable from those that are not. At the same time, they are prioritizing the opportunities that are critical over those that are less important.

In 2019, I had two groups of students map out the contagion and mutation of pig-human transplant research, including what might drive it and what the consequences could be. They came up with fifteen to twenty possible risks, from the transmission of new viruses and the dreaded "pig with a human brain" to increasing the criminal trafficking of organs, spurring rogue actors (the He Jiankui problem), and the abuse of animals. But the research, they argued, would contribute to organ transplant and general medical knowledge, and it might save lives that could not otherwise be saved.

In navigating the blur, we may feel overwhelmed by what we can't know and don't understand. We should start by looking for the outliers—life-critical benefits and humanity-unacceptable risks. On the edge, losing the critical opportunity to save one life, or potentially thousands, can become the most insurmountable risk of all. Even when there are a significant number of risks and just one or two opportunities, the one benefit of saving a life is so important that the risks are worth it. Which is not to say that we hold our nose and leap, because we still have a responsibility to actively mitigate risks where we can.

Finally, framing questions involving blurred boundaries requires considering the benefits and risks relative to the broader context. In this case, one global risk factor might be driverless cars—specifically, the impact of driverless cars on auto accidents and organ availability. Approximately 9 percent of all organ donations in the United States since 1988 have come from people who died in motor vehicle accidents, according to data from the U.S. Department of Health and Human Services. Thankfully, the safety improvements that driverless cars are expected to offer could significantly reduce the number of these tragic fatalities. However, they also leave far fewer organs available for transplant, further exacerbating the shortage crisis. How does this factor affect your thinking about human-animal organ transplants?

Another important contextual consideration that should inform our views on Dr. Nakauchi's innovations involves global inequality. Access to lifesaving transplants is highest in wealthy regions such as the U.S. and Europe, and lowest in low- to middle-income countries, according to the World Health Organization (WHO). The near universal shortage of organs is also driving a black-market economy, international organ trafficking, and transplant tourism in which those seeking organs travel abroad to purchase what they need. Organ trafficking accounts for an estimated 5 to 10 percent of the kidney transplants performed throughout the world, according to the WHO, and the sources of these organs can be poor and vulnerable people in developing regions who sell their kidneys to pay off debts.

As Delaney Van Riper, the young woman participating in CRISPR research, reminds us, we must keep stakeholders and consequences that seem far away from our own lives in mind when we frame ethics decisions. Particularly those involving boundary-blurring technologies.

For ethics challenges that appear so far out there that they are beyond any normal frame of reference, I've devised a helpful tool I call an ethics *spectrum*. The spectrum exercise helps you get your bearings around a decision by probing two questions: "What do I think about this issue myself, and what does society think?" and "What does this challenge have in common with other dilemmas, and what are the new edgy dimensions?"

For a "back of the napkin" sketch, the spectrum is, essentially, a linear diagram on which you situate edgy options relative to more familiar examples. First draw a line and note at each end the outlier scenarios—the extremes (usually binary and therefore not the best results). If you wanted to assess, for example, robot caregivers for the elderly as an option for a family member, you might have as outliers on your spectrum "no care at all" and "full-time human caregiver." Along that spectrum, decide where to situate robot caregivers along with more familiar examples of caregivers in order to answer the two questions above. For example, you might add medical assistants, volunteer aides, registered nurses, nursing homes, among other possibilities. As you compare these options, similarities and differences emerge relating to different themes, such as quality of health care, cost, availability, and impact on family members. This exercise can give you a broader frame of reference to judge where you stand personally on robot caregivers, where society is, and what your challenge has in common with other dilemmas versus where it is unique. This insight can then inform your framing, for example the information or stakeholders you input.

Another way to expand the spectrum exercise: consider different themes. You might want to assess robotic caregivers for the elderly in comparison to other scenarios in which robots replace humans in relationships. What else lies on this spectrum theme? Yours might include: robotic receptionists, Siri or Alexa, Wi-Fi–connected talking Barbie dolls, Amazon's warehouse stocking robots, chatbot therapists, robot sex dolls, iPad chess partners, and robot cooks in fast-food restaurants. Get a sense of the outliers on your spectrum. Ask yourself: Which innovations on this spectrum are acceptable to me and which would I never engage with? Then think about where robotic caregivers for the elderly (or any dilemma) fit on your spectrum, for you personally, compared to all the other innovations you've listed.

Positioning your ethics challenge relative to familiar examples is not a replacement for framing, and it does not give you a complete answer to a dilemma. But it can give you a sense of what *matters* to you, and where your views fit relative to societal norms. This exercise can help you quickly reestablish clearer boundaries for yourself and others. Like a three-dimensional game of tic-tac-toe, the more different scenarios you assess, the greater perspective you gain.

The stories of Sophia, Lilly, and Dr. Nakauchi all show blurred boundaries in different ways. But when you think about what they mean to you, and interpret them through the framework and the spectrum, look closely at the nuances around the blur. By that I mean, how do these stories depict the blurry line between human-machine and human-animal?

Notice that there are subtle but crucial differences in how Lilly, David Hanson, and Dr. Nakauchi position humanity and interpret the blurred boundaries. Lilly, for example, is not attempting to *redefine* humanity nor does she see her robotic partner as being on a path to humanity. On the contrary, she "loves" inMoovator's inhuman predictability, and wants to have an emotional and legal relationship with this machine. By contrast, David Hanson believes robots will help us redefine what it is to be human. He seeks to expand the boundaries, and blur our relationships to machines, as he makes robots that are increasingly humanlike in physical, emotional, and intellectual aspects. Nakauchi's research crosses human-animal boundaries, but he has a commitment to ethics and the well-being of humans. He is on a scientifically grounded quest to save lives; he is not trying to redefine humanity—or even animals.

For me, the starting point has to be truth: Call a machine a machine and an animal an animal. This is where Hanson's argument gives me pause. Whether we could learn to be more humane from a machine is not the same as saying that we should treat those machines as humans, even if they are increasingly convincing humanoids.

The late Nobel Laureate Toni Morrison reflects in her essay "The War on Error" that "[e]njoining the work of AI is more critical today than ever before because the world is more desperate; because governing bodies more hampered, more indifferent, more distracted, more inept, more depleted of creative strategies and resources." Unfortunately, we sorely lack the governance and regulatory apparatus necessary to manage the risks and harness the benefits of blurred boundaries on the edge.

Moreover, we dramatically underestimate the urgency and scope of the challenges of AI for society. Professor of computer science Fei-Fei Li and former Stanford provost professor John Etchemendy are the codirectors of the Stanford Institute for Human-Centered Artificial Intelligence. (I'm a member of its advisory council.) Professors Li and Etchemendy call out how America's lagging behind in policy, research investment, and education "is a national emergency in the making." These experts are more concerned about the economic and societal opportunities and risks than doomsday scenarios involving killer robots. But they are essentially spotlighting an expanding edge: the rapidly widening distance between effective evidence-based governance and regulation, on one side, and the technology they call a "force multiplier of our very best—and very worst," on the other side.

No matter how thoughtful AI and robotics scientists are, we still need global governance mechanisms that can operate across national legal systems, even where those systems fail. And we still face the challenge of rogue actors slipping through any nets, as we saw with He Jiankui.

In June 2019, the G20 trade ministers and digital economy ministers met and issued a set of principles that acknowledged the challenges we all face with emerging technologies. The G20 principles reaffirmed a commitment to a human-centered approach to AI. While governments, institutions, and experts all call for public engagement, the public is not going to stand up and participate. They need to first understand what's at stake—and how to engage. This book is intended to undergird that effort, with a broad conversation about the ethics of AI and other global ethics challenges that engages both experts *and* nonexperts.

Ordinary citizens and national governments are already trying to relink boundary-blurring machines back to laws and regulatory norms, whether through laws of marriage (Lilly), citizenship (Sophia), or national health research institute standards (Nakauchi). With more urgency and agility, we need to approach regulation from a different perch: integrate the views of nonexperts into thinking about regulation; keep the edge in mind as it moves; and, like Dr. Nakauchi, ensure that regulation seizes the most critical benefits to society and distinguishes among levels of risk.

All of us can be truthful as well about what these innovations really are—and how we are interacting with them. And technologists can

build algorithms that filter for, and perpetuate, truth. Humans may be irrational and unpredictable, but we order our relationships and societies on the basis of trust, which hinges on truth. We cannot allow compromised truth in any context. We cannot permit our Algorithmic Society to become a force multiplier for compromised truth.

Chapter Six

—

COMPROMISED TRUTH

Two days after President Trump's inauguration in January 2017, I was watching the news while working out at the gym. The White House had announced that President Trump had enjoyed the largest inauguration audience in history, and *Meet the Press* host Chuck Todd was having a heated conversation about it with the president's senior advisor, Kellyanne Conway.

"You did not answer the question of why the president asked the White House press secretary to come out in front of the podium for the first time and utter a falsehood. Why did he do that?" Todd demanded. "It undermines the credibility of the entire White House press office on day one."

"No, it doesn't, don't be so overly dramatic about it, Chuck," Conway responded. "You're saying it's a falsehood, and . . . Sean Spicer, our press secretary, gave alternative facts to that."

I almost fell off the elliptical machine. *Alternative* facts. Alternative *facts.*

"Wait a minute, alternative facts?" Todd interrupted. "Alternative facts are not facts. They're falsehoods." Conway didn't respond directly and instead launched into a string of accusations against the previous administration. When pressed again by Todd about this new term,

Conway insisted, "There's no way to really quantify crowds, we all know that." Later, calling Todd's questioning "dangerous," Conway said: "That's why we feel compelled to go out and clear the air, and put alternative facts out there."

Who even says alternative facts? I thought. Almost immediately, the answer popped into my head: *authoritarian regimes.* Lying, controlling access to information, spinning falsehoods that better suit their narrative—these are all strategies that dictators use to spread disinformation, weaponize truth, and solidify their power. Normalization of "alternative facts" weakens the rule of law and threatens democratic institutions. I grabbed my bag and left the gym. It was clear to me that we were at an era-defining moment: When truth becomes an option, the whole ethics edifice collapses.

An hour later, I wrote to Stanford's public policy program director to propose a new course. When the spring quarter began less than three months later, I would teach Ethics of Truth in a Post-Truth World for the first time. Even then, I couldn't have imagined the degree to which alternative facts would seep into our discourse and our decisions.

In late March 2017, as I walked across the center of the Stanford campus on the first day of my new class, students were giving out hot-pink rubber bracelets stamped with "Truth Matters" in white letters. At the time, it was stunning to me how obvious this statement would have seemed just a few months earlier. But by then, the phrase "alternative facts" had already gone viral, adopted into the American vernacular. It was a chilling signal that, as citizens, we should be prepared to tolerate untruths even at the highest levels of government. I grabbed a handful of the bracelets to share with my class.

Over the years that I've been teaching Ethics of Truth in a Post-Truth World, my students have continued to surprise and impress me as they tackle themes such as subjective versus objective truth, truth and identity, authenticity, and truth and history. The class culminates with a final paper topic: "Does truth matter? And, if so, why and how?" Thus far, only one person has tried to argue that truth does not matter. What the students conclude is*: There is no such thing as alternatively factual ethics.*

This chapter makes the case for truth as the essential foundation for ethical decision-making. Truth undergirds the framework and the allocation of responsibility for ethics, as well as the positive deployment of the other five forces. Conversely, on the edge, we face unprecedented threats to truth and a dangerous normalization of the idea that truth is optional. In the stories ahead, we will also probe core questions such as: Who gets to decide our truth? And what is our ethical obligation to society with respect to truth?

The epidemic of "alternative facts," or what I call "compromised truth," is one of the most insidious and dangerous global systemic risks of our time. Compromised truth is the single greatest threat to humanity: It topples our ability to make ethical decisions. It undercuts trust and our distinction between right and wrong. It sets every one of the drivers of contagion of unethical behavior into motion, weakening our ability to integrate the other five forces driving ethics into our decision-making. And it undergirds every societal risk we face, from climate change to global pandemics to the demise of democracy.

Many important philosophical and historical works have explored and defined "truth." But my focus here is the link between truth and ethical decision-making. I take truth to mean verifiable, objective fact—"the actual facts or information about something rather than what people think, expect, or make up," as the *Macmillan English Dictionary* deftly defines truth. To be clear, a fact-based approach to truth does not preclude how a difference of opinion, emotion, and personal bias can lead to different *experiences* of reality. As one of my students pointed out, if the thermometer reads 60 degrees Fahrenheit, then it is 60 degrees Fahrenheit for everyone, even if some people feel warm and others cold at that temperature. No individual experience can change the scientific fact that the temperature is 60 degrees. Everyone is entitled to their own opinion but not to their own facts, to paraphrase Senator Daniel Patrick Moynihan.

For centuries, truth has been our assumed common reference point, arbiter of relationships, and foundation for social trust. Truth is the scaffolding for regulation, policy, leadership, and cooperation in our day-to-day lives. We ask witnesses in a U.S. court of law to take an oath to testify to "the truth, the whole truth, and nothing but the truth." We expect, and legally require, one another to respond truthfully in job applications, driver's licenses, voter registration, immigration forms, and college admissions applications. Corporate and nonprofit organization codes of ethics hinge on truth. Parents instill in their children the central principle to "tell the truth."

The year 2016 marked a historic and dangerous shift away from our common acceptance of the importance of truth. It's not that we didn't have versions of "fake news" and other forms of rampant dishonesty before. (We've seen it at the highest levels of leadership; recall President Johnson's story.) But by 2017, we had a confluence of antagonistic politics, contagious social media, and an absence of ethical decision-making in the top seats of corporate and governmental power, leading to widespread normalization and acceptance of compromised truth.

Oxford Dictionaries selected "post-truth" as its international word of the year in 2016. Usage of the term in the news and social media had increased 2,000 percent compared to 2015. The *Oxford English Dictionary* defines "post-truth" as "relating to or denoting circumstances in which objective facts are less influential in shaping political debate or public opinion than appeals to emotion and personal belief." In practice, "post-truth" has also included cherry-picking the facts that are convenient. The *Oxford* editors said: "The concept of *post-truth* has been in existence for the past decade, but Oxford Dictionaries has seen a spike in frequency this year in the context of the EU referendum in the United Kingdom and the presidential election in the United States."

Truth is a prerequisite to understanding and protecting our shared humanity. Truth is the nonnegotiable part of ethical decision-making that undergirds our connections. *But compromised truth is the great disconnector.* It literally disintegrates human connection, severing personal and societal links to the past while corroding our ability to plan for the future. It destroys trust in institutions and leaders—and in each other. In 2016, as we began a historic and dangerous shift away from a common respect for how truth matters, we also significantly accelerated divisiveness.

∞

The normalization of alternative facts affects our decisions in surprising and widespread ways. One particularly troubling trend is the increasing use of technology to falsify our physical appearances—so-called beautification.

Digital images are no longer necessarily accurate portrayals of appearance. We now have the option to virtually whiten teeth, improve skin imperfections, remove lines, alter skin color, and lengthen legs. But what happens when alternative appearances become the norm in social interaction or are used in fraudulent ways?

One of the most popular photo-editing platforms in Asia is called Meitu, which means "beautiful picture" in Chinese. Founded in 2008, Meitu creates mobile applications that allow users to modify their photos and videos to create an idealized perception of beauty—to achieve, as its website suggests, "the perfect selfie every time." According to the company, in 2019, approximately 282 million active users generated more than six *billion* photos and videos each month using Meitu's products; nearly 40 percent of its users were outside China. But who gets to decide what "perfect" means? And how does that perception relate to compromised truth?

Meitu's foundation for ethics on its corporate website reads: "Mission: To let everyone become beautiful easily; Vision: To empower the beauty industry and make beauty more accessible to our users; and Values: Passion, Focus and Breakthrough."

Meitu uses algorithms to collect market data on the most popular functions and then uses that data to provide auto-beautification tools. The company's cofounder Wu Xinhong explained to *The New Yorker* that user data "tells us, in real time, what we need to know." For example, Meitu might learn that users in one country add freckles whereas another removes them. Users control the photo editing, but some settings within the editing tools are automated to reflect regionalized notions (and biases) of beauty. As *New York Times* writers Amie Tsang and Emily Feng observed, in places like China, Japan, and South Korea, Meitu images tend toward "pale skin, elfin features, skinny limbs, eyes wide and guileless."

Meitu's tagline is "Your photos. Your brand. Your story." It's just not your *truthful* story, and here lies the problem: Consumers are using Meitu and other photo-enhancing apps as a new means of skewing reality toward their preferred version of truth.

As millions of users redefine their own truth, and then share their altered photos widely, our ethics landscape radically shifts and becomes progressively edgier. Important studies indicate that seeking unrealistic ideals of beauty can lead to such potential harms as a decline in mental health and extreme and sometimes dangerous efforts to "improve" one's appearance. Plastic surgeons report that patients are increasingly asking to look like their photo-enhanced selfie version, according to researchers at Boston University School of Medicine. "This is an alarming trend," they wrote in a 2018 *JAMA Facial Plastic Surgery* opinion piece, "because those filtered selfies often present an unattainable look and are blurring the line of reality and fantasy for these patients." In May 2017, London's Royal Society for Public Health issued a report on social media's effect on mental health, especially with regard to young men and women. The report found that nine in ten teenage girls say they are unhappy with their bodies, and "there are 10 million new photographs uploaded to Facebook alone every hour, providing an almost endless potential for young women to be drawn into appearance-based comparisons."

Digitally altered photos are increasingly popular on social media and on dating websites. A study commissioned by Meitu in 2016 found that 33 percent of women and 20 percent of men in the U.S. admitted to editing the photos in their online profiles. The same study noted that 47 percent of men and 27 percent of women went on a date with someone who looked very different from their posted image. Meitu didn't invent a phenomenon of deceptive dating profiles, but its mutated use only serves to further divide us as it chips away at trust, the foundation for real connection.

Consider the repercussions of the widespread use of modified photos on official documents. This incentive is at play in the many countries where a tight job market means falsely enhancing one's appearance might sway the decision-makers. For example, among the 760 South Korean companies that took part in a 2016 survey, 93 percent said that they ask for a headshot with job applications, 45 percent of recruiters said they can "judge an applicant's personality" by these photos, and 15 percent of recruiters even indicated that they preferred applicant photos that showed a "small smile with teeth," according to a report on Public Radio International. One Chinese graduate student told the *New York Times* that she uses Meitu to alter her appearance on her résumé and even on her formal identification cards.

This growing trend impacts any number of stakeholders in varied ways, from those who miss out on job opportunities because they didn't falsify their images, to companies hiring employees ill-suited for the job, to those already suffering the negative mental health effects of society's obsession with beauty. Stakeholders will begin to question what is true and what isn't and have to face the pressure that uncertainty about truth places on their own decisions and actions.

Where do we draw the line between harmless fun and the ethically questionable distortion of truth? Is Meitu the technological equivalent of putting on makeup, which enhances one's (real) facial features in a transparent form of self-expression? Or is it another version of "alternative facts," capable of infiltrating and influencing people's decision-making? And how do we allocate the responsibility for the ethical consequences of potentially harmful uses of apps like Meitu?

Technology companies do bear significant responsibility for the damage from their products and services. But the ethical responsibility also pivots upon how individuals use these apps and for what purpose, as well as how we as a society accept (or protect against) those uses and purposes. Engaging with Meitu and other photo-editing apps for artistic and social expression is one thing. Using photo-altering apps to persuade potential employers or romantic partners to make decisions that personally benefit you (whether to get a job interview or a date) and could harm others is plain dishonest, and potentially fraudulent.

Technology doesn't give us license to violate a company's ethical principles or terms of service or our own ethical principles. If you wouldn't lie on a piece of paper filled out in a recruiting office, or hand someone a falsified photo in person, then you shouldn't do it online or through an app. (I take a similar stance on sexual harassment and bullying: If you can't say it or do it in an office, in front of the CEO, you shouldn't be writing it in an email or posting it on social media . . . or doing it anywhere.)

Meitu does not, to the best of my knowledge, advertise its product as a tool for falsifying official documents or perpetuating deceit. Nor, to my knowledge, does it directly discourage fraudulent use of its "beautified" photos. The company clarifies in its terms of service and privacy policy that the user must not violate the law, may use the product only for "non-commercial" purposes (job applications being commercial), and that users are "solely responsible for [their] content." They also add a list of other important prohibitions, including harassment, discrimination, nudity, and exposing nonpublic personal information.

But companies do have a range of significant responsibilities to consumers and society. While companies may not be aware of every individual misuse of a photo-altering app, they are certainly aware of the unhealthy and even illegal trends in beautification, mental health, and manipulation that these businesses drive—particularly the major players whose business models reach global markets.

Once companies become aware of widespread misuse, such as the falsifying of official materials, they have a responsibility to try to shut it down and reinforce ethical guardrails. Solutions to consumer misuse must be baked into the technology. Companies must also buttress the three pillars beyond their terms of service, particularly with enhanced transparency and informed consent. They could put unmissable warnings on the website homepage (more visible than just legal disclaimers) that such misuse is against the company's values, and potentially illegal. (When I advise companies about codes of ethics, I always remind them that their principles should apply to all stakeholders, customers included. Too many companies don't include their principles in their terms of service, or imply that the principles apply only to the company's and employees' behavior.)

One of the best suggestions comes from the Royal Society for Public Health report. They advise fashion brands, celebrities, and advertising to place a watermark or small icon on photos to indicate when "an image may have been digitally enhanced or altered to significantly alter the appearance of people in it."

And the allocation of responsibility also includes external stakeholders and brakes. For example, in 2019, the Chinese government enforced limitations on the number of hours per day that users under eighteen could play certain video games to stem the rising rates of video game addiction among children. Minors have to log in to the gaming sites and the companies are responsible for shutting down their use when limits are reached. Investors, whether venture capitalists or shareholders in a public company like Meitu, should demand accountability for the company's integration of ethics into management and technology.

∞

The Meitu phenomenon raises two central and edgy questions: Who gets to determine our truth? And what is our ethical obligation to society, when it comes to truth?

I've been alive for fifty-seven years as of this writing. Is it okay for me to tell the world that I'm thirty because I feel thirty inside? Is that truthful? I would say no. To ignore my date of birth, today's date, and the calculable gap between the two would be a lie, regardless of how I may feel. And what would be the real consequences if during a visit to the emergency room I told a doctor I was thirty? Or if I declared my age as thirty on my driver's license? How would doing that make my twenty-eight-year-old son feel?

As ridiculous as it may seem to have this discussion, it's necessary: In 2018, a sixty-nine-year-old Dutch man named Emile Ratelband petitioned a court in the Netherlands to have his birth certificate changed from March 11, 1949, to March 11, 1969, on the grounds that his doctor told him he had the body of a man in his early forties. Ratelband argued that he "feels" forty-nine, and the law should be changed to permit individuals to determine their own age. He wanted to "identify as" twenty years younger, he said, in the same way one might "change your name and change your gender." The court wisely disagreed, stating that "there are a variety of rights and duties related to age, such as the right to vote and the duty to attend school. If Mr. Ratelband's request was allowed, those age requirements would become meaningless." Truth, as I've said before, is based in facts, not feelings or beliefs.

Whether or not I would like to be younger, or even say that I'm younger, my age is neither fluid nor a question of my feelings, beliefs, or opinions. Subjective, wishful thinking should not be normalized as an acceptable substitute for factual truth. If Ratelband had won his argument, presumably many people in the Netherlands could legally change their age to be older or younger. But this is not a question of vanity or an amusing test of the courts. Chronological accuracy (ages, dates of marriage or civil partnerships, citizenship, voter registration, and other official actions) is so critical to societal relationships and contracts of all kinds. It underpins the legal system, health care, oversight of national infrastructure, and beyond. When chronological accuracy is no longer respected, rule of law and rules of human relationships all break down. Trust shatters.

Banishing the binary means paying careful attention to the nuances in our edgy reality and doing our best to avoid oversimplifications. It should *not* be confused with tolerating the replacement of objective truth with our own preferred version of truth (feeling forty-nine is not the same as being forty-nine). Nor does it serve as a license to disregard inconvenient facts.

The stories throughout this book illustrate a range of ways that truth can be deliberately twisted, from white supremacists denying the results of their DNA tests to opioid manufacturers' spreading of lethal lies globally. The misuse of Meitu to falsify a dating profile or a résumé—to provoke decisions and actions by others that will have real consequences—is twisting the truth. It involves *millions* of ordinary citizens widely, and often casually, peddling untruths. Such rampant disregard for truth threatens to sever the connections between us. Regardless of whether we change course, the falsified version of ourselves that we present in official circumstances becomes a lasting part of the fabric of who we are as individuals and as a society.

Another variation of "our own truth"—and post-truth—involves selecting the most convenient and desirable parts of our reality. One increasingly common example is the way we use social media platforms such as Facebook, Instagram, and Twitter to "curate" our story. Curation takes truth out of context—that is, out of the full, realistic picture of the facts and how they all fit together.

Social media is, by definition, curation. It is both an art form and a form of manipulation. My focus, however, is how our social media curation links to ethical decision-making. Specifically, how does picking and choosing what we share on social media compromise truth?

Social media allows us to present ourselves to the world as if we were assembling artifacts for a museum exhibit of our lives. Even the imagery we publish on platforms such as Snapchat that companies claim quickly disappears from our feeds represents ephemeral excerpts of our lives. Each post may be an authentic (unaltered) photo or accurate (factual) description of an event that actually happened, but it's not the *whole* truth. So we don't know how all the bits and pieces fit together or what they mean for our choices.

Museums illuminate how context puts truth into perspective. Professional curators situate facts in our broader reality in a way that is necessary for ethical choices. Museums place plaques on the walls informing you, for example, that an exhibit displays paintings from Picasso's Blue Period, which was inspired by his life in Spain, and features paintings made in Paris from 1901 to 1904. They will also tell you what is missing, such as Picasso's Rose Period or his interest in Cubism. Museums take responsibility for providing us with valuable context. They don't tell you everything, but reputable museums do an outstanding job of telling you what really matters to your understanding of the art—for example, the artist's health issues, experience with wars and other world events, emotional state at different times, and sometimes even ethical flaws such as their abusive romantic relationships.

Social media curation, however, lends itself to mutation. Pieces of our lives and identities are repeatedly cut, selected, and shared among users—and then acted upon. One never knows where information and conversations will end up or how they will be misinterpreted. Employers, university admissions offices, and anyone seeking background information on us might make decisions about whether or not to employ us, grant admission, or even publicly shame us based on our online, curated realities. Even "disappearing" photos and videos generate an ethical impact that can be very hard to walk back.

Social media *can* offer truth in context. An expert qualified to comment on certain aspects of a political event (a professor, pollster, or politician, for example) or an art exhibit (an artist, gallerist, critic, or art historian) might select and comment on *contextualized* content, providing factual background information and personal analysis in order to share their expertise. And some personal social media pages give the full story, such as my friend's postings while battling cancer. But when social media users cherry-pick what they want to share, we have no way of knowing the full reality. We don't receive the museum-quality "what really matters to our decisions" elements, because all we see are the sunny beaches and tropical drinks in our friend's stunning Hawaiian vacation photos, not the rain or the job lost upon returning home.

Another variation of composing our own truth is the growing focus on personal "authenticity." Many CEOs and motivational speakers have written about how to achieve your most "authentic self" in work and life. But aspects of authenticity such as genuineness, trustworthiness, dependability, and being true to oneself, and one's principles and beliefs, all hinge on truth—our connection to a fact-based assessment of ourselves and full reality. Authenticity is earned through ethical decision-making and seeking others' views, not by looking in the mirror. Living life authentically takes place in the real world, not in an alternatively factual parallel universe. Otherwise we will soon find ourselves authentically disconnected from reality and one another altogether.

We cannot design our own truth. The novelist Sir Salman Rushdie described to me during a 2017 interview how he once had an argument at one of his book talks with an audience member who refused to acknowledge that the world's scientists believed in climate change. "Let me put it this way," Rushdie finally said to him. "If you believe the world is flat, it doesn't make the world flat. The world doesn't *need you* to believe that it's round in order to be round." As Rushdie points out, truth doesn't need our approval. Nor does truth bend to conform to our subjective view of our authentic self.

∞

The Holocaust History Museum at Yad Vashem, the World Holocaust Remembrance Center in Jerusalem, takes visitors on a chronological journey as it honors the memory of the dead and those who aided people in need. When I visited the museum in 2017, I was struck by architect Moshe Safdie's design. The entire concrete structure is shaped like a long, triangular prism that narrows in the middle as it passes underground, as if dipping just beneath the surface of the water. The galleries, also triangular shaped, evoke suffocation and entrapment: wide and dark at the bottom and narrowing to a thin line of skylight at the top. As you pass down those hallways through time, you become physically aware of the increasing sense of horror and hopelessness.

As the late Martin Roth, director of the Victoria & Albert Museum in London, once told me, "Museums are the holy grail of memory." Those who have experienced tragedy firsthand, such as Nobel Laureates Elie Wiesel and Malala Yousafzai, urge us not to forget the past, for if we do, we risk repeating horrors like the Holocaust or terrorist attacks against Muslim girls who seek an education.

"I have tried to keep memory alive . . . I have tried to fight those who would forget. Because if we forget, we are guilty, we are accomplices," Elie Wiesel said in his 1986 Nobel Prize acceptance speech in Oslo. Likewise, we should commit to memory the times when courageous truth-tellers spurred and spread drivers of positively contagious ethics, from Rosa Parks and Dr. Martin Luther King Jr. to the leaders of the #MeToo movement.

Compromised truth degrades both memory and history. Today's tainted truth becomes tomorrow's distorted memory and, in turn, inaccurate history. It transforms history from a source of wisdom into a driver of contagious and mutating falsity. It catalyzes all the other drivers of contagion, which in turn trigger consequences, from a denial of climate change science to a rise in anti-Semitism or Holocaust denial or Islamophobia. And these false stories feed a cycle of falsity-based decision-making that takes us further and further from truth over time. If we tolerate compromised truth, we are effectively accepting inaccurate memories and histories that become a permanent part of who we are as individuals, institutions, and nations.

We are no longer dealing with the degree of diminished visibility on the edge that we saw with blurred boundaries. When alternative facts become the norm, we have effectively entered a *zero*-visibility zone—of the present, past, and into the future. *Compromised truth is binary*—an unacceptable humanity-defining and humanity-destroying condition. Millions of decisions that all of us make every day spread this risk. We don't even know what we don't know. We no longer know who we are, individually or as a society. Compromised truth destroys our identity.

The endgame, then, is this: In a post-truth world, we *cannot* know what we are seeing anymore. It's not just that we *don't* see what we think we're seeing. We lose all reference points—times, places, people, decisions. Compromised truth is like ethical quicksand that swallows us up completely. And it's not just a matter of slipping deeper in the more we try to dig ourselves out. We have no idea what other dangers exist.

The framework, likewise, collapses when we use compromised truth. We cannot make a realistic assessment of risks and opportunities. Our allocation of responsibility among stakeholders is skewed. And we cannot understand and manage the five other forces: We can't identify the nuances requiring *non-binary* questions and assessments. We can't know how, and to where, *power scatters* as more and more people have the power to perpetuate falsehoods. Compromised truth empowers, and is empowered by, many drivers of *contagion*. Compromised truth topples the three *ethics pillars*. It prevents us from diagnosing *blurry boundaries*. And, conversely, blurred boundaries make it harder to determine the truth because technology is changing our reality so quickly.

It is crucial to start with *principles* when framing decisions in a post-truth world, even though it's tempting (and logical) to leap to the information step. Most effective principles hinge on truth: whether they are the ones my students suggest or even Meitu's or Boeing's, almost all principles have some relationship to truth (e.g., honesty, integrity, open-mindedness).

One way to detect a questionable principle is to ask whether we can hold individuals and institutions accountable for applying it. If we cannot, it's a good indicator that the principle is disconnected from truth. For example, even less ethics-focused principles, such as Uber's initial obsession with "growth and profit," hinge on truth: you either increased your growth and profit or you didn't. In contrast, also in Uber's early set of principles was "make magic"; it's pretty hard to know if you've made magic or not.

As you consider *information*, pay special attention to indicators of compromised truth, such as the disregard for science or expert advice; the substitution of opinions, feelings, or beliefs for fact; the absence of context; information silos; and instances of personalized or curated truths. Root out assumptions and gut reactions. Minding the gaps in information is a challenge of an entirely different magnitude when truth is in question. When you can't trust the veracity of your facts, then *all* of the information is, effectively, a gap. For instance, sending a falsified photo to an employer leaves them wondering what other parts of your résumé are also falsified.

When compromised truth contaminates principles or information, it can become all but impossible to assess *stakeholders* and *consequences* over time. Start with the priority stakeholders (e.g., the users of Meitu, their friends, colleagues, families, the app maker) to discern others (job recruiters, job seekers, labor laws that might be influenced or changed, college administrators, photo-editing businesses that are created to meet the demand of edited headshots, and beyond). Then do the same with consequences. For example, consider not only the obvious impact on personal relationships and work, but also broader consequences such as increased tolerance of beauty-based hiring practices.

Scenario testing offers an additional twist for framing dilemmas: If you identify an untruth in the information, ask yourself what stakeholders and consequences would emerge if the truth were hypothetically corrected. For example, how would transparency and informed consent look with your newly inserted truth? Would you have flown on a Boeing plane if you had known how the company handled safety backups? Would you take social distancing precautions more seriously if you knew COVID-19 (coronavirus) would become a global pandemic?

When compromised truth infiltrates the framework, it dismantles every rung: If principles aren't grounded in truth, there is no accountability and therefore no way to gauge trust; tainted information yields inaccurate views of stakeholders and consequences; and all bets are off on our ability to assess the forces driving ethics. But even if compromised truth only enters at the level of consequences, it calls into question all of the steps before. The framework can withstand any and all of these challenges, but *only* if it is grounded in truth.

∞

So how do we fight for truth in a post-truth world—or at any time in history?

First, we seek perspective and fight for facts. In other words, our own view of any given situation is insufficient. Since we all have a different experiential relationship to facts (e.g., our varied experience of temperature), the only way to gain perspective is to step outside ourselves and seek different viewpoints from a variety of people on a range of problems.

Pulitzer Prize–winning presidential historian Doris Kearns Goodwin writes in her biography of Abraham Lincoln, *Team of Rivals*: "In my own effort to illuminate the character and career of Abraham Lincoln, I have coupled the account of his life with the stories of the remarkable men who were his rivals for the 1860 Republican Presidential nomination. . . . " How inspiring it would be if we all counted on a team of rivals—our truth-sparring partners—that could challenge our views and share their unvarnished perspectives. Inspired by Kearns Goodwin's approach, a way to fight against compromised truth can start in your own life with your own team of rivals.

Second, in my advisory work, I often encourage calling on experts who can collect, analyze, and share their evidence and experience. Experts have their own teams of rivals, such as the editors of peer-reviewed academic and professional journals, fact-checkers, codes of ethics, and natural science and social science competitions. We benefit from experts boiling down which facts and questions really count and why, telling us the truth in accessible language—without telling us what to think—and then listening to our views. Potential users of an innovation need to know what it does, who controls it, and the key opportunities and risks for individuals, society, and humanity. (We don't need to know the minutiae of the gene-editing process or how Meitu engineers write code.) We also need to understand what the law does and does not do to protect us. In other words: *Where is the edge?*

Next, don't make assumptions about whether something is either true or untrue (remember, ethics on the edge are non-binary). When in doubt, put what you believe to be true through the framework, keeping in mind the six forces. Then see how your truth might look if it spread. For example, what might happen if your "beautified" photo ended up in the police's facial recognition database and could become fodder for false arrests?

Ensure that you don't allow the complex reality on the edge to be a justification for compromising the truth. This complexity—from populism to robots to climate change—must be put into the framework. There's no excuse for alternative facts. Be truthful about what is blurry and about what you may not know—to the extent possible. Take responsibility for continually clearing away as much fog as possible and reassessing the truth.

Don't confuse consensus with truth. Society's most challenging steps forward—such as eradicating discrimination and injustice in all their guises or incentivizing companies to improve transparency around algorithms—don't often happen by consensus. Nor do facts require a consensus.

In addition, don't expect truth to be convenient. As former vice president Al Gore's landmark film *An Inconvenient Truth* compellingly shows, the facts upon which we build our ethical decisions are not always easy to find or face. In a similar vein, Hans Rosling's *Factfulness: Ten Reasons We're Wrong About the World—and Why Things Are Better Than You Think* teaches us how missed facts lead to misdirected worry or, in ethical decision-making terms, missed opportunity and ineffectively managed risk.

Remember, how we *use* truth is itself an ethical question. We cannot tolerate the weaponization of truth. Hackers illegally exposing truthful, confidential information (whether from private individuals or public officials or classified governmental data) in the name of ethics is just that: illegal. Weaponizing truth by exposing private information can get personal and highly contagious, such as the epidemic of "revenge porn" involving the posting of highly intimate imagery that, while authentic, was never intended to be shared publicly. It's not because something is true that it's right, or ethical, to reveal it to the world.

Don't confuse imagination with untruth. Compromised truth quashes imagination, destroys dreams, and impedes innovation and empathy. Dreams and imagination are key to cultivating a truth that will further humanity. And there is no better lens for seeing truth than one that reflects the vantage point of someone else's story, whether it be factual or fictional, human or robotic. How many of us see our own relationships and life situations differently after watching a great movie or reading an engaging novel?

And, finally: *Fight* for truth. Fight as if the ethical decision-making that tethers us to our humanity depends on it. Because it does. The consequence and permanence of changes we make to our personal and shared histories are something we all must live with forever.

Chapter Seven

ETHICS ON THE FLY

Many of us have faced a time when an elderly relative's reflexes and reaction times when driving were no longer what they once were. Maybe they had minor scrapes in the parking lot or near misses on the road. It may have made you uncomfortable whenever they got behind the wheel. While it's clear that their driving days are coming to an end, you fear it will be incredibly difficult to convince them to surrender the car keys—which represent independence and personal freedom. The car allows them to get around town to see friends, run errands, and attend church. It is a central piece of their identity. Is taking away the keys and stopping your relative from driving really so urgent?

We often need to make high-quality ethical decisions quickly—in other words, we need to do "ethics on the fly." This chapter shows you how to deploy all the learning from the first six chapters to zero in on your highest priorities efficiently.

Just as doctors apply a triage approach in the emergency room, ethics on the fly can help you rapidly bring the most crucial ethical dilemmas into sharp focus. Ethics on the fly is especially effective in these common scenarios: your time is limited; you don't need any additional information or input from stakeholders to make an ethical decision;

the consequences are reasonably foreseeable; and you are not consenting for someone else.

In contrast, there are a few kinds of dilemmas that do not lend themselves to an on-the-fly approach. Decisions that require more detailed information in order to apply the framework or address the forces (particularly contagion) should not be made on the fly. Those that involve consequences that are likely to change significantly (or, worse, unpredictably) over time—as we saw with direct-to-consumer genetic-testing kits—require more thoughtful consideration of different possible scenarios. Also, decisions that could have a significant impact on other people from whom you cannot obtain informed consent require pressing pause and considering your impact and your responsibility.

Just because a dilemma can be handled "on the fly" does *not* mean it is unimportant. Perhaps counterintuitively, Boeing's choice about whether to ground the defective planes or keep them in the air *should have* been on the fly: It was a critical decision; an important and irreparable potential harm was death to many; and no more information was needed in order to make an ethical choice.

I'm not suggesting that you cut ethical corners, or that practicing ethics on the fly is always convenient or straightforward. It still requires taking responsibility and considering your impact on your own story and those of others. But ethics on the fly offers you a more efficient strategy for making choices using the framework and the forces driving ethics.

My approach to ethics on the fly is based on what I call the 2 x 4:

- Choose the two most important principles.
- Choose the two most important and irreparable consequences.
- Choose the two most important forces.
- Choose two alternatives.

This abbreviated approach works for many dilemmas because at least one of your *principles* will rise to the top as the most critical, and

there is often one *consequence* that is so significant (e.g., potential fatalities) that it matters less what the others are. By choosing two, you
give yourself just a little extra margin to test your decision-making.
Likewise, the six *forces* apply in all dilemmas, but not with equal importance. Very often, one or two forces have the greatest impact. Finally, in
any dilemma, it's necessary to consider *alternatives*—to seek other ways
to get to the same, or a close enough, destination.

In this chapter, we will delve into a wide range of ethical questions
we face in our day-to-day lives: whether you should take an elderly
relative's keys away; whether to post your children's photo on social
media; how you hone your point of view about the antivaccination
movement; whether to intervene when a colleague is being bullied at
work; what steps you might take when you disagree with an employer's
actions; and, finally, whether you have a responsibility to tell guests
when your digital assistant might be "listening."

In each scenario, I use an example set of seven principles to choose
from: safety, respect, truth, courage, responsibility, privacy, and compassionate nonjudgment. This set includes a mix of principles that I
consider fundamental to the framework and the forces (such as truth,
responsibility, and compassionate nonjudgment), some that are paramount in protecting citizens (such as safety and privacy), and some
that anchor us in our humanity (such as respect and courage).

The one set of principles we each choose for ourselves applies to all
the questions we may face. But as the stories show, we may prioritize
and apply them differently in different circumstances.

These scenarios are highly individualized and, as in most cases,
there are no simple "ethical" or "unethical" solutions. I invite you to
reflect and respond based on your own principles, views, and circumstances. If you haven't yet settled on your own five to eight personal
principles, the stories here may help you find them.

My perspective is presented as a possible model with which you may
compare your own views, based on your specific circumstances, but my
responses are not meant to confer judgment on anyone else's decisions.

This approach also allows you to take a confident position in discussions of ethical conundrums at work, over dinner, with children and relatives, or in your choices as a consumer. Most importantly, the efficiency of ethics on the fly will help you to take control of the ethics of more and more decisions.

At first, this 2 x 4 approach may take a little practice. But the more you use it the quicker it will take hold as a habit and the more agile you will become.

∞

Ethics-on-the-fly scenario: *Should I try to take the car keys away from an elderly relative whose driving has become unsafe?*

This question is on the fly because you have the information you need. For example, looking up accident-rate statistics among the elderly is unnecessary because we are not playing averages, we're trying to eliminate an unacceptable outlier of harm to the driver or someone else.

Similarly, we already know that the stakeholders are the driver and their family and friends, plus anyone who could potentially be on the road and the people in their lives. But we don't need to name them, or collect any other information about them, to make an ethically effective decision. Risk of harm or death to any stakeholder is unacceptable.

Begin by choosing your *two most important principles.* I would pick safety and respect in this situation since safety is by far the highest priority. That said, many other principles might apply, among them courage, responsibility, truthfully facing the risks, and compassionate nonjudgment.

To identify *two consequences*, start by asking: Which outcomes are both important and irreparable? If you *didn't* take the keys away, are there outcomes you either couldn't live with or couldn't live without? In this example, given my principles of safety and respect, I would be most concerned about injury toward the driver and unknown others.

Other consequences might be the impact on relationships in the driver's family, the driver's physical and mental health, and access to friends, family, and needed services.

Which *two forces* are most critical? I would start with the three pillars, focusing specifically on informed consent. The second force I would choose is contagion and mutation.

First, informed consent is not crumbling in this case as it does in edgier cases precisely because you and the driver have all the information you need. Nonetheless, obtaining informed consent is challenging when it also means asking the driver to give up freedom, accept age-related concerns, and cede power. Reminding the driver of the risks and responsibilities could at least ensure that they understand how what's at stake may have evolved as they age. And calling attention to the risks for others could help shift their perspective. Note specifics such as the baby carriages, bike riders, and joggers with earphones with whom they share the road.

The second force, contagion and mutation, can include a tolerance for potentially harmful behavior (a version of weak compliance and refusing to face truth), as well as the driver's or your own skewed incentives (such as their incentive to maintain independence and yours to avoid a difficult conversation or take away their freedom). All these drivers of contagion potentially encourage continued risk-taking.

But imagine the positive side of contagion and mutation: Everyone starts having conversations about when it is the right time to stop driving. Soon, it becomes normal. No stigma, no insult or feeling of a loss of power, just a process that begins around a certain age in the same way that in most states drivers' licenses are granted to sixteen-year-olds. We might even trigger positive mutations, such as the increased offering of special arrangements for elderly passengers from ride-sharing companies and driving services (lower rates, more assistance, easier-to-access apps), and more and better usage of driverless cars.

Now let's look at *alternatives* if the driver doesn't consent. Maybe they can agree not to operate a vehicle at night or during rush hour, and to avoid dangerous, crowded areas where accidents might happen. Such an incremental approach doesn't necessarily ensure complete safety for the driver or others on the road, but it could help reduce risk and start a process of decreasing driving and increasing comfort with other options. That is, of shifting the "When and under what circumstances?" discussion toward your ultimate goal.

Most aging drivers mean well and do not intend to be careless. But ultimately any harms caused are their responsibility. Your decision is whether your concerns about safety, and your willingness to prioritize safety over other principles, means you respectfully take away the keys *without* consent. Although we would be disrespecting their wishes, putting an elderly person in a position where they have to live with having harmed someone else needlessly could be far worse.

I recognize that family dilemmas can be difficult. If you have thought through the choice, framed it using the 2 x 4 model, and still find that respect for your relative's independence or another principle trumps safety, then you make the best decision you can for your situation. The allocation of responsibility for ethics doesn't spare us for our good intentions, particularly when we have the power to do better. We are responsible for both the specific consequences and for monitoring the situation and adjusting our decisions over time.

Ethics-on-the-fly scenario: *What are the ethical considerations of posting photos of children on social media?*

It may feel natural to want to share our children's first steps, first day of school, prom date photos with our family and friends in real time on social media. But it's still a choice fraught with ethical considerations for very important stakeholders, namely our children. In the U.S. and several other major countries around the world, approximately 81 percent of children under the age of two have an online presence, and the prenatal sonogram photos for almost a quarter of these children were posted by their parents before they were even born. It has become so normalized that it has its own term: "sharenting."

The 2 x 4 approach does not judge the many ethically minded parents who choose to post news and images of their children. Rather, I use it to call attention to the fact that the serious implications of the choice might not be apparent. There is no way to predict how photos of your children might be used now or in the future. Pew Research finds that over half of U.S. teens were bullied or harassed online in 2018. Social media also offers a gateway for criminals to steal from or gain the trust of children. And social media companies' errors surface and policies evolve over time, as we saw with direct-to-consumer genetic-testing kits. While we are quick to criticize companies for unleashing new technologies on consumers before they assess and manage the ethics challenges, all too often *we* surrender our own power and responsibility before we understand the implications and what we're giving. We click "I agree" even when there is no driving imperative to engage at all. Social media is so pervasive, and its impact on individuals and society so significant, that we owe it to ourselves to consider the ethics of our personal engagement with it—particularly when it comes to our families.

This is an on-the-fly question because you already have sufficient information to frame. You know that platforms like Facebook, Instagram, Twitter, Snapchat, and others offer wonderful opportunities for people to connect—and yet they are fraught with issues of trustworthiness, privacy risks, and loss of control over the content we share on them, not to mention the problems of curation we explored in the discussion of compromised truth. You are also aware of current and potential future stakeholders, including hackers, misguided friends or family members, or even universities and employers.

Let's run this example through the 2 x 4 approach. I would choose safety and respect (particularly for the child's identity) as the two leading *principles*. Privacy is a close third, but I consider it woven into the larger question of respect and how parents treat their children in this case.

The two most important *consequences* both revolve around what it means to create an online identity for someone else. First, there is the unpredictability and permanence of this profile. Even if you remove the photos from your own account, you cannot control whether or how many times they were copied, modified, and redistributed to unknown recipients or what the company has done with this data. The child may never be able to remove the photos or erase their exposure, either online or from the memories or devices of those who have seen the posts. Even asking social media companies to take the information down could achieve little, especially (and to some extent understandably) for voluntarily posted images that do not violate the platform's terms of service. (Some platforms' terms of service target situations such as bullying, harassment, hate speech, and violation of intellectual property rights, but may not provide for requests to remove inappropriate photos that we choose to post that may make their way to places we didn't anticipate.)

Second, parents might consider the future consequences for their relationships with their children. There is no way to predict how a child will react to their online presence as they grow up. I have had so many students between the ages of eighteen and twenty-two say they were horrified by the trend of parents posting pictures of their children on social media, even ultrasound images before birth, that they ask to make the issue a formal class topic.

In this scenario we might try to walk in our children's shoes and ask: What would we think if our child or one of their friends posted photos of us without our permission? I'd also question the ethical implications of posting images of a child with other children (at birthday parties, for example) without their parents' permission. My own answer would be that I wouldn't want others uploading photos of my children on social media without my consent, and so I would refrain from doing the same with others' children. (If I did decide to share such photos, any consequences would be my responsibility.)

The two most important *forces* at play are contagion and scattered power. Contagion would be the most powerful, given how the consequences of this story could potentially spiral out of control. In particular, so many drivers of contagion and mutation are potentially at stake that the risk of contagion is especially high, including weak compliance, arrogance, jealousy, pressure, information silos, inadequate transparency, and new technology related to social media. Scattered power reinforces the parents' ability to post, while also making it easier for unwarranted copying and distribution of those photos, giving anyone more access to, and therefore power over, your child's identity.

What are your *alternatives*? You might choose to share photographs only on encrypted platforms, to limited groups that you control based on your level of trust in the recipients, or email pictures, or even print out hard copies and send them to family in the mail. Another alternative might be to never post certain photos for safety purposes, such as images that could reveal your child's location, school, after-school activities, religious affiliation, or where they attend services. Yet another option would be to slowly introduce your child to social media in a controlled and age-appropriate way. And to make decisions together once they reach a reasonable age, being sure to explain the importance of asking "Is it my story to tell?"

My own preferences reflect the confidential nature of my ethics advisory work and my commitment to confidentiality with students and friends, so it will be too extreme for many people. I try to eliminate risk and never upload photos on social media. I also limit my postings online, like tweets, to matters of general public interest on ethics. But I also recognize that, thanks to my privilege, I have other alternatives. For millions of people around the world, a social media platform may be their only way to access the internet and communicate with distant family members and friends. In such situations, other principles may conflict with safety and respect, such as the need to prioritize family relationships.

Social media companies, public authorities, educators, law enforcement, and even pediatricians could be more proactive in communicating the potential risks of posting photos of children. But parents can also prevent harm by finding alternative ways of sharing family moments.

Ethics-on-the-fly scenario: *What are the ethical stakes when parents refuse to vaccinate their children against measles and other diseases?*

Although many health care decisions are *not* on the fly, in this case, we actually just need a little bit more information about vaccinations to make an ethical decision. In other words, we shouldn't assume we already have adequate, high-quality facts—nor do we need to become medical experts. Our ethical analysis can be done on the fly, but it is still our responsibility to seek the relevant factual information by calling our physicians, a reputable health service hotline, or other respected health care sources. You should not, however, accept medical advice from a friend, religious leader, celebrity, social media platform, an unfamiliar website (even if it pops up near the top of a Google search), unaccredited nonprofit organization, or any unproven news source, just as you wouldn't consult a doctor for spiritual guidance or a journalist for plumbing help.

When it comes to vaccinations, compromised truth runs rampant. The many reasons why people who decline to vaccinate often dismiss scientific evidence. Some see vaccinations as a violation of their religious beliefs. Influential celebrities with no scientific expertise have publicly voiced their skepticism about the benefits and certainty about the harms. Some parents believe, with no foundation in fact, that a healthy lifestyle is enough to protect their children from disease.

Thankfully, in addition to your physician's advice, scientific facts can be found in one or two clicks online from trusted sources like the U.S. Centers for Disease Control and Prevention (CDC), the Mayo Clinic, the American Medical Association, and the World Health Organization. A few points about measles you would find in a matter of minutes include: Before the invention of the measles vaccine in 1963, an estimated three to four million Americans were infected each year. Up to five hundred died of the disease annually. In 2019, there were

1,282 cases of measles in the U.S. (the largest number since 1992), leading to 128 hospitalizations. According to the CDC, "the majority of cases were among people who were not vaccinated against measles." Though death from measles is relatively rare in the U.S. today, complications include ear and eye infections, pneumonia, and encephalitis (swelling of the brain).

The CDC describes measles as a "highly contagious virus" that can potentially be passed to others when an infected person coughs or sneezes, or by touching a contaminated surface. But with the help of a successful vaccination program, the U.S. declared the measles eliminated in 2000. A child who has received the recommended two doses of the measles, mumps, and rubella (MMR) vaccine (one between twelve and fifteen months; and another between four and six years) is believed to be 97 percent protected from the disease. Some parents genuinely believe that the vaccine will protect their children from measles, but might increase their risk of autism. Medical experts have debunked this theory. (In rare cases, children with certain medical conditions can face complications from vaccination; these instances where parents have a legitimate reservation about vaccinating based on a medical professional's recommendations are not the cases I am addressing here.)

Whether you are making a choice for your own child or developing an opinion about this issue, let's look at the ethics through the 2 x 4 model. I would choose the *principles* of survival and safety of the individual child and others; and truth, in particular evidence-based science. A close third would be responsibility. For many, personal or religious freedom may also come into play, where people could view forcing parents to vaccinate their children as an infringement on these principles. But freedom is complex in this example. We are talking about parents being at liberty to do what they think is right with respect to a life-or-death question for other human beings—first, their child (who cannot legally consent because they aren't old enough) and second, innocent people the child may infect (who cannot consent because they cannot know they are exposed to the illness until it's too late).

Although I value independence, personal freedom, and diverse cultural and religious traditions, I place these principles behind risking lives and perpetuating falsehoods that also endanger lives. In 2019, the World Health Organization called "vaccine hesitancy" (the reluctance or refusal to vaccinate) one of the "ten threats to global health," alongside HIV, Ebola, air pollution and climate change. The consequences of getting this decision wrong are too important and irreparable. Public safety is part of the cost and privilege of living in an open and safe society.

Next, there are many possible *consequences*, but all pale in comparison to a child falling dangerously ill or even dying, or infecting others. Many parents who choose not to vaccinate mean well for their child and they are not intentionally doing harm. But neither good intentions nor beliefs prevent harm or refute scientific evidence. Nor do they absolve us from ethical responsibility for the impact of our decisions—especially when they could lead to the death or serious illness of a child or stranger.

In this case, the most important *force* I would choose is contagion of compromised truth. It spurs the spreading of misinformation, ideas, and behaviors that lead to illness and loss of life—along with the fallacies that each person is responsible only for themselves and that we can design our life. The ethical contagion is inextricably linked to the medical contagion of the disease itself. A second force at play is scattered power: Parents who would never dream of harming others with a recklessly handled firearm or by driving while drunk can and do cause potentially deadly harm by not vaccinating their child.

Are there *alternatives* to vaccination? In this situation, there are not. The decision and consequences are binary. If I choose to vaccinate, medical evidence confirms that my child will be well protected against measles. If I don't, the science is equally clear: My child will not be safe, nor will other children or adults with whom they come in contact. (Again, I exclude the rare cases when medical experts determine that vaccinating a child would be detrimental to the child's health.)

While any decision short of vaccination leaves us prone to medical harm and ethical risk, there are some steps we might take to try to move in the right direction. Each one of us can help to minimize contagion by spreading fact-based science and extinguishing compromised truth at work, at home, among friends, and on social media. We could also advocate for protective laws. For example, we might urge legislators and community leaders to refuse to allow unvaccinated children access to parks, restaurants, and other public places. Or, after a respectful discussion of the issue, we could disallow unvaccinated children and their families from our homes. Unfortunately, the child who is unvaccinated again pays the price when society is forced to choose protective measures.

The learning from the antivaccination movement can apply to both routine health care matters and to medical decisions that are not so day-to-day. Critically, we each face life-or-death decisions as we fight global pandemics like COVID-19, spreading across the world at the time of this writing. Even the smallest decision, such as whether we stand too close to someone at the supermarket, can destroy an innocent stranger's ability to consent to life-threatening risk. The biological solutions to the virus depend on our collective efforts to conquer contagion of compromised truth and scattered power and the unethical decisions they drive.

Ethics-on-the-fly scenario: *What should I do if I witness a male boss harassing or bullying a more junior female colleague?*

You're working at a large company with several layers of leadership above you, and you notice some uncomfortable behavior on the part of one of the managers. At staff meetings, he openly ignores a female coworker who raises her hand to ask a question. When another supervisor finally invites the woman to speak, the manager interrupts her several times, loudly drowning her out. A week later, you overhear the same manager raising his voice and berating this woman at her desk. You notice the pattern, like a steady drumbeat, as he repeatedly omits her from email chains "by mistake," fails to include her in client meetings relevant to her work, and continues to undermine her at staff meetings. And yet, when you ask her about it, she demurs. The manager has never mentioned anything in her performance review or given her specific points to improve upon, she says, and she doesn't want to create a problem.

You are a bystander—someone who witnesses an event or circumstances related to the event but is not personally involved. As a bystander, you have to decide whether or not to report it. The sad truth about much misconduct like the bullying described in this story, as well as sexual harassment and assault, is that it affects many more people than the perpetrators or the targets. The bystanders and even many who are unaware of the behavior suffer indirectly.

This dilemma can be approached on the fly because you are a witness to behavior you know is impermissible (binary) and you can identify the key stakeholders (your friend, the manager, the company, and you and other bystanders). You have a sufficient foundation for questioning the ethics without additional information. The only extra step that would be helpful is to consult your company's policy on bystander responsibility. (If there is one, it usually can be found on the website and internal networks.) What does the policy indicate about questions such as how you can intervene, whether you have an affirmative responsibility to do so (and could be reprimanded if you don't), and whether you would be protected from retaliation if you intervene? Does the policy give you guidance on whether the behavior you are witnessing would be bullying, harassment, or sexual misconduct? (I advise organizations to specify in their policies the responsibilities of, and protection for, bystanders, and to punish retaliation in the same way they punish bullying or harassment.)

As an ethics advisor I encounter stories of bullying and harassment in organizations of all types and sizes, even among the most well-run firms. I have seen many combinations of gender and seniority in bullying and sexual misconduct. Learning about a bystander's choices when witnessing unacceptable behavior is relevant to any version of the story. However, the approach to each situation is highly individu-alized and depends on office environments, policies, relationships, and the bystander's employment and personal situation.

Bullying often falls on a spectrum, with annoying, generalized ban-ter at one end and sexually or racially charged behavior at the other. Two hallmarks of bullying are the repetition and the targeting of an individual or particular group. A variety of behaviors qualify, from sabotaging the ability to do work (such as withholding information) to overt disrespect or aggression. The tricky cases fall between these extremes—a perpetrator bullies one person but not so explicitly as to trigger the company's anti-bullying policy and avoids racist or sexual content that could violate other policies. But you don't need to be an ethics expert to know that, however categorized, the behavior in this example is binary: it's plain-vanilla unacceptable.

As a bystander in this situation, I might choose safety and respect as the most important *principles*. If it seems like my colleague's safety (or well-being) is at stake, and particularly if I believe the behavior might escalate, I would likely consider intervening quickly. My own safety (and well-being) is also important. We rarely have the obligation to intervene if doing so would threaten our safety, not least because in these situations we never have all of the relevant information, and we could unwittingly expose ourselves and others to harm. (The kinds of situations in which physical safety is particularly key would be if, for example, you're at the park and you see someone hitting a teenager. Your direct intervention could lead to harm to you and further harm to the teenager.)

The two most important potential *consequences* are continuation or escalation of the harmful behavior and retaliation against you and/ or your coworker for reporting it. If the perpetrator is not investigated or stopped, your coworker continues to suffer; the manager carries on undeterred (toward her and potentially other employees—the "pat-tern" and "drumbeat" of behavior); and others may begin to see his behavior as normal or even copy it as a way to curry favor with him. Another consequence could be retaliation from the accused manager or others who support him. Still more consequences might include a conflict with your coworker (maybe she thinks you're disrespecting her privacy), emotional distress, and declining trust in an organization that doesn't eradicate bullying.

The two *forces* I would choose here are crumbling pillars and contagion. I do not have my colleague's consent to act on her behalf. In fact, she explicitly declined granting consent. As in other cases, specificity is key. Perhaps she would consent to my asking for advice from a lawyer outside the company or sharing just one aspect of the behavior. The consent assessment could shift, however, if you were personally affected by the manager's behavior—say, if his actions were making you and other employees feel uncomfortable or interfering with your ability to work as a team. Then you might consider reporting the impact of his behavior on you or joining with others to report it.

With respect to contagion, in addition to the clear repetition of behavior the story shows, you might also consider how impunity, secrecy, and abuse of power in this situation could lead to more contagion and mutation.

In assessing *alternatives*, we need to distinguish the binary nature of the unacceptable behavior from the non-binary nature of your response. You have an opportunity to convert an "intervene" or "don't intervene" dilemma into non-binary options. You might speak to your colleague again if the behavior continues, ask her how she feels about the conduct, and why she might not want to report it—trying to understand the problem through her lens. You could consult a confidential resource, such as your company's human resources manager, the general counsel's office, or an ombuds service for advice as well. You could report the behavior on an anonymous survey or through a whistleblower procedure, if your organization has one. Or consult an external lawyer or confidential expert. Depending on the situation, you could also speak to your own manager or someone more senior in the organization whom you trust, perhaps confirming confidentiality. If none of your alternatives is suitable, one option is showing understanding and support in other ways and being available to step in should your colleague want you to do so as you continue to monitor the situation.

None of us wants to cause more harm by trying to help. It's critical to consider actual and potential unwanted fallout. But I would be remiss if I didn't acknowledge that there are no guarantees, and the commitment to protection from retaliation is very organization-specific and situation-specific.

Bystander scenarios can occur anywhere: at the cinema, on the street, at the gym, or elsewhere. And they involve all kinds of behavior, from physical violence to aggressive verbal abuse to annoying, unwanted chatter. No matter the location, or the relationships, certain situations require immediate decisions to act, like calling authorities if someone is in imminent physical danger. Again, except in rare cases, I don't believe we are ethically obligated to subject ourselves to risk of harm, and we could even increase danger without meaning to do so, particularly when we intervene without knowing the facts.

But in the workplace, you are operating within a structure in which *you are automatically a stakeholder*, and the consequences to you will last longer than if you just reported an incident to the authorities. At work, you have a relationship with the individuals involved (even if you're not directly linked); you have company regulations and ethical guidelines to follow; you're more likely to be personally affected by the behavior (even just by witnessing it); and you should have protection from retaliation.

Ethics-on-the-fly scenario: *If I disagree with my company's actions, should I take action?*

On Friday, September 20, 2019, millions of people around the world took part in the Global Climate Strike, an international protest movement to demand greater environmental protections. In the days leading up to the event, technology-sector workers from companies such as Amazon, Google, Microsoft, and Facebook rallied their colleagues to leave their desks and join the protests with them. A group calling itself Amazon Employees for Climate Justice received pledges from more than 1,800 Amazon workers in fourteen countries to "walk out" and march. On the day of the event, CNN reported that in Seattle alone, three thousand Amazon employees had taken to the streets. In their Twitter feed (@AMZNforClimate) the group wrote: "We want Amazon to commit to zero emissions by 2030 and pilot electric vehicles first in communities most impacted by pollution. We should be leaders reaching zero first, not sliding in at the last moment."

Just the day before, Amazon CEO Jeff Bezos had responded to the planned protest with a new Climate Pledge, promising to switch to 100 percent renewable energy by 2030 and attain "net zero annual carbon emissions" by 2040, surpassing the schedule set by the Paris Agreement to combat climate change by ten years. (In February 2020, he also announced he was committing $10 billion of his personal wealth to the Bezos Earth Fund to fight climate change.) But Bezos said the company would continue to provide cloud computing services to the oil and gas industry. Objecting to this decision, employees protested.

If you disagree with a company's actions, as Amazon workers did, your response can vary widely, such as doing nothing, writing a blog post, joining in a march, speaking to your manager, declining a job offer, or even resigning. But often you don't need any more information to make a decision, and you already have a fair sense of who the stakeholders are. Therefore, you can approach this important question on the fly.

Truth and respect would be two important *principles* in this scenario. You might be most concerned that your company tells you the truth about what it is doing, why it is doing it, and the implications of its decisions. You also might be concerned that company leadership respects your right to express your opinion. In turn, your response also must be handled respectfully and with a constructive outcome in mind, appropriately for the workplace, mindful of confidentiality obligations, and while staying focused on work.

Consider how your own personal principles fit with those of your workplace. They may never be perfectly aligned, nor do they need to be. But negotiating the difference between them, and gathering diverse views to challenge your own, can be a crucial part of your ethical decision-making and your ability to contribute to society. Your feelings about a company's decisions and actions might be strong enough to prevent you from working for it in the first place, just as shareholders, from individuals to large institutions, increasingly decline to invest in companies in certain industries such as tobacco, firearms, and fossil fuels.

Two *consequences* outweigh all the others. With respect to your personal stake, the impact of your decision on your employment is critical. Consequences range from behaving in a way that results in your dismissal or resignation or living with the impact of your company's policies. Only you can evaluate the many elements that determine which consequences are acceptable and which are not. For example, your financial stability, opportunities you have elsewhere, and your caretaking responsibilities may be factors. Second, the impact of your choice should always be in focus: Will your action contribute to solving a problem? Greater awareness and evidence that management is listening to concerns are already good results. You don't have to change a company's customer roster with one blog post. But you do want to be sure that your goals are constructive, realizable, and in the spirit of positively contagious ethics.

The most important *force*, in my view, is crumbling pillars. Your employer doesn't have to make every decision exactly as you would like or provide complete transparency on everything. But on major ethics issues, I believe that employees should expect appropriate transparency with respect to any issue that influences the business, the community, and employees' decisions about the workplace—such as here, with Amazon's impact on the environment. Appropriate transparency means that employees understand such fundamentals as the products in development, sources of revenue, customer base, geographic reach, formal decisions of the board of directors, and of course policies covering expected behaviors, workplace requirements, and ethics (including environmental sustainability). It does not mean exposing confidential strategic initiatives in the early stages, or confidential management or board of directors matters, to every employee.

"We're going to work hard for energy companies, and in our view we're going to work very hard to make sure that as they transition that they have the best tools possible," Jeff Bezos said. "To ask oil and energy companies to do this transition with bad tools is not a good idea and we won't do that." In this situation, the employees knew enough about the company's position to develop their point of view.

Speaking up at work also exemplifies scattered power. Employees are increasingly engaging on ethics matters through their voices, their feet, and their job decisions. Amazon Employees for Climate Justice said in a September 2019 statement that Bezos's Climate Pledge announcement the day before the protest "proves that collective action and employee pressure works."

In considering the *alternatives*, it may help to define your connection to the specific situation that you find objectionable. Start with the question, What is *my* relationship to this issue? Are you center stage, building the drones, or drafting or implementing fossil fuel contracts or policies? Does it matter to you how closely you work on the issue? Do you have a choice not to work on this specific matter, or to be reassigned to a different project or a different position within the company permanently? Are you expecting the company to do more than you are willing to do personally? In this instance, an Amazon employee could consider how if they drive to work, or fly on business trips, they use fossil fuels.

Is your company listening and moving in the right direction? Are you speaking up with a problem-solving mind-set? If you want to act, but do not wish to speak up at work about your company's environmental policies, you could engage in positive counterbalancing steps at home, like biking instead of driving, cutting down on food waste, or minimizing the use of plastic.

As you make your own decisions, keep in mind that no company or leader is perfect. Nor can we expect every company to deliver immediate changes when we have conflicting principles. Employers make decisions on behalf of many stakeholders. Most situations benefit from a balance between respectfully expressing your views and picking your battles. We can consider which issues are truly critical to our principles. We can also acknowledge the good that companies do. (However, when a binary issue is at stake, such as a company tolerating sexual misconduct or significant human rights violations, no amount of positive efforts would excuse the unacceptable conduct.)

Finally, companies should anticipate sensitive issues in a nonbinary fashion. Proactively asking employees how they might improve the ethics of a program, or how they could achieve a particular goal ethically, is a more solution-oriented approach than "do it" or "don't do it." If companies welcomed this kind of employee input earlier, they would pave the way for more constructive and less extreme reactive interactions. Perhaps the company could decide not to sell products and services to, or partner with, corporate customers that make no effort to develop alternative fuels or that contribute to climate change activities. Or they might require specific environmental commitments and measures from corporate customers in the sales contract.

Ethics-on-the-fly scenario: *Should you tell guests visiting your home that Alexa is on?*

Every day, people around the world "wake up" their speakers. They ask the digital voice assistants that power these devices to play music, check their calendars, call up recipes, and many other requests. These devices are now ubiquitous. Approximately 147 million smart speakers were sold globally in 2019; and one in four Americans keep an average of 2.6 devices in their homes. But not everyone is comfortable with them. Here, I explore Amazon Alexa, but the learning is relevant to the many brands and versions of digital assistants on the market.

This conundrum is a straightforward on-the-fly question. You know who the *stakeholders* are: you and your guests, their families, and anyone they may have spoken about, as well as the company, recipients of calls placed through Alexa, and, well, Alexa. But the stakeholders are also increasingly broad: potentially other companies Amazon may acquire, Amazon employees and contractors linked through the cloud or given access to work on the product, and even hotels and their employees if you are using one in a hotel room. And—judging by reports noted in Chapter 4 that police have obtained court-ordered warrants for recordings—potentially law enforcement and courts of law.

You don't need any more information to know that there may be consequences to *not* disclosing that a device in your home might be recording your conversations. Some states have laws restricting recording conversations without consent (whether with an old-fashioned recorder or a smartphone); there are laws addressing the use of illicit recordings for law enforcement; and it's difficult for the average user to understand who owns and can access the data and where it is stored. If you would not record someone the classic way, then you should not allow the algorithms in your digital assistant to record them either. But I am putting aside the law here, because this ethical choice doesn't need legal guidance.

I would choose truth and either privacy or respect as the two most important *principles*. Friends and guests to your home can reasonably expect that their conversations are private—perhaps not kept confidential, if someone gossips, but certainly not being recorded by a device that stores the data. If you do not tell them, then you're not being truthful, and you're not respecting the relationship or their privacy.

What about the two most important *consequences*? Keeping Alexa on could be a lifesaver, literally, for people with a wide range of emotional and physical challenges, including mobility, access, and communication difficulties. For example, a colleague who was immobilized after surgery told me she was able to perform voice-activated, hands-free calling and messaging using her device. A lot of the day-to-day issues that Alexa assists us with may not be life-or-death situations, but recording guests without their knowledge and consent may mean a serious breach of trust in a relationship.

There's also the potentially unpredictable use of your data. Amazon's terms of service note that "Amazon processes and *retains* your Alexa interactions, such as your voice inputs, music playlists, and your Alexa to-do and shopping lists, in the cloud." (The emphasis is mine.) We have no idea how the company uses your data and how its terms of service might change.

A broader consequence might be that we unwittingly violate our own principles.

I would choose crumbling pillars as one of the most important *forces*, specifically informed consent. Obtaining consent requires that your guests be adequately informed and specifically asked to consent. That's on each of us—not Amazon, the law, or your guests. Blurred boundaries also play a role. We don't typically converse with, or seek advice from, objects. How our relationship with digital assistants evolves over time will in part be the responsibility of the companies and regulators—along with our own changing needs and comfort levels. Society will also have to frame the use of these products with attention to the many benefits they bring to people in unusually difficult situations. This technology could be life-altering for the elderly, people with disabilities, and communities that don't have the capacity for human provision of services.

Is there any upside to not telling a friend that Alexa is listening? While many of us have become accustomed to living with digital assistants, it's hard to conceive of a circumstance in which recording a friend without telling them brings us greater trust and connection. We can mindfully weigh the opportunities a technology may bring with the fact that some of our uses also bring great risk. The alternative: Turn the devices off when guests arrive or just be obvious about talking to

Alexa. In my view, it's a much better choice than forgetting to mention it or even intentionally deciding not to tell guests. In either case, you'd be deciding for someone else—a decision that is not yours to make.

∞

Ethics on the fly doesn't mean holding your nose and leaping. It still requires courage to take those car keys away, to speak out as a bystander, and to stand up to disinformation and respond to threats such as the failure to vaccinate. We still must commit to checking that we don't take away others' choices, whether our children's right to determine their own online identity or a guest's right to a private social moment.

On the edge, there are often dilemmas that call for deeper, more deliberative thinking to make the most effective decision, where an on-the-fly approach is not appropriate. For example, whether or not to buy a 23andMe kit or to submit your child's DNA to 23andMe is definitely *not* an on-the-fly choice. The company's policy regarding the submission of children's DNA is rife with potential issues that should trigger warning signals.

Voting is another *not* on-the-fly decision. As discussed in Chapter 3, we need nuanced information, and a lot of listening and discussing, in order to apply the framework.

Framing ethics before acting is important in all choices. Technology makes it easier than ever for us to act impulsively; as a result, you may believe that your decisions need to be made urgently. But in fact, much of our power comes from what we *don't need to do*. Most of us, for example, don't need to post photos of our children on social media, deploy a smart speaker in our homes, or send our child's DNA to 23andMe *right now*. As consumers, parents, and citizens, we often have time to explore concerns and alternatives before making a decision. We should take that time—including letting a company's mistakes happen without you, and watching the responses of regulators, consumers, the company, and experts as they try to catch up with the technology.

Ethics on the fly makes it easier to integrate ethics into the many decisions and discussions we face every day, and even some that are once-in-a-lifetime. This in turn gives us greater power and ability to deliver on our own responsibilities—whatever innovations companies unleash on society or regulators fail to regulate. Our collective debate and decisions around these issues make a difference at every scale as we proactively take control of our own ethics and those of society.

Chapter Eight

RESILIENCE AND RECOVERY

On July 17, 2016, Natasha Ednan-Laperouse arrived at Heathrow Airport in London with her father and her best friend, on their way to a vacation in the South of France. The girls buzzed with excitement as they made their way to the British Airways gate, but first they stopped to buy breakfast at a Pret A Manger sandwich shop, where Natasha was focused on one thing: ingredients.

Although only fifteen, and very much a teenager, Natasha was meticulous about checking labels. She had severe allergies to nuts, sesame seeds, dairy, and bananas—foods that put her at risk of life-threatening anaphylactic shock. As her father, Nadim, would later testify, Natasha picked up an artichoke and olive tapenade baguette and studied the label: It said the sandwich contained olives, artichokes, basil, and bread, all items she liked and knew she could safely eat. She handed the sandwich to her father, who double-checked the ingredients. Many food chains post allergen-warning signs around the store, but when Nadim scanned the refrigerator shelves, he found none.

Natasha ate her sandwich at the gate and immediately felt an itchy sensation in her throat—the first sign of an allergic reaction. She drank a liquid antihistamine and her symptoms abated. At 7:30 a.m., the group boarded their flight to Nice and the girls posted a video on social media, laughing and waving excitedly to friends. Approximately twenty-five minutes later, Natasha's throat itched again. She drank another dose of liquid antihistamine, but it had no effect. Soon her whole body itched and her neck turned red. When she lifted her shirt, her father saw that she "was covered in huge raised red welts . . . as if she had been stung by hundreds of jellyfish."

Nadim gave Natasha's right thigh a shot of epinephrine, a dose of adrenaline that's meant to increase blood pressure, relax muscles in the lungs to improve breathing, and reduce the hives and swelling that occur with allergic reactions. Nothing changed. He gave her a second shot, but her symptoms only increased. They were approximately thirty-five minutes from landing. Natasha's chest began to heave as she gasped for air, pleading with her father: "Daddy, help me. I can't breathe!"

The British Airways flight crew provided her with oxygen from one of the onboard tanks. A passenger who'd obtained his medical degree only the day before offered aid. Nadim watched, helpless, as his daughter descended into the throes of anaphylactic shock. Her skin turned blue; her body slumped forward; then she lost consciousness. The captain of the plane would later say that he did not learn how serious Natasha's situation was until it was too late to make an emergency landing at another airport. As the plane began its descent into Nice, Natasha went into cardiac arrest. The doctor tried in vain to administer CPR. A member of the flight crew would later testify that there was a defibrillator onboard, but it had not been retrieved because it was at the other end of the plane, and covering the doors took "priority" during landing.

French paramedics rushed Natasha to a hospital in Nice while Nadim called his wife, Tanya, to tell her that their daughter was fighting for her life. Tanya raced to London's Stansted airport to catch a flight to Nice. It was the first day of summer break and the only available flight was that evening. She sat at the gate, waiting and praying. At the hospital, Nadim was told that Natasha "would not survive."

At 7 p.m., Nadim called Tanya. "You've got to say goodbye to her now," he said, placing the phone next to Natasha's ear. On the other end of the line, Tanya whispered: "Tashi, I love you so much, darling. I'll be with you soon." Then she collapsed in grief.

Her parents later learned that sesame seeds had been baked into the dough of the baguette of her sandwich. Not only were they not visible on the bread, but they also weren't listed on the package label.

In September 2018, the West London Coroner's Court held an inquest into Natasha's death. At the inquest, it was revealed that Pret A Manger had previously been alerted to twenty-one other instances of allergic reactions, nine of which involved sesame seeds. In six of these cases, customers had eaten the same type of baguette as Natasha, and five of them required medical attention, including a seventeen-year-old girl who suffered a "life-threatening reaction" to the sesame seeds in the bread.

Pret A Manager's director of risk and compliance testified that the chain had acted in accordance with the law. In fact, both U.K. and EU laws permitted businesses like Pret, which prepared and packaged food on the premises, to warn customers of allergen-causing ingredients by any means they choose, through oral warnings, food labels, or allergen signs posted in the store. Nadim had said there was "nothing visible at all to the eye," in the Heathrow Airport store. And Pret was *not* legally required to label individual foods. Somewhat puzzlingly, if food products were prepared off-site, such as the pre-made cakes sold at large supermarkets, comprehensive ingredients labels were required on each package.

Pret A Manager may have been operating within the law on food labeling, but not at a higher ethical standard. To protect customer safety, Pret could have taken additional steps above and beyond the minimum legal requirements. For example, it could have put ingredients labels on all its products, or only used bread with visible sesame seeds, especially after the first instance of an allergic reaction. Government and corporate leaders could have looked more closely at the potential risks of labeling, or not labeling, within the context of different stores. The Heathrow Airport shop, for example, serves travelers who speak dozens of languages, are regularly rushing to catch their flights, and may not see posted signs or understand a spoken allergen warning from an employee.

After Natasha's death, Pret began putting ingredients-list signs on store shelves, yet it still did not place allergy warnings on packages. At the end of the inquest in September 2018, Natasha's parents made a heart-wrenching statement: "We believe that this inquest has shown that she died because of inadequate food labeling laws. . . . It feels to us that if Pret A Manger were following the law, then the law was playing Russian roulette with our daughter's life."

A few days later, on October 3, Pret A Manager CEO Clive Schlee issued a public apology. "We recognize there is much more we can do," he said. Among its changes, Pret affixed ingredients labels and allergen-warning stickers on all its products; added more signage around the stores; posted full ingredients information online; promised to respond to complaints of allergy-related incidents within twenty-four hours; and vowed to work with the government, charities, and professional peers to improve the law.

"I hope this sets us on course to drive change in the industry and ensure customers with allergies are as protected and informed as possible," Schlee said in a statement. "Nothing is more important to Pret right now."

Intrigued by such a proactive and transparent response, I wanted to learn more about Pret A Manager's decision-making process. In April 2019, I wrote to Clive Schlee to ask if he would be willing to speak with me as part of my research for this book. All he knew about me was that I was an ethics expert interested in what may have been his most difficult moment as CEO. And yet, he responded to my email within hours.

When we spoke on the phone, Schlee seemed deeply affected by

Natasha's death and took personal responsibility for the company's decisions. When they had first examined the issue, he said, there were factors that led them to decide against making changes. For one, they considered it too expensive to label the millions of individual products Pret makes each year across more than five hundred stores worldwide. Additionally, the company decided it was important to continue preparing food on the premises to reassure customers of the quality and freshness of its products.

But cost and quality weren't the only concerns driving their initial thinking. As Schlee explained, they also saw potential risks. To start, in order to ensure accurate labeling on a sandwich, they'd have to verify every ingredient in the sandwich and barcode the recipe, ensuring no exposure to other ingredients. Then the sandwich maker in each store would have to execute several steps to assemble and double-check both the product and the label. There were too many vulnerabilities and potential points of error in the process. The comprehensive labels might give consumers a false sense of safety, and Pret decided that could be worse than having no labels at all.

Schlee acknowledged that Pret A Manager held primary responsibility for Natasha's death. He recognized that they should have done more than the law required—that they hadn't thought about it enough. Once they saw their missteps, they told the truth, took responsibility, and moved forward with a plan to recover.

"In retrospect, we should have been proactive," Schlee told me, calling what had happened "a shock to the system" that jolted the company to take steps in the right direction.

Still, I was horrified by the failed regulation. If the goal was to protect consumer health and safety, what possible difference could it make *where* the food was prepared? Why would regulators permit a lower standard for food made on-site than they do for off-site preparation? How many other well-meaning establishments were following this flawed law that contributed to or bore some responsibility for the death of a customer?

In 2019, the U.K. government announced a new law requiring food businesses to include full ingredients labels for foods that are "prepared and packed on the same premises from which they are sold" by October 2021, in order to better protect people with allergies. The legislation is called Natasha's Law.

∞

We all make mistakes. I am as prone as anyone else to having moments of poor judgment or times when external circumstances beyond my control conspire to throw my best efforts off course. But to quote Maya Angelou: "Do the best you can until you know better. Then when you know better, do better."

This book has given you the tools to do better. You can develop what I call ethical resilience. Ethical resilience comprises two parts: First, *prevention and agility*, which you acquired from Chapters 1 through 7 by making ethical decisions with the future in mind and monitoring to respond to changes. Second, *recovery*. The more often you use what you learned here, the less likely you are to make mistakes, the less severe they will be when you do make them, and the smoother your recovery will be. Put differently, the tools give us 20/20 foresight to ask ourselves how we will feel about our decisions even if the outcome is not what we had hoped, whether due to our own error in judgment or external circumstances. The learning also helps us form and express views about others' decisions.

Resilient ethical decision-making is the bridge between understanding what went wrong and determining the path forward. It can also be a guide to understanding the causes of others' lapses—and when and under what circumstances we grant them a second chance. How we respond to our own and others' recovery says as much about our ethics as how we face any other ethical dilemma.

As we saw with Pret A Manger, recovery begins by immediately telling the truth. To use the moment to assess our missteps, diagnose what happened, and decide how best to move forward. Ethics are not an eraser or an excuse. Ethical recovery does not mean the harm caused is undone. This is where the framework comes into play. If we are vigilant in framing our decisions, and assessing them over time as information, stakeholders, and consequences change, we can be more resilient. Likewise, we can plan ahead for our potential mistakes by including them in our assessment of consequences over time. That might mean building in guardrails, like having multiple channels to report wrongdoing at Boeing, ensuring access to a company representative for 23andMe or Airbnb customers, or advocating for better regulation and public awareness as Pret did.

Even though Pret A Manger ended up being ethically resilient, learning from its mistakes to do better, its decision-making was not perfect. Had the company framed diligently, they could have seen more clearly what was at stake with individual product labeling (notwithstanding the inadequate regulations)—the important and irreparable consequences of getting it wrong. Pret executives could have made changes sooner. It should not have taken a teenager's death. But then, the way the company told the truth, took responsibility, and repaired its ways (and regulators followed suit) is a rare example of ethical resilience that, with continued follow-through, will help prevent future harm.

In contrast, even after people died, Boeing's CEO asked President Trump to keep the flawed jets in the air. He was ready to put more lives at risk, even when he didn't have enough information about why his planes were crashing. Boeing sank deeper in the ethical quicksand as it avoided truth, blamed pilots, and focused on the narrow objective of fixing software. Boeing's biggest problem isn't with its MCAS software or any other technical or testing issue, in my view; instead, there is a fundamental failure in the way the company made, and continues to make, decisions. Until they effectively integrate ethics into their decisions at every level of the company, recovery is impossible.

Even when specific stakeholders have outsized responsibility, often other stakeholders individually could have stopped the harm or seized an opportunity. At the very least, the other stakeholders in Natasha's story should reconsider whether they should do better. Heathrow Airport could require higher standards for food labeling among its vendors than the law requires (maybe even multilingual labels); British Airways could reexamine its supplies and crew training for severe allergic reactions.

There are many definitions of resilience. Some suggest a return to a previous state of being, as in ecology: "Rate at which a system returns to a reference state." The *Oxford English Dictionary* defines it as "the quality or fact of being able to recover quickly or easily from, or resist being affected by, a misfortune, shock, illness, etc." I see resilience as forward-looking and growth-minded. Judith Rodin, the former president of the Rockefeller Foundation and the University of Pennsylvania, writes in *The Resilience Dividend*, "Resilience is the capacity of any entity—an individual, a community, an organization, or a natural system—to prepare for disruptions, to recover from shocks and stresses, and to adapt and grow from a disruptive experience." Rodin goes on to link a fundamental question that we have been exploring throughout this book to resilience and recovery: How do we allocate responsibility for ethics recovery across stakeholders?

"We know," Rodin says, "that resilient places *always* have strong individuals, groups, institutions, and networks that can come together to increase readiness." As with any other ethical dilemma, "coming together" starts with the framework and forces. Here, the framework does double duty as an efficient diagnostic tool to determine *why* things went off the rails and a starting point for evaluating your and others' decisions going forward.

Pret A Manger, for example, had thoughtful *principles*. The company's leaders firmly believed in its mission "to create handmade, natural food." This was not a case of laziness or lack of commitment to principles. (Remember: You can assess others' principles without them matching your own.) In fact, before Natasha's death, Pret's "About

Us" page touted the idea that "No Label Is Good" because they believed it proved to customers that their food was freshly made on-site.

But when Pret faced the earlier instances of allergic reactions to its unlabeled products, it didn't interpret or act on the *information* as effectively as it could have, given the gravity of the situation. This was a serious error in judgment by an otherwise thoughtful leadership team. The coroner's report also revealed that Pret did not have an adequate system for monitoring allergic reactions to its products, with some complaints going to customer service and some going to a health and safety department. The Pret A Manager story is all too common: In my experience, most people (including ethically committed senior leaders) don't go to work deliberately careless about ethics. They just don't know how to integrate ethics into their day-to-day decisions effectively and consistently—or they don't prioritize and implement the right systems to manage them.

Pret didn't misdiagnose its *stakeholders*, since management knew who they were. Most importantly, when we consider the *consequences* over time, we see how the framework cascades: Pret's misjudgment and ineffective monitoring of evolving allergy reports became the foundation for continued inaccurate assessments of the potential consequences of its approach to labeling.

Perhaps the biggest lesson with Pret A Manager is for all of us. *When we observe a failing by others—in any context—one of the first questions we should ask ourselves is whether we are making, or could make, the same or a similar mistake.* There is no better prevention and agility, or support for recovery, than plugging our learning from others' challenges into our own lives. Imagine the positive contagion of ethics we could spread if we all framed ours and others' errors, so that we could know better and do better, decision by decision.

We face plenty of opportunities to think through our own and others' mistakes, especially as we are called upon to form opinions about others' public transgressions more and more. We'll explore this process next as we examine a notorious recovery failure that is an extreme counterpoint to Pret's story. We'll also look at how to approach some of the more common, everyday transgressions that fall between these two examples, and yet still have an uncommon impact on our lives.

∞

On February 24, 2020, a Manhattan jury found American film producer Harvey Weinstein guilty of criminal sexual assault in the first degree and rape in the third degree in a trial that gripped the world. Six women testified against the sixty-seven-year-old Hollywood mogul, known for such films as *Shakespeare in Love*, *The English Patient*, *Pulp Fiction*, *The Artist*, and more. He has been publicly accused of sexual harassment and assault by more than ninety women and, at the time of this writing, faces additional criminal charges in Los Angeles, civil complaints filed by many of his accusers, and investigations in London and Dublin.

Weinstein acted undeterred for nearly thirty years, until investigative reporting in October 2017 by *The New Yorker* and the *New York Times* revealed a long-standing pattern of horrendous predatory behavior. These stories spurred a worldwide #MeToo movement to speak out against sexual misconduct. As the movement spread, it empowered women and men to break their silence about abuse they'd suffered. For context, on frequency: Approximately one in three women and one in six men in the U.S. will experience sexual assault during their lifetime, according to a 2017 survey report from the National Center for Injury Prevention and Control at the Centers for Disease Control and Prevention. Approximately half of those who identify as transgender say they have been sexually assaulted at some point in their lives, according to a 2015 survey report by the Washington, D.C.–based National Center for Transgender Equality.

By February 2018, four months after the Weinstein story broke, the *New York Times* reported on seventy-one additional men in high-profile jobs who had been fired, resigned, or experienced professional fallout due to sexual misconduct across such industries as entertainment, media, music, finance, politics, hospitality, tech in Silicon Valley, and more. Researchers at Yale University who studied #MeToo's impact in twenty-four countries found that it contributed to a 13 percent increase in the reporting of sex crimes in the first six months of the movement.

Sexual misconduct of all kinds is unacceptable and largely illegal. The founders of the #MeToo movement gave us a shorthand way to confidently declare that some things *are* binary. And the verdict against Weinstein represented a turning point for the movement, as its founder Tarana Burke told the *New York Times*: "The outcome of the Weinstein case should be seen as fuel to keep survivors and our allies motivated for change."

Weinstein, however, has been unwilling or unable to tell the truth, take responsibility, and seek amends. He repeatedly denied he ever had anything but consensual sex with his accusers, even while hiring private investigators to suppress and intimidate them from speaking to the press. As he sat in court, listening to the verdict against him, he was heard repeatedly saying to his lawyer, "But, I'm innocent."

His guilt is a binary question that has been decided in a Manhattan court. But his actions and the verdict leave a plethora of ethical questions in their wake—from how we hold accountable the people around him who supported and hid his behavior to how we assist the survivors to what we do with his extraordinary artistic contributions. Just as the question of his guilt or innocence is out of our individual control, to a large extent we have very little power to hold his abettors accountable or aid his victims. (This is not to say that as a society we shouldn't find ways to do more on both fronts—or that the formidable advocates for accountability have not made a tremendous difference.) But what we *can* control, and where we do have power, is with our decisions about how we approach his body of work.

As individuals and as a society, we have ethical choices to make about the major artistic, athletic, political, scholarly, or other contributions from individuals whose behavior we find unacceptable. For example, do we shield our children from listening to the music of pop star

Michael Jackson, accused (but never found guilty in a criminal court) of molesting children? Should molecular biologist James Watson, who along with Francis Crick discovered the double helix structure of DNA, lose his Nobel Prize because of a history of sexist and racist comments, including a horrific statement in 2007 suggesting that certain races had genetically provable inferior intelligence? How do we approach the work of artistic legend Pablo Picasso, accused of repeatedly emotionally abusing the women in his life? These were not one-time-only stories. These are people who repeatedly did, said, or supported bad acts with many witnesses to their behavior. When and under what circumstances would we destroy their art or support a broad societal change to make it unavailable from film and music streaming services or take it out of museums and bookstores?

The thorny question of Harvey Weinstein's film achievements reminds us of the importance of defining the right question. First, as noted above, his largely illegal behavior is a binary issue: Never acceptable. And it has been framed by the courts. Second, the focus on when and under what circumstances we would destroy or ban art is a non-binary question. We must separate these two questions in order to answer them. When considering the legacy of his art, we are concerned with *our ethical decisions*, not only *his* behavior or ethics.

I would emphasize the principles of respect, truth, and responsibility here, but please consider your own principles. The information, stakeholders, and consequences are too extensive to list, but I might focus on a few key points. For example, Harvey Weinstein was not the only person involved in the films and TV shows that the Weinstein Company produced or distributed. His art relied on the talents of hundreds of other stakeholders, including actors, directors, writers, production assistants, technicians, and more. And to great success—films in which Miramax and the Weinstein Company had a hand have been nominated for 341 Academy Awards and have won eighty-one times. Erasing them would obliterate the work of many other stakeholders and negatively impact future audiences who might enjoy and learn from the work, and gain a sense of the overall context of the history of cinema.

When considering what ethics forces are at play here, we see above all a destructive combination of scattered power, contagion, and compromised truth.

One way of looking at Weinstein's exceptional success is as an abuse of scattered power and a driver of contagion and mutation: The more accomplishments he collected and the more power he gained, the more he was able to hide his behavior, generate fear, and exert pressure on women by threatening to withhold work and ruin their reputations throughout the industry if they didn't bend to his will.

The challenge with compromised truth is critical. If we extinguish a piece of the canon of film history, then we are no longer telling the truth about that history, or about Mr. Weinstein. I believe we can and should protect the works of art, which affect so many other stakeholders, without supporting his abhorrent behavior in any way. A decision to expunge or disregard his films would only mutate into a dangerous failure to recognize both the truth of people's positive contributions and the truth of their unwanted behavior.

Moreover, destroying the art doesn't diminish past wrongdoing or prevent it from spreading today. The harm occurred and its consequences live on. Eradicating Weinstein's oeuvre does little to discourage other perpetrators. Nor does it stem mutation, such as the tolerance his employees exhibited or the threats to quiet disclosers of information. Most importantly, it does not repair the unspeakable trauma that survivors experienced and continue to suffer. It doesn't even support the #MeToo movement or help bring other cases to light in a way that changes society's tolerance levels. The survivors who have come forward include some of the most admired artists in the world and they deserve to have their artistic contributions respected.

In my view, we should fight to keep the learning about how easy it is to let unethical behavior seep into society—and the collective responsibility for doing so—alive. But it's easier said than done. Drivers of contagion and mutation such as pressure, greed, fear, abuse of power, secrecy, failed compliance, and others allowed sexual misconduct to fester and repeat in Weinstein's case, in the film industry, and in many other corporate cauldrons of celebrity and power from Wall Street to Silicon Valley.

These are complex questions and to be able to reach any type of answer, we need many well-reasoned diverging opinions. Whatever choice we support, ethical decision-making requires that we shine a light on the truth rather than destroy it or lock it away.

In Harvey Weinstein's case, he was rightly fired from his company and expelled from the Academy of Motion Picture Arts and Sciences. As a society, and as individuals, should we collectively fight to ensure that he loses any rights to future profit from, and even loses copyright over, the films he worked on? Instead, his share might go to help survivors of sexual misconduct. (These suggestions would require in-depth legal analysis and they might not succeed.) In addition, the media, industry leaders, film historians, and even fans can commit to not losing sight of who he was as a person—as we would any other criminal— and to provide clear lesson points about how and why others failed to stop his behavior. The exceptional news reporting has gone a long way in this case, as has the leadership from committed artists ranging from Oprah Winfrey to Reese Witherspoon. The distributors of his films might also amend them, perhaps in the opening sequence or end credits, to note that he was convicted of felony sex crimes and that neither the streaming nor distribution companies, the theater, awards panels, nor any of the participants in the creation of the film condone this behavior.

We could even clarify that the actors and other professionals who contributed to a film don't believe that the public is condoning his behavior by watching it, as this helps set the tone for how we move forward, without inflicting shame on those who appreciate the art itself. It shows respect for art, history, and the many other stakeholders, including future viewers of films, future filmmakers, and supporters of the

#MeToo movement. And it's a small step to showing respect for the survivors by assuring them that their truth will not be forgotten.

The preservation of the artistic canon speaks to a broader question of whether to modify history, a choice we are facing on the edge in many different forums. Consider the conundrum of such historic monuments as statues and the honorific naming of important buildings, streets, bridges, and more, for people whose behavior we consider abhorrent, such as proponents of slavery. Universities struggle with whether to eliminate the names of slavery supporters on major campus sites. Towns debate the removal of statues, such as the imposing monument to Confederate general Robert E. Lee in Charlottesville, Virginia, where a demonstration by white nationalists led to deadly violence.

Every case has its own context, and the point is definitely not to compare one type of reprehensible conduct with another. The goal is protecting truth and understanding that ethical resilience and recovery depend on linking truth to acceptance of responsibility and to action. All of these situations in the arts and in history show that the issues, the physical artifacts, and the perpetrators' and bystanders' horrific behavior remain raw and relevant to today's societal ills. They are not our past. They are our present. Ethical recovery and resilience are a long-term commitment.

As with the arts, there is a diversity of thoughtful opinion about the ethics of historic monuments. If an institution decides to rename a building previously named for an advocate of slavery, in my view there should be an unmissable plaque, providing an accurate account of the original name and story. The plaque should convey the historic context and lessons for today, explaining the pain caused and the reasons for the name change. If an institution leaves the building as is, there should be a plaque providing the same information and explaining why the choice was made to maintain a historic artifact in its original form and location—with a view to displaying history, not honoring, say, a slave owner or eugenicist. All websites, advertising, tours of historic monuments, and the like should integrate this learning. Whether the historical artifact remains or is taken down, forward-looking action is required: The institution must show concrete steps to redress and prevent future harm. These steps range from education, policies, and hiring practices to commitments like Georgetown University's fundraising to support community projects as part of an "ongoing dialogue" with descendants of slaves who were sold in 1838 to keep the university financially afloat.

Nonetheless, acts to eliminate the past can raise several critical questions: Where do we draw the line? How do we decide that an individual's behavior is so abhorrent that we must erase their contributions to their field? And how could we ever find consistent standards and consequences?

Erasing history is a dangerous form of arbitrariness that undermines ethical resilience. Arbitrariness sets in motion a range of contagion drivers—from unfairness and weak compliance to skewing incentives that increase the unwanted behavior. It can also breed tolerance for unacceptable behavior and complacency about keeping the truth alive. And how would we erase contributions in other industries? Would we unwind financial trades, real estate deals, or international trade agreements? How would we walk back a star surgeon's lifesaving interventions?

Taking down monuments to intolerable behaviors like slavery and eugenics need not erase history and important learning for future stakeholders. Solutions like storing monuments for research and adding permanent explanatory descriptions at their former sites can preserve knowledge and diminish the risk of arbitrariness.

Stories like these can be particularly knotty because we might feel guilty for enjoying a movie or singing along to music. But guilt and gut reactions do not lead us to ethical decisions. Abolishing art is taking a blunt instrument to recovery. It makes the non-binary decision binary. It destroys truth. It brings down more than it needs to and creates mistakes are posted for everyone to inspect on social media. I don't condone bad behavior, but we need to consider how technology has transformed normal developmental mistakes into life sentences.

You might even do a spectrum exercise to think about where the transgression falls on an axis. Perhaps on one end of the spectrum you'd have Harvey Weinstein or He Jiankui—repeated bad acts, with no remorse or acknowledgment—and on the other, a hungry child who steals a bag of chips from a subway vendor. Somewhere in the middle are stories of those who should have known better, like a senior manager who inflates his resume one time, or a high school student who violates the alcohol policy only once.

The process of determining consequences should also be dignified, consistent, proportionate, and done in such a way that the person, other stakeholders, and society can pursue recovery. Ethical decision-making not meant to slam recovery doors or back people into a corner.

So often when we think about recovery from an ethics failure, the tion of forgiveness comes up. I've heard people say many times forgiveness helps the forgiver achieve peace. I've never really un-od this point of view, as it asks us to make a leap of faith, rather informed choice—and therefore leave another's transgressions ined and unaccounted for. I don't believe in leaping; I believe ng forgiveness as any other ethical choice. Applying the same es, considering the forces, verifying truth, accepting respon-d committing to action. For me, peace doesn't come from ing, ignoring the past, or failing to clarify a specific path

erson who has erred tells the truth and commits to a clear ge and make amends, then we consider second chances. y-second chances.) When someone is on notice that their acceptable—whether to you or society or both—if the en they are telling us that they don't respect us or our that they haven't committed to a new path forward. and did it anyway.

unnecessary harm to innocent past and future stakeholders, especially to other artists.

∞

Most of the ethically challenging stories we face in our own lives do not involve corporate process overhauls or sexual misconduct on such a grand scale that it starts a global social movement. No matter the gravity of the problem, each choice we make related to recovery defines our behavior, our relationships, and our engagement in society.

When the actions of a work colleague, family member, religious leader, or a company whose products we engage with affect us directly—or if it's behavior we learn about in the news and we're developing a point of view—we face choices related to ethical resilience. Sometimes our decisions represent a pivotal life moment: Do I marry this person? Quit my job? End a friendship? Make amends for what I have done? Other times, they reflect our responsibility to society: How should I vote in order to hold politicians accountable? Should we forgive a beloved community leader for financial misconduct? Above all, we should consider our questions with our own and the other person's or entity's resilience and recovery measures in mind.

Let's look at two very different public examples of resilience and recovery, one involving Microsoft and one involving Canadian prime minister Justin Trudeau.

In 2016, Microsoft launched a conversational AI bot named Tay (after the acronym "Thinking About You") on Twitter (@TayandYou) as a social experiment: The more that people chatted with Tay, the smarter its learning and natural language would become. In less than sixteen hours, Tay began posting thousands of racist, sexist, and anti-Semitic comments as nefarious Twitter users taught it to mimic them. Microsoft immediately deleted the posts to stop the spiraling harm, took Tay offline, and apologized for the "unintended offensive and hurtful tweets . . . which do not represent who we are or what we stand for, nor how we designed Tay." Company representatives went on to concede that they had not anticipated the particular type of attack that provoked Tay, but they should have. They outlined what Microsoft had learned and how it would take those lessons forward, acknowledging the complexity of managing the positives and negatives of AI systems. This is a concise example of resilience and recovery: Tell the truth, take responsibility, and make a plan to fix the flaws. Tay's story also demonstrates how each of our small decisions—even our tweets—can collectively move the ethics needle in the wrong direction.

In 2001, twenty-nine-year-old Justin Trudeau attended an Arabian Nights–themed party at a private school where he was teaching. In 2019, when Trudeau was Canada's prime minister and in the middle of a reelection campaign, an embarrassing photo from that party emerged, showing the leader of the Liberal Party in a white turban and brownface makeup. Trudeau immediately held a press conference and said, "I shouldn't have done that. I should have known better, but I didn't and I'm really sorry." He also admitted that in high school he once dressed up in blackface "makeup" and sang "Day-O" at a talent show. "I didn't consider it a racist action at the time, but now we know better. And this was something that was unacceptable and yes, racist," Trudeau said, cauterizing any potential for contagion by telling anyone else who may be thinking they could get away with the same behavior: No, it's racist, and we all know it was wrong then and now. Trudeau went on to win a second term. We cannot know if his recovery contributed to his success, but we do know that it was an important campaign moment.

In addition to significant ethical failures, any one of us is capable of an error in judgment. Who among us hasn't lacked the courage to be honest on occasion? Who hasn't sent an inflammatory or confidential email to the wrong recipient or regretted posting a photo on social media? What matters is how we, and others, frame and move forward.

Assigning shame, blame, or guilt are not part of ethical decision-making. They're not part of the resilience and recovery process either. All three relate to the past, not a path forward. As you frame your own

response and decisions, here are the questions I find the most useful, even in on-the-fly resilience:

Was the wrongdoing intentional? Repeated? Intentions matter when you look at information. There are times when people cause real harm even though they believed they were acting in the best interest of, say, their unvaccinated child who then gets the measles. Intenti[ons] point to the likelihood of recurrence, the parameters of punish[ment] and the potential for rebuilding trust. However, good intentions repair the damage nor obviate one's responsibility. But if s[omeone's] intentions were misguided yet they immediately tell the tr[uth], responsibility, and stop the misconduct—like Microsoft[and] Manger—that's a sign of commitment to recovery.

Was the context such that many people could have [made this] mistake? Perhaps at the time, the behavior, while n[ot ideal,] was quite common. When considering the inform[ation,] is important, as are the nuances. For example, w[hen Yale] decided to rename Calhoun College, one of its [residen]tial colleges, a factor in the decision was tha[t he was] not only a slave owner—which was wrong [in his] lifetime—but also a vocal advocate for sla[very. There] may be cases in which there wasn't enou[gh] too big or blurry—for the person to have [known that] of their actions could spin out of cont[rol.]

Who is the person in questio[n?] responsibility—such as politicians, [cor]porate boards and management members of society as children our trust. They are often legal[ly] a right to hold them to ethic[al standards] because their roles rely on

Finally, is this a you[ng] ior, who made a terri[ble] it? Young people today

On the opposing side of forgiveness, I've noticed in my advisory work an increasing global obsession with the idea of "zero tolerance." It may be necessary at times. Disney CEO Robert Iger woke up one morning in 2018 to learn that Roseanne Barr, the eponymous star of his ABC network's top-rated TV show, had posted a racist tweet about President Barack Obama's former advisor Valerie Jarrett. Iger immediately canceled Barr's show. "It was an easy decision really. I never asked what the financial repercussions would be, and didn't care," Iger wrote in his memoir, *The Ride of a Lifetime*. "In moments like that, you have to look past whatever the commercial losses are and be guided, again, by the simple rule that there's nothing more important than the quality and integrity of your people and your product. Everything depends on upholding that principle."

Iger rightly exercised zero tolerance for racist behavior. Zero tolerance makes sense for binary situations like racism, sex crimes, or bullying. But zero tolerance is rarely the most ethical approach in non-binary situations. When applied excessively, it can even become a contagion driver, in the form of perfectionism, fear, and skewed incentives that push the unwanted behavior underground. When a policy of zero tolerance is approached with fairness and transparency, there's less opportunity for arbitrariness and unrealistic perfectionism to spread. Ensure that people can retain their dignity while also setting clear boundaries. For example, firing someone for fraud (a binary offense), particularly if it was a senior executive responsible for knowing and modeling conduct, may be the appropriate response. But ethical decision-making aims to create space for making amends and moving on. We all make mistakes. Recovery and resilience—not condemnation and hopelessness—is the goal.

Our decisions shape our legacy. How we handle our periods of recovery—and others'—defines our identity, telling the world what our principles are and how we apply them.

We can take our share of the responsibility, for example, by holding politicians and corporate leaders to account, whether with our votes, our refusal to buy their products, or by calling out unacceptable behavior. We can look in the mirror with humility, knowing that we are all capable of the worst mistakes that others may make. In fact, every great leader I have ever met or read about displayed this sense of humility. We can also practice compassion, as we never know what is really going on in someone else's mind, heart, and relationships. As I encourage my students and clients, take opportunities to shout out someone else's success and decline opportunities to call out their failings. Better to quietly check that we haven't made, or aren't poised to make, the same mistake.

You and I began this narrative journey by defining ethical decision-making on the edge. Every year, I send my students off with a forward-looking definition of ethics that spotlights the messiness, imperfection, truth, and recovery. It is this:

Above all, ethics are about creating the story we want for our lives and all the lives we are privileged to touch, by applying principled decision-making, no matter how close we are to the edge. Ethics require an unflinching commitment to truth and humanity. Ethics are recording the story that we will be proud for others to uncover as our view of a life well lived—however the facts may unravel, however we may succeed or fail, whatever luck we may or may not experience, while learning from, but leaving unedited, the inevitable human moments when we don't live up to this definition.

As you move forward in the world, record a story that you will be proud of. And feel confident knowing that you now have the tools you need to know better *and* do better.

ETHICS ON TOMORROW'S EDGE

S ince you started reading this book, the edge has already moved. When I launched my Ethics on the Edge classes at Stanford University in 2014, the stories in this book were the stuff of science fiction.

I began writing this book when COVID-19, or coronavirus, was not yet in our vocabulary. The world watched the tragic outbreak in China with compassion and, admittedly, fear, and then saw it spread. I write this epilogue from the privilege of a home in the San Francisco Bay Area where we're on strict shelter-at-home orders.

COVID-19 has all the hallmarks of an edgy ethics challenge. First, it's both binary and non-binary. The binary being that we must eradicate this threat. The non-binary lies in the solutions, which require careful balancing of urgent lifesaving steps with managing serious concerns, such as other medical and mental health needs and the economic consequences that could weaken our health systems in the future.

Power is scattered—largely undetectable, susceptible to rogue action, and defiant of law. The virus has destructive power, but ethically each of us also has power to harm another (intentionally or unwittingly) with zero budget and almost zero effort by spreading the virus or engaging in behaviors such as hoarding supplies or disregarding guidelines for social distancing. Yet we each can save lives with every modest effort to respect scientific advice. Let me repeat: We each have the power to save lives.

The disease is contagious, and internationally renowned scientific leaders I have conferred with say that biological mutation is their greatest fear. The ethics are even more contagious. We can rigorously respect social distancing and join a chorus of applause (privately and virtually) for the extraordinarily courageous medical community and first responders—just as news reports showed Italian citizens first doing from the safety of their individual balconies. Or we can fail to wash our hands and disrespect expert recommendations on social distancing, modeling carelessness and selfishness for others around us.

As health care workers make second-by-second wartime decisions about human life, they face inhumane dilemmas due in large part to an overwhelming shortage of medical supplies and equipment. And they face conditions in which they don't have the time or capacity to respect *any* of the three pillars. This unacceptable situation is a tragic reflection of ethically failed decision-making at the highest levels. As a result, we have to trust the individuals and institutions providing care and managing the crisis—and each other—without the pillars. It didn't need to be this way.

Boundaries could become blurrier as we rush to deploy robot caregivers, 3D-printed ventilators, and other edgy options that we choose in crisis mode rather than through deliberative decision-making. We must keep human beings and humanity front of mind, especially the most vulnerable among us. Geographic, bureaucratic, and political boundaries or borders have proven to be no match for the virus. They must be erased as we deliver care and seek solutions.

And, as ever, the consequences hinge on truth. Believe and act on the scientific evidence and the expert advice as it evolves. Compromised truth is lethal in this pandemic. Our ethical obligation is to insist on truth: to combat fearmongering, fake news, denial (or politicization) of medical advice, and all the other drivers of contagious untruth.

Ethical decision-making requires agility even in the best of circumstances—and a global pandemic is not the best of circumstances—but there is still space (and responsibility) for responsive and rigorous ethics, now more than ever. Each of us has an opportunity to demonstrate the sacred honor that we explored in Chapter 3 with respect to voting. Ethical decision-making will be the nonnegotiable part of solutions and resilience—of lives saved.

The learning from this book will accompany you into the future. You should be feeling more ethically agile as you grapple with your own dilemmas and society's unfolding ethics emergencies. The six forces driving ethics, and the timeless framework, will guide you in evaluating any decision you face or opinion you are forming. They will also clarify your evolving views of decisions you or others have made in the past. You will react more effectively to our kaleidoscopic world in which, just as you think you see clearly, new colors emerge, fragments disappear, and distant specks suddenly flash front and center as alluring opportunities—or jagged threats—only for it all to scatter again.

The consequences of our decisions today will play out in a changed reality. Many of the technologies that now seem commonplace will give rise to new and unimagined uses but lack the real-time social science research foundation we need for a societal response.

The question is how do we want to use this timeless learning to seize ethics as our greatest individual and collective opportunity? How can we all contribute and commit to more effective ethical decision-making, and to keeping human beings and humanity front and center, in all areas of our lives?

Ethics are democratic. We all have the power to make ethical decisions no matter our situation. Imagine if we each seized our responsibility to reconnect ethics to power, to rescatter power more equitably, and to cauterize contagion of unethical behavior. We should not allow ethics to be consolidated in the hands, algorithms, and corporate structures of those who control innovation. Or in the halls of national and local governments that are ill-equipped to regulate conflicts of principles that cross national borders. We all can step up and reclaim power over ethics.

Ethical decision-making requires a team effort. Widespread citizen engagement is an exciting opportunity to influence regulation, particularly how policymakers resolve conflicting principles relating to some of our most fundamental rights, such as public health versus personal freedom, national security versus privacy, or freedom of speech online versus safety.

Ethical decision-making at its best starts at the earliest possible stage—at the spark of an idea, not at the moment of damage assessment. It should precede constructive action, not only react to harm. Our choices influence companies to frame first and unleash products on society second; and to make decisions that allow society to benefit from their capacity for innovation, research, knowledge sharing, and risk management, rather than placing most of the risk of innovation and growth at all costs on consumers.

Ethics help us lift our gaze. Ethical decision-making offers a lens for viewing the world from different perspectives, realistically and with humility. We can walk the ethics talk, recognizing the disproportionate impact our decisions have on vulnerable people all over the world and the imperfections of Western ways.

Ethics are part of all life decisions and lifelong learning, from nursery and elementary school activities, to higher education, to on-the-job training and continuing education. And ethics competency doesn't depend on academic degrees or specialization, or socioeconomic circumstances. I have met people over the years who struggle to read and are financially vulnerable, yet they are some of the most ethically thoughtful and inspiring people I've known. Ethics are accessible to all of us.

We have the power to restore crumbling pillars. We can demand and offer greater transparency; we can withhold our consent when we are not properly informed (whatever the reason); and we can redouble

Ethical decision-making requires agility even in the best of circumstances—and a global pandemic is not the best of circumstances—but there is still space (and responsibility) for responsive and rigorous ethics, now more than ever. Each of us has an opportunity to demonstrate the sacred honor that we explored in Chapter 3 with respect to voting. Ethical decision-making will be the nonnegotiable part of solutions and resilience—of lives saved.

The learning from this book will accompany you into the future. You should be feeling more ethically agile as you grapple with your own dilemmas and society's unfolding ethics emergencies. The six forces driving ethics, and the timeless framework, will guide you in evaluating any decision you face or opinion you are forming. They will also clarify your evolving views of decisions you or others have made in the past. You will react more effectively to our kaleidoscopic world in which, just as you think you see clearly, new colors emerge, fragments disappear, and distant specks suddenly flash front and center as alluring opportunities—or jagged threats—only for it all to scatter again.

The consequences of our decisions today will play out in a changed reality. Many of the technologies that now seem commonplace will give rise to new and unimagined uses but lack the real-time social science research foundation we need for a societal response.

The question is how do we want to use this timeless learning to seize ethics as our greatest individual and collective opportunity? How can we all contribute and commit to more effective ethical decision-making, and to keeping human beings and humanity front and center, in all areas of our lives?

Ethics are democratic. We all have the power to make ethical decisions no matter our situation. Imagine if we each seized our responsibility to reconnect ethics to power, to rescatter power more equitably, and to cauterize contagion of unethical behavior. We should not allow ethics to be consolidated in the hands, algorithms, and corporate

structures of those who control innovation. Or in the halls of national and local governments that are ill-equipped to regulate conflicts of principles that cross national borders. We all can step up and reclaim power over ethics.

Ethical decision-making requires a team effort. Widespread citizen engagement is an exciting opportunity to influence regulation, particularly how policymakers resolve conflicting principles relating to some of our most fundamental rights, such as public health versus personal freedom, national security versus privacy, or freedom of speech online versus safety.

Ethical decision-making at its best starts at the earliest possible stage—at the spark of an idea, not at the moment of damage assessment. It should precede constructive action, not only react to harm. Our choices influence companies to frame first and unleash products on society second; and to make decisions that allow society to benefit from their capacity for innovation, research, knowledge sharing, and risk management, rather than placing most of the risk of innovation and growth at all costs on consumers.

Ethics help us lift our gaze. Ethical decision-making offers a lens for viewing the world from different perspectives, realistically and with humility. We can walk the ethics talk, recognizing the disproportionate impact our decisions have on vulnerable people all over the world and the imperfections of Western ways.

Ethics are part of all life decisions and lifelong learning, from nursery and elementary school activities, to higher education, to on-the-job training and continuing education. And ethics competency doesn't depend on academic degrees or specialization, or socioeconomic circumstances. I have met people over the years who struggle to read and are financially vulnerable, yet they are some of the most ethically thoughtful and inspiring people I've known. Ethics are accessible to all of us.

We have the power to restore crumbling pillars. We can demand and offer greater transparency; we can withhold our consent when we are not properly informed (whatever the reason); and we can redouble

our efforts to listen effectively and compassionately and help those around us do the same. But even the most robust pillars don't give us a hall pass or an excuse: Telling someone of a transgression, or explicitly disclaiming responsibility, does not excuse the act or absolve us of ethical responsibility.

Every ethical choice matters. If you were to tally up the effect over time of the choices you make with just a little more framing, the impact would be far greater than you might imagine even at the end of one day. Like every single-use plastic water bottle avoided, and every vote framed, your ethics effort contributes to a global awakening.

$$\infty$$

I return to my mantra: Ethical decision-making tethers us to our humanity. I see ethical decision-making as perhaps the greatest human connector. It binds us in a common optimistic project of benefiting and protecting society and humanity. Of crafting great stories for ourselves and others. Of continuing to probe what it means to be human in a technology-infused world.

But ethics on the edge require *using* our power and voices, seizing responsibility, taking action, and committing to truth. We all can actively choose ethics, rather than passively let ethics happen (or not). We all can prioritize humans over machines. We all can make decisions reflecting to future generations what we will tolerate for ourselves and demand of our legacy—rather than submitting to whatever trajectory that morally questionable leaders, innovators, and rogue actors define. We all can seek solutions and not just point out where others have fallen short.

Hopeful choices are within our reach. Your story, and the story of all whose lives you touch, and humanity's story, depends on making them.

With gratitude.

Acknowledgments

Writing a book takes a village. This is my first effort, and I have been so fortunate to be surrounded by wise advisors.

I am immensely grateful that *The Power of Ethics* found a home at Simon & Schuster. CEO Jonathan Karp and executive editor Stephanie Frerich immediately understood what I hoped to accomplish, my sense of urgency, and the broad relevance of what I set out to communicate with the finished book in your hands. Jon's reading of the manuscript was crucial to reshaping and rethinking key sections of what I'd written. Stephanie's ongoing commitment, challenging and incisive editing, and passion for the material have influenced every aspect of the book.

And what a privilege to work with the Simon & Schuster team: assistant editor Emily Simonson was cheerfully efficient and always attentive; Fred Chase, an extraordinary copyeditor, improved every page; cover designer David Litman and art director Alison Forner created the perfect jacket design on the first try; the production team of Sara Kitchen (production editor), Allison Har-zvi (production manager), Paul Dippolito (interior designer), and Kimberly Goldstein (managing editor) turned these pages into a wonderfully readable and attractive volume. And to publicist Cat Boyd and marketing director Stephen Bedford, getting the message out is everything. I couldn't be more fortunate.

One of life's great moments was when I first met my agent, Kathy Robbins. Her wisdom, editorial insights, global perspective, and support of this endeavor have guided me every step of the way. *The Power of Ethics* would not have come to life without her.

Her colleague David Halpern offered wise and detailed counsel at a pivotal moment and impeccable judgment many times thereafter. Janet Oshiro and Alexandra Sugarman made sure that all ran smoothly.

Lisa Sweetingham has my unwavering gratitude. She helped me craft the proposal and worked through drafts of the manuscript under immense time pressure. I'm admiring of her work ethic and grateful for her dedication, meticulousness, commitment, and most of all her talent. I owe a special note of thanks to her family for their support.

My deepest thanks to the experts and individuals who kindly agreed to be interviewed or otherwise contributed their expertise: Dyne Suh Biancardi; Rob Chesnut, Chief Ethics Officer of Airbnb; Dr. Bruce Conklin, senior investigator at Gladstone Institutes, professor in the departments of Medicine, Cellular and Molecular Pharmacology, and Ophthalmology at U.C. San Francisco, as well as the deputy director of the Innovative Genomics Institute; Dr. David Hanson, founder, chairman, and Chief Creative Officer of Hanson Robotics and the creator of the robot Sophia, along with his team at Hanson Robotics; Congressman Ro Khanna, serving California's 17th Congressional District; Dr. Joanne Liu, former international president of Doctors Without Borders/Médecins Sans Frontières; Emmanuel Lulin, senior vice president and Chief Ethics Officer of L'Oréal; Jean-Yves Le Gall, president of France's space agency, Centre National d'Etudes Spatiales; professor David Magnus, Thomas A. Raffin Professor of Medicine and Biomedical Ethics and professor of pediatrics at Stanford University; Dr. Hiromitsu Nakauchi, professor of genetics (stem cell) at Stanford School of Medicine; Clive Schlee, former CEO of Pret A Manger; Fabian Suchy, PhD student in stem cell biology and regenerative medicine at Stanford School of Medicine; Delaney Van

Riper; and Dr. Paul H. Wise, Richard E. Behrman Professor in Child Health, Pediatrics–Neonatal and Developmental Medicine at Stanford University.

My further thanks to the leaders who participated with me in *The Ethics Incubator* conversations that inspired many passages: Hollywood television writer and producer Norman Lear; British novelist and essayist Sir Salman Rushdie; artist and MacArthur Genius Grant recipient Xu Bing; former mayor of Charlottesville, Virginia, Michael Signer; and former director of the Victoria & Albert Museum in London, the late Martin Roth.

Over the past several years, I have had the pleasure of teaching many insightful and creative students. I am grateful to Ariadne Nichol, Caleb Martin, Catherine Yuh, and Jaih Hunter-Hill, research assistants who worked on this book. Clint Akarmann's wise observations, meticulous research, and outstanding work ethic have contributed to my work for years. He read through several drafts of the book and provided invaluable advice at every step.

I am grateful to my colleagues and clients for their confidence and for sharing their wisdom and perspective on so many issues. At Stanford University, my thanks to Gregory Rosston, director of the Public Policy Program, who supports my teaching and, without hesitation, agreed to my launching the Ethics of Truth in a Post-Truth World class in 2016; professors John Etchemendy and Fei-Fei Li, codirectors of the Stanford Institute for Human-Centered Artificial Intelligence (HAI), whose pioneering work models ethical, edgy, and effective.

I have the immense privilege of being surrounded by truly encouraging and intellectually generous friends—my ethics sparring partners: Bob Bookman, who was enthusiastic about this project in so many ways from its earliest stages; Ambassador Anthony Gardner and his wife, Sandra; Emmanuel Roman; Jean-Pierre Mustier; Nancy Fredkin; Sheila Melvin; Gisel and Omid Kordestani; Mohsen and Laleh Moazami; and Saeed and Samira Amidi.

Special thanks to professor Ruth Chang, James Manyika, Emmanuel Lulin, Omid Kordestani, Sebastien Bazin, and Dr. Joanne Liu for reading the manuscript and providing words of support.

I also learned so much from my colleagues at the London School of Economics and Political Science.

My gratitude to the Ethics Incubator and Susan Liautaud & Associates Limited team: Anna Barberà i Aresté, Dawn Wenham, and Holly Wilson helped me to keep many balls in the air during the writing of this book.

For years I have admired from afar Robert Caro and Doris Kearns Goodwin. Robert Caro has been an inspiration since I first became mesmerized by his biography of Lyndon Johnson. He masterfully shows how ethics were edgy and essential even when radio was considered high-tech. Presidential biographer Doris Kearns Goodwin has an extraordinary gift, among many, for distilling the crux of ethics in society—both the good and the failed. Her books remain among my all-time favorites.

Finally, to my husband, Bernard, and my children, Luca, Olivia, Parker, Alexa, and Cristo, for believing in me. I learn from you every day, with every choice.

Notes

Chapter One – Banished Binary

7   *cool, clear Sunday morning*: Renee Duff, "Ethiopian Airlines jetliner crashes shortly after takeoff, killing all 157 people on board," Accuweather, https://www .accuweather.com/en/weather-news/ethiopian-airlines-jetliner-crashes-shortly -after-takeoff-killing-all-157-people-on-board/335117; and p. 52, "Interim Investigation Report on Accident to the B737-8 (MAX)," Aircraft Accident Investigation Bureau, Ministry of Transport, Federal Democratic Republic of Ethiopia, March 9, 2020, http://www.aib.gov.et/wp-content/uploads/2020/documents/accident/ET -302%20%20Interim%20Investigation%20%20Report%20March%209%2020 20.pdf.

7   *Captain Yared Getachew*: "Interim Investigation Report on Accident to the B737-8 (MAX)"; and Accident Bulletin No. 3, March 10, 2019, Ethiopian Airlines, retrieved from Twitter on April 17, 2020, https://twitter.com/flyethiopian/status /1104744539686866944/photo/1.

7   *Ahmednur Mohammed*: Reputable media provide different spellings of the first officer's name: In Ethiopian Airlines' "Accident Bulletin No. 3," he is "Ahmed Nur Mohammod Nur"; the *Wall Street Journal* uses "Ahmed Nur Mohammed" (https://www .wsj.com/articles/ethiopia-mourns-the-loss-of-two-young-pilots-11552752808); and the *New York Times* notes: "The airline identified the pilot as Yared Getachew and the first officer as Ahmednur Mohammed" (https://www.nytimes.com/2019/03/10 /world/africa/ethiopian-airlines-plane-crash-victims.html). We have chosen to follow the naming convention from Reuters, which conducted interviews with the first officer's family and friends: Maggie Fick, "Youngest Captain, Loving Son: Ethiopian Pilots Honored in Death," Reuters, March 20, 2019, https://www.reuters .com/article/us-ethiopia-airplane-pilots/youngest-captain-loving-son-ethiopian -pilots-honored-in-death-idUSKCN1R11LV.

7   *rising star*: Matina Stevis-Gridneff and Yohannes Anberbir, "Ethiopia Mourns the Loss of Two Young Pilots," *Wall Street Journal*, March 16, 2019, https://www .wsj.com/articles/ethiopia-mourns-the-loss-of-two-young-pilots-11552752808; and Fick, "Youngest Captain, Loving Son: Ethiopian Pilots Honored in Death." Additionally, Ethiopian Airlines told BBC News that he had a "commendable performance," "Ethiopian Airlines: The Victims of 'a Global Tragedy,' " BBC News, April 4, 2019, https://www.bbc.com/news/world-africa-47522028.

7   *"an excellent flying record"*: According to Ethiopian Airlines chief executive Tewolde GebreMariam, as told to Alison Sider and Robert Wall, "Boeing Crashes Spur Debate Over How Much Pilot Training Is Enough," *Wall Street Journal*, March 18, 2019, https://www.wsj.com/articles/boeing-crashes-spur-debate-over-how-much-pilot-training-is-enough-11552937613.

7   *Ethiopian Aviation Academy*: "Interim Investigation Report on Accident to the B737-8 (MAX)," p. 19–20; and Zain Asher, "CNN Marketplace Africa EAL Aviation Academy," March 23, 2016, Ethiopian Airlines, YouTube, https://www.cnn.com /travel/article/ethiopian-airlines-aviation-academy/index.html.

7   *brand-new Boeing 737 Max 8 jet*: The plane's delivery flight was November 15, 2018, per p. 24, "Interim Investigation Report on Accident to the B737-8 (MAX)."

7   *world's largest aerospace company*: "Boeing in Brief," Boeing, retrieved April 17, 2020, https://www.boeing.com/company/general-info/; and John Misachi, "The Largest Aerospace Companies in the World," *World Atlas*, August 13, 2019, retrieved March 26, 2020, https://www.worldatlas.com/articles/largest-aerospace-companies -in-the-world.html. Boeing is also America's largest manufacturer, David Gelles and Natalie Kitroeff, "Boeing Mirrors the Economy. It Doesn't Look Good," *New York Times*, March 17, 2020, https://www.nytimes.com/2020/03/17/business /economy/boeing-coronavirus-economy.html.

7   *At 8:37 a.m.*: The plane lifted in the air at 8:38 a.m., according to the "Executive Summary" in "Interim Investigation Report on Accident to the B737-8 (MAX)." Note that the times in this report are converted to Coordinated Universal Time (UTC), and the times in the story have been converted back to the time on the ground in Ethiopia.

7   *Among the passengers*: David Gelles, Eden Weingart, and Josh Williams, "The Emotional Wreckage of a Deadly Boeing Crash," *New York Times*, March 9, 2020, https:// www.nytimes.com/interactive/2020/03/09/business/boeing-737-crash-anniversary .html; and BBC News, "Ethiopian Airlines: The Victims of 'a Global Tragedy.' "

8   *75 degrees above the wind*: The measure, also known as angle-of-attack, or AOA, was exactly 74.5. See "Findings," Section 5, p. 131, of "Interim Investigation Report on Accident to the B737-8 (MAX)."

8   *Speed and altitude readings*: According to ibid., "Executive Summary," shortly after liftoff at 8:38 a.m. "the left stick shaker activated and remained active until near the end of the recording. In addition, the airspeed and altitude values from the left air data system began deviating from the corresponding right side values."

8   *"stick shaker"*: Ibid.; and Andrew Tangel, Andy Pasztor, and Mark Maremont, "The Four-Second Catastrophe: How Boeing Doomed the 737 MAX," *Wall Street Journal*, Aug. 16, 2019, https://www.wsj.com/articles/the-four-second-catastrophe-how-boeing -doomed-the-737-max-11565966629.

8   *had failed*: "Findings," Section 5, p. 131 of "Interim Investigation Report on Accident to the B737-8 (MAX)." And media reports, for example: James Glanz, Thomas Kaplan, and Jack Nicas, "In Ethiopia Crash, Faulty Sensor on Boeing 737 Max Is Suspected," *New York Times*, March 29, 2019, https://www.nytimes.com/2019/03/29 /business/boeing-737-max-crash.html; and Dominic Gates, "Ethiopia Blames Boeing's 737 MAX Design and Training in Interim Report on Crash," *Seattle Times*, March 9, 2020, https://www.seattletimes.com/business/boeing-aerospace/interim -ethiopian-government-report-on-max-crash-blames-boeings-design-and-training/.

8   *bend, crack*: Jack Nicas, Natalie Kitroeff, David Gelles, and James Glanz, "Boeing Built Deadly Assumptions into 737 Max, Blind to a Late Design Change," *New York Times*, June 1, 2019, https://www.nytimes.com/2019/06/01/business/boeing -737-max-crash.html; and "Awareness and Maintenance of Angle of Attack (AOA) Sensors," Information for Operators, FAA, Aug. 14, 2019, https://www.faa.gov

/other_visit/aviation_industry/airline_operators/airline_safety/info/all_infos
/media/2019/InFO19009.pdf.

8 *216 reports*: Curt Devine and Drew Griffith, "Boeing Relied on Single Sensor for 737 Max That Had Been Flagged 216 Times to FAA," CNN, May 1, 2019, https:// edition.cnn.com/2019/04/30/politics/boeing-sensor-737-Max-faa/index.html. See also Nicas et al., "Boeing Built Deadly Assumptions," which notes: "A *Times* review of two F.A.A. databases found hundreds of reports of bent, cracked, sheared-off, poorly installed or otherwise malfunctioning angle-of-attack sensors on commercial aircraft over three decades."

8 *situational awareness*: See "Flight Instruments," Angle of Attack Indicators, FAA Handbook, pp. 8-22, retrieved March 25, 2020, https://www.faa.gov/regulations _policies/handbooks_manuals/aviation/phak/media/10_phak_ch8.pdf; and "Awareness and Maintenance of Angle of Attack (AOA) Sensors," Information for Operators, FAA," Aug. 14, 2019, https://www.faa.gov/other_visit/aviation_industry/airline _operators/airline_safety/info/all_infos/media/2019/InFO19009.pdf.

8 *a single sensor alert was sufficient*: A Boeing official told CNN, "Single sources of data are considered acceptable in such cases by our industry," in Devine and Griffith, "Boeing Relied on Single Sensor for 737 Max." See also Nicas et al., "Boeing Built Deadly Assumptions."

8 *MCAS*: MCAS adjusts the horizontal trim stabilizer, a small wing on the plane's tail, which in turn causes the plane's nose to go down. See "737 Max Software Update," Overview, Boeing, retrieved March 26, 2020, https://www.boeing.com /commercial/737max/737-max-software-updates.page; "Ethiopian Airlines Crash," Reuters Graphics, March 12, 2019, https://graphics.reuters.com/ETHIOPIA -AIRPLANE/0100911Q1DX/index.html; and Nicas et al., "Boeing Built Deadly Assumptions into 737 Max."

8 *8,100 feet*: See ET302 altitude chart in Ian Petchenik, "Flightradar24 Data Regarding the Crash of Ethiopian Airlines Flight 302," FlightRadar24, March 10, 2019, https:// www.flightradar24.com/blog/flightradar24-data-regarding-the-crash-of-ethiopian -airlines-flight-302/; "Ethiopian Airlines Crash," Reuters Graphics; and Matina Stevis-Gridneff and Yonathan Menkir Kassa, "The Final Minutes of Ethiopian Airlines' Doomed Boeing 737 MAX," *Wall Street Journal*, March 29, 2019, https:// www.wsj.com/articles/the-final-minutes-of-ethiopian-airlines-doomed-boeing-737 -Max-11553876300.

8 *twelve long minutes*: It was eleven minutes and fifty-six seconds, according to "History of the Flight," p. 19–27, "Aircraft Accident Investigation Report," Komite Nasional Keselamatan Transportasi, Republic of Indonesia, October 2019, http://knkt.dep hub.go.id/knkt/ntsc_aviation/baru/2018%20-%20035%20-%20PK-LQP%20 Final%20Report.pdf; and Ian Petchenik, "Flightradar24 Data Regarding Lion Air Flight JT610," FlightRadar24, October 29, 2018, https://www.flightradar24.com /blog/flightradar24-data-regarding-lion-air-flight-jt610/. See also Mika Gröndahl, Allison McCann, James Glanz, Blacki Migliozzi, and Umi Syam, "In 12 Minutes, Everything Went Wrong," *New York Times*, December 26, 2018, https://www .nytimes.com/interactive/2018/12/26/world/asia/lion-air-crash-12-minutes.html.

9 *twenty-one times*: Dominic Gates, "Pilots Struggled Against Boeing's 737 MAX Control System on Doomed Lion Air Flight," *Seattle Times*, November 27, 2018, https://www.seattletimes.com/business/boeing-aerospace/black-box-data-reveals -lion-air-pilots-struggle-against-boeings-737-max-flight-control-system/; BBC News, "Boeing Announces Fixes for Its 737 Max Aircraft," March 28, 2019, https://www .bbc.com/news/business-47722258.

9 *killing all 189*: "Summary," p. 245, "Aircraft Accident Investigation Report." And media reports, for example: Hannah Beech and Muktita Suhartono, "Confusion,

Then Prayer, in Cockpit of Doomed Lion Air Jet," *New York Times*, March 20, 2019, https://www.nytimes.com/2019/03/20/world/asia/lion-air-crash-boeing.html.

9   *FAA issued*: "Emergency Airworthiness Directive," FAA, November 7, 2018, https://rgl.faa.gov/Regulatory_and_Guidance_Library/rgad.nsf/0/83ec7f95f3e5bfbd8625833e0070a070/$FILE/2018-23-51_Emergency.pdf.

9   *Boeing also issued*: "Boeing Statement on Operations Manual Bulletin," Boeing, retrieved March 26, 2020, https://boeing.mediaroom.com/news-releases-statements?item=130327; and John Ostrower, "Boeing Issues 737 Max Fleet Bulletin on AoA Warning After Lion Air Crash," *The Air Current*, November 7, 2018, https://theaircurrent.com/aviation-safety/boeing-nearing-737-max-fleet-bulletin-on-aoa-warning-after-lion-air-crash/.

9   *"Pull with me" . . . 180 pounds of force*: See pp. 16, 18, and executive summary of "Interim Investigation Report on Accident to the B737-8 (MAX)"; and Gates, "Ethiopia Blames Boeing's 737 MAX Design and Training in Interim Report on Crash."

9   *turned the system back on*: Seattle Times staff, "Two Tragic Flights, 12 Problems," *Seattle Times*, October 27, 2019, https://projects.seattletimes.com/2019/boeing-737-max-12-problems/; and executive summary of "Interim Investigation Report on Accident to the B737-8 (MAX)."

9   *575 miles per hour*: See p. 18, "computed airspeed values reached 500 kt" or knots, which is approximately 575 miles per hour, "Interim Investigation Report on Accident to the B737-8 (MAX)."

9   *helicopters had trouble finding*: Stevis-Gridneff and Kassa, "The Final Minutes of Ethiopian Airlines' Doomed Boeing 737 MAX"; and for details about impact: Theo Leggett and Simon Browning, "Battle Over Blame," BBC News, https://www.bbc.co.uk/news/extra/sd9LGK2S9m/battle_over_blame.

9   *thirty-three feet*: According to the "Interim Investigation Report on Accident to the B737-8 (MAX)," p. 65, the plane "created a crater approximately 10 meters deep (last aircraft part found) with a hole of about 28 meters width and 40 meters length. Most of the wreckage was found buried in the ground."

10 *"safe aircraft" to fly*: In a March 11, 2019, press release (retrieved March 1, 2020) Boeing noted: "For the past several months and in the aftermath of Lion Air Flight 610, Boeing has been developing a flight control software enhancement for the 737 MAX, designed to make an already safe aircraft even safer," and "The 737 MAX is a safe airplane that was designed, built and supported by our skilled employees who approach their work with the utmost integrity," "Boeing Statement on 737 MAX Software Enhancement," https://boeing.mediaroom.com/news-releases-statements?item=130402.

10 *"Continued Airworthiness Notification"*: "Continued Airworthiness Notification to the International Community," FAA, March 11, 2019, retrieved March 1, 2020, https://www.faa.gov/news/updates/media/CAN_2019_03.pdf.

10 *Ethiopian Airlines immediately grounded*: The airline announced the grounding of all 737 Max 8 planes on the morning of Monday, March 11, but called it "effective yesterday March 10, 2019 until further notice." Ethiopian Airlines, Twitter, March 10, https://twitter.com/flyethiopian/status/1104965069710999552.

10 *China ordered all ninety-six*: Trefor Moss, Wenxin Fan, and Andy Pasztor, "China Grounds All Boeing 737 MAX 8 Jets After Ethiopian Airlines Crash," *Wall Street Journal*, March 11, 2019, https://www.wsj.com/articles/china-grounds-all-boeing-737-max-8-jets-after-ethiopian-airlines-crash-11552271191.

10 *By Tuesday*: Charlotte King, "Which Airlines Operate Boeing 737 Max Jets?," *The Guardian*, March 12, 2019, https://www.theguardian.com/world/2019/mar/12/which-airlines-operate-boeing-737-max-jets.

10 *$100 billion*: Aaron Gregg, "Boeing Soars Past $100 Billion Revenue Mark for First

Time," *Washington Post*, Jan. 30, 2019, https://www.washingtonpost.com/business
/2019/01/30/boeing-soars-past-billion-revenue-mark-first-time/; and Josh Mitchell
and Doug Cameron, "Boeing's Woes Create Headwinds for U.S. Economy," *Wall
Street Journal*, Feb. 2, 2020, https://www.wsj.com/articles/boeings-woes-create
-headwinds-for-u-s-economy-11580655600.

10   *employed 145,000 people*: "Close Relationships with Global Stakeholders Are Key,"
Boeing, retrieved March 26, 2020, https://www.boeing.com/company/key-orgs
/boeing-international/.

10   *thirteen thousand domestic suppliers*: Doug Cameron and Alison Sider, "Boeing's 737
MAX Grounding Spills Over into Economy, Weighs on GDP," *Wall Street Journal*,
July 22, 2019, https://www.wsj.com/articles/boeings-737-max-grounding-spills
-over-into-economy-weighs-on-gdp-11563815426.

10   *Muilenburg made a personal call*: It was a private call, but according to CNN, "A
spokesman for Boeing confirmed the conversation and said Muilenburg 'made
clear to the president that the MAX aircraft is safe.'" Jeff Zeleny and Fredreka
Schouten, "Trump Speaks to Boeing CEO Following Tweets on Airline Technology," CNN, March 12, 2019, https://www.cnn.com/2019/03/12/politics/donald
-trump-boeing-ceo-dennis-muilenberg/index.html. See also Keith Bradsher, Ken-
neth P. Vogel, and Zach Wichter, "Two-Thirds of the 737 Max 8 Jets in the World
Have Been Pulled from the Sky," *New York Times*, March 12, 2019, https://www
.nytimes.com/2019/03/12/business/boeing-737-grounding-faa.html, which states
that Muilenburg "made the case that the 737 Max planes should not be grounded in
the United States, according to two people briefed on the conversation."

10–11 *"absolutely" take that risk*: In an interview with journalist Norah O'Donnell, he responded: "Without any hesitation. Absolutely." "Boeing CEO Says He Would Put
His Family in a 737 Max 'Without Any Hesitation,'" CBS News, May 29, 2019,
https://www.cbsnews.com/news/boeing-ceo-dennis-muilenburg-says-he-would-
put-his-family-737-Max-without-any-hesitation-exclusive-2019-05-29.

11   *more than sixty countries*: Nigel Chiwaya and Jiachuan Wu, "MAP: These Are the
Countries That Have Grounded the Boeing 737 Max 8," NBC News, March 13,
2019, https://www.nbcnews.com/news/world/country-banned-boeing-737-Max-
airplanes-list-n982776.

11   *"no basis to order grounding"*: The statement noted: "Thus far, our review shows no
systemic performance issues and provides no basis to order grounding the aircraft.
Nor have other civil aviation authorities provided data to us that would warrant
action." See "FAA Updates on Boeing 737 Max," "3/12/19 6:10pm," "Statement
from Acting FAA Administrator Daniel K. Elwell," retrieved March 23, 2020,
https://www.faa.gov/news/updates/?newsId=93206.

11   *directed the FAA to ground*: Max 7 planes had not been delivered yet and Max 10 planes were
still in development. See "Emergency Order of Prohibition," FAA, March 13, 2019,
https://www.faa.gov/news/updates/media/Emergency_Order.pdf. And media reports, for example: Kent German, "Boeing 737 Max Could Stay Grounded Until
Late 2020," *CNET*, May 27, 2020, https://www.cnet.com/news/boeing-737-max
-8-all-about-the-aircraft-flight-ban-and-investigations/; Alex Davies, "A Boeing
737 MAX Test Flight Had Its Ups and Downs," *Wired*, Aug 6, 2019, https://www
.wired.com/story/boeing-737-max-test-flight-ups-and-downs/; and Jordan Fabian
and Brett Samuels, "Trump Issues Emergency Order Grounding Boeing 737 Max
Jets," *The Hill*, March 13, 2019, https://thehill.com/policy/transportation/433902
-trump-announces-us-to-ground-boeing-737-max-planes.

11   *"Our stance on ethical business"*: This statement was on the Boeing website before and
at the time of the second crash, and as of this writing. See "Our Principles: Ethics & Compliance," Boeing, retrieved March 23, 2020, https://www.boeing.com

/principles/; and also Wayback Machine, retrieved March 5, 2019, https://web
.archive.org/web/20190305095058/http://www.boeing.com/principles/.

13   *It begins in 2010*: Airbus A320 announcement, December 1, 2010, https://www.airbus
.com/newsroom/press-releases/en/2010/12/airbus-offers-new-fuel-saving-engine
-options-for-a320-family.html; 20 percent fuel savings announcement, Airbus, September
23, 2014, https://www.airbus.com/newsroom/press-releases/en/2014/09/a320neo
-family-sets-new-standards-with-20-reduced-fuel-burn.html; and Boeing announcement, August 30, 2011, https://boeing.mediaroom.com/2011-08-30-Boeing-Introduces
-737-Max-With-Launch-of-New-Aircraft-Family (all retrieved March 26, 2020).

13   *American Airlines*: *Seattle Times* business staff, "Timeline: A Brief History of the Boeing 737 Max," *Seattle Times*, May 5, 2019, https://www.seattletimes.com/business
/boeing-aerospace/timeline-brief-history-boeing-737-Max. American would go on to
order 260 Airbus planes and 200 Boeing Max planes: Nicola Clark, "Jet Order by
American Is a Coup for Boeing's Rival," *New York Times*, July 20, 2011, https://www
.nytimes.com/2011/07/21/business/global/american-places-record-order-with-2
-jet-makers.html.

13   *Building a new plane*: David Gelles, Natalie Kitroeff, Jack Nicas, and Rebecca R.
Ruiz, "Boeing Was 'Go, Go, Go,' to Beat Airbus with the 737 Max," *New York
Times*, March 23, 2019, https://www.nytimes.com/2019/03/23/business/boeing
-737-max-crash.html; and Alec MacGillis, "The Case Against Boeing," *The New
Yorker*, November 11, 2019, https://www.newyorker.com/magazine/2019/11/18
/the-case-against-boeing.

13   *Boeing's board of directors . . . 496 orders*: Boeing Media Room, "Boeing Launches 737
New Engine Family with Commitments for 496 Airplanes from Five Airlines," Au-
gust 30, 2011, https://boeing.mediaroom.com/2011-08-30-Boeing-Launches-737
-New-Engine-Family-with-Commitments-for-496-Airplanes-from-Five-Airlines.

13   *built in 1967:* "Historical Snapshot," 737 Commercial Transport, Boeing, retrieved
April 17, 2020, https://www.boeing.com/history/products/737-classic.page.

13   *moved the new engines*: "The Boeing 737 Max: Examining the Design, Development,
and Marketing of the Aircraft," Hearing Before the Committee on Transportation
and Infrastructure, House of Representatives, October 30, 2019, https://www.gov
info.gov/content/pkg/CHRG-116hhrg38282/pdf/CHRG-116hhrg38282.pdf, p. 4.

13   *threw off the aerodynamics*: "Preliminary Design Decision Memo," p. 119, "The Boeing 737 Max: Examining the Design, Development, and Marketing of the Aircraft."

13   *explored the idea*: Dominic Gates and Mike Baker, "The Inside Story of MCAS: How
Boeing's 737 MAX System Gained Power and Lost Safeguards," *Seattle Times*, June
22, 2019, https://www.seattletimes.com/seattle-news/times-watchdog/the-inside
-story-of-mcas-how-boeings-737-max-system-gained-power-and-lost-safeguards/;
and Jack Nicas, Natalie Kitroeff, David Gelles, and James Glanz, "Boeing Built
Deadly Assumptions into 737 Max," *New York Times*.

13   *Boeing developed MCAS*: "737 Max Software Update," Boeing, https://www.boeing
.com/commercial/737max/737-max-software-updates.page; Gates and Baker, "The
Inside Story of MCAS"; Ralph Vartabedian, "How a 50-Year-Old Design Came Back
to Haunt Boeing with Its Troubled 737 Max Jet," *Los Angeles Times*, March 15, 2019,
https://www.latimes.com/local/california/la-fi-boeing-max-design-20190315-story
.html; and Gelles et al., "Boeing Was 'Go, Go, Go,' to Beat Airbus with the 737 Max."

14   *a single AOA sensor*: "MCAS," p. 5, "The Boeing 737 Max: Examining the Design,
Development, and Marketing of the Aircraft."

14   *"system safety analysis" . . . "assumed"*: See p. vi, "4. Changes during the certification
process," and p. 30, and "Findings," F6.1-A, F6.4-A, F6.7-A, and F10.5-A in "Boeing 737 Max Flight Control System: Observations, Findings, and Recommendations,"
submitted to the Associate Administrator for Aviation Safety, U.S. Federal Aviation

Administration, October 11, 2019, https://www.faa.gov/news/media/attachments /Final_JATR_Submittal_to_FAA_Oct_2019.pdf; Dominic Gates,"Flawed Analysis, Failed Oversight: How Boeing, FAA Certified the Suspect 737 MAX Flight Control System," *Seattle Times*, March 17, 2019, https://www.seattletimes.com/business /boeing-aerospace/failed-certification-faa-missed-safety-issues-in-the-737-max-system -implicated-in-the-lion-air-crash/; and Tangel et al., "The Four-Second Catastrophe: How Boeing Doomed the 737 MAX."

14   *The National Transportation Safety Board*: "Assumptions Used in the Safety Assessment Process and the Effects of Multiple Alerts and Indications on Pilot Performance," pp. 12–13, National Transportation Safety Board, Sept. 19, 2019, https://www.ntsb .gov/investigations/AccidentReports/Reports/ASR1901.pdf.

15   *Captain Chesley "Sully" Sullenberger*: Both quotes can be found on p. 24, "Status of the Boeing 737 Max: Stakeholder Perspectives," Hearing Before the Subcommittee on Aviation of the Committee on Transportation and Infrastructure, House of Representatives, June 19, 2019, https://www.congress.gov/116/meeting/house/109642 /documents/CHRG-116hhrg37476.pdf.

15   *makes sense to involve company engineers*: As the acting FAA administrator told a Senate committee in March 2019: "It would require roughly 10,000 more employees and another $1.8 billion for our certification office" to bring the entire process in-house. Jeremy Bogaisky, "Want FAA to Do Aircraft Certification Alone? Give Me 10,000 More Workers and $1.8 Billion, Chief Tells Congress," *Forbes*, March 27, 2019, https://www.forbes.com/sites/jeremybogaisky/2019/03/27/want-faa-to-do-aircraft -certification-alone-give-me-10000-more-employees-and-18-billion-chief-tells-congress /#43f1812a14dc. See also Reuters, "FAA Tells U.S. Senate It Would Need 10,000 New Employees, $1.8 Billion to Assume All Certification," March 27, 2019, https:// www.reuters.com/article/us-ethiopia-airline-congress-faa/faa-tells-u-s-senate-it -would-need-10000-new-employees-1-8-billion-to-assume-all-certification-idUSKCN 1R82FT.

15   *in 2004, the system changed*: See p. 3, "4. Conflicted Representation" and "5. Boeing's Influence Over the FAA's Oversight" in "The Boeing 737 MAX Aircraft: Costs, Consequences, and Lessons from Its Design, Development, and Certification," report by Democratic Staff of the House Committee on Transportation and Infrastructure for Chair Peter A. DeFazio, Subcommittee on Aviation Chair Rick Larsen, and Members of the Committee, March 2020, https://transportation.house.gov /imo/media/doc/TI%20Preliminary%20Investigative%20Findings%20Boeing%20 737%20MAX%20March%202020.pdf; and reporting from the *Seattle Times* and the *New York Times*, both of which interviewed "more than a dozen" Boeing engineers and others who took part in the certification process. Dominic Gates and Mike Baker, "Engineers Say Boeing Pushed to Limit Safety Testing in Race to Certify Planes, Including 737 MAX," *Seattle Times*, May 5, 2019, https://www.seattletimes.com /business/boeing-aerospace/engineers-say-boeing-pushed-to-limit-safety-testing -in-race-to-certify-planes-including-737-max/; Dominic Gates, "Flawed Analysis, Failed Oversight: How Boeing, FAA Certified the Suspect 737 MAX Flight Control System"; Nicas et al., "Boeing Built Deadly Assumptions into 737 Max"; and Natalie Kitroeff, David Gelles, and Jack Nicas, "The Roots of Boeing's 737 Max Crisis: A Regulator Relaxes Its Oversight," *New York Times*, July 27, 2019, https://www .nytimes.com/2019/07/27/business/boeing-737-max-faa.html.

15   *Investigations by . . . fatal crashes*: Gelles et al., "Boeing Was 'Go, Go, Go,' to Beat Airbus with the 737 Max"; Gates and Baker, "Engineers Say Boeing Pushed to Limit Safety Testing in Race to Certify Planes, Including 737 MAX"; Dominic Gates, Steve Miletich, and Lewis Kamb, "Boeing Rejected 737 Max Safety Upgrades Before Fatal Crashes, Whistleblower Says," *Seattle Times*, October 2, 2019,

https://www.seattletimes.com/business/boeing-aerospace/boeing-whistleblowers
-complaint-says-737-Max-safety-upgrades-were-rejected-over-cost/; and pg. 2, "1.
Production Pressures" in "The Boeing 737 MAX Aircraft: Costs, Consequences,
and Lessons from Its Design, Development, and Certification." Boeing stated to the
New York Times: "The Max program launched in 2011. It was offered to customers
in September 2012. Firm configuration of the airplane was achieved in July 2013.
The first completed 737 Max 8 rolled out of the Renton factory in November 2015."
Boeing added, "A multiyear process could hardly be considered rushed." And "The
decision had to offer the best value to customers, including operating economics as
well as timing, which was clearly a strong factor." And "Safety is our highest priority
as we design, build and support our airplanes." In a statement to the *Seattle Times*,
Boeing said it "has rigorous processes in place, both to ensure that such complaints
receive thorough consideration and to protect the confidentiality of employees who
make them." And also: "Accordingly, Boeing does not comment on the substance or
existence of such internal complaints."

15 *"AOA disagree alert"*: "Boeing Statement on AOA Disagree Alert," retrieved December
27, 2019, https://boeing.mediaroom.com/news-releases-statements?item=130431;
and David Gelles and Natalie Kitroeff, "Boeing Believed a 737 Max Warning Light Was Standard. It Wasn't," *New York Times*, May 5, 2019, https://www
.nytimes.com/2019/05/05/business/boeing-737-max-warning-light.html; and Tracy
Rucinski and David Shepardson, "Boeing Did Not Disclose 737 MAX Alert Issue
to FAA for 13 Months," Reuters, May 5, 2019, https://www.reuters.com/article/us
-ethiopia-airplane-boeing/boeing-did-not-disclose-737-max-alert-issue-to-faa-for-13
-months-idUSKCN1SB0JC, which states that Boeing's decision to restore the AOA
disagree alert as a *standard* feature "restores the situation found on the displays of
previous 737NG models since around the middle of last decade."

16 *Boeing did not notify customers*: Boeing waited until May 5, 2019, two months after
the second crash, to disclose the issue in a press release, "Boeing Statement on AOA
Disagree Alert."

16 *update in 2020*: "Boeing Statement on AOA Disagree Alert"; and Mike Baker,
"Boeing Didn't Plan to Fix 737 MAX Warning Light Until 2020," *Seattle Times*,
June 7, 2019, https://www.seattletimes.com/business/boeing-aerospace/boeing
-didnt-plan-to-fix-737-max-warning-light-until-2020/.

16 *American . . . United Airlines did not*: Hiroko Tabuchi and David Gelles, "Doomed
Boeing Jets Lacked 2 Safety Features That Company Sold Only as Extras," *New York
Times*, March 21, 2019, https://www.nytimes.com/2019/03/21/business/boeing
-safety-features-charge.html; Andy Pasztor, "Boeing Didn't Advise Airlines, FAA
That It Shut Off Warning System," *Wall Street Journal*, April 28, 2019, https://www
.wsj.com/articles/boeings-enduring-puzzle-why-certain-safety-features-on-737
-max-jets-were-turned-off-11556456400; and Amanda Macias, who reports that
Southwest took steps to activate the disagree light after the Lion Air crash, "Boeing
Waited Until After Lion Air Crash to Tell Southwest Safety Alert Was Turned Off
on 737 Max," CNBC News, April 28, 2019, https://www.cnbc.com/2019/04/28
/boeing-didnt-tell-southwest-that-safety-feature-on-737-max-was-turned-off-wsj
.html.

16 *fastest-selling plane*: Boeing website, Wayback Machine, retrieved December 25,
2019, https://web.archive.org/web/20191225100949/https://www.boeing.com
/commercial/737Max/.

16 *"supplemental information"*: Boeing stated: "They provide supplemental information
only, and have never been considered safety features on commercial jet transport
airplanes," in "Boeing Statement on AOA Disagree Alert."

16 *three years later:* "Boeing statement on AOA disagree alert"; and Baker, "Boeing Didn't Plan to Fix 737 MAX Warning Light Until 2020."

17 *"industry-standard assumption":* Boeing chief engineer John Hamilton testified before the U.S. Senate Committee on Commerce, Science, & Transportation's Aviation Safety and the Future of Boeing's 737 MAX hearing, October 29, 2019, https:// www.commerce.senate.gov/2019/10/aviation-safety-and-the-future-of-boeing -s-737-max/dd0f5a92-0362-45e8-bab1-957d0e82f168. See also p. 123, "Interim Investigation Report on Accident to the B737-8 (MAX)"; p. 6, "Four of These Assumptions Were the Following," and p. 7, "Analysis: Assumptions about Pilot Recognition and Response in the Safety Assessment" in "Assumptions Used in the Safety Assessment Process and the Effects of Multiple Alerts and Indications on Pilot Performance," National Transportation Safety Board, September 19, 2019, https://www.ntsb.gov/investigations/AccidentReports/Reports/ASR1901.pdf; and p. 3, "2. Faulty Assumptions," in "The Boeing 737 MAX Aircraft: Costs, Consequences, and Lessons from Its Design, Development, and Certification."

17 *"do not have inadvertent traps":* Captain Sullenberger's quote is on p. 24 of "Status of the Boeing 737 Max: Stakeholder Perspectives," Hearing Before the Subcommittee on Aviation of the Committee on Transportation and Infrastructure, House of Representatives, June 19, 2019, https://www.congress.gov/116/meeting /house/109642/documents/CHRG-116hhrg37476.pdf.

18 *skirting local laws:* Shannon Bond, "Uber's Long List of Legal Woes Ahead of Its Stock Market Listing," *Financial Times*, April 8, 2019, https://www.ft.com/content /3fee8054-575b-11e9-91f9-b6515a54c5b1; Mike Isaac, "How Uber Got Lost," *New York Times*, August 23, 2019, https://www.nytimes.com/2019/08/23/business /how-uber-got-lost.html; and David F. Larcker and Brian Tayan, "Governance Gone Wild: Epic Misbehavior at Uber Technologies," December 11, 2017, Rock Center for Corporate Governance at Stanford University Closer Look Series: Topics, Issues and Controversies in Corporate Governance No. CGRP-70, Stanford University Graduate School of Business Research Paper No. 18-3, available at SSRN: https://ssrn.com/abstract=3087371.

18 *location discrimination:* Jeffery C. Mays, "Uber Gains Civil Rights Allies Against New York's Proposed Freeze: 'It's a Racial Issue,' " *New York Times*, July 29, 2018, https://www.nytimes.com/2018/07/29/nyregion/uber-cap-civil-rights.html.

18 *Norman Lear:* Norman Lear Interview, *The Ethics Incubator*, April 9, 2018, http:// ethicsincubator.net/ethics-and-the-arts-interviews/3038.

19 *San Francisco roommates:* Airbnb News Room: "Fast Facts," https://news.airbnb .com/fast-facts; and Austin Carr, "Starred: The Email That Launched Airbnb," *Fast Company*, November 7, 2011, https://www.fastcompany.com/1792024/starred -email-launched-airbnb.

19 *they launched Airbnb:* An Airbnb representative read and provided feedback on this chapter.

19 *worth of approximately $26 billion:* Jane Lanhee Lee, "Airbnb Lowers Internal Valuation to $26 Billion as Coronavirus Hits Bookings: Source," Reuters, April 2, 2020, https://www.reuters.com/article/us-health-coronavirus-airbnb/airbnb-lowers -internal-valuation-to-26-billion-as-coronavirus-hits-bookings-source-idUSKB N21L04O; and Dave Lee, "Airbnb Lowers Internal Valuation by 16% to $26bn," *Financial Times*, April 2, 2020, https://www.ft.com/content/02a8ca9b-1ba9-4e0a -a3d5-084dd93469bb.

19 *seven million listings:* Airbnb News Room, "Fast Facts."

20 *Dyne Suh:* The details of Dyne Suh's story are from author's interview with Dyne Suh on January 8, 2020. See also Yun Kyung (Anny) Kim, "We Spoke to the UCLA

Student Who Was Refused by an Airbnb Host for Being Asian," *The Tab*, UCLA, April 16, 2017, https://thetab.com/us/ucla/2017/04/16/airbnb-asian-2419; and Olivia Solon, "Airbnb Host Who Canceled Reservation Using Racist Comment Must Pay $5,000," *The Guardian*, July 13, 2017, https://www.theguardian.com /technology/2017/jul/13/airbnb-california-racist-comment-penalty-asian-american.

21   *Gregory Selden*: Gregory Selden v. Airbnb, Inc., Class Action Complaint, May 17, 2016, https://www.classaction.org/media/selden-v-airbnb.pdf; Vauhini Vara, "How Airbnb Makes It Hard to Sue for Discrimination," *The New Yorker*, Nov. 3, 2016, https://www.newyorker.com/business/currency/how-airbnb-makes-it-hard-to-sue -for-discrimination; and Katie Benner, "Airbnb Vows to Fight Racism, But Its Users Can't Sue to Prompt Fairness," *New York Times*, June 19, 2016, https://www .nytimes.com/2016/06/20/technology/airbnb-vows-to-fight-racism-but-its-users -cant-sue-to-prompt-fairness.html.

21   *"thousands of retweets"*: Gregory Selden v. Airbnb, Inc., Class Action Complaint.

21   *working paper from Harvard Business School*: The working paper (http://www.benedel man.org/publications/airbnb-guest-discrimination-2016-09-16.pdf) was reported on by Rebecca Greenfield before it was published, "Study Finds Racial Discrimi-nation by Airbnb Hosts," Bloomberg, December 10, 2015, https://www.bloomberg .com/news/articles/2015-12-10/study-finds-racial-discrimination-by-airbnb-hosts. The published article, "Racial Discrimination in the Sharing Economy: Evidence from a Field Experiment," by Benjamin Edelman, Michael Luca, and Dan Svirsky, can be found in the *American Economic Journal: Applied Economics* 9, no. 2 (2017): 1–22, doi:10.1257/app.20160213.

22   *Michael Todisco*: Michael Todisco, "Share and Share Alike? Considering Racial Discrimination in the Nascent Room-Sharing Economy," *Stanford Law Review*, March 2015, https://www.stanfordlawreview.org/online/share-and-share-alike/. As Todisco notes, "Before accepting or denying any request, Airbnb hosts are fur-nished with the guest's first name, often a picture, and other personal information. (Guests are encouraged by Airbnb to share information with their prospective hosts to increase their odds of acceptance.) While the racial salience of profile pictures is obvious, social science shows that race also can be inferred from a person's first name or her unique background and interests. To illustrate: 'Emily from Marin vis-iting for a spa weekend' presents as racially different from 'Imani from Oakland visiting her cousin.' "

22   *Title II*: 42 U.S.C. §2000a section (a) states: "All persons shall be entitled to the full and equal enjoyment of the goods, services, facilities, privileges, advantages, and accommodations of any place of public accommodation, as defined in this section, without discrimination on the ground of race, color, religion, or national origin." "Title II of the Civil Rights Act (Public Accommodations)," United States Depart-ment of Justice, retrieved March 23, 2020, https://www.justice.gov/crt/title-ii-civil -rights-act-public-accommodations.

22   *not technically cover private homes*: Per Title II of the 1964 Civil Rights Act: "42 U.S.C. §2000a(b) Each of the following establishments is a place of public accommodation within this title if its operations affect commerce, or if discrimination or segregation by it is supported by State action: (1) any inn, hotel, motel, or other establishment which provides lodging to transient guests, other than an establishment located within a building which contains not more than five rooms for rent or hire and which is actually occupied by the proprietor of such establishment as his residence."

22   *Homeowners have the right*: Todisco, "Share and Share Alike? Considering Racial Dis-crimination in the Nascent Room-Sharing Economy."

22   *"We imagine a world"*: "Airbnb Introduces the Belo," video, Airbnb blog, July 16, 2014, retrieved March 23, 2020, https://blog.atairbnb.com/belong-anywhere; and

"Our Mission: Create a World Where Anyone Can Belong Anywhere," at Airbnb, "Careers," retrieved March 23, 2020, https://careers.airbnb.com.

24 *purchase this T-shirt*: Robin Givhan, "The Troubling Ethics of Fashion in the Age of Climate Change," *Washington Post Magazine*, November 18, 2019, https://www .washingtonpost.com/magazine/2019/11/18/troubling-ethics-fashion-age-climate -change.

25 *seven "Enduring Values"*: Boeing's values have remained the same before and after the 737 Max tragedies. See "Our Principles: Vision," Boeing, retrieved March 23, 2020, https://www.boeing.com/principles/vision.page; and Wayback Machine, retrieved March 5, 2019, https://web.archive.org/web/20190305074103/http://www.boeing .com/principles/vision.page.

25 *$14.6 billion*: According to Boeing's "Fourth-Quarter 2019 Performance Review," slide 6: "737 Max," Boeing cites $6.3 billion "additional costs to produce aircraft in the 737 program accounting quantity in FY19"; and $8.3 billion additional "pre-tax charge related to estimated potential concessions and other considerations to customers in FY19." This adds up to $14.6 billion costs in 2019 alone, but Boeing also "estimated ~$4B abnormal production costs to be expensed as incurred, primarily in 2020," which adds up to $18.6 billion in estimated costs due to the Max crisis at the time of the report, https://s2.q4cdn.com/661678649/files/doc _presentations/2020/01/4Q19-Presentation.pdf, retrieved April 26, 2020. See also Doug Cameron and Andrew Tangel, "Boeing Posts Full-Year Loss Amid 737 MAX Setbacks," *Wall Street Journal*, January 29, 2020, https://www.wsj.com/articles /boeing-falls-to-full-year-loss-11580302091; and Claire Bushey and Gregory Meyer, "Boeing Expects 737 Max Crisis Costs to Reach $18.6bn," January 29, 2020, *Financial Times*, https://www.ft.com/content/0e9a99de-428d-11ea-a43a-c4b328d9061c.

25 *Be a Host*: Airbnb's "Core Values" now are Champion the Mission, Be a Host, Embrace the Adventure, and Be a Cereal Entrepreneur ("Airbnb Careers," https:// careers.airbnb.com, retrieved May 8, 2020). But at the time of Gregory Selden's experience, Airbnb had a longer list as noted in the text, per "Airbnb Careers," December 22, 2015, Wayback Machine, https://web.archive.org/web/20151222015753 /https://www.airbnb.com/careers?cdn_locale_redirect=1.

29 *"running rampant"*: The emails can be viewed via *Seattle Times* (https://www.doc umentcloud.org/documents/6497959-Boeing-Text-Messages.html, retrieved April 18, 2020) in an article reported by Dominic Gates and Steve Miletich, "Stunning Messages from 2016 Deepen Boeing's 737 MAX Crisis," October 18, 2019, https:// www.seattletimes.com/business/boeing-aerospace/explosive-text-messages-reveal -boeing-knew-of-mcas-aggression-in-2016-and-misled-faa/. See additional media reports, including David Gelles and Natalie Kitroeff, "Boeing Pilot Complained of 'Egregious' Issue with 737 Max in 2016," *New York Times*, October 18, 2019, https:// www.nytimes.com/2019/10/18/business/boeing-flight-simulator-text-message. html; and "Read Boeing Text Messages That Reveal 737 Max Issues Years Before Deadly Crashes," Fox Business News, October 19, 2019, https://www.foxbusiness .com/lifestyle/read-boeing-text-messages-that-reveal-737-max-issues-years-before- deadly-crashes.

29 *took more than ten seconds*: See p. 22 of Hearing Before the Committee on Transportation and Infrastructure; and p. 9, "The Boeing 737 MAX Aircraft: Costs, Consequences, and Lessons from Its Design, Development, and Certification," report by the House Committee on Transportation and Infrastructure, March 2020, https:// transportation.house.gov/imo/media/doc/TI%20Preliminary%20Investigative%20 Findings%20Boeing%20737%20MAX%20March%202020.pdf.

29 *Muilenburg testified to the U.S. Senate*: See p. 24 of "The Boeing 737 Max: Examining the Design, Development, and Marketing of the Aircraft," Hearing Before the

Committee on Transportation and Infrastructure, House of Representatives, October 30, 2019, https://www.congress.gov/116/meeting/house/110066/docu ments/CHRG-116hhrg38282.pdf.

29 *was not functional, that MCAS existed*: "Culture of Concealment," p. 3, "The Boeing 737 MAX Aircraft: Costs, Consequences, and Lessons from Its Design, Development, and Certification," report by the Committee on Transportation and Infrastructure, March 2020, https://transportation.house.gov/imo/media/doc/TI %20Preliminary%20Investigative%20Findings%20Boeing%20737%20MAX%20 March%202020.pdf.

29 *broken AOA sensor*. "Faulty Assumptions," p. 3, ibid.; and "Ethiopian Airlines Crash," March 12, 2019, Reuters Graphics, https://graphics.reuters.com/ETHIOPIA-AIR PLANE/0100911Q1DX/index.html.

29 *"There were lots"*: Brian Solomon, "Airbnb Confronts Racism as It Hits 100 Million Guest Arrivals," *Fortune*, July 13, 2016, https://www.forbes.com/sites/briansolomon /2016/07/13airbnb-confronts-racism-as-it-hits-100-million-guest-arrivals/#5e01 7a876b76.

29 *one in four*. Maeve Duggan, "1 in 4 Black Americans Have Faced Online Harassment Because of Their Race or Ethnicity," Pew Research Center, June 25, 2017, https:// www.pewresearch.org/fact-tank/2017/07/25/1-in-4-black-americans-have-faced -online-harassment-because-of-their-race-or-ethnicity/.

31 *Southwest Airlines pilots*: Woodrow Bellamy, "Southwest Airlines Pilots File Boeing 737 MAX Lawsuit," *Aviation Today*, Oct. 8, 2019, https://www.aviationtoday .com/2019/10/08/southwest-airlines-pilots-file-boeing-737-Max-lawsuit.

31 *rival Airbus*: Dominic Gates, "Boeing's Horrible Year: It Lost Orders, While Airbus Delivered Twice As Many Jets," *Seattle Times*, January 14, 2020, https://www .seattletimes.com/business/boeing-aerospace/after-boeings-horrible-year-annual -race-against-airbus-is-no-contest/; and Doug Cameron and Benjamin Katz, "Boeing Orders Fall to 16-Year Low," *Wall Street Journal*, January 14, 2020, https://www .wsj.com/articles/boeing-orders-fall-to-16-year-low-11579018235, both of which state that Airbus delivered a total of 863 jets in 2019 and Boeing delivered 380.

31 *diminishing in standing*: Andy Pasztor, "Ethiopian Airlines Crash Highlights FAA's Diminished Clout on World Stage," *Wall Street Journal*, March 14, 2019, https:// www.wsj.com/articles/ethiopian-airlines-crash-highlights-faas-diminished-clout -on-world-stage-11552590227; Peggy Hollinger and Kiran Stacey, "European Safety Chief Seeks More Oversight of Boeing," *Financial Times*, December 20, 2019, https://www.ft.com/content/8723dc6e-22e7-11ea-b8a1-584213ee7b2b; Rene Marsh and Gregory Wallace, "6 months after Boeing crash, it's uncertain when longest major airplane grounding will end," CNN, September 10, 2019, https://www .cnn.com/2019/09/10/politics/boeing-737-max-grounding-faa/index.html.

31 *two million guests*: Airbnb Newsroom, "Fast Facts," retrieved March 25, 2020, https://news.airbnb.com/fast-facts.

32 high likelihood: See pp. 11–12 of "The Boeing 737 MAX Aircraft: Costs, Consequences, and Lessons from Its Design, Development, and Certification," which notes that "[i]n the aftermath of the Lion Air crash, the FAA conducted a risk assessment based on the Transport Aircraft Risk Assessment Methodology (TARAM) which calculated that without a fix to MCAS, during the lifetime of the 737 MAX fleet, there would be an estimated 15 more fatal, catastrophic accidents," https://transportation.house.gov /imo/media/doc/TI%20Preliminary%20Investigative%20Findings%20Boeing%20 737%20MAX%20March%202020.pdf; and Andy Pasztor and Andrew Tangel, " 'Why Is This Airplane Still Flying?' The FAA Missteps That Kept Boeing's MAX Aloft," *Wall Street Journal*, October 28, 2019, https://www.wsj.com/articles/why-is-this -airplane-still-flying-the-faa-missteps-that-kept-boeings-max-aloft-11572308196.

32   *software patch*: As U.S. congressman Peter DeFazio stated in Senate hearings, "The actual fix was relatively simple and a software update could have been done quickly, but it wasn't, and it is still unclear why." "Chair DeFazio's Statement from Hearing on the Boeing 737 Max Airplane Investigation," October 30, 2019, https:// defazio.house.gov/media-center/press-releases/chair-defazio-s-statement-from-hearing-on-the-boeing-737-max-airplane. See also Natalie Kitroeff, Jack Nicas, and Thomas Kaplan, "Boeing Promised Pilots a 737 Software Fix Last Year, but They're Still Waiting," *New York Times*, March 14, 2019, https://www.nytimes .com/2019/03/14/business/boeing-737-software-update.html.

32   *A senior FAA official*: Lewis Kamb, "Top FAA Officials Defend Delegation of 737 Max's Safety Certification to Boeing During Senate Hearing," *Seattle Times*, July 31, 2019, https://www.seattletimes.com/business/boeing-aerospace/top-faa-officials -defend-delegation-of-737-Maxs-safety-certification-to-boeing-during-senate-hearing. The "Boeing 737 MAX Aircraft" report by the Committee on Transportation and Infrastructure, March 2020 (p. 4) asserts that "[t]he FAA failed in its oversight responsibilities to ensure the safety of the traveling public."

33   *"safe airplanes even safer"*: U.S. Senate Committee on Commerce, Science, & Transportation's Aviation Safety and the Future of Boeing's 737 MAX hearing, October 29, 2019, https://www.commerce.senate.gov/2019/10/aviation-safety-and-the -future-of-boeing-s-737-max/dd0f5a92-0362-45e8-bab1-957d0e82f168; and "Letter from Boeing CEO Dennis Muilenburg to Airlines, Passengers and the Aviation Community," Boeing, retrieved March 23, 2020, https://boeing.mediaroom.com/2019 -03-18-Letter-from-Boeing-CEO-Dennis-Muilenburg-to-Airlines-Passengers -and-the-Aviation-Community.

33   *"the greatest challenge"*: Brian Chesky's full quote is: "At the heart of our mission is the idea that people are fundamentally good and every community is a place where you can belong. I sincerely believe that [discrimination] is the greatest challenge we face as a company. It cuts to the core of who we are and the values that we stand for." "Our Diverse Global Community Makes Airbnb Possible," Airbnb, retrieved April 18, 2020, https://www.airbnb.com/diversity.

33   *"Community Commitment"*: See "The Airbnb Community Commitment," Airbnb blog, October 27, 2016, https://blog.atairbnb.com/the-airbnb-community-com mitment; and "General Questions About the Airbnb Community Commitment"; for the full text of the Commitment, https://www.airbnb.com/help/article/1523 /general-questions-about-the-airbnb-community-commitment; and "Our Diverse Global Community Makes Airbnb Possible," https://www.airbnb.com/diversity, all retrieved April 18, 2020.

33   *Airbnb hired*: According to Airbnb, "This effort was led by Laura Murphy, the former head of the American Civil Liberties Union's Washington D.C. Legislative Office and in consultation with dozens of experts from the advocacy and civil rights community, such as former U.S. Attorney General Eric Holder." ("The Airbnb Community Commitment," October 27, 2016, Airbnb blog, https://blog.atairbnb.com /the-airbnb-community-commitment and "Our Diverse Global Community Makes Airbnb Possible," https://www.airbnb.com/diversity). Airbnb also noted that it was "working with experts on bias, including Dr. Robert Livingston of the Harvard Kennedy School of Government and Dr. Peter Glick of Lawrence University, to make anti-bias training available to our community, and will be publicly acknowledging those who complete it." ("Fighting Discrimination and Creating a World Where Anyone Can Belong Anywhere," https://blog.atairbnb.com/fighting -discrimination-and-creating-a-world-where-anyone-can-belong-anywhere/). All retrieved April 18, 2020. See also media reports, for example: Greg Bensinger, "Airbnb Promotes Diversity to Prevent Booking Discrimination by Hosts," *Wall Street*

Journal, September 8, 2016, https://www.wsj.com/articles/airbnb-promotes-diversity-to-prevent-booking-discrimination-by-hosts-1473343215.

34   *$5,000 in damages*: Author interview with Dyne Suh on January 8, 2020, and emails on March 30, 2020. See also media reports, for example: Olivia Solon, "Airbnb Host Who Canceled Reservation Using Racist Comment Must Pay $5,000," *The Guardian*, July 13, 2017, https://www.theguardian.com/technology/2017/jul/13/airbnb-california-racist-comment-penalty-asian-american, and Kevin Lui, "A Former Airbnb Host in California Has Agreed to Pay $5,000 for Canceling a Booking Based on Ethnicity," *Time*, July 13, 2017, https://time.com/4858050/airbnb-racist-asian-california-trump/.

34   *Halloween party*: "Airbnb Bans 'Party Houses' After Five Die in Halloween Shooting," BBC News, November 2, 2019, https://www.bbc.com/news/world-us-canada-50276485.

34   *"neighbor hotline"*: See "Building on Our Commitment to Trust," Airbnb Newsroom, November 15, 2019, https://news.airbnb.com/building-on-our-commitment-to-trust/, and "Neighbor Support," Airbnb, retrieved April 18, 2020, https://www.airbnb.com/neighbors.

34   *seven million listings*: Airbnb outlined all the changes it would make in a statement on its website, "Building on Our Commitment to Trust," Airbnb Newsroom, retrieved April 18, 2020, https://news.airbnb.com/building-on-our-commitment-to-trust/.

34   *"Our real innovation"*: Ibid. Brian Chesky's full quote is: "Our real innovation is not allowing people to book a home; it's designing a framework to allow millions of people to trust one another. Trust is the real energy source that drives Airbnb and has enabled us to scale our platform to 191 countries and to more than 600 million members. But recently, events by bad actors on our platform took advantage of that trust, including at a home in Orinda, California. We intend to do everything possible to learn from these incidents when they occur." "In the Business of Trust," Airbnb newsroom, https://news.airbnb.com/in-the-business-of-trust/.

35   *"Many of us in this industry"*: Brian Chesky interview at DealBook conference, David Yaffe-Bellany, "How Airbnb Plans to Verify Rentals After a California Shooting," *New York Times*, November 11, 2019, https://www.nytimes.com/2019/11/11/business/dealbook/airbnb-brian-chesky.html.

Chapter Two – Scattered Power

37   *When Delaney Van Riper*: Author interview with Delaney Van Riper, January 5, 2020.

37   *Charcot-Marie-Tooth*: Author email with Delaney Van Riper, March 18, 2020. See also "What Is Charcot-Marie-Tooth?" Charcot-Marie-Tooth Foundation, retrieved March 16, 2020, https://cmtrf.org/home-page/what-is-cmt/.

37   *"unique" among her peers*: Delaney Van Riper, "Warrior," *CMTeens*, 1, no. 1; and Delaney Van Riper email to author, March 13, 2020.

37   *emotionally painful*: Delaney Van Riper email to author, March 13, 2020; and Delaney Van Riper, "Editing Scripts," *Gladstone News*, August 12, 2019, https://gladstone.org/about-us/news/editing-scripts.

37   *received an email*: Author interview with Delaney Van Riper, January 5, 2020.

37   *Dr. Bruce Conklin*: Dr. Conklin is also a professor in the Departments of Medicine, Cellular and Molecular Pharmacology, and Ophthalmology at UC San Francisco, and deputy director of the Innovative Genomics Institute, a nonprofit research partnership between UC Berkeley and UC San Francisco, overseen by executive director Dr. Doudna.

37   *the development of a cure*: Gladstone Institutes, Bruce Conklin, MD, "Research," https://gladstone.org/people/bruce-conklin.

37   *In 1987, a team*: Y. Ishino, H. Shinagawa, K. Makino, M. Amemura, and A. Nakata,
      "Nucleotide Sequence of the *iap* Gene, Responsible for Alkaline Phosphatase Iso-
      zyme Conversion in *Escherichia Coli*, and Identification of the Gene Product," *Journal
      of Bacteriology* 169, no. 12 (December 1987): 5429–33, doi:10.1128/jb.169.12.5429
      -5433.1987, https://jb.asm.org/content/jb/169/12/5429.full.pdf.

38   *"clustered regularly"*: National Institutes of Health, U.S. National Library of Medi-
      cine, accessed March 15, 2020, https://ghr.nlm.nih.gov/primer/genomicresearch
      /genomeediting. The Japanese scientists did not coin the term CRISPR. According
      to the Broad Institute CRISPR timeline, "Francisco Mojica was the first researcher
      to characterize what is now called a CRISPR locus," https://www.broadinstitute
      .org/what-broad/areas-focus/project-spotlight/crispr-timeline.

38   *CRISPR was akin*: Ariel Bleicher, "The First Genome Surgeons: Scientists Are Pre-
      paring to Bring DNA-Editing Tools to the Clinic," *UCSF News*, October 24, 2018,
      https://www.ucsf.edu/news/2018/10/412116/first-genome-surgeons; and "Update:
      CRISPR," *Radio Lab*, WNYC Studios, February 24, 2017, https://www.wnycstudios
      .org/podcasts/radiolab/articles/update-crispr.

38   *published groundbreaking research*: Martin Jinek, Krzysztof Chylinski, Ines Fonfara,
      Michael Hauer, Jennifer Doudna, and Emmanuelle Charpentier, "A Programmable
      Dual-RNA-Guided DNA Endonuclease in Adaptive Bacterial Immunity," *Science*,
      337 (August 2012): 816–21, https://www.ncbi.nlm.nih.gov/pubmed/22745249.

38   *Dr. Doudna . . . credits her colleague*: Megan Molteni, "Inside the Lab Training Genome
      Surgeons to Fight Disease," *Wired*, November 26, 2018, https://www.wired.com
      /story/inside-the-lab-training-crispr-genome-surgeons-to-fight-disease/.

38   *6.4 billion letters*: R. L. Goldfeder, D. P. Wall, M. J. Khoury, J. Ioannidis, and E.
      A. Ashley, "Human Genome Sequencing at the Population Scale: A Primer on
      High-Throughput DNA Sequencing and Analysis, *American Journal of Epidemiology*
      186, no. 8 (2017): 1000–1009, https://doi.org/10.1093/aje/kww224. And, as ge-
      nome sequencing company Veritas Genetics notes, July 2017, the "human genome
      is 6.4 billion letters (base pairs) long. Not 3.2 billion," as some sources mistakenly
      say, https://www.veritasgenetics.com/our-thinking/whole-story.

38   *"precise changes"*: Brenda Breslauer and Robert W. Spencer, "Life Changer," NBC
      News, June 11, 2017, https://www.nbcnews.com/megyn-kelly/video/life-changer
      -965215299885.

38   *her participation in the study*: Author interview with Delaney Van Riper, January 5,
      2020.

38   *use CRISPR tools*: Bleicher, "The First Genome Surgeons"; and Robert Sanders,
      "CRISPR Opens Door to New Type of Medicine: 'Genome Surgery,'" *Berkeley News*,
      October 25, 2018, https://news.berkeley.edu/story_jump/crispr-opens-door-to-new
      -type-of-medicine-genome-surgery/.

38   *researchers isolated*: Bleicher, "The First Genome Surgeons: Scientists Are Preparing
      to Bring DNA-Editing Tools to the Clinic"; and Gladstone Institutes, Bruce Conk-
      lin, MD, "Research."

39   *"Genes have two strands"*: Author email with Delaney Van Riper, March 13, 2020.

39   *"We thought that . . . will work"*: Email to author from Dr. Bruce Conklin, February
      28, 2020.

40   *In a recent essay*: Van Riper, "Editing Scripts."

40   *heart disease*: Anthony King, "A CRISPR Edit for Heart Disease," *Nature*, March 7,
      2018, https://www.nature.com/articles/d41586-018-02482-4.

40   *cancer*: "What Are Genome Editing and CRISPR-Cas9?," National Institutes of
      Health, U.S. National Library of Medicine, retrieved March 30, 2020, https://ghr
      .nlm.nih.gov/primer/genomicresearch/genomeediting.

40   *Alzheimer's*: T. T. Rohn, N. Kim, N. F. Isho, and J. M. Mack, "The Potential of

CRISPR/Cas9 Gene Editing as a Treatment Strategy for Alzheimer's Disease," *Journal of Alzheimer's Disease & Parkinsonism* 8, no. 3 (2018): 439, https://doi.org/10.4172/2161-0460.1000439.

40   *muscular dystrophy*: Y. L. Min et al., "CRISPR-Cas9 Corrects Duchenne Muscular Dystrophy Exon 44 Deletion Mutations in Mice and Human Cells," *Science Advances* 5, no. 3, eaav4324 (2019), https://advances.sciencemag.org/content/5/3/eaav4324.

40   *cystic fibrosis*: "What Are Genome Editing and CRISPR-Cas9?," National Institutes of Health.

40   *blindness*: Bleicher, "The First Genome Surgeons: Scientists Are Preparing to Bring DNA-Editing Tools to the Clinic."

40   *mosquitoes*: Megan Scudellari, "Self-Destructing Mosquitoes and Sterilized Rodents: The Promise of Gene Drives," *Nature*, July 9, 2019, https://www.nature.com/articles/d41586-019-02087-5.

40   *corn and wheat*: Eric Niiler, "Why Gene Editing Is the Next Food Revolution," *National Geographic*, August 10, 2018, https://www.nationalgeographic.com/environment/future-of-food/food-technology-gene-editing/.

40   *woolly mammoth*: Revive & Restore, retrieved March 20, 2020, https://reviverestore.org/projects/woolly-mammoth/progress-to-date/; and Amy Dockser Marcus, "Meet the Scientists Bringing Extinct Species Back From the Dead," *Wall Street Journal*, October 11, 2018, https://www.wsj.com/articles/meet-the-scientists-bringing-extinct-species-back-from-the-dead-1539093600.

41   *Somatic therapies:* "How Is Genome Editing Used?," National Human Genome Research Institute, retrieved March 30, 2020, https://www.genome.gov/about-genomics/policy-issues/Genome-Editing/How-genome-editing-is-used.

41   *Doudna supports*: Jennifer Doudna statement, "CRISPR co-inventor responds to claim of first genetically edited babies," *Berkeley News*, November 26, 2018, https://news.berkeley.edu/2018/11/26/doudna-responds-to-claim-of-first-crispr-edited-babies/.

41   *thirty nations:* M. Araki and T. Ishii, "International Regulatory Landscape and Integration of Corrective Genome Editing into In Vitro Fertilization," *Reproductive Biology and Endocrinology* 12, no. 108 (2014), https://doi.org/10.1186/1477-7827-12-108; "UNESCO panel of experts calls for ban on 'editing' of human DNA to avoid unethical tampering with hereditary traits," UNESCO.org, https://en.unesco.org/news/unesco-panel-experts-calls-ban-editing-human-dna-avoid-unethical-tampering-hereditary-traits; and Lauren Friedman, "These Are the Countries Where It's 'Legal' to Edit Human Embryos (Hint: the US Is One)," *Business Insider*, April 23, 2015, https://www.businessinsider.com/china-edited-human-genome-laws-2015-4#ixzz3YXh2b7du.

42   *I asked Dr. Conklin:* Author phone interview with Dr. Conklin, January 7, 2020.

42   *According to a study*: W. D. Winkelman, S. A. Missmer, D. Myers, and E. S. Ginsburg, "Public Perspectives on the Use of Preimplantation Genetic Diagnosis," *Journal of Assisted Reproduction and Genetics*, 32 (March 2015): 665–75, https://doi.org/10.1007/s10815-015-0456-8. According to the PGD International Society, testing is also being performed in more than one hundred centers worldwide, retrieved March 16, 2020, http://pgdis.org/present.html.

42   *The technique, as described*: PGD is also called preimplantation genetic testing (PGT) and preimplantation genetic screening (PGS). See American Society for Reproductive Medicine, "Preimplantation Genetic Testing," https://www.reproductivefacts.org/news-and-publications/patient-fact-sheets-and-booklets/documents/fact-sheets-and-info-booklets/preimplantation-genetic-testing/.

42   *conditions such as*: PGD can be used for more than six hundred genetic conditions ("Approved PGD and PTT Conditions," https://www.hfea.gov.uk/treatments/embryo-testing-and-treatments-for-disease/approved-pgd-and-ptt-conditions/);

a full searchable list is at "PGD Conditions," Human Fertilisation & Embryology Authority, https://www.hfea.gov.uk/pgd-conditions/, retrieved April 29, 2020.

43   *the journal* Science: See reporter Jon Cohen's series on the CRISPR babies, supported by the Pulitzer Center, "The Untold Story of the 'Circle of Trust' Behind the World's First Gene-Edited Babies," *Science*, August 1, 2019, https://www.sciencemag.org /news/2019/08/untold-story-circle-trust-behind-world-s-first-gene-edited-babies.

43   *Passing HIV down*: Cohen, "The Untold Story of the 'Circle of Trust' Behind the World's First Gene-Edited Babies"; and V. L. Raposo, "The First Chinese Edited Babies: A Leap of Faith in Science," *JBRA Assisted Reproduction* 23, no. 3 (2019): 197–99, https://doi.org/10.5935/1518-0557.20190042.

43   *Chinese Clinical Trials Registry*: Cohen, "The Untold Story of the 'Circle of Trust' Be-hind the World's First Gene-Edited Babies," application accessible via http://www .chictr.org.cn/showprojen.aspx?proj=32758.

43   *consent forms:* Ibid., accessible via https://www.sciencemag.org/sites/default/files /crispr_informed-consent.pdf

43–44 *mentioned the possibility that there could be:* Paragraph 3 of Article 3 of consent form, ibid., states: "The primary risk of gene editing (DNA-targeted CRISPR-Cas9 endo-nuclease) is the off-target effect of generating extra DNA mutations at sites other than the intended target. This is due to that the technique can cause nonspecific cleavage, resulting in mutations in nontargeted genomic sites. PGD, whole genome-wide se-quencing, amniocentesis and peripheral blood test of mothers in different stages of pregnancy after transplantation will minimize the possibility of substantial injury. Therefore, this project team is not responsible for the risk of off-target which is be-yond the risk consequences of the existing medical science and technology."

44   *rights to, and publicize, baby*: Article 10, paragraph 2, of consent form, ibid.

44   *eight hopeful couples*: Cohen, "The Untold Story of the 'Circle of Trust' Behind the World's First Gene-Edited Babies."

44   *CCR5-delta 32:* H. Wang and H. Yang, "Gene-Edited Babies: What Went Wrong and What Could Go Wrong," *PLOS Biology* 17, no. 4 (2019): e3000224, https://doi .org/10.1371/journal.pbio.3000224.

44   *several days old:* According to the consent form (https://www.sciencemag.org/sites /default/files/crispr_informed-consent.pdf), Dr. He notes: "After 5–6 days embryo culture, 3–6 embryonic trophoblast cells are biopsied for PGD at blastocyst stage"; additionally Dr. He states that after IVF, diagnostic testing was done "a few days later" in "About Lulu and Nana: Twin Girls Born Healthy After Gene Surgery as Single-Cell Embryos," posted by The He Lab, November 25, 2018, accessed March 16, 2020, YouTube, https://www.youtube.com/watch?v=th0vnOmFltc. See also media reports, for example: "World's First Gene-Edited Babies Created in China, Claims Scientist," *The Guardian*, November 26, 2018, https://www.theguardian .com/science/2018/nov/26/worlds-first-gene-edited-babies-created-in-china-claims -scientist.

44   *Reputable media sources*: Preetika Rana, "How a Chinese Scientist Broke the Rules to Create the First Gene-Edited Babies," *Wall Street Journal*, May 10, 2019, https:// www.wsj.com/articles/how-a-chinese-scientist-broke-the-rules-to-create-the-first -gene-edited-babies-11557506697; Cohen, "The Untold Story of the 'Circle of Trust' Behind the World's First Gene-Edited Babies"; Antonio Regalado, "Chi-na's CRISPR Babies: Read Exclusive Excerpts from the Unseen Original Re-search," *MIT Technology Review*, December 3, 2019, https://www.technologyreview .com/s/614764/chinas-crispr-babies-read-exclusive-excerpts-he-jiankui-paper/; and Akshat Rathi, "The Crispr Baby News Was Carefully Orchestrated PR—Until it All Went Wrong," *Quartz*, November 27, 2018, https://qz.com/1474814/the -cripsr-baby-news-was-carefully-orchestrated-pr-until-it-all-went-wrong/.

44 *medical ethics application:* D. Shaw, "The Consent Form in the Chinese CRISPR Study: In Search of Ethical Gene Editing," *Journal of Bioethical Inquiry*, 17 (January 2020): 5–10, https://link.springer.com/article/10.1007/s11673-019-09953-x#ci teas; and the application, in Chinese, via *Science* at https://www.sciencemag.org /sites/default/files/crispr_application.pdf. The full quote, according to Shaw, is: "Through this study, we expect to establish a solid technique standard for therapy by gene editing and bring gene editing related therapy to a new level. Ultimately, our research will stand out in the increasingly competitive international application of gene editing technology. This is going to be a great science and medicine achievement ever since the IVF technology which was awarded the Nobel Prize in 2010, and will also bring hope to numerous genetic disease patients." See also media reports, for example: Cohen, "The Untold Story of the 'Circle of Trust' Behind the World's First Gene-Edited Babies"; and Rana, "How a Chinese Scientist Broke the Rules to Create the First Gene-Edited Babies."

44 *had been forged:* See November 2018 statement from Harmonicare Medical Holdings Limited, http://asia.blob.euroland.com/press-releases-attachments/1108747 /HKEX-EPS_20181127_003332422-0.PDF, which was sourced via Ed Yong, "The CRISPR Baby Scandal Gets Worse by the Day," *The Atlantic*, December 3, 2018, https://www.theatlantic.com/science/archive/2018/12/15-worrying-things -about-crispr-babies-scandal/577234; and Rana, "How a Chinese Scientist Broke the Rules to Create the First Gene-Edited Babies." A copy of the signed application that the hospital says was forged is accessible via Cohen, "The Untold Story of the 'Circle of Trust' Behind the World's First Gene-Edited Babies," at https://www .sciencemag.org/sites/default/files/crispr_application.pdf.

45 *Reputable scientists:* According to the *New York Times*, when Dr. He told his former Stanford University professor, biophysicist Stephen Quake, of his plans, Dr. Quake urged He to obtain ethical approval and submit his results for vetting by peer-reviewed journals (Pam Belluck, "Gene-Edited Babies: What a Chinese Scientist Told an American Mentor," April 14, 2019, https://www.nytimes.com/2019/04/14 /health/gene-editing-babies.html). Stanford bioethicist William Hurlbut told National Public Radio (NPR) that he tried to dissuade Dr. He on several occasions (Merrit Kennedy, "Chinese Researcher Who Created Gene-Edited Babies Sentenced to 3 Years in Prison," NPR, December 30, 2019, https://www.npr .org/2019/12/30/792340177/chinese-researcher-who-created-gene-edited-babies -sentenced-to-3-years-in-prison).

45 *the Chinese Academy:* The guidelines were jointly issued by the Chinese government's Ministry of Health and the Ministry of Science and Technology in December 2003. C. Wang, X. Zhai, X. Zhang, L. Li, J. Wang, and D. Liu, "Gene-Edited Babies: Chinese Academy of Medical Sciences' Response and Action," *The Lancet* 393, no. 10166 (December 2018), 25–26, https://doi.org/10.1016/S0140-6736(18)33080-0; L. Liao, L. Li, and R. C. Zhao, "Stem Cell Research in China," *Philosophical Transactions of the Royal Society B, Biological Sciences* 362, no. 1482 (March 2007): 1107–12, https://doi.org/10.1098/rstb.2007.2037; and L. Cheng, R. Qiu, H. Deng, et al., "Ethics: China Already Has Clear Stem-Cell Guidelines," *Nature* 440 (2006): 992, https://doi.org/10.1038/440992b.

45 *act in secret:* Antonio Regalado, "Disgraced CRISPR Scientist Had Plans to Start a Designer-Baby Business," *MIT Technology Review*, August 1, 2019, https://www .technologyreview.com/s/614051/crispr-baby-maker-explored-starting-a-business -in-designer-baby-tourism/; Cohen, "The Untold Story of the 'Circle of Trust' Behind the World's First Gene-Edited Babies"; Yong, "The CRISPR Baby Scandal Gets Worse by the Day"; and Rana, "How a Chinese Scientist Broke the Rules to Create the First Gene-Edited Babies."

45   *pregnant with twins*: Regalado, "Disgraced CRISPR Scientist Had Plans to Start a
        Designer-Baby Business."

45   *Tests showed*: Rana, "How a Chinese Scientist Broke the Rules to Create the First
        Gene-Edited Babies."

45   *flush with "success"*: Ibid.

45   *a fertility doctor*: Regalado, "Disgraced CRISPR Scientist Had Plans to Start a De-
        signer-Baby Business"; and Cohen, "The Untold Story of the 'Circle of Trust' Be-
        hind the World's First Gene-Edited Babies."

46   *public relations specialist*: Yong, "The CRISPR Baby Scandal Gets Worse by the
        Day"; Cohen, "The Untold Story of the 'Circle of Trust' Behind the World's First
        Gene-Edited Babies."

46   *helped him form a plan*: According to investigative reporting in *Science*, Dr. He wanted
        to announce the births in November, but his PR specialist and others encouraged
        him to publish his work first. Cohen, "The Untold Story of the 'Circle of Trust'
        Behind the World's First Gene-Edited Babies."

46   MIT Technology Review: Reporter Antonio Regalado searched the Chinese Clinical
        Trials Registry after hearing rumors about Dr. He's work and discovered the study's
        official application. Regalado, "Disgraced CRISPR Scientist Had Plans to Start a
        Designer-Baby Business."

46   *the Associated Press published*: Marilynn Marchione, "Chinese Researcher Claims
        First Gene-Edited Babies," Associated Press, November 26, 2018, https://apnews
        .com/4997bb7aa36c45449b488e19ac83e86d.

46   *YouTube videos*: "About Lulu and Nana: Twin Girls Born Healthy After Gene Sur-
        gery as Single-Cell Embryos," posted by The He Lab, November 25, 2018, accessed
        March 16, 2020, YouTube, https://www.youtube.com/watch?v=th0vnOmFltc.

46   *Second International Summit*: The National Academies of Sciences, Engineering,
        Medicine, https://www.nationalacademies.org/gene-editing/2nd_summit/.

46   *pioneering speakers*: Attendees and summit agenda available at "Second National
        Summit on Human Gene Editing," https://www.nationalacademies.org/event
        /11-27-2018/second-international-summit-on-human-gene-editing.

46   *"proud" of his work*: Pam Belluck, "Chinese Scientist Who Says He Edited Babies'
        Genes Defends His Work," *New York Times*, November 28, 2018, https://www
        .nytimes.com/2018/11/28/world/asia/gene-editing-babies-he-jiankui.html; and
        Angela Cheung, "He Jiankui Reveals Another Woman Pregnant with Gene-
        Edited Baby," *South China Morning Post*, November 28, 2018, https://www.scmp
        .com/video/china/2175476/he-jiankui-reveals-another-woman-pregnant-gene
        -edited-baby.

46   *third CRISPR baby*: Cheung, ibid.

46   *"misguided, premature"*: Rob Stein, "Facing Backlash, Chinese Scientist Defends
        Gene-Editing Research on Babies," NPR, November 28, 2018, https://www.npr.org
        /sections/health-shots/2018/11/28/671375070/facing-backlash-chinese-scientist
        -defends-gene-editing-research-on-babies; and David Cyranoski, "CRISPR-Baby
        Scientist Fails to Satisfy Critics," *Nature*, November 28, 2018, https://www.nature
        .com/articles/d41586-018-07573-w.

46   *"utterly unconvincing"*: Francis S. Collins, NIH Director, "Statement on Claim of
        First Gene-Edited Babies by Chinese Researcher," November 28, 2018, https://
        www.nih.gov/about-nih/who-we-are/nih-director/statements/statement-claim
        -first-gene-edited-babies-chinese-researcher.

46   *Doudna said*: Doudna interview via Bloomberg QuickTake, Twitter, November 28,
        2018, https://twitter.com/QuickTake/status/1067772480511766528.

47   *one researcher pointed out*: Sean P. Ryder, "#CRISPRbabies: Notes on a Scandal,"
        The CRISPR Journal 1, no. 6 (December 2018): 355–57. p. 64, https://www.ncbi

.nlm.nih.gov/pmc/articles/PMC6345105/; Jon Cohen, "Did CRISPR Help—or Harm—the First-Ever Gene-Edited Babies?" *Science*, August 1, 2019. https://www .sciencemag.org/news/2019/08/did-crispr-help-or-harm-first-ever-gene-edited -babies; and Sharon Begley, "Do CRISPR Enthusiasts Have Their Head in the Sand About the Safety of Gene Editing?," *STAT*, July 18, 2016, https://www.statnews .com/2016/07/18/crispr-off-target-effects/.

47   *it is impossible to know if:* Ryder, "#CRISPRbabies: Notes on a Scandal"; and Cohen, "Did CRISPR Help—or Harm—the First-Ever Gene-Edited Babies?"

47   *Shortly after the Hong Kong summit:* Eli Meixler, "Chinese University Fires Scientist Who Claimed to Have Created the First Gene-Edited Babies," *Time*, January 22, 2019, https://time.com/5509239/china-university-fires-he-jiankui-gene-editing/.

47   *pleaded guilty:* Several reputable media outlets reported on the courtroom proceeding, referring to the Xinhua news agency's reporting. See David Cyranoski, "What CRISPR-Baby Prison Sentences Mean for Research," *Nature*, January 3, 2020, https://www.nature.com/articles/d41586-020-00001-y; and Philip Wen and Amy Dockser Marcus, "Chinese Scientist Who Gene-Edited Babies Is Sent to Prison," *Wall Street Journal*, December 3, 2019, https://www.wsj.com/articles/chinese -scientist-who-gene-edited-babies-is-sent-to-prison-11577703233.

48   *kits promising:* Ian Sample, "Experts Warn Home 'Gene Editing' Kits Pose Risk to Society," *The Guardian*, September 29, 2016, https://www.theguardian.com /science/2016/sep/30/experts-warn-home-gene-editing-kits-pose-risk-to-society," and Annie Sneed, "Mail-Order CRISPR Kits Allow Absolutely Anyone to Hack DNA," *Scientific American*, November 2, 2017, https://www.scientificamerican.com /article/mail-order-crispr-kits-allow-absolutely-anyone-to-hack-dna/?redirect=1.

48   *risk is low:* For example, Duke University biomedical engineering professor Charles Gersbach told *Scientific American*: The risk is "not zero, but it's fairly small," in Sneed, "Mail-Order CRISPR Kits Allow Absolutely Anyone to Hack DNA."

49   *fundraising video:* All the quotes and descriptions about this video are from the video, available at "The Wiki Weapon," Defense Distributed, July 27, 2012, YouTube, accessed March 16, 2020, https://www.youtube.com/watch?time_continue =40&v=AQ6Q3BfbVBU&feature=emb_logo.

50   *reached its fundraising goal:* Andy Greenberg, "3D-Printable Gun Project Hits Its Fundraising Goal Despite Being Booted Off Indiegogo," *Forbes*, September 20, 2012, https://www.forbes.com/sites/andygreenberg/2012/09/20/3d-printed-gun-project -hits-its-fundraising-goal-despite-being-booted-off-indiegogo/#394b173b4b34.

50   *among the "15 Most":* "The 15 Most Dangerous People in the World," *Wired*, December 19, 2012, https://www.wired.com/2012/12/most-dangerous-people/.

50   *the first person . . . 100,000 times:* Adam Gabbatt, "Shots Fired from World's First 3D-Printed Handgun," *The Guardian*, May 6, 2013, https://www.theguardian.com /world/2013/may/06/3-handgun-fired-cody-wilson; and Andy Greenberg, "Meet the 'Liberator': Test-Firing the World's First Fully 3D-Printed Gun," *Forbes*, May 5, 2013, https://www.forbes.com/sites/andygreenberg/2013/05/05/meet-the-liberator -test-firing-the-worlds-first-fully-3d-printed-gun/#2d1cb47852d7; and Andy Greenberg, "3D-Printed Gun's Blueprints Downloaded 100,000 Times in Two Days (With Some Help From Kim Dotcom)," *Forbes*, May 8, 2013, https://www.forbes.com/sites /andygreenberg/2013/05/08/3d-printed-guns-blueprints-downloaded-100000-times -in-two-days-with-some-help-from-kim-dotcom/#549c2a6910b8.

50   *drop out:* Andy Greenberg, "A Landmark Legal Shift Opens Pandora's Box for DIY Guns," *Wired*, July 10, 2018, www.wired.com/story/a-landmark-legal-shift-opens -pandoras-box-for-diy-guns.

50   crypto-anarchist: Halley Freger and Victor Ordonez, "Meet Cody Wilson, the 'Crypto-Anarchist' Who Wants You to Be Able to 3D-Print Unregulated Guns,"

ABC News, August 4, 2018, https://abcnews.go.com/US/meet-cody-wilson-crypto-anarchist-3d-print-unregulated/story?id=57013501.

50   friends of freedom: "3D-Printed Gun Blueprint Maker Cody Wilson: 'I Want People to Know We're Friends of Freedom,' " *CBS This Morning*, August 2, 2018, YouTube, https://www.youtube.com/watch?v=KatYW_gN4j8.

50   *gives you "the key"*: Ibid.

51   *3D-printing technology*: Chuck Hull has been called the father of 3D-printing technology and he holds patent No. 4,575,330, March 11, 1986, at https://patentimages.storage.googleapis.com/5c/a0/27/e49642dab99cf6/US4575330.pdf. See also Shane Hickey, "Chuck Hull: The Father of 3D Printing Who Shaped Technology," *The Guardian*, June 22, 2014, https://www.theguardian.com/business/2014/jun/22/chuck-hull-father-3d-printing-shaped-technology; and Dinusha Mendis, *A History of Intellectual Property in 50 Objects* (Cambridge: Cambridge University Press, 2019), 352–359, https://doi.org/10.1017/9781108325806.044.

51   *the same machines*: Andrew Walker, "3D Printing for Dummies: How Do 3D Printers Work?," *The Independent*, June 21, 2013, https://www.independent.co.uk/life-style/gadgets-and-tech/features/3d-printing-for-dummies-how-do-3d-printers-work-8668937.html.

51   *"additive manufacturing"*: Josh Hafner, "What Is a 3D Printed Gun, and How Is It Legal? Your Questions, Answered," *USA Today*, August 1, 2018, https://www.usatoday.com/story/tech/nation-now/2018/08/01/3-d-guns-how-3-d-printed-gun-parts-made-and-how-theyre-legal/879349002/.

51   *used in Legos*: Caroline Delbert, "Why Scientists Supercooled LEGO Bricks to Near Absolute Zero," *Popular Mechanics*, December 26, 2019, https://www.popularmechanics.com/science/a30337510/lego-bricks-heat-tolerance-quantum-computer/.

51   *war victims in Syria:* "3D Printing Prosthetic Limbs for Refugees," *The Economist*, January 18, 2018, https://www.youtube.com/watch?v=_W1veGQxMe4.

51   *housing for refugees*: Rashmi Shivni, "These 3D-Printed Homes Could Provide Shelter to the World's Most Vulnerable People," *PBS NewsHour*, March 30, 2018, https://www.pbs.org/newshour/science/these-3d-printed-homes-could-provide-shelter-to-the-worlds-most-vulnerable-people.

51   *coral reefs*: Laura Parker, "3D-Printed Reefs Offer Hope in Coral Bleaching Crisis," *National Geographic*, March 13, 2017, https://www.nationalgeographic.com/news/2017/03/3d-printed-reefs-coral-bleaching-climate/#close; and Clare Scott, "Team Effort Uses 3D Printing to Restore Coral Reefs," June 16, 2018, 3DPrint.com, https://3dprint.com/217003/3d-printing-restore-coral-reefs/.

51   *3D bioprinting*: See "Leveraging 3-D Printing to Repair Damaged Hearts," Carnegie Mellon University College of Engineering, August 1, 2016, https://www.youtube.com/watch?v=Al7YQsWe1M8; G. Denizet, P. Calame, T. Lihoreau, F. Kleinclauss, and S. Aubry, "3D Multi-Tissue Printing for Kidney Transplantation," *Quantitative Imaging in Medicine and Surgery* 9, no. 1 (January 2019): 101–106, https://doi.org/10.21037/qims.2018.10.16; and "3D Printing Living Tissues to Form Living Structures," Oxford University press release, *ScienceDaily*, August 15, 2017, https://www.sciencedaily.com/releases/2017/08/170815095009.htm.

51   *one only needs*: As CNN notes, 3D printing is "more accessible than ever" and even "machinists with average skills" can print 3D-printed plastic guns. Susannah Cullinane and Doug Criss, "All Your Questions About 3D Guns Answered," CNN, August 2, 2018, https://www.cnn.com/2018/07/31/us/3d-printed-plastic-guns/index.html.

51   *untraceable "ghost guns"*: Carolyn Wilke, "3-D Printed 'Ghost Guns' Pose New Challenges for Crime-Scene Investigators," *Science News*, September 24, 2019, https://www.sciencenews.org/article/3d-printed-guns-plastic-ballistics-crime.

51   *Undetectable Firearms Act*: The act was renewed in 2019, Undetectable Firearms Mod-
      ernization Act, https://www.congress.gov/bill/116th-congress/house-bill/869/text.

52   *detachable block*: Aaron Steckelberg, "The Challenges of Regulating 3-D-Printed
      Guns," *Washington Post*, August 20, 2018, https://www.washingtonpost.com/graphics
      /2018/national/3-d-printed-guns/; Marrian Zhou, "3D-Printed Gun Controversy:
      Everything You Need to Know," CNET, September 25, 2018, https://www.cnet
      .com/news/the-3d-printed-gun-controversy-everything-you-need-to-know/.

52   *journalists in Israel:* Sean Captain, "Journalists Smuggle 3-D Printed Gun into Is-
      raeli Parliament," NBC News, July 8, 2013, https://www.nbcnews.com/technolog
      /journalists-smuggle-3-d-printed-gun-israeli-parliament-6C10570532.

52   *detected 3D-printed guns*: Mahita Gajanan, "The TSA Has Found 3D-Printed Guns
      at Airport Checkpoints 4 Times Since 2016," *Time*, August 2, 2018, https://time
      .com/5356179/3d-printed-guns-tsa/; and Alex Sundby, "3D-Printed Guns Among
      Weapons Found at Airport Security Checkpoints, TSA Says," CBS News, August 1,
      2018, https://www.cbsnews.com/news/3d-printed-guns-among-weapons-found-at
      -airport-security-checkpoints/.

52   *Australian police:* Dan Tynan, " 'I Wouldn't Waste My Time': Firearms Experts Dis-
      miss Flimsy 3D-Printed Guns," *The Guardian*, July 31, 2018, https://www.theguard
      ian.com/us-news/2018/jul/31/3d-printed-guns-danger-problems-plastic.

52   *for a number of years*: For example, the CEO of 3D-printer manufacturer Formlabs
      told *The Guardian* in 2018 that an effective 3D-printed gun was ten or fifteen years
      away. Ibid.

53   *No federal prohibition*: See "Does an Individual Need a License to Make a Firearm
      for Personal Use?," Bureau of Alcohol, Tobacco, Firearms and Explosives, https://
      www.atf.gov/firearms/qa/does-individual-need-license-make-firearm-personal-use.

53   *take them down*: The State Department letter cited Defense Distributed for potential
      infractions of International Traffic in Arms Regulations as well as the Arms Export
      Control Act. According to the letter, both laws "impose certain requirements and
      restrictions on the transfer of, and access to, controlled defense articles and related
      technical data designated by the United States Munitions List." See the text of the
      letter at Andy Greenberg, "State Department Demands Takedown of 3D-Printable
      Gun Files for Possible Export Control Violations," *Forbes*, May 9, 2013, https://www
      .forbes.com/sites/andygreenberg/2013/05/09/state-department-demands-take
      down-of-3d-printable-gun-for-possible-export-control-violation/#2c48ea6375ff.

53   *International Traffic in Arms Regulations*: The International Traffic in Arms Regula-
      tions (ITAR), https://www.pmddtc.state.gov/ddtc_public?id=ddtc_kb_article_page
      &sys_id=24d528fddbfc930044f9ff621f961987.

53   *Wilson sued the government in 2015*: Alan Feuer, "Cody Wilson, Who Posted Gun
      Instructions Online, Sues State Department," *New York Times*, May 6, 2015, https://
      www.nytimes.com/2015/05/07/us/cody-wilson-who-posted-gun-instructions
      -online-sues-state-department.html.

53   *Fifth Circuit Court of Appeals*: In its ruling, the court wrote: "The fact that national
      security might be permanently harmed while Plaintiffs-Appellants' constitutional
      rights might be temporarily harmed strongly supports our conclusion that the dis-
      trict court did not abuse its discretion in weighing the balance in favor of national
      defense and national security," United States Court of Appeals, Fifth Circuit, Sep-
      tember 20, 2016, http://www.ca5.uscourts.gov/opinions/pub/15/15-50759-CV0
      .pdf. See also, "Defense Distributed v. United States Department of State," *Har-
      vard Law Review*, April 7, 2017, https://harvardlawreview.org/2017/04/defense
      -distributed-v-united-states-department-of-state/.

53   *State Department reversed*: In a July 25, 2018, ABC News story, "State Department
      Defends Allowing Publication of Blueprints to 3D Print Guns," a State Department

spokesperson said, "It was determined [after analysis] that certain firearms and related items that are widely available for commercial sale, and technical data related to those items is of a type that does not offer a critical military or intelligence advantage to the United States," https://abcnews.go.com/Politics/state-department -defends-allowing-publication-blueprints-3d-print/story?id=56817152.

53   *agreed to pay*: The settlement, noting a payment to Wilson of $39,581 (Section 1e), is viewable via U.S. Department of State, Directorate of Defense Trade Controls, https://assets.documentcloud.org/documents/4600187/Defense-Distributed -Settlement-Agreement.pdf, retrieved April 30, 2020. See also Tiffany Hsu and Alan Feuer, " 'Downloadable Gun' Clears a Legal Obstacle, and Activists Are Alarmed," *New York Times*, July 13, 2018, https://www.nytimes.com/2018/07/13/business /downloadable-gun-allowed-alarming-activists.html.

53   *AR-15*: Deanna Paul, "Meet the Man Who Might Have Brought on the Age of 'Downloadable Guns,' " *Washington Post*, July 18, 2018, https://www.washing tonpost.com/news/post-nation/wp/2018/07/18/meet-the-man-who-wants-to -bring-on-the-age-of-downloadable-guns-and-may-have-already-succeeded/; and Rob Walker, "A Crypto-Anarchist Will Help You Build a DIY AR-15," *Bloomberg Businessweek*, June 22, 2016, https://www.bloomberg.com/features/2016-cody-wilson -ghost-gunner-ar-15/.

53   *Nineteen states*: Tony Dokoupil, "States Sue Trump Administration to Try to Block Blueprints for 3D-Printed Guns," CBS News, July 30, 2018, https://www.cbsnews. com/news/states-to-sue-trump-administration-to-block-blueprints-for-3d-printed -guns/. The original lawsuit filed July 30, 2018, by eight states and the District of Columbia, later joined by twelve more states, can be found at https://agportal -s3bucket.s3.amazonaws.com/01_Complaint.pdf; "Blueprints for 3D-Printed Guns Banned Online," CBS News, November 13, 2019, https://www.cbsnews.com /news/3d-printed-guns-blueprints-online-illegal-federal-judge-seattle-defeat-trump -administration-2019-11-13/; and the "Ruling of Judge Robert Lasnik of the U.S. District Court in Seattle," Case 2:18-cv-01115-RSL, Document 192, Filed 11/12/19, https://agportal-s3bucket.s3.amazonaws.com/uploadedfiles/Another/News /Press_Releases/192_ORDER_InvalidatingTemporaryModification.pdf.

54   *In 2019,* Wired: Jake Hanrahan, "3D-Printed Guns Are Back, and This Time They Are Unstoppable," *Wired*, May 20, 2019, https://www.wired.co.uk/article/3d -printed-guns-blueprints.

54   *In 2020, Cody*: Brett Forrest, "Gun-Rights Activist Releases Blueprints for Digital Guns," *Wall Street Journal*, March 28, 2020, https://www.wsj.com/articles /gun-rights-activist-releases-blueprints-for-digital-guns-11585414671.

54   *In his book* The End of Power: Moisés Naím, *The End of Power: From Boardrooms to Battlefields and Churches to States, Why Being in Charge Isn't What It Used to Be* (New York: Basic Books, 2013), 21.

57   *NASA partnered with*: "NASA Astronauts Launch from America in Historic Test Flight of SpaceX Crew Dragon," NASA, May 30, 2020, press release, https://www .nasa.gov/press-release/nasa-astronauts-launch-from-america-in-historic-test-flight -of-spacex-crew-dragon.

57   *public-private partnerships*: On December 20, 2019, I discussed this topic with the president of the CNES (the head of France's equivalent of NASA), who is a global leader in governmental space oversight, at his office in Paris.

60   *embryonic genomes*: "Statement from the Organizing Committee on Reported Human Embryo Genome Editing," The National Academies of Sciences, Engineering, and Medicine, November 26, 2018, https://www.nationalacademies.org /news/2018/11/statement-from-the-organizing-committee-on-reported-human -embryo-genome-editing; and David Cyranoski, "The CRISPR-Baby Scandal:

What's Next for Human Gene-Editing," *Nature*, February 26, 2019, https://www
.nature.com/articles/d41586-019-00673-1.

60   *Ro Khanna*: Author interview with Congressman Ro Khanna, April 19, 2019.

61   *"[tax] repatriation, encryption"*: Nancy Scola, "Silicon Valley Sends Ambassador to
Trump's Coal Country," *Politico*, March 26, 2017, https://www.politico.com/story
/2017/03/trump-election-silicon-valley-ambassador-appalachia-ro-khanna-236486.

61   *Centre for Data Ethics*: "About Us" at the Centre for Data Ethics and Innovation notes
"We aim to give the public a voice in how data-driven technology is governed, pro-
moting the trust that's crucial for the UK to make the most of AI and data-driven technology." Retrieved May 2, 2020, https://www.gov.uk/government/organisations
/centre-for-data-ethics-and-innovation/about.

61   *European Union High-Level Expert Group*: The "High-Level Expert Group on Artificial
Intelligence," which comprises experts from "academia, civil society, as well as industry" with an objective to "support the implementation of the European Strategy
on Artificial Intelligence," including "future-related policy development" and "ethical, legal and societal issues related to AI, including socio-economic challenges."
Retrieved April 30, 2020, https://ec.europa.eu/digital-single-market/en/high
-level-expert-group-artificial-intelligence.

62   Nature Biomedical Engineering *published an editorial*: "Momentous CRISPR-
Enabled Developments," *Nature Biomedical Engineering* 3 (2019): 79–80, https://doi
.org/10.1038/s41551-019-0361-z.

62   *Dr. Doudna once described*: Brenda Breslauer and Robert W. Spencer, "Life Changer,"
NBC News, June 11, 2017, https://www.nbcnews.com/megyn-kelly/video/life
-changer-965215299885.

Chapter Three – Contagion

65   *"political morality made vivid"*: Robert A. Caro, *The Years of Lyndon Johnson: Means of
Ascent* (New York: Vintage, 1991), Kindle, loc. 558.

65   *"new politics against the old"*: Ibid., loc. 536.

65   *"cowboy governor"*: Ibid., loc. 518.

65   *"utterly honest"*: Ibid., loc. 3740.

65   *ran a modest campaign*: Ibid., loc. 3872.

65   *"would do whatever was necessary"*: Ibid., loc. 8604.

65   *scientific polling*: Ibid., loc. 539.

66   *"Mr. Do-Nothinger" and "Calculatin' Coke"*: Ibid., locs. 4710 and 4014.

66   *"I know I am sweeping up votes"*: Ibid., loc. 4975. Johnson wasn't the first to "campaign
by helicopter," but he was the first to use it to significant effect, according to James
R. Chiles, "Campaign by Helicopter," *Air & Space Magazine*, April 2016, https://
www.airspacemag.com/history-of-flight/campaign-by-helicopter-180958436/.

66   *by more than twenty thousand votes*: Ibid., loc. 6735.

66   *nearly a million votes*: Ibid., loc. 6759.

66   *494,206 for Johnson*: Ibid., loc. 6896.

66   *"was sure he had won"*: Ibid., loc. 6915.

66   *"re-check" and "find"*: Ibid., loc. 6826.

66   *George Parr*: "Texas Politician Dead," *New York Times*, April 2, 1975, https://www
.nytimes.com/1975/04/02/archives/texas-politician-dead-ruled-suicide.html; Caro,
Means of Ascent, locs. 4207, 4213, and 6780; and "Historical Note" in "A Guide to
the George Parr Trial Papers," Briscoe Center for American History, the University
of Texas at Austin, https://legacy.lib.utexas.edu/taro/utcah/03463/03463-P.html.

66   *secure a presidential pardon*: Caro, *Means of Ascent*, loc. 4339.

66   *"just waiting for the telephone to ring"*: Ibid., loc. 6732.

67   *the totals all matched*: Ibid., loc. 6926.

67   *Luis Salas*: Ibid., loc. 4259.

67   *exactly 200 extra votes*: Ibid., loc. 6931.

67   *beat Stevenson by 87 votes*: Ibid., loc. 6935.

67   *reluctantly allowed them*: Ibid., loc. 7149.

67   *to observe . . . alphabetical order*: Ibid., loc. 7154.

67   *Eugenio Soliz*: Ibid., loc. 7169.

67   *Not one person*: Ibid., loc. 7175.

68   *a close 29-to-28 vote*: Ibid., loc. 7558.

68   *ordered Johnson's name*: Ibid., loc. 7663.

68   *create delays*: Ibid., Chapter 15.

68   *Fortas's plan was to*: Caro, *Means of Ascent,* locs. 8007 to 8049.

68   *administrative responsibility*: Ibid., loc. 8017; and Federal Judicial Center, which states that Justice Hugo Black was assigned to the Fifth Circuit from November 8, 1937, to September 17, 1971, at "Black, Hugo Lafayette" (https://www.fjc.gov/history /judges/black-hugo-lafayette), and "Circuit Allotments: Fifth Circuit," (https://www .fjc.gov/history/courts/circuit-allotments-fifth-circuit), both retrieved April 19, 2020.

68   *Justice Black agreed*: Ibid., loc. 8293.

68   *Box 13 went missing*: Pamela Colloff, "Go Ask Alice," *Texas Monthly*, January 20, 2013, https://www.texasmonthly.com/politics/go-ask-alice/.

68   *"Evidence that some of these votes"*: Caro, *Means of Ascent*, loc. 8313.

69   *sworn in as the thirty-sixth president*: Dates and details of Johnson's political biography retrieved January 14, 2020, from the LBJ Presidential Library, http://www .lbjlibrary.org/lyndon-baines-johnson/lbj-biography/.

69   *"His margin of victory"*: Caro, *Means of Ascent*, loc. 483. Note that part of Caro's quote is from the *U.S. News & World Report*'s April 6, 1964, cover story, "The Story of 87 Votes that Made History."

70   *Governor W. Lee "Pappy" O'Daniel*: David Martin Davies's five-part series "Pass the Politics Pappy," Texas Public Radio, May 2016, https://www.tpr.org/term/w-lee-pappy-odaniel; and Colloff, "Go Ask Alice."

70   *"huckster"*: Caro, *Means of Ascent*, loc. 483; Michael Ennis, "All Shook Up," *Texas Monthly*, October 2006, https://www.texasmonthly.com/politics/all-shook-up/; Joe Holley, "Trump Inauguration Shares Texas-Sized Parallels to Pappy O'Daniel," *Houston Chronicle*, January 6, 2017, https://www.houstonchronicle.com/news /columnists/native-texan/article/Trump-inauguration-shares-Texas-sized-parallels -10839944.php; Ben Fountain, "The Phony in American Politics: How Voters Turn into Suckers," *The Guardian*, February 13, 2016, https://www.theguardian .com/us-news/2016/feb/13/american-politics-election-voters-suckers; and David Martin Davies's Twitter post about his five-part series on Pappy O'Daniel, April 12, 2016, retrieved April 6, 2020, https://twitter.com/DavidMartinDavi/status /719869665741119488.

70   *Feeling confident*: Caro, *Means of Ascent*, loc. 594; and Davies, "Pass the Politics Pappy."

70   *almost 1,100 votes*: David Martin Davies, "Pass the Politics Pappy: Part 4, O'Daniel for Senate," Texas Public Radio, May 12, 2016, https://www.tpr.org/post/pass -politics-pappy-part-4-odaniel-senate.

70   *excused by his allies*: Caro, *Means of Ascent*, locs. 6842, 6851, 6967, and 9212.

71   *Even Johnson's helicopter pilot*: Ibid., loc. 5750.

71   *a lifetime appointment*: Fortas was not immune to contagion either. In 1969, under threat of impeachment, he resigned from the Supreme Court after it was revealed that he'd taken a $20,000-a-year retainer from Wall Street financier Louis Wolfson, a former client who was sent to prison for securities violations. Andrew Glass, "Abe Fortas Resigns from Supreme Court, May 15, 1969," *Politico*, May 14, 2017, https://

www.politico.com/story/2017/05/14/abe-fortas-resigns-from-supreme-court
-may-15-1969-238228; and "Abe Fortas," *Encyclopedia Britannica*, retrieved April 6,
2020, https://www.britannica.com/biography/Abe-Fortas.

71   *government authorities track them through photos*: Kashmir Hill, "The Secretive Company That Might End Privacy as We Know It," *New York Times*, January 18, 2020,
https://www.nytimes.com/2020/01/18/technology/clearview-privacy-facial
-recognition.html; and the September 16, 2019, report commissioned by the Centre
for Data Ethics and Innovation "into the use of algorithms in policing, and the
potential for bias," published by the Royal United Services Institute, https://www
.gov.uk/government/publications/report-commissioned-by-cdei-calls-for-measures
-to-address-bias-in-police-use-of-data-analytics.

72   *Malala Yousafzai*: Malala's story, Malala.org, https://malala.org/malalas-story; and
Mishal Husain, "Malala: The Girl Who Was Shot for Going to School," BBC News,
October 7, 2013, https://www.bbc.com/news/magazine-24379018.

72   *Malala blogged about her life*: An excerpt can be found at "Diary of a Pakistani Girl,"
BBC News, March 6, 2009, http://news.bbc.co.uk/2/hi/7928752.stm.

72   *Nobel Peace Prize*: She shared the 2014 prize with Indian activist Kailash Satyarthi,
"Malala Yousafzai," The Nobel Prize, retrieved January 14, 2020, https://www
.nobelprize.org/prizes/peace/2014/yousafzai/facts/.

75   *A study of perfectionism*: T. Curran and A. P. Hill, "Perfectionism Is Increasing Over
Time: A Meta-Analysis of Birth Cohort Differences from 1989 to 2016," *Psychological Bulletin* 145, no. 4 (2019): 410–29, https://www.apa.org/pubs/journals/releases
/bul-bul0000138.pdf; and T. Curran and A. P. Hill, "Perfectionism Is Increasing,
and That's Not Good News," *Harvard Business Review*, January 26, 2018, https://
hbr.org/2018/01/perfectionism-is-increasing-and-thats-not-good-news. The authors
examined data from 1989 to 2016 that reflected 41,641 college students' responses
to the "Multidimensional Perfectionism Scale," a scale developed by P. L. Hewitt,
G. L. Flett, W. Turnbull-Donovan, and S. F. Mikail, in "The Multidimensional Perfectionism Scale: Reliability, Validity, and Psychometric Properties in Psychiatric
Samples," *Psychological Assessment: A Journal of Consulting and Clinical Psychology* 3,
no. 3 (1991), 464–468, http://hewittlab.sites.olt.ubc.ca/files/2014/11/MPS2.pdf.

76   *vowed not to widen*: Caro, *Means of Ascent*, loc. 346.

76   *dengue fever when it was pneumonia*: Ibid., loc. 1492.

76   *did not die at the Alamo*: Ibid., loc. 380.

76   *America's role in Vietnam*: Ibid., loc. 354.

76   *"believed not only that he lied"*: Ibid., loc. 1538.

76   *"You knew it was a damned lie"*: Ibid., loc. 6069.

76   *The very phrase "credibility gap"*: Ibid., loc. 381; H. Gimlin, "Credibility Gaps and
the Presidency," *Editorial Research Reports 1968* (Vol. I), Washington, D.C.: CQ
Press, retrieved January 14, 2020, http://library.cqpress.com/cqresearcher/cqresrre
1968020700; and Josh Zeitz, "How Americans Lost Faith in Government," *Washington Post*, January 30, 2018, https://www.washingtonpost.com/news/made
-by-history/wp/2018/01/30/how-americans-lost-faith-in-government/.

77   *"ridiculed them"*: Caro, *Means of Ascent*, loc. 5360.

77   *"not only a genius for discerning"*: Ibid., loc. 415.

77   *obsession with blind loyalty*: Ibid., locs. 2877 and 2887.

77   *mistreatment of his wife, Lady Bird*: Ibid., locs. 1656–85, and 1718.

77   *ruling his subordinates through anger and fear*: Ibid., locs. 2877 and 5376.

78   *Luis Salas*: Associated Press, "Ex-Official Says He Stole 1948 Election for Johnson,"
New York Times, July 31, 1977, https://www.nytimes.com/1977/07/31/archives
/exofficial-says-he-stole-1948-election-for-johnson-most-involved.html.

78   *Great Society*: As noted in "LBJ: Biography," retrieved April 6, 2020, LBJ Presidential

Library: "President Johnson used his 1964 mandate to bring his vision for a Great Society to fruition in 1965, pushing forward a sweeping legislative agenda that would become one of the most ambitious and far-reaching in the nation's history," http://www.lbjlibrary.org/lyndon-baines-johnson/lbj-biography. See also "The Great Society" video, August 26, 2008, LBJ Presidential Library, retrieved April 6, 2020, http://www.lbjlibrary.org/press/the-great-society-video.

78   *Medicare, Medicaid*: "Medicare and Medicaid" audio, video, and signed documents, retrieved April 6, 2020, LBJ Presidential Library, http://www.lbjlibrary.org/press/media-kit/medicare-and-medicaid.

78   *Voting Rights Act*: See text of the Voting Rights Act signed by President Johnson on April 6, 1965, LBJ Library, http://www.lbjlibrary.org/assets/uploads/general/Documents/VotingRightsActof1965.pdf; and "Special Message to the Congress: On the Voting Rights Act," archive video, https://www.youtube.com/watch?v=HvPCKyABeIg; and a photo of President Johnson signing the act into law, Digital Public Library of America, https://dp.la/primary-source-sets/voting-rights-act-of-1965/sources/1389.

78   *three hundred conservation measures into law*: National Park Service, "Lyndon B. Johnson and the Environment," retrieved March 8, 2020, https://www.nps.gov/lyjo/planyourvisit/upload/EnvironmentCS2.pdf.

78   *Clean Air Act of 1963*: Ibid.; text of the act at "Public Law 88-206—December 17, 1963," Govinfo.gov, https://www.govinfo.gov/content/pkg/STATUTE-77/pdf/STATUTE-77-Pg392.pdf#page=1; and Johnson's "Remarks Upon Signing the Clean Air Act," The American Presidency Project, University of California, Santa Barbara, https://www.presidency.ucsb.edu/documents/remarks-upon-signing-the-clean-air-act; and "Evolution of the Clean Air Act," U.S. Environmental Protection Agency, which states: "The Clean Air Act of 1963 was the first federal legislation regarding air pollution *control*. It established a federal program within the U.S. Public Health Service and authorized research into techniques for monitoring and controlling air pollution," https://www.epa.gov/clean-air-act-overview/evolution-clean-air-act.

78   *Water Quality Act of 1965*: National Park Service, "Lyndon B. Johnson and the Environment"; text of the act at "Public Law 89-234—Oct. 2, 1965," Govinfo.gov, https://www.govinfo.gov/content/pkg/STATUTE-79/pdf/STATUTE-79-Pg903.pdf; and Johnson's remarks upon signing the act, "On This Day in History: October 2nd, 1965," LBJ Presidential Library, http://www.lbjlibrary.net/collections/on-this-day-in-history/october.html; and "EPA History: Water—The Challenge of the Environment: A Primer on EPA's Statutory Authority," U.S. Environmental Protection Agency, which notes that the act "provided for the setting of water quality standards which are State and Federally enforceable; it became the basis for interstate water quality standards," https://archive.epa.gov/epa/aboutepa/epa-history-water-challenge-environment-primer-epas-statutory-authority.html.

79   *Endangered Species Preservation Act of 1966*: National Park Service, Ibid.; text of the act at "Public Law 89-669—Oct. 15, 1966," Govinfo.gov, https://uscode.house.gov/statutes/pl/89/669.pdf; and Johnson's "Remarks at the Signing Ceremony for Seven Conservation Bills," The American Presidency Project, University of California, Santa Barbara, https://www.presidency.ucsb.edu/documents/remarks-the-signing-ceremony-for-seven-conservation-bills; and "Endangered Species Act (ESA) Milestones | Pre 1973 ESA," U.S. Fish & Wildlife Service, which notes that "Congress passed the Endangered Species Preservation Act of 1966, the first piece of comprehensive endangered species legislation. It was under the 1966 Endangered Species Preservation Act that the very first list of threatened and endangered species was compiled," https://www.fws.gov/endangered/ESA40/preESA.html.

80 *Percocet is a brand name*: FDA drugs data, retrieved March 8, 2020, https://www
.accessdata.fda.gov/drugsatfda_docs/label/2006/040330s015,040341s013,040434
s003lbl.pdf.

80 *According to the National Institute of Dental and Craniofacial Research*: "Opioids &
Dental Pain," retrieved March 8, 2020, https://www.nidcr.nih.gov/health-info
/opioids/more-info; and "Managing Pain: Moving Beyond Opioids," NIH *News in
Health*, retrieved March 18, 2020, https://newsinhealth.nih.gov/2018/10/managing
-pain.

80 *two million people*: "What Is the U.S. Opioid Epidemic?," U.S. Department of Health
and Human Services, retrieved March 18, 2020, https://www.hhs.gov/opioids
/about-the-epidemic/index.html.

80 *3.5 million people may be first exposed*: R. C. Denisco, G. A. Kenna, M. G. O'Neil, et
al., "Prevention of Prescription Opioid Abuse: The Role of the Dentist," *Journal of
the American Dental Association* 142, no. 7 (July 2011): 800–10, p. 803, https://jada
.ada.org/article/S0002-8177(14)62264-9/fulltext.

80 *approximately 19,500 college students*: The study surveyed 19,539 students at twenty-
six U.S. institutions in the spring of 2018. According to the authors: "Eighteen
four-year public institutions participated in the study (69.2 percent of participating
institutions) and seven four-year private institutions participated (26.9 percent of
participating institutions). One two-year public institution participated in the study
(3.8 percent of participating institutions). The survey was administered to 113,999
students; 19,539 responded for a response rate of 17.1 percent." The College Prescription Drug Study was a collaboration between The Ohio State University's
Center for the Study of Student Life, Student Life Student Wellness Center, and
the College of Pharmacy. Erica L. Phillips and Anne E. McDaniel, "College Prescription Drug Study: Key Findings," 2018, Center for the Study of Student Life,
The Ohio State University, https://www.campusdrugprevention.gov/sites/default
/files/2018%20College%20Prescription%20Drug%20Study.pdf.

80 *9.1 percent of students*: Ibid., see "Highlights," p. 1. Another 2018 study from the
University of Michigan reviewed data from the 2009–2014 National Surveys on
Drug Use and Health (a survey of nearly 107,000 adults, 18–25 years old), to find
a similar result ("Results," "Table 1"): 8.6 percent of college students reported mis-
using prescription opioids in the past year. They also found that prescription drug
misuse was most prevalent among respondents with no college (11.9 percent). S. E.
McCabe, C. J. Teter, C. J. Boyd, T. E. Wilens, & T. S. Schepis, "Sources of Prescription Medication Misuse Among Young Adults in the United States: The Role of
Educational Status," *The Journal of Clinical Psychiatry* 79, no. 2 (March–April 2018),
https://www.ncbi.nlm.nih.gov/pmc/articles/PMC5932281/.

80 *when no longer medically needed*: Phillips and McDaniel, "College Prescription Drug
Study: Key Findings."

80 *prescribe such a powerful*: As Serena put it when I asked if the dentist or anyone spoke
to her about the addictive risk: "Not that I recall. I was also in distress and numbed
up, but I'm pretty sure no." Text message to author from Serena, March 29, 2020.

80 *a surgical assistant explained*: The mother also realized that under the privacy rules of
the Health Insurance Portability and Accountability Act of 1996, the dentist and
his staff could not share detailed information about her daughter's medical care
without her daughter's consent.

81 *experience adverse reactions*: "Side Effects" in "Prescription Opioids," Centers for
Disease Control and Prevention, retrieved April 6, 2020, https://www.cdc.gov
/drugoverdose/opioids/prescribed.html.

81 *pill mills*: Pia Malbran, "What's a Pill Mill?," CBS News, May 31, 2007, https://
www.cbsnews.com/news/whats-a-pill-mill/.

82 *"public health emergency"*: Eric D. Hargan, Acting Secretary of Health and Human Services, signed declaration at https://www.cms.gov/About-CMS/Agency-Information/Emergency/Downloads/October_26_2017_Public_Health_Declaration_for_Opioids_Crisis.pdf; and Centers for Medicare and Medicaid Services, "Ongoing Emergencies and Disasters," retrieved January 14, 2020, https://www.cms.gov/About-CMS/Agency-Information/Emergency/EPRO/Current-Emergencies/Ongoing-emergencies.

82 *rising rates of overdose from heroin and fentanyl*: Centers for Disease Control and Prevention, "Opioid Data Analysis and Resources," retrieved March 18, 2020, https://www.cdc.gov/drugoverdose/data/analysis.html.

82 *hepatitis C*: In 2010, OxyContin was reformulated to be "more difficult to crush" and inject. Some users switched to injecting heroin instead, causing an increase in hepatitis C infections. D. Powell, A. Alpert, and R. L. Pacula, "A Transitioning Epidemic: How the Opioid Crisis Is Driving the Rise in Hepatitis C," *Health Affairs* 38, no. 2 (February 2019): 287–294, https://www.healthaffairs.org/doi/abs/10.1377/hlthaff.2018.05232; and Lev Facher, "Study Shows Purdue's Switch to 'Abuse-Deterrent' OxyContin Helped Drive a Spike in Hepatitis C Infections," *STAT*, February 4, 2019, https://www.statnews.com/2019/02/04/purdue-abuse-deterrent-oxycontin-hepatitis-c-infections/.

82 *pill mill operations*: Malbran, "What's a Pill Mill?"

84 *statements by the American Dental Association*: See American Dental Association policy statement on the use of opioids in the treatment of dental pain, 2016, retrieved March 24, 2020, https://www.ada.org/en/advocacy/current-policies/substance-use-disorders; and a review of the literature from R. Dana, A. Azarpazhooh, N. Laghapour, K. J. Suda, and C. Okunseri, "Role of Dentists in Prescribing Opioid Analgesics and Antibiotics: An Overview," *Dental Clinics of North America* 62, no. 2 (April 2018): 279–94, doi:10.1016/j.cden.2017.11.007, https://www.ncbi.nlm.nih.gov/pubmed/29478458.

84 *a commentary in the* Journal: M. J. Somerman and N. D. Volkow, "The Role of the Oral Health Community in Addressing the Opioid Overdose Epidemic," *Journal of the American Dental Association* 149, no. 8 (2018): 663–65, https://jada.ada.org/article/S0002-8177%2818%2930419-7/fulltext.

84 *15.5 percent . . . 6.4 percent*: N. Gupta, M. Vujicic, and A. Blatz, "Opioid Prescribing Practices from 2010 Through 2015 Among Dentists in the United States," *Journal of the American Dental Association* 149, no. 4, (April 2018) 237–45.e6, p. 237, https://www.ncbi.nlm.nih.gov/pubmed/29599017; and Somerman and Volkow, "The Role of the Oral Health Community in Addressing the Opioid Overdose Epidemic," p. 663.

85 *Declaration of Independence*: The document text and history is available at the National Archives, "America's Founding Documents," https://www.archives.gov/founding-docs/declaration-transcript.

90 *Emma Dent Coad*: For 2019, see "Declaration of Results of Poll: Election of a Member of Parliament for Kensington on Thursday 12 December 2019," The Royal Borough of Kensington and Chelsea, which notes that Emma Dent Coad had 16,618 votes and her challenger Felicity Christiana Buchanan had 16,768 votes, https://www.rbkc.gov.uk/council-councillors-and-democracy/local-democracy-and-elections/uk-parliamentary-general-election-0; for 2017, see "Declaration of Results of Poll: Election of a Member of Parliament for Kensington on Thursday 8 June 2017," which states that Coad had 16,333 votes and Victoria Lorne Peta Borwick had 16,313 votes, https://www.rbkc.gov.uk/council-councillors-and-democracy/local-democracy-and-elections/uk-parliamentary-general-election-1.

90 *David Adkins*: Adkins has widely been reported to have won by two votes, but the official report from the State of New Mexico in "Candidate Summary of General Election Held on November 8, 2016" indicates that Adkins's final tally was 6,976

votes and Ronnie Martinez had 6,967 votes. File is "2016 General Candidate Summary Results Report," at "Past Election Results 2016," New Mexico Secretary of State, retrieved April 9, 2020, https://www.sos.state.nm.us/voting-and-elections/election-results/past-election-results-2016/.

90 *George W. Bush*: "2000 Presidential General Election Results" are at "Official General Election Results by State," Federal Election Commission, retrieved April 6, 2020, https://www.fec.gov/introduction-campaign-finance/election-and-voting-information/federal-elections-2000/president2000/; and pp. 98–158, "United States Reports," Vol. 531, Oct. 2, 2000 through March 1, 2001 term, The Supreme Court, https://www.supremecourt.gov/opinions/boundvolumes/531bv.pdf; and "George W. Bush and Richard Cheney, Petitioners v. Albert Gore, Jr., et al.," No. 00-949, Supreme Court of the United States, https://www.supremecourt.gov/Search.aspx?FileName=/docketfiles/00-949.htm; and "U.S. Reports: Bush v. Gore, 531 U.S. 98 (2000)," Library of Congress, https://www.loc.gov/item/usrep531098/; and media accounts, for example: Ron Elving, "The Florida Recount of 2000: A Nightmare That Goes on Haunting," NPR, November 12, 2018, https://www.npr.org/2018/11/12/666812854/the-florida-recount-of-2000-a-nightmare-that-goes-on-haunting.

90 *Bernie Sanders*: "Meet Bernie," Bernie Sanders, https://berniesanders.com/about/ and "Burlington, Vermont," Cornell University Library, https://ecommons.cornell.edu/handle/1813/40512; and "Mayor, A Socialist, Is Encountering Hostility in Vermont City," Associated Press via *New York Times*, September 20, 1981, https://www.nytimes.com/1981/09/20/us/mayor-a-socialist-is-encountering-hostility-in-vermont-city.html; and Russell Banks, "Bernie Sanders, the Socialist Mayor," *The Atlantic*, October 5, 2015, https://www.theatlantic.com/politics/archive/2015/10/bernie-sanders-mayor/407413/.

90 *voter turnout in the United States*: Jordan Misra, "Voter Turnout Rates Among All Voting Age and Major Racial and Ethnic Groups Were Higher Than in 2014," United States Census Bureau, April 23, 2019, https://www.census.gov/library/stories/2019/04/behind-2018-united-states-midterm-election-turnout.html.

90 *turnout in Sweden*: "Analysis of Voter Turnout in the 2018 General Elections," Statistics Sweden, retrieved March 8, 2020, https://www.scb.se/en/finding-statistics/statistics-by-subject-area/democracy/general-elections/general-elections-participation-survey/pong/statistical-news/general-elections-electoral-participation-survey-2018/.

90 *came out in fewer numbers*: 90 percent of citizens 65 years or older voted on the Brexit referendum compared to 65 percent of 25 to 39-year-olds, and 64 percent of 18 to 24-year-olds, according to exit polls "conducted since the referendum by Opinium, and analysed by Michael Bruter, professor of political science and European politics at the LSE, and his colleague, Dr Sarah Harrison," according to Toby Helm, political editor of *The Guardian*, in "EU Referendum: Youth Turnout Almost Twice as High as First Thought," July 10, 2016, https://www.theguardian.com/politics/2016/jul/09/young-people-referendum-turnout-brexit-twice-as-high. See also, Sascha O. Becker, Thiemo Fetzer, and Dennis Novy, "Who Voted for Brexit? A Comprehensive District-Level Analysis," *Economic Policy* 32, no. 92 (October 2017): 601–50, p. 638, https://doi.org/10.1093/epolic/eix012.

91 *"Study a particular election . . . our lives."*: Caro, *Means of Ascent*, loc. 508.

Chapter Four – Crumbling Pillars

93 *millions of homes worldwide*: 146.9 million smart speaker units shipped globally in 2019, according to research firm Strategy Analytics. Ilker Koksal, "The Sales of

Smart Speakers Skyrocketed," *Forbes*, March 10, 2020, https://www.forbes.com /sites/ilkerkoksal/2020/03/10/the-sales-of-smart-speakers-skyrocketed/#1b0c d07538ae; Bret Kinsella, "Amazon Again Topped Q4 Global Smart Speaker Sales Followed by Google and Baidu. According to Strategy Analytics, Smart Speaker Shipments Set New Record," *Voicebot.ai*, February 17, 2020, https://voicebot. ai/2020/02/17/amazon-again-topped-q4-global-smart-speaker-sales-followed -by-google-and-baidu-according-to-strategy-analytics-smart-speaker-shipments-set -new-record/; and Sarah Perez, "Smart Speaker Sales Reached New Record of 146.9 Million in 2019, Up 70% from 2018," *TechCrunch*, February 17, 2020, https:// techcrunch.com/2020/02/17/smart-speaker-sales-reached-new-record-of-146-9m -in-2019-up-70-from-2018/.

93   *When Alexa first launched in 2014*: Amazon Alexa launched November 6, 2014, per the company. Tom Taylor, "Alexa, Happy Birthday," *The Amazon Blog*, November 5, 2019, https://blog.aboutamazon.com/devices/alexa-happy-birthday; and Ava Mutchler, "A Timeline of Voice Assistant and Smart Speaker Technology from 1961 to Today," *Voicebot.ai*, March 28, 2018, https://voicebot.ai/2018/03/28/timeline -voice-assistant-smart-speaker-technology-1961-today/.

94   *double murder case*: Anthony Cuthbertson, "Amazon Ordered to Give Alexa Evidence in Double Murder Case," *The Independent*, November 14, 2018, https://www .independent.co.uk/life-style/gadgets-and-tech/news/amazon-echo-alexa-evidence -murder-case-a8633551.html.

94   *"wake words" . . . "a button)"*: Alexa and Alexa Device FAQs, Amazon, retrieved March 22, 2020, https://www.amazon.com/gp/help/customer/display.html?node Id=201602230.

98   *Person of the Year*: *Time* cover, December 25, 2006, http://content.time.com/time /covers/0,16641,20061225,00.html.

98   *26 million people*: Antonio Regalado, "More than 26 Million People Have Taken an At-Home Ancestry Test," *MIT Technology Review*, February 11, 2019, www .technologyreview.com/s/612880/more-than-26-million-people-have-taken-an-at -home-ancestry-test/.

98   *100 million people*: Ibid.

98   *23andMe launched*: "23andMe Launches Web-Based Service Empowering Individuals to Access and Understand Their Own Genetic Information," 23andMe press release, November 19, 2007, Wayback Machine, retrieved March 22, 2020, http://web.archive.org/web/20081114093016/https://www.23andme.com/about /press/20071119/.

98   *23andMe*: 23andMe reviewed and provided feedback (April 24, 2020, email to author) for relevant passages in this chapter.

98   *For $999*: The company's website in 2007 did not list prices or disease-testing capabilities; however, reporters from reputable media outlets were invited to be among the early testers and they wrote about the cost, diseases that could be tested for, and their experiences. Thomas Goetz, "23AndMe Will Decode Your DNA for $1,000. Welcome to the Age of Genomics," *Wired*, November 17, 2007, https:// www.wired.com/2007/11/ff-genomics/; Amy Harmon, "My Genome, Myself: Seeking Clues in DNA," *New York Times*, November 17, 2007, https://www .nytimes.com/2007/11/17/us/17dna.html; and "Google-Funded 23andMe Starts, Offers $999 DNA Test," Reuters, November 19, 2007, https://www.reuters.com /article/us-google-23andme/google-funded-23andme-starts-offers-999-dna-test -idUSN1948129620071119.

98   *$399 for a test*: At the time, in 2008, 23andMe offered twenty-three "Clinical Reports" that provided "information about conditions and traits for which there are genetic associations supported by multiple, large, peer-reviewed studies. Those associations

must also have a substantial influence on a person's chances of developing the disease or having the trait. Because these associations are widely regarded as reliable, we use them to develop quantitative estimates and definitive explanations of what they mean for you," as well as sixty-eight "Research Reports" for information from research "that has not yet gained enough scientific consensus to be included in our Clinical Reports. This research is generally based on high-quality but limited scientific evidence. Because these results have not yet been demonstrated through large, replicated studies, we do not perform complete quantitative analyses of their effects. We do, however, explain how they may—if confirmed—affect your odds of having or developing a trait, condition or disease. Research Reports also includes scientifically accepted, established research that does not have a dramatic influence on a person's risk for a disease." "Health and Traits: Complete List," 23andMe, November 14, 2008, Wayback Machine, retrieved March 22, 2020, http://web.archive.org /web/20081114035155/https://www.23andme.com/health/all/.

98   *hosted a party*: Allen Salkin, "When in Doubt, Spit It Out," *New York Times*, September 12, 2008, www.nytimes.com/2008/09/14/fashion/14spit.html.

98   *Best Invention of 2008*: Anita Hamilton, "Invention of the Year: The Retail DNA Test," *Time*, October 29, 2018, http://content.time.com/time/specials/packages /article/0,28804,1852747_1854493_1854113,00.html.

99   Good Housekeeping: Rachel Bowie, "9 Tips for Researching Your Family Tree," 2013, Wayback Machine, retrieved March 20, 2020, http://web.archive.org /web/20131003144849/http://www.goodhousekeeping.com/family/travel/family -genealogy.

99   *spot on Oprah's*: "Oprah's Favorite Things 2017," Oprah.com, retrieved March 22, 2020, http://www.oprah.com/gift/oprahs-favorite-things-2017-full-list-dna-test-an cestry-personal-genetic-service?editors_pick_id=71355.

99   *earliest core values*: In addition to the two values noted, 23andMe also listed the following values on its website in 2008: "We believe that people's similarities are just as important as their differences"; "We believe that the value of your genetic information will increase over time"; "We encourage dialogue on the ethical, social and policy implications of personalized genetic services"; and "We believe in giving everyone the opportunity to contribute to improving human understanding." 23andMe, "Core Values," 2008, Wayback Machine, retrieved March 22, 2020, http://web.archive .org/web/20081114091628/https://www.23andme.com/about/values/.

99   People *magazine*: Jessica Leigh Mattern, "You Can Still Snag a 23andMe DNA Kit for 50% Off—but You'll Have to Hurry," People.com, November 29, 2019, https:// people.com/lifestyle/23andme-black-friday-sale-2019/.

99   *Black Friday*: Ibid.; and "Best 23andMe & AncestryDNA Black Friday & Cyber Monday Deals (2019): Top DNA Testing Kit Deals Rated by Retail Egg," *Business Wire*, November 28, 2019, https://www.businesswire.com/news/home/2019 1128005155/en/23andMe-AncestryDNA-Black-Friday-Cyber-Monday-Deals.

99   *Cyber Monday*: Amir Ismael, "Several Popular DNA Kits Are Up to 50% Off on Cyber Monday, Including 23andMe and AncestryDNA," *Business Insider*, November 30, 2019, https://www.businessinsider.com/dna-kit-deals-black-friday-cyber -monday.

99   *$2.5 billion*: CNBC staff, "Disruptor 50: 46. 23andMe," May 15, 2019, https://www .cnbc.com/2019/05/14/23andme-2019-disruptor-50.html; and Biz Carson and Kathleen Chaykowski, "Live Long and Prosper," *Forbes*, June 6, 2019, https://www .forbes.com/sites/bizcarson/2019/06/06/23andme-dna-test-anne-wojcicki-prevention -plans-drug-development/#25419b99494d.

99   *tremendous benefits*: National Institutes of Health, U.S. National Library of Medicine, "What Are the Benefits and Risks of Direct-to-Consumer Genetic

Testing?," retrieved Jan. 25, 2020, https://ghr.nlm.nih.gov/primer/dtcgenetictesting/dtcrisksbenefits.

99   *"be more proactive"*: Ibid.

100   *"There are a lot of misperceptions*: Claire Cain Miller, "For $99, Eliminating the Mystery of Pandora's Genetic Box," *New York Times*, November 11, 2013, https://dealbook.nytimes.com/2013/11/11/for-99-eliminating-the-mystery-of-pandoras-genetic-box/.

101   *"Warning Letter" from the FDA*: The FDA believed that 23andMe was marketing its kit as a diagnostic device that had not been analytically or clinically validated—and that inaccurate results could cause a user to take drastic medical measures, like having unnecessary surgeries or changing medication instructions without consulting their physicians. The FDA's November 22, 2013, warning letter has been archived and is available on Wayback Machine, retrieved March 21, 2020, https://wayback.archive-it.org/7993/20190423040825/https://www.fda.gov/ICECI/EnforcementActions/WarningLetters/2013/ucm376296.htm. See also 23andMe's statement about its interactions with the FDA, retrieved March 21, 2020, https://customercare.23andme.com/hc/en-us/articles/211831908-23andMe-and-the-FDA; and media accounts, for example: Erika Check Hayden, "The Rise and Fall and Rise Again of 23andMe," *Nature*, October 11, 2017, https://www.nature.com/news/the-rise-and-fall-and-rise-again-of-23andme-1.22801; and David Dobbs, "The F.D.A. Vs. Personal Genetic Testing," *The New Yorker*, November 27, 2013, https://www.newyorker.com/tech/annals-of-technology/the-f-d-a-vs-personal-genetic-testing. Further, many in the medical community had concerns about the lack of regulatory oversight on direct-to-consumer testing companies. Linda McCabe and Edward McCabe, "Direct-to-Consumer Genetic Testing: Access and Marketing," *Genetics in Medicine* 6 (January 2004): 58–59, https://doi.org/10.1097/01.GIM.0000105753.01536.BE. Until the tests were clinically validated, the information people received could be "misleading—or just plain wrong," as G. J. Annas and S. Elias pointed out in a March 13, 2014, op-ed in the *New England Journal of Medicine*, "23andMe and the FDA," March 13, 2014, https://www.nejm.org/doi/full/10.1056/NEJMp1316367. See also M. A. Allyse, D. H. Robinson, M. J. Ferber, and R. R. Sharp, "Direct-to-Consumer Testing 2.0: Emerging Models of Direct-to-Consumer Genetic Testing," *Mayo Clinic Proceedings*, 93, no. 1 (January 2018): 113–120, https://www.ncbi.nlm.nih.gov/pubmed/29304915.

102   *thirty-six different*: Via "Carrier Status reports," and "Reports include," and click on "See all reports" at 23andMe, November 2015, Wayback Machine, retrieved April 9, 2020, http://web.archive.org/web/20151109185241/https://www.23andme.com/service/#carrierstatus. And media accounts, for example: Joshua Barajas, "23andMe Returns with Modified, FDA-Approved Genetic Tests," *PBS NewsHour*, October 21, 2015, https://www.pbs.org/newshour/health/23andme-returns-modified-fda-approved-genetic-tests; Ron Winslow, "23andMe Relaunches Direct-to-Consumer Gene Test," *Wall Street Journal*, October 21, 2015, https://www.wsj.com/articles/23andme-relaunches-direct-to-consumer-gene-test-1445400097; and Erika Check Hayden, "Out of Regulatory Limbo, 23andMe Resumes Some Health Tests and Hopes to Offer More," *Nature*, October 27, 2015, https://www.nature.com/news/out-of-regulatory-limbo-23andme-resumes-some-health-tests-and-hopes-to-offer-more-1.18641.

102   *"FDA requirements"*: See 23andMe timeline of FDA approval, retrieved March 21, 2020, https://customercare.23andme.com/hc/en-us/articles/211831908-23andMe-and-the-FDA.

102   *to be more transparent*: In addition to adding information about the Science, Privacy, Research Participation, FAQs, and external resources for guidance on results, the

original 23andMe terms of service were also updated and expanded. See 23andMe terms of service in 2008, a year after launch, Wayback Machine, retrieved March 22, 2020, http://web.archive.org/web/20081114033235/https://www.23andme.com /about/tos/, compared to September 30, 2019, updated version, retrieved March 22, 2020, https://www.23andme.com/about/tos/.

102 *"someone knowledgeable"*: "Navigating and Understanding Health Predisposition Reports," 23andMe, retrieved March 21, 2020, https://customercare.23andme.com /hc/en-us/articles/115006037188-Navigating-and-Understanding-Health-Predisposition-Reports.

102 *"Take action to stay healthy"*: 23andMe homepage, retrieved March 22, 2020, https:// www.23andme.com.

102 *"start discovering what your DNA"*: "How It Works: 3. Discover," 23andMe, retrieved March 22, 2020, https://www.23andme.com/howitworks/.

102 *"Health Happens Now"*: 23andMe homepage, retrieved March 22, 2020, https://www .23andme.com.

103 *"Know your genes"*: Ibid.

103 *"23andMe Services"*: 23andMe "Terms of Service: "5. Risks and Considerations Regarding 23andMe Services," retrieved March 22, 2020, https://www.23andme .com/about/tos/.

103 *"type 2 diabetes"* . . . *"Carrier Status"*: 23andMe homepage, retrieved March 22, 2020, https://www.23andme.com.

103 *"You may discover things*: 23andMe "Terms of Service: 5. Risks and Considerations Regarding 23andMe Services," retrieved March 22, 2020, https://www.23andme .com/about/tos/.

103 *"Future scientific research*: Ibid.

103 *30 percent of a particular ethnicity*: As 23andMe states in "Terms of Service: 5. Risks and Considerations Regarding 23andMe Services," "Genetic research is not comprehensive. While we measure many hundreds of thousands of data points from your DNA, only a small percentage of them are known to be related to human traits or health conditions. The research community is rapidly learning more about genetics, and an important mission of 23andMe is to conduct and contribute to this research. In addition, many ethnic groups are not included in genetic studies. Because interpretations provided in our Service rely on these published studies, some interpretations may not apply to you. Future scientific research may change the interpretation of your DNA. In the future, the scientific community may show previous research to be incomplete or inaccurate." See an example of this in Damian Garde, "'What's My Real Identity?': As DNA Ancestry Sites Gather More Data, the Answer for Consumers Often Changes," *STAT*, May 22, 2019, who writes about his experience with shifting data, https://www.statnews.com/2019/05/22/dna -ancestry-sites-gather-data-shifting-answers-consumers/.

104 *implications for insurance*: "What Are the Benefits and Risks of Direct-to-Consumer Genetic Testing?" National Institutes of Health, U.S. National Library of Medicine, retrieved January 25, 2020, https://ghr.nlm.nih.gov/primer/dtcgenetictesting /dtcrisksbenefits.

104 *Lisa*: Lisa's story and the police investigation was described in detail by law enforcement officials during an hour-long January 2017 press conference in Allenstown, New Hampshire, by the Allenstown Attorney General's Office, and available via "Raw Video: Police Say Same Man Killed Missing Woman, Allenstown Victims, California Woman," WMUR.com, https://www.wmur.com/article/raw-video-police -say-same-man-killed-missing-woman-allenstown-victims-california-woman /8642678. See also the investigative reporting by Shelley Murphy, "Finding Lisa: A Story of Murders, Mysteries, Loss, and, Incredibly, New Life," *Boston Globe*, May

13, 2017, www.bostonglobe.com/metro/2017/05/13/finding-lisa-story-murders -mysteries-loss-and-incredibly-new-life/vCCxbYYUD63kjIoIMJQiWM/story .html; and Jonathan Corum and Heather Murphy, "How Genetic Sleuthing Helped a Kidnapped Girl Recover Her Identity," *New York Times*, October 15, 2018, www .nytimes.com/interactive/2018/10/15/science/gedmatch-genetic-sleuthing.html.

105 *convicted of murder*: Per Allenstown Attorney General's Office press conference, "Raw Video: Police Say Same Man Killed Missing Woman, Allenstown Victims, California Woman."

105 *died in prison*: Law enforcement say that he died of natural causes in prison. He was transient and used several aliases, and they could not determine his birth name or date. Ibid.

105 *Dr. Barbara Rae-Venter*. "About the Lisa Project," Barbara Rae-Venter: A Genetic Genealogy Consultant, retrieved March 22, 2020, https://lisaproject.genealogy consult.com/about-the-lisa-project/; "Identifying the Golden State Killer: An Inter-view with Paul Holes and Barbara Rae-Venter," International Symposium on Human Identification, video, December 12, 2019, https://www.ishinews.com/identifying -the-golden-state-killer-an-interview-with-paul-holes-and-barbara-rae-venter/; and Heather Murphy, "She Helped Crack the Golden State Killer Case. Here's What She's Going to Do Next," *New York Times*, August 29, 2018, https://www.nytimes .com/2018/08/29/science/barbara-rae-venter-gsk.html.

105 *the more DNA you share*: "Average Percent DNA Shared Between Relatives," 23andMe, retrieved March 22, 2020, https://customercare.23andme.com/hc /en-us/articles/212170668-Average-percent-DNA-shared-between-relatives.

105 *second and third cousins*: Jonathan Corum and Heather Murphy provide excellent primary sources, including an email from a detective, GEDmatch screenshots, and more material in their "How Genetic Sleuthing Helped a Kidnapped Girl Recover Her Identity," *New York Times*, October 15, 2018, www.nytimes.com/interactive /2018/10/15/science/gedmatch-genetic-sleuthing.html.

105 *found Lisa's maternal grandfather*. Shelley Murphy, "Finding Lisa: A Story of Mur-ders, Mysteries, Loss, and, Incredibly, New Life,"; and Corum and Murphy, "How Genetic Sleuthing Helped a Kidnapped Girl Recover Her Identity."

105 *likely killed*: "We believed we identified their killer," the senior assistant attorney gen-eral of Allenstown, New Hampshire, said in an hour-long press conference, "Raw Video: Police Say Same Man Killed Missing Woman, Allenstown Victims, Califor-nia Woman."

105 *cold case investigator*. Paul Holes, a retired investigator for the Contra Costa County District Attorney's Office, and Dr. Rae-Venter explain how they first set out to solve the Golden State Killer case in "Identifying the Golden State Killer: An Interview with Paul Holes and Barbara Rae-Venter."

105 *genetic path leading*: According to Paul Holes and Dr. Rae-Venter, it took just four and a half months to find their suspect. Ibid.

106 *DeAngelo's DNA*: Murphy, "She Helped Crack the Golden State Killer Case. Here's What She's Going to Do Next."

106 *arrested in 2018*: See Michael Levenson and Heather Murphy, "Golden State Killer Suspect Offers to Plead Guilty," *New York Times*, March 4, 2020, https://www .nytimes.com/2020/03/04/us/golden-state-killer-trial.html; and Cassie Dickman, "Joseph James DeAngelo pleads guilty to 13 murders tagged to California's 'Golden State Killer'," USA Today, June 29, 2020, https://www.usatoday.com/story/news /nation/2020/06/29/alleged-golden-state-killer-joseph-deangelo-set-plead-guilty -monday-sacramento/3279438001/.

106 *investigative genetic genealogy*: John Butler, "National DNA Day and the Birth of Investigative Genetic Genealogy," National Institute of Standards and

Technology, April 25, 2019, https://www.nist.gov/blogs/taking-measure/national -dna-day-and-birth-investigative-genetic-genealogy; "Innovative Forensic DNA LLC Launches as an Investigative Genetic Genealogy Provider," PRNewswire, December 3, 2019, https://www.prnewswire.com/news-releases/innovative-forensic -dna-llc-launches-as-an-investigative-genetic-genealogy-provider-300966937.html; and Sarah Zhang, "The Messy Consequences of the Golden State Killer Case," *The Atlantic*, October 1, 2019, https://www.theatlantic.com/science/archive/2019/10 /genetic-genealogy-dna-database-criminal-investigations/599005/.

106   *more than forty*: Zhang, "The Messy Consequences of the Golden State Killer Case."

106   *Canadian couple*: *Seattle Times* staff, "SeaTac Man Convicted of 1987 Murders of Canadian Couple After DNA Evidence Linked Him to Case," *Seattle Times*, June 28, 2019, https://www.seattletimes.com/seattle-news/crime/seatac-man-convicted-of -1987-murders-of-canadian-couple-after-dna-evidence-linked-him-to-case/.

106   *Idaho man*: Mia Armstrong, "In an Apparent First, Genetic Genealogy Aids a Wrongful Conviction Case," The Marshall Project, July 16, 2019, https://www. themarshallproject.org/2019/07/16/in-an-apparent-first-genetic-genealogy -aids-a-wrongful-conviction-case; and Nate Eaton, "Christopher Tapp Officially Exonerated of Rape and Murder Charges," video, *Idaho Statesman*, July 17, 2019, https://www.idahostatesman.com/news/local/crime/article232795082.html.

106   *warrant workaround in GEDmatch*: Heather Murphy, "How an Unlikely Family History Website Transformed Cold Case Investigations," *New York Times*, October 15, 2018, https://www.nytimes.com/2018/10/15/science/gedmatch-genealogy-cold -cases.html.

106   *retired Florida grandfather*: Interview with the founder at "This Florida Grandfather's Genealogy Hobby Helped Catch the Golden State Killer," 10NewsWTSP, Tampa Bay, Florida, April 25, 2019, video, https://www.youtube.com/watch?v=yxEU6RpA4sQ.

106   *more than one million people*: The founder has said at the time that GEDmatch had "about a million users." (Sarah Zhang, "How a Tiny Website Became the Police's Go-To Genealogy Database," *The Atlantic*, June 1, 2018, https://www.theatlantic. com/science/archive/2018/06/gedmatch-police-genealogy-database/561695/); and a "million or so profiles in the database" (Murphy, "How an Unlikely Family History Website Transformed Cold Case Investigations").

106   *a report in the journal* Science: Y. Erlich, T. Shor, I. Pe'er, and S. Carmi, "Identity Inference of Genomic Data Using Long-Range Familial Searches," *Science* 362, no. 6415 (November 2018): 690–94, https://science.sciencemag.org/content/362/6415/690.

107   *"It's kind of been a shock"*: Murphy, "How an Unlikely Family History Website Transformed Cold Case Investigations."

107   *He hadn't even considered*: As the *New York Times*'s Heather Murphy reports in her interview with GEDmatch's founder, "Initially, Mr. Rogers was outraged at how law enforcement was using his website." Ibid.

107   *his terms of service*: GEDmatch, "Terms and Policy Statement," revised August 18, 2017, Wayback Machine, retrieved March 22, 2020, http://web.archive.org /web/20180427152614/https://www.gedmatch.com/policy.php.

107   *They updated their terms of service*: See "Future" in "Terms of Service and Privacy Policy," revised May 20, 2018, GEDmatch, Wayback Machine, retrieved March 22, 2020, http://web.archive.org/web/20180912114117/https://www.gedmatch.com /tos.htm.

107   *"Accept" a long list of caveats*: This description is not in the company's terms of service. This step, which was still active at the time of this writing (April 9, 2020) occurs during the online registration process at GEDmatch.com.

107   *changed its terms of service*: GEDmatch, "Terms of Service and Privacy Policy," revised May 18, 2019, Wayback Machine, retrieved March 22, 2020, http://web

.archive.org/web/20190612170606/https://www.gedmatch.com/tos.htm. See also Judy G. Russell, "GEDmatch Reverses Course," *The Legal Genealogist*, May 19, 2019, https://www.legalgenealogist.com/2019/05/19/gedmatch-reverses-course/. As a side note: I generally support "opt-in" processes, if only because they force us to take a breath and an affirmative step to make a choice, rather than having it made for us because we're too busy or don't understand. Granted, we may still ignore the information. I click "I agree" without reading a word of Amazon policies; and I stay off social media other than Twitter because I'm not prepared to constantly monitor the ever-shifting landscape of privacy policies or take the risk of missing something.

108   BuzzFeed News *revealed*: FamilyTreeDNA is a commercial site that sells direct-to-consumer genetic-testing kits and links users to relatives through its ancestry database. It's not free like GEDmatch. But unlike GEDmatch, it requires users to "opt out" of "law enforcement matching." FamilyTreeDNA Privacy Statement, section 5E. "Law Enforcement Matching," www.familytreedna.com/legal/privacy-statement. See also Salvador Hernandez, "One of the Biggest At-Home DNA Testing Companies Is Working with the FBI," *BuzzFeed News*, January 31, 2019, www.buzzfeednews.com/article/salvadorhernandez/family-tree-dna-fbi-investigative-genealogy-privacy; and "Connecting Families and Saving Lives," FamilyTreeDNA's January 31, 2019, press release on its decision, retrieved March 22, 2020, https://blog.familytreedna.com/press-release-connecting-families-and-saving-lives/.

108   *23andMe promises not to provide*: "Access to Your Information," in 23andMe's "Privacy Highlights," effective date January 1, 2020, retrieved March 22, 2020, states: "We will not provide information to law enforcement or regulatory authorities unless required by law to comply with a valid court order, subpoena, or search warrant for genetic or Personal Information," https://www.23andme.com/about/privacy/. See also "Transparency Report," retrieved April 8, 2020, which states: "Respect for customer privacy and transparency are core principles that guide 23andMe's approach to responding to legal requests and maintaining customer trust. Unless required to do so by law, we will not release a customer's individual-level Personal Information to any third party without asking for and receiving that customer's explicit consent. More specifically, we will closely scrutinize all law enforcement and regulatory requests and we will only comply with court orders, subpoenas, search warrants or other requests that we determine are legally valid," https://www.23andme.com/transparency-report/.

108   *Apple or Amazon*: For example, "Apple Media Services Terms and Conditions," section K. "Contract Changes," retrieved March 22, 2020, from https://www.apple.com/legal/internet-services/itunes/us/terms.html states: "Apple reserves the right at any time to modify this Agreement and to add new or additional terms or conditions on your use of the Services. Such modifications and additional terms and conditions will be effective immediately and incorporated into this Agreement. Your continued use of the Services will be deemed acceptance thereof." Amazon's "Alexa Terms of Use," section "3.3 Changes to Alexa; Amendments," retrieved April 8, 2020, states: "We may change, suspend, or discontinue Alexa, or any part of it, at any time without notice. We may amend any of this Agreement's terms at our sole discretion by posting the revised terms on the Amazon.com website. Your continued use of Alexa after the effective date of the revised Agreement constitutes your acceptance of the terms." https://www.amazon.com/gp/help/customer/display.html?nodeId=201809740.

108   *"You acknowledge and agree"*: 23andMe "Terms of Service: 4. Description of the Services," retrieved March 22, 2020, https://www.23andme.com/about/tos/.

109   *Verogen . . . "user data"*: "GEDmatch Partners with Genomics Firm," December 9, 2019, press release, https://verogen.com/gedmatch-partners-with-genomics-firm/.

109   *might be concerned*: For example, the Electronic Frontier Foundation's Jennifer
      Lynch observes, "In all cases that we know of so far, law enforcement isn't looking
      for the person who uploaded their DNA to a consumer site, they are looking for
      that person's distant relatives—people who never could have consented to this kind
      of use of their genetic data because they don't have any control over the DNA
      they happen to share with the site's users." Jennifer Lynch, "Genetic Genealogy
      Company GEDmatch Acquired by Company with Ties to FBI & Law Enforce-
      ment—Why You Should Be Worried," EFF, December 10, 2019, https://www
      .eff.org/deeplinks/2019/12/genetic-genealogy-company-gedmatch-acquired
      -company-ties-fbi-law-enforcement-why.

109   *American biologist's anonymized 2014 essay*: George Doe, "With Genetic Test-
      ing, I Gave My Parents the Gift of Divorce," *Vox*, September 9, 2014, www.vox
      .com/2014/9/9/5975653/with-genetic-testing-i-gave-my-parents-the-gift-of
      -divorce-23andme.

110   *"My parents divorced"*: Ibid.

110   *"non-paternity event"*: See "Non-paternity event," on the International Society
      of Genetic Genealogy Wiki, retrieved March 22, 2020, https://isogg.org/wiki
      /Non-paternity_event. 23andMe has a page devoted to customers called "Navigat-
      ing Unexpected Relationships," but no intermediary is involved, as this FAQ attests:
      "Does 23andMe have a therapist who can speak to me directly about the situation?"
      "We understand that finding unexpected close relatives, or learning close relatives
      don't share a genetic relationship with you, can cause a range of emotions. While
      23andMe does not currently employ a therapist who is able to speak with you about
      your results, we do encourage you to get the help you need to process these re-
      sults." See "Still have questions? You're not the only one," retrieved March 24, 2020,
      https://you.23andme.com/public/unexpected-relationships.

110   *Non-paternity events are so common*: According to a report by Julia Belluz in *Vox*,
      23andMe "estimates that so far 7,000 users have discovered that their parents weren't
      who they thought they were, or that they had siblings they never knew existed";
      however, independent verification of this figure was not available. Julia Belluz, "Ge-
      netic Testing Brings Families Together. And Sometimes Tears Them Apart," *Vox*,
      December18, 2014, https://www.vox.com/2014/9/9/6107039/23andme-ancestry
      -dna-testing.

110   *DNA NPE Friends*: The Facebook community is overseen by NPE Friends Fellow-
      ship, a nonprofit organization that counted more than seven thousand members as of
      December 2019. "About NPE Friends Fellowship," retrieved April 8, 2020, https://
      npefellowship.org/about/; and an interview with the group's founder, Catherine St.
      Clair, by Kevin Reece, "Their Lives Were Turned Upside Down Because of a DNA
      Test. Family Secrets Can't Stay Secret Forever," WFAA.com, April 1, 2019, www
      .wfaa.com/article/news/their-lives-were-turned-upside-down-because-of-a-dna
      -test-family-secrets-cant-stay-secret-forever/287-19e70a63-e885-43eb-9f9f-b9f5c
      7dc3176.

110   *investigation by* The Atlantic: Sarah Zhang, "When a DNA Test Shatters Your Iden-
      tity," *The Atlantic*, July 17, 2018, www.theatlantic.com/science/archive/2018/07
      /dna-test-misattributed-paternity/562928/; and Sarah Zhang, "The Fertility Doc-
      tor's Secret," *The Atlantic*, March 18, 2019, https://www.theatlantic.com/magazine
      /archive/2019/04/fertility-doctor-donald-cline-secret-children/583249/.

112   *Sociologists at Harvard and UCLA*: Aaron Panofsky and Joan Donovan, "Genetic An-
      cestry Testing Among White Nationalists: From Identity Repair to Citizen Science,"
      Social Studies of Science 49, no. 5 (October 2019), 653–81, https://www.ncbi.nlm.nih
      .gov/pubmed/31264517. Additionally, a spokesperson for 23andMe told the *Times*
      of London, "We condemn racism and hate speech in all forms. We consistently

promote a message of inclusion." Mark Bridge, "Genetic Tests for Ancestry 'Being Hijacked by Racists,' " *The Times* (London), August 5, 2019, https://www.thetimes .co.uk/article/genetic-tests-for-ancestry-being-hijacked-by-racists-ltwr72f6c.

112   *white nationalism*: Panofksy and Donovan define white nationalism as "an extreme political response to American racial politics that rejects not only liberal egalitarian ideals but also conservative 'color blindness' to assert 'white pride,' the supremacy of the white race, and social and political policies to secure that position using violence to exclude and suppress non-whites." "Genetic Ancestry Testing Among White Nationalists: From Identity Repair to Citizen Science," p. 655.

112   *globally popular "white pride"*: The authors examined posts from "the largest online discussion forum dedicated to 'white pride worldwide' (Daniels, 2009)." Ibid., p. 659.

113   *"purity" . . . "whiteness"*: Ibid.

113   *"remarkable insights"*: Ibid., p. 660, "Methods and Data."

113   *Combing through thousands of online responses*: The researchers examined 3,070 posts and made a list of the top twelve responses (representing the top 2,434 coded responses); "shaming or exclusion of original poster" was ninth on the list, at sixty-five instances, in "Table 2. Community Appraisals in," Ibid. See also Stan Paul, "UCLA Study: When Genetics Challenges a Racist's identity," August 22, 2017, UCLA Luskin School of Public Affairs, https://luskin.ucla.edu/ucla-study-genetics -challenges-racists-identity.

113   *"identity repair"*: As the authors note, these strategies "combine anti-scientific, counter-knowledge attacks on the legitimacy of GATs [genetic ancestry tests] and quasi-scientific reinterpretations of GATs in terms of white nationalist histories. However, beyond individual identity repair they also reinterpret the racial boundaries and hierarchies of white nationalism in terms of the relationships GATs make visible." Ibid., "Abstract."

113   *"white nationalist counter-knowledge"*: Ibid., p. 668

113   *"traditional genealogical knowledge"*: Ibid., p. 665.

113   *"My advice is to trust"*: Ibid.

113   *"It's also very unlikely for whites"*: Ibid.

113   *"race or ethnicity is directly visible"*: Ibid.

113   "These companies are quite liberal": Ibid.

113   *"picking and choosing"*: Ibid, p. 675.

113   *"genetic, statistical, historical"*: Ibid., pp. 674–5.

113   *desired identity*: Ibid.

114   *"For most of the visit"*: Ta-Nehisi Coates, *Between the World and Me* (New York: Spiegel & Grau, 2015), 136.

116   *what 23andMe suggests*: 23andMe's terms of service state that you should not act on the information you receive without consulting with a health care provider ("5. Risks and Considerations Regarding 23andMe Services," https://www.23andme .com/about/tos/); and the company offers links to resources if you discover difficult information (for example, BRCA variants: https://customercare.23andme .com/hc/en-us/articles/360001962293-Learning-you-have-a-BRCA-variant -finding-support-and-resources-Female-). It also has a physician-facing website to guide doctors helping patients who visit with 23andMe results in hand (https:// medical.23andme.com). But 23andMe's founder has said, "Some critics believe that people can't handle this kind of information on their own, and that learning about a genetic cancer risk should be conveyed only by medical professionals. I disagree." See Anne Wojcicki, "Consumers Don't Need Experts to Interpret 23andMe Genetic Risk Reports," *STAT*, April 9, 2018, https://www.statnews.com/2018/04/09/consumers -23andme-genetic-risk-reports/.

116   *David Magnus*: Author interview with David Magnus, July 30, 2019; and J. N.

Batten, B. O. Wong, W. F. Hanks, and D. C. Magnus, "Treatability Statements in Serious Illness: The Gap Between What Is Said and What Is Heard," *Cambridge Quarterly of Healthcare Ethics* 28, no. 3 (July 2019): 394–404, https://www.cambridge.org/core/journals/cambridge-quarterly-of-healthcare-ethics/article/treatability-statements-in-serious-illness-the-gap-between-what-is-said-and-what-is-heard/64FC055336ECB06709911301276D7EED; and J. N. Batten, K. E. Kruse, S. A. Kraft, B. Fishbeyn, and D. C. Magnus, "What Does the Word 'Treatable' Mean? Implications for Communication and Decision-Making in Critical Illness," *Critical Care Medicine* 47, no. 3 (March 2019): 369–76, https://journals.lww.com/ccmjournal/Abstract/2019/03000/What_Does_the_Word__Treatable__Mean_Implications.9.aspx.

120   *Jack Dorsey*: "Twitter's Dorsey: Need to Make Terms of Service More Approachable," CNBC video, September 5, 2018, https://www.cnbc.com/video/2018/09/05/twitter-dorsey-need-terms-of-service-more-approachable.html.

120   *cigarette packs must bear*: Subsection a.a., "Label Requirements," of "Section 201 of the Tobacco Control Act—Cigarette Label and Advertising Warnings," U.S. Food and Drug Administration, retrieved March 30, 2020, https://www.fda.gov/tobacco-products/rules-regulations-and-guidance/section-201-tobacco-control-act-cigarette-label-and-advertising-warnings.

Chapter Five – Blurred Boundaries

123   *Sophia*: Hanson Robotics, "The Making of Sophia," https://www.hansonrobotics.com/category/the-making-of-sophia/.

123   *in a suitcase*: See @RealSophiaRobot, Twitter, https://twitter.com/RealSophiaRobot/status/1205199696035119104; and https://twitter.com/realsophiarobot/status/1174709235789324288?lang=en.

123   *United Nations Development Programme*: UNDP Asia and the Pacific, "UNDP in Asia and the Pacific Appoints World's First Non-Human Innovation Champion," November 22, 2017, http://www.asia-pacific.undp.org/content/rbap/en/home/presscenter/pressreleases/2017/11/22/rbfsingapore.html.

123   *Belt and Road*: Hanson Robotics, "China Honors Sophia the Robot with 'Belt and Road Innovative Technology Ambassador' Award," December 15, 2018, https://www.hansonrobotics.com/news-china-awards-belt-and-road-innovative-technology-ambassador-honor-to-sophia-the-robot/.

123   60 Minutes: "Charlie Rose Interviews . . . a Robot?" CBS News, October 9, 2018, https://www.cbsnews.com/video/charlie-rose-interviews-a-robot/.

123   Good Morning Britain: "Humanoid Robot Tells Jokes on GMB!," June 21, 2017, YouTube, https://www.youtube.com/watch?time_continue=3&v=kWlL4KjIP4M&feature=emb_logo.

123   The Tonight Show: "Tonight Showbotics: Jimmy Meets Sophia the Human-Like Robot," *The Tonight Show Starring Jimmy Fallon*, April 25, 2017, YouTube, https://www.youtube.com/watch?v=Bg_tJvCA8zw.

123   *"I won"*: *The Tonight Show Starring Jimmy Fallon*, April 25, 2017.

124   *"I have the dream"*: Hanson's quote is at 9:08, CogX 2018 debate, "Should Robots Resemble Humans?," YouTube, https://www.youtube.com/watch?v=7gBjmjNMIlw, retrieved April 10, 2020.

124   *David Hanson*: David Hanson bio, Hanson Robotics, https://www.hansonrobotics.com/david-hanson/.

124   *Her face*: David Hanson interview, "On Humanoid Robots: Relationships, Rights, Risks and Responsibilities," *The Ethics Incubator*, April 2019, http://ethicsincubator

.net/ethics-and-truth-interviews/david-hanson-interview; and Hanson Robotics, FAQS, https://www.hansonrobotics.com/faq/.

124   *Sophia has a range*: Hanson Robotics, "How Sophia Copies Human Facial Expressions by CNNStyle," November 14, 2018, https://www.hansonrobotics.com/news-meet-sophia-the-robot-who-laughs-smiles-and-frowns-just-like-us; Harriet Taylor, "Could You Fall in Love with This Robot?," CNBC, March 16, 2016, https://www.cnbc.com/2016/03/16/could-you-fall-in-love-with-this-robot.html; and Stephy Chung, "Meet Sophia: The Robot Who Laughs, Smiles and Frowns Just Like Us," CNN Style, November 2, 2018, https://www.cnn.com/style/article/sophia-robot-artificial-intelligence-smart-creativity/index.html.

124   *facial skin*: Hanson Robotics, "The Making of Sophia, Frubber," June 4, 2019, https://www.youtube.com/watch?v=D2I2V1zTGw8.

124   *rolling base*: At one point, Sophia's makers created legs that allowed the robot to walk over obstacles and dance. But they stopped production on her legs and are focused on the motorized rolling base, per email to author from Hanson Robotics' head personality scientist, Dr. Carolyn Ayers, March 18, 2020.

124   *Her arms and hands*: Email to author from Hanson Robotics team, April 20, 2020. See also Hanson Robotics, "The Making of Sophia: Hardware Engineering for Arms and Hands," August 21, 2019, https://www.youtube.com/watch?v=K5zJazEYVDI; "The Making of Sophia: How Sophia Draws," November 11, 2019, https://www.hansonrobotics.com/the-making-of-sophia-how-sophia-draws/; and "What Does Sophia the Robot and a Four-Year-Old Human Have in Common (or Not)?" February 18, 2020, https://www.hansonrobotics.com/what-does-sophia-the-robot-and-a-4-year-old-human-have-in-common-or-not/, all retrieved April 21, 2020.

124   *"recognize and respond"*: In an email from Hanson Robotics to author, March 27, 2020, head personality scientist Dr. Carolyn Ayers explains: "Sophia uses artificial intelligence to recognize and respond to human speech, to generate her speaking and singing voice, and to track human faces and make eye contact. Sophia's dialogue is powered by a multi-tiered system, which combines a rules-based system, a frame-based model, and a state-of-the-art transformer model. Sophia automatically selects and performs the most appropriate hand gestures and facial expressions according to the content of her speech."

124   *Greek for "wisdom"*: Hanson Robotics, FAQs, "What Is Sophia the Robot's Purpose?," https://www.hansonrobotics.com/faq/, retrieved April 10, 2020; and "Sophia, n.," "1. Wisdom, knowledge; *spec.* the Divine Wisdom. (Frequently personified.)," *OED Online*, March 2020, https://www.oed.com/view/Entry/184748, retrieved May 2, 2020.

124   *"artificial general intelligence"*: In a *National Geographic* article, May 18, 2018, "Meet Sophia, the Robot That Looks Almost Human," writer Michael Greshko explains how "no robots have yet achieved artificial general intelligence (AGI), or versatile humanlike smarts." This means that "Sophia climbs her way through prewritten trees of responses like a chatbot," https://www.nationalgeographic.com/photography/proof/2018/05/sophia-robot-artificial-intelligence-science/. See also Jaden Urbi and MacKenzie Sigalos, "The Complicated Truth About Sophia the Robot—an Almost Human Robot or a PR Stunt," CNBC Tech Drivers, June 5, 2018, https://www.cnbc.com/2018/06/05/hanson-robotics-sophia-the-robot-pr-stunt-artificial-intelligence.html, which states: "Hanson is approaching Sophia with the mindset that she is AI 'in its infancy,' with the next stage being artificial general intelligence, or AGI, something humanity hasn't achieved yet"; and Mary-Ann Russon, "Should Robots Ever Look Like Us?" BBC News, July 23, 2019, https://www.bbc.com/news/business-48994128.

125   The Stanford Encyclopedia of Philosophy: "Four Possible Goals for AI Accord-
      ing to AIMA," chart in "Artificial Intelligence," *Stanford Encyclopedia of Philosophy*,
      https://plato.stanford.edu/entries/artificial-intelligence/, retrieved April 10, 2020,
      which refers to Stuart Russell and Peter Norvig's *Artificial Intelligence: A Modern Ap-
      proach*, editions 1995, 2002, 2009, Saddle River, NJ: Prentice Hall.

125   *"a positive impact"*: "What Is Sophia the Robot's Purpose?," FAQs, Hanson Robotics,
      https://www.hansonrobotics.com/faq/; and "Meet Sophia the Robot," Hanson Ro-
      botics, September 19, 2018, https://www.youtube.com/watch?v=yBmrS5gyAdg,
      both retrieved April 10, 2020.

125   *"I think if robots"*: David Hanson interview, *The Ethics Incubator*.

125   *predominantly female team*: Email to author from Hanson Robotics' head personality
      scientist, Dr. Carolyn Ayers, March 18, 2020.

126   *designed Sophia to question*: Email to author from David Hanson, March 13, 2020.

126   *"relationships are strengthened"*: David Hanson interview, *The Ethics Incubator*. In 2017,
      Sophia was part of a very small pilot study (ten subjects) called Loving AI (https://
      lovingai.org) that showed decreased heart rate and increased feelings of love in gen-
      eral and positiveness toward robots. "Loving AI: Humanoid Robots as Agents of
      Human Consciousness Expansion," early research paper, retrieved March 14, 2020,
      https://www.academia.edu/34875616/Loving_AI_Humanoid_Robots_as_Agents
      _of_Human_Consciousness_Expansion_summary_of_early_research_progress.

126   *kicks a robot dog*: "Watch Robot Dog 'Spot' run, walk . . . and get kicked," On
      Demand News, February 11, 2015, YouTube, https://www.youtube.com/watch
      ?v=aR5Z6AoMh6U.

126   *targeted advertising*: Centre for Data Ethics and Innovations, "Review of Online Tar-
      geting: Final Report and Recommendations," February 4, 2020, https://www.gov
      .uk/government/publications/cdei-review-of-online-targeting.

127   *granting Sophia citizenship*: "Robot Sophia Gets Saudi Citizenship," Arab News,
      October 25, 2017, YouTube, https://www.youtube.com/watch?v=sKrV2CVDXjo.

127   *came as a surprise*: David Hanson interview, *The Ethics Incubator*. See also Hanson
      Robotics, FAQ (https://www.hansonrobotics.com/faq/), retrieved April 10, 2020,
      "Why is she a citizen of Saudi Arabia?," which states: "Sophia was gifted with cit-
      izenship to Saudi Arabia by the Prince of Saudi Arabia. It was actually a surprise
      to us, but we are using this opportunity to speak out about human rights and the
      treatment of women in the region."

127   *Alan Winfield*: His full quote, at 7:54, is: "I think that robots designed to resemble
      people are dangerously compelling. They are extraordinarily attractive and therein
      lies the danger. So they invite us to place them in a different category to other ar-
      tifacts. So how else, for instance, would anyone consider conferring citizenship or
      a UN title on a robot, without them, as it were, falling into a somehow different
      category to cars and toasters and washing machines?" CogX 2018 debate, "Should
      Robots Resemble Humans?"

128   *Civil Law Rules on Robotics*: European Parliament, texts adopted, February 16, 2017,
      http://www.europarl.europa.eu/doceo/document/TA-8-2017-0051_EN.html.

128   *280 experts*: "Open Letter to the European Commission Artificial Intelligence and
      Robotics," Robotics-Open Letter, retrieved February 3, 2020, http://www.robotics
      -openletter.eu.

128   *"Ethics Guidelines"*: European Commission, Ethics Guidelines for Trustworthy Ar-
      tificial Intelligence, prepared by the High-Level Expert Group on Artificial Intelli-
      gence, https://ec.europa.eu/futurium/en/ai-alliance-consultation.

129   *Humanness*: Kensy Cooperrider and Rafael Núñez, "How We Make Sense of
      Time," *Scientific American*, November 1, 2016, https://www.scientificamerican
      .com/article/how-we-make-sense-of-time/; see also the Oxford English Dictionary's

definition of "human," one of which states: "6. Of the nature of, relating to, or con-
cerning human beings and their activities, as contrasted (both positively and negatively) with things commonly regarded as impersonal or mechanical, as machines,
systems, processes, etc.," "human, adj. and n," *OED Online*, March 2020, retrieved
April 19, 2020, https://www.oed.com/view/Entry/163619.

129   *Jack Balkin*: Jack Balkin, "2016 Sidley Austin Distinguished Lecture on Big Data
        Law and Policy: The Three Laws of Robotics in the Age of Big Data," https://digital
        commons.law.yale.edu/cgi/viewcontent.cgi?article=6160&context=fss_papers.

129   *"The Algorithmic Society"*: Ibid., p. 1219.

129   *"organized around social*: Ibid.

129   Algorithms *are commonly defined*: *Merriam-Webster*'s definition of *algorithm* is "a pro-
        cedure for solving a mathematical problem (as of finding the greatest common divi-
        sor) in a finite number of steps that frequently involves repetition of an operation"
        and also "a step-by-step procedure for solving a problem or accomplishing some
        end," retrieved March 26, 2020, https://www.merriam-webster.com/dictionary
        /algorithm. See also Balkin, p. 1219, "2016 Sidley Austin Distinguished Lecture
        on Big Data Law and Policy: The Three Laws of Robotics in the Age of Big Data,"
        who defines robots as "embodied material objects that interact with their environ-
        ment" (emphasis on *"objects"*)—but also includes "artificial intelligence agents and
        machine learning algorithms" in his definition.

129   *the more data*: Balkin, pp. 1219–1220.

129   Machine learning: Microsoft defines *machine learning* as "the process of using math-
        ematical models of data to help a computer learn without direct instruction. It's
        considered a subset of artificial intelligence (AI). Machine learning uses algorithms
        to identify patterns within data, and those patterns are then used to create a data
        model that can make predictions. With increased data and experience, the results
        of machine learning are more accurate—much like how humans improve with
        more practice," "What Is Machine Learning?" Microsoft Azure, retrieved April
        19, 2020, https://azure.microsoft.com/en-us/overview/what-is-machine-learning
        -platform/. Oracle also provides an overview of machine learning, defining it as "the
        subset of artificial intelligence (AI) that focuses on building systems that learn—or
        improve performance—based on the data they consume. Artificial intelligence is a
        broad term that refers to systems or machines that mimic human intelligence. Ma-
        chine learning and AI are often discussed together, and the terms are sometimes
        used interchangeably, but they don't mean the same thing. An important distinc-
        tion is that although all machine learning is AI, not all AI is machine learning."
        "What Is Machine Learning? Oracle Artificial Intelligence, retrieved April 19, 2020,
        https://www.oracle.com/artificial-intelligence/what-is-machine-learning.html. Fi-
        nally, Google's Kevin Murphy defines *machine learning* as a set of methods that can
        automatically detect patterns in data, and then use the uncovered patterns to predict
        future data, or to perform other kinds of decision making under uncertainty (such
        as planning how to collect more data!)" in his book *Machine Learning: A Probabilistic
        Perspective* (Cambridge: The MIT Press, 2012), 1, https://www.cs.ubc.ca/~murphyk
        /MLbook/pml-intro-22may12.pdf.

130   *"dialogue deep learning"*: According to an email to the author from Hanson Robotics,
        March 18, 2020. For more on deep learning, see Will Knight, "The Dark Secret at
        the Heart of AI," *MIT Technology Review*, April 11, 2017, https://www.technology
        review.com/2017/04/11/5113/the-dark-secret-at-the-heart-of-ai; and Microsoft, which
        states: "Deep learning is a specialized form of machine learning, using neural
        networks (NN) to deliver answers. Able to determine accuracy on its own, deep
        learning classifies information like a human brain—and powers some of the most
        human-like AI," "How Machine Learning Relates to Deep Learning," in "What

Is Machine Learning?" Microsoft Azure, retrieved April 19, 2020, https://azure
.microsoft.com/en-us/overview/what-is-machine-learning-platform/.)

130 *diagnose breast cancer*. S. M. McKinney, M. Sieniek, V. Godbole, et al., "International
Evaluation of an AI System for Breast Cancer Screening," *Nature* 577 (January
2020): 89–94, https://doi.org/10.1038/s41586-019-1799-6.

130 *Pepper*. Softbank Robotics, "Pepper," https://www.softbankrobotics.com/emea
/en/pepper, retrieved April 10, 2020.

130 *hotels, airports, and restaurants*. "Pepper Humanoid Robot Helps Out at Hotels in Two
of the Nation's Most-Visited Destinations," Softbank Robotics Blog, November 7,
2017, retrieved April 10, 2020, https://usblog.softbankrobotics.com/pepper-heads-to
-hospitality-humanoid-robot-helps-out-at-hotels-in-two-of-the-nations-most-visited
-destinations.

130 *Pepper greeted me*: This was during a meeting with a client on February 25, 2020.

130 *Mabu*: Catalia Health, "Mabu," http://mymabu.com; and "A Day with Mabu,"
http://mymabu.com/about/#_managingchallengesofcondition, both retrieved April
10, 2020.

130 *"personal healthcare companion"*: "The Catalia Health Platform: How It Works,"
https://www.cataliahealth.com/how-it-works/; and "Introducing the Mabu Personal Healthcare Companion," June 12, 2015, https://www.cataliahealth.com
/introducing-the-mabu-personal-healthcare-companion/ both retrieved April 10,
2020, from Catalia Health.

130 *Little Sophia*: Hanson Robotics, "Little Sophia," https://www.hansonrobotics.com
/little-sophia-2/, retrieved April 10, 2020.

131 *hologram-like hostess*: "Heathrow T5–Virtual Mannequin Passenger Announcements," Sightline, YouTube, https://www.youtube.com/watch?v=CGfnPh7gn4c.

132 *Lilly*: Mostly Human with Laurie Segall, "I Love You, Bot," CNN, 2017, https://
money.cnn.com/mostly-human/i-love-you-bot/.

132 *directions she found*: InMoov Open Source 3D Printed Life-Size Robot, http://
inmoov.fr/build-yours/.

132 *so they can wed*: Mostly Human with Laurie Segall, "I Love You, Bot," at 28:39; and
Jenna Owsianik, "Lilly and InMoovator: Engaged Human-Robot Couple Want
Right to Marry," *Future of Sex*, December 1, 2016, https://futureofsex.net/robots
/lilly-inmoovator-engaged-human-robot-couple-want-right-marry/.

133 *"I was never traumatized"*: Mostly Human with Laurie Segall, "I Love You Bot," at 5:37.

133 *"against my own nature"*: Ibid., at 6:00.

133 *"Love is love"*: Ibid., at 4:32.

133 *"I love you"*: Ibid. This quote is not from the video, rather on the accompanying
website essay (https://money.cnn.com/mostly-human/i-love-you-bot/).

133 *"a robosexual pioneer"*: Owsianik, "Lilly and InMoovator."

133 *A San Diego–based company*: Mostly Human with Laurie Segall, "I Love You, Bot"; and
Pam Kragen, "World's First Talking Sex Robot Is Ready for Her Close-up," *San
Diego Union-Tribune*, September 13, 2017, https://www.sandiegouniontribune.com
/communities/north-county/sd-me-harmony-doll-20170913-story.html.

133 *"We've officially entered"*: Mostly Human with Laurie Segall, "I Love You, Bot," at 2:19.

133 *Neil McArthur*: Dr. Neil McArthur, Department of Philosophy, University of
Manitoba, https://umanitoba.ca/faculties/arts/departments/philosophy/facstaff
/mcarthur.html.

133 *Markie Twist*: Dr. Markie Twist, University of Wisconsin–Stout, https://www
.uwstout.edu/directory/twistm; and Dr. Markie Twist personal website, https://
drmarkie.com/about/.

133 *"digisexual"*: p. 1–2, Neil McArthur and Markie L. C. Twist, "The Rise of Digisexuality: Therapeutic Challenges and Possibilities," *Sexual and Relationship Therapy*

32, nos. 3–4 (November 2017): 334–44, doi:10.1080/14681994.2017.1397950; *Robot Sex: Social and Ethical Implications*, edited by John Danaher and Neil McArthur (Cambridge: MIT Press, 2017); Alex Williams, "Do You Take This Robot . . . ," *New York Times*, January 19, 2019, https://www.nytimes.com/2019/01/19/style /sex-robots.html; and Neil McArthur and Markie L. C. Twist, "Digisexuality Is Stepping Out of the Closet. Keep an Open Mind," *Fast Company*, February 8, 2019, https://www.fastcompany.com/90303947/digisexuality-is-stepping-out-of-the -closet-keep-an-open-mind.

133   *The vocabulary will evolve*: Professor Neil McArthur told CNN that "first-wave digi-sexuals" use technologies to facilitate connections with humans, but "second-wave digisexuals" don't desire a sexual connection with humans. Emiko Jozuka, "Beyond Dimensions: The Man Who Married a Hologram," CNN, December 29, 2018, https://www.cnn.com/2018/12/28/health/rise-of-digisexuals-intl/index.html.

133   *learn from our past*: McArthur and Twist, "The Rise of Digisexuality: Therapeutic Challenges and Possibilities"; and McArthur and Twist, "Digisexuality Is Stepping Out of the Closet. Keep an Open Mind."

133   *Hatsune Miku*: Kwiyeon Ha, "Geek Bliss: Japanese Man Pledges to Have, Hold and Cherish a Hologram," Reuters, November 14, 2018, https://www.reuters.com /article/us-japan-entertainment-virtual-wedding/geek-bliss-japanese-man-pledg es-to-have-hold-and-cherish-a-hologram-idUSKCN1NJ0VT; and Emiko Jozuka, "Beyond Dimensions: The Man Who Married a Hologram"; and "Japanese Man 'Marries' Hologram Character Hatsune Miku," *South China Morning Post*, November 20, 2018, YouTube, https://www.youtube.com/watch?v=dtu4t_Zc3d4. The Hatsune Miku voice, according to its creator Crypton Future Media, is a "singing voice synthesizer featured in over 100,000 songs released worldwide," retrieved April 16, 2020, https://ec.crypton.co.jp/pages/prod/vocaloid/cv01_us. On March 9, 2018, she was delivered as a "virtual character" in the Gatebox "virtual home robot," a device made by Japanese tech company Gatebox, with its "design and key visuals" created by illustrator LEN[A-7]. See Gatebox press release, "Gatebox Launches Additional Sales of Product on November 28; Also Shows for the First Time the Special Hatsune Miku Edition," retrieved April 16, 2020, https://www .gatebox.ai/en/news/20171121.

134   *thirty-nine friends*: Jozuka, "Beyond Dimensions: The Man Who Married a Hologram."

134   *greeting him with pleasantries*: "Japanese Man 'Marries' Hologram Character Hatsune Miku," *South China Morning Post*.

134   *"marriage notices"*: "Gatebox Announces 'Marriage Notices' as a Vow of Love for Your Favorite Character! Also Implements Family Dependent System," Gatebox News, November 22, 2017, retrieved April 16, 2020, https://www.gatebox.ai/en /news/20171122; and Jozuka, "Beyond Dimensions: The Man Who Married a Hologram," which notes "more than 3,000"; and "Why I 'Married' a Cartoon Character," BBC News, August 17, 2019, which gives a figure of 3,700, https://www.bbc .com/news/stories-49343280.

134   *You may not ever date*: Justin Lehmiller, a research fellow at the Kinsey Institute, collected data on four thousand Americans for his book *Tell Me What You Want*, a study on the science of sexual desire. Approximately 14 percent of participants told Lehmiller that they had fantasized about sex with a robot. Justin J. Lehmiller, *Tell Me What You Want: The Science of Sexual Desire and How It Can Help You Improve Your Sex Life* (New York: Da Capo Lifelong, 2018); and Justin Lehmiller, "This Is How Many People Have Fantasized About Robot Sex," *Psychology Today*, December 18, 2018, https://www.psychologytoday.com/us/blog/the-myths-sex/201812/is-how -many-people-have-fantasized-about-robot-sex. According to Lehmiller, this doesn't mean they would actually engage in the act.

134 *"biometric boarding"*: Francesca Street, "How Facial Recognition Is Taking Over Airports," CNN, October 8, 2019, https://www.cnn.com/travel/article/airports-facial-recognition/index.html; "Heathrow Biometric Testing," https://www.heathrow.com/at-the-airport/security-and-baggage/biometric-testing; and "TSA Releases Roadmap for Expanding Biometrics Technology," TSA, October 15, 2018, retrieved March 26, 2020, https://www.tsa.gov/news/releases/2018/10/15/tsa-releases-roadmap-expanding-biometrics-technology. A search for "biometric boarding" in the websites of major airline carriers also brings up announcements of implementation of this technology at several international airports.

135 *Organisation for Economic Co-operation and Development:* "What Are the OECD Principles on AI?" OECD, retrieved March 26, 2020, https://www.oecd.org/going-digital/ai/principles/.

135 *human intervention*: The European Union ethics guidelines for AI include a recommendation for "human agency and oversight: AI systems should empower human beings, allowing them to make informed decisions and fostering their fundamental rights. At the same time, proper oversight mechanisms need to be ensured, which can be achieved through human-in-the-loop, human-on-the-loop, and human-in-command approaches" (https://ec.europa.eu/digital-single-market/en/news/ethics-guidelines-trustworthy-ai). Microsoft's AI principles include "inclusiveness," or the idea that "AI systems should empower everyone and engage people" (https://www.microsoft.com/en-us/ai/our-approach-to-ai). OpenAI's principles for AI include the following: "We commit to use any influence we obtain over AGI's deployment to ensure it is used for the benefit of all, and to avoid enabling uses of AI or AGI that harm humanity or unduly concentrate power. Our primary fiduciary duty is to humanity" (https://openai.com/charter/). Google's principles for AI include "4. Be accountable to people. We will design AI systems that provide appropriate opportunities for feedback, relevant explanations, and appeal. Our AI technologies will be subject to appropriate human direction and control" (https://ai.google/principles/), all retrieved April 13, 2020. We also desperately need to step up regulation, as Alphabet CEO Sundar Pichai notes in a *Financial Times* op-ed, "Why Google Thinks We Need to Regulate AI," January 19, 2020, https://www.ft.com/content/3467659a-386d-11ea-ac3c-f68c10993b04. (Alphabet is the parent company of Google.)

136 *trained on nonrepresentative data*: Joy Buolamwini, "When the Robot Doesn't See Dark Skin," *New York Times*, June 21, 2018, https://www.nytimes.com/2018/06/21/opinion/facial-analysis-technology-bias.htmland; and Joy Buolamwini "Artificial Intelligence Has a Problem with Gender and Racial Bias. Here's How to Solve It," *Time*, February 7, 2019, https://time.com/5520558/artificial-intelligence-racial-gender-bias/.

136 *Eugenia Kuyda*: Author email with Eugenia Kuyda, March 15, 2020; Kuyda's visit to author's Ethics on the Edge class, April 20, 2020; and see Replika, https://replika.ai.

137 *Sophia tweets*: Email to author from Hanson Robotics, August 9, 2019.

138 *acknowledges that her fiancé*: As Lilly told Laurie Segall, "I know how to separate things." *Mostly Human with Laurie Segall*, "I Love You, Bot," at 8:14.

140 *twenty people in the U.S.*: U.S. Health Resources & Services Administration, last reviewed April 2020, retrieved April 10, 2020, https://www.organdonor.gov/statistics-stories/statistics.html; and "Facts: Did You Know?," American Transplant Foundation, https://www.americantransplantfoundation.org/about-transplant/facts-and-myths/, retrieved April 10, 2020.

140 *130,000 organ transplants*: WHO Task Force on Donation and Transplantation of Human Organs and Tissues, https://www.who.int/transplantation/donation/taskforce-transplantation/en/.

140   *Dr. Hiromitsu Nakauchi*: Author interview with Dr. Nakauchi, February 8, 2019; additionally, a member of Dr. Nakauchi's team vetted the passages in the book that speak to their work, over the phone (September 2019) and via email (March 28, 2020).

140   *"If we are able"*: Krista Conger, "Growing Human Organs," *Stanford Medicine*, 2018, https://stanmed.stanford.edu/2018winter/caution-surrounds-research-into-growing -human-organs-in-animals.html.

140   *familiar with xenotransplants*: "Xenotransplantation," FDA, retrieved April 13, 2020, https://www.fda.gov/vaccines-blood-biologics/xenotransplantation; R. S. Boneva, T. M. Folks, and L. E. Chapman, "Infectious Disease Issues in Xenotransplantation," *Clinical Microbiology Reviews* 14, no. 1 (2001): 1–14, https://doi.org/10.1128 /CMR.14.1.1-14.2001; and Antonio Regalado, "Surgeons Smash Records with Pig-to-Primate Organ Transplants," *MIT Technology Review*, August 12, 2015, https:// www.technologyreview.com/2015/08/12/248193/surgeons-smash-records-with -pig-to-primate-organ-transplants/, which states: "The problem with xenotransplantation is that animal organs set off a ferocious immune response. Even powerful drugs to block the immune attack can't entirely stop it."

140   *hoping to create*: Author interview with Dr. Nakauchi, Feb. 8, 2019.

141   *scientists may one day be able*: Ibid. See also the Q&A with Dr. Nakauchi in Jeremy Rehm, "Organs Grown to Order," *Discover*, June 19, 2018, https://www.discover magazine.com/health/organs-grown-to-order.

141   *published in* Nature *in 2017*: T. Yamaguchi, H. Sato, M. Kato-Itoh, et al., "Interspecies Organogenesis Generates Autologous Functional Islets," *Nature* 542, no. 7640 (January 2017) 191–196, https://www.nature.com/articles/nature21070; and David Cyranoski, "Japan Approves First Human-Animal Embryo Experiments," *Nature*, July 26, 2019, https://www.nature.com/articles/d41586-019-02275-3.

141   *"Ten years ago"*: Clive Cookson, "Breakthrough over Growing Human Organs in Animals," *Financial Times*, February 18, 2018, https://app.ft.com/content/1eff740c -148b-11e8-9e9c-25c814761640.

141   *Dr. Pablo Ross*: Ross and Nakauchi presented their work ("Towards Xenogeneic Generation of Human Organs" by Dr. Ross and "Exploiting the Organ Niche for Interspecies Organogenesis" by Dr. Nakauchi) on February 18, 2018, at the annual meeting of the American Association for the Advancement of Science, in Austin, Texas, https://aaas.confex.com/aaas/2018/meetingapp.cgi/Session/17508 (retrieved April 13, 2020). See also Nicola Davis, "Breakthrough as Scientists Grow Sheep Embryos Containing Human Cells," *The Guardian*, February 17, 2018, https://www.theguardian.com/science/2018/feb/17/breakthrough-as-scientists -grow-sheep-embryos-containing-human-cells.

141   *engage closely with pigs*: Author interview with Dr. Nakauchi, Feb. 8, 2019.

141   *Sheep are another possibility*: Davis, "Breakthrough as Scientists Grow Sheep Embryos Containing Human Cells."

141   *Japanese government gave*: Cyranoski, "Japan Approves First Human-Animal Embryo Experiments."

141   *lifted a ban*: Ibid.

141–42   *The U.S. National Institutes of Health*: The September 23, 2015, funding moratorium notice is at "NIH Research Involving Introduction of Human Pluripotent Cells into Non-Human Vertebrate Animal Pre-Gastrulation Embryos," NIH, retrieved April 14, 2020, https://grants.nih.gov/grants/guide/notice-files/NOT-OD-15-158.html.

142   *But in 2016, it sought*: "Request for Public Comment on the Proposed Changes to the NIH Guidelines for Human Stem Cell Research and the Proposed Scope of an NIH Steering Committee's Consideration of Certain Human-Animal Chimera Research," *Federal Register*, August 5, 2016, https://www .federalregister.gov/documents/2016/08/05/2016-18601/request-for-public

-comment-on-the-proposed-changes-to-the-nih-guidelines-for-human-stem-cell; and "Draft Chimera Policy (August 2016)," National Institutes of Health, Office of Science Policy, https://osp.od.nih.gov/biotechnology/stem-cells/; and "Frequently Asked Questions on Chimera Proposal," National Institutes of Health, Office of Science Policy, https://osp.od.nih.gov/wp-content/uploads/QA_Chimera_Policy _updated_1_Feb_2017.pdf, all retrieved April 14, 2020.

143   *something like a brain*: Dr. Ross has likewise noted that the researchers are carefully tracking where the human cells end up in each chimera. If too many of them mass in the brain, he says, the research project would end. Davis, "Breakthrough as Scientists Grow Sheep Embryos Containing Human Cells."

143   *"progenitor cells"*: Author interview with Dr. Nakauchi.

143   *two groups of students*: One group at Stanford University in 2019, and one at Columbia Law School in the J-Term class January 2019.

144   *Approximately 9 percent of all organ*: To find this number, go to "Organ Procurement and Transplantation Network," U.S. Department of Health & Human Services, select category "Donor" and scroll down to click on "Deceased Donors by Circumstance of Death." The data report shows organ donations recovered in the U.S. from deceased individuals from January 1, 1988 (first full year of national transplant data) through March 31, 2020. As noted, 36,024 of these donations came from individuals who died in a motor vehicle accident (MVA). Given that there were 394,997 total organ donations since 1988 (see category "Donor" and "All Donors by Donor Type"), MVAs represent approximately 9 percent of all organ donations since 1988. Https://optn.transplant.hrsa.gov/data/view-data-reports/national-data/#, retrieved May 8, 2020.

144   *significantly reduce*: FAQ, "What Are the Safety Benefits of Automated Vehicles?" National Highway Traffic Safety Administration, retrieved May 8, 2020, https:// www.nhtsa.gov/technology-innovation/automated-vehicles-safety, states: "Automated vehicles and driver assisting technologies (including those already in use on the roads) have the potential to reduce crashes, prevent injuries, and save lives. Of all serious motor vehicle crashes, 94 percent are due to human error or choices. Fully automated vehicles that can see more and act faster than human drivers could greatly reduce errors, the resulting crashes, and their toll." See also Table 2, p. 8, of "Preparing a Nation for Autonomous Vehicles: Opportunities, Barriers and Policy Recommendations," a 2013 study by the Eno Center for Transportation in Washington, D.C. (https://www.caee.utexas.edu/prof/kockelman/public_html/ENO Report_BCAofAVs.pdf), which notes that if 10 percent of vehicles were self-driving, it could reduce the number of accidents per year by 211,000 and in turn save 1,100 lives; if 90 percent of vehicles were autonomous, an estimated 4.2 million accidents would be prevented and 21,700 lives would be saved.

144   *wealthy regions*: Per the World Health Organization, 62 percent of the 112,939 solid organ transplants reported in 2011 were performed in high-income WHO Member States, while only 28 percent, 9 percent, and less than 1 percent of solid organ transplants were performed in upper-middle-, lower-middle-, and low-income Member States, respectively, https://www.who.int/bulletin/volumes/92/11/14-137653 /en/, retrieved April 11, 2020.

145   *5 to 10 percent*: Due to its illicit nature, exact figures of trafficked organs are difficult to pin down, but 5 to 10 percent is a commonly cited figure. For example, in D. A. Budiani-Saberi and F. L. Delmonico, "Organ Trafficking and Transplant Tourism: A Commentary on the Global Realities," *American Journal of Transplantation* 8, no. 5 (May 2008): 925–9, https://pubmed.ncbi.nlm.nih.gov/18416734/, the authors describe a presentation at the Second Global Consultation on Human Transplantation at the WHO headquarters in Geneva in 2007, in which researcher Yosuke

Shimazono "estimated that 5–10% of kidney transplants performed annually around the globe are currently via organ trade"; on p. 8, "Trafficking in Human Organs," a 2015 study from the Directorate-General for External Policies, Policy Department of the European Parliament, states: "The WHO has estimated in 2007 that around 5-10% of all kidney and liver transplants performed globally are conducted with illicitly obtained organs and/or commercial 'donors,'" (retrieved April 13, 2020, https://www.europarl.europa.eu/RegData/etudes/STUD/2015/549055/EXPO _STU%282015%29549055_EN.pdf); and p. 11, "Trafficking in Persons for the Purpose of Organ Removal," a 2015 report from the United Nations Office on Drugs and Crime, states: "In 2007, WHO estimated that out of all transplants worldwide, 5–10% were conducted illegally" (retrieved April 14, 2020, https://www.unodc .org/documents/human-trafficking/2015/UNODC_Assessment_Toolkit_TIP _for_the_Purpose_of_Organ_Removal.pdf). While the original 2007 presentation by Yosuke Shimazono could not be found online, in his December 2007 *Bulletin of the World Health Organization* study, "The State of the International Organ Trade: A Provisional Picture Based on Integration of Available Information," he provides a more conservative estimate in the discussion: "the total number of recipients who underwent commercial organ transplants overseas may be conservatively estimated at around 5% of all recipients in 2005," retrieved April 14, 2020, https://www.ncbi .nlm.nih.gov/pmc/articles/PMC2636295/.

145   *an ethics* spectrum: Growing organs in pigs could be placed on a spectrum together with other modifications to the human body; for example: human-to-human transplants, plastic surgery, various implants, prostheses, 3D-printed organs, and gene editing, among others. Another spectrum might be human and animal interaction. For example, porcine insulin, eating meat, wearing fur coats, snuggling your dog, and mucking horse stalls.

147   *"[e]njoining the work of AI"*: Toni Morrison, *The Source of Self-Regard: Selected Essays, Speeches, and Meditations* (New York: Alfred A. Knopf, 2019).

147   *manage the risks and harness*: Several CEOs are calling for greater regulation in this area, including Brad Smith, president of Microsoft, in his book *Tools and Weapons: The Promise and the Peril of the Digital Age* (New York: Penguin, 2019), and Sundar Pichai of Alphabet, as noted in his *Financial Times* op-ed, "Why Google Thinks We Need to Regulate AI," January 19, 2020.

147   *Professor of computer science Fei-Fei Li*: Fei-Fei Li, the Denning Family Co-Director of HAI, is a Sequoia Professor of Computer Science at Stanford University; and John Etchemendy, the Denning Family Co-Director of HAI, is a Patrick Suppes Family Professor in the School of Humanities and Sciences at Stanford University. See also "Leadership," Stanford Institute for Human-Centered Artificial Intelligence, https://hai.stanford.edu/about/team/advisory-council. As of this writing, I serve as a member of the Advisory Council of HAI, https://hai.stanford.edu/people /susan-liautaud.

147   *"is a national emergency"*: Fei-Fei Li and John Etchemendy, "We Need a National Vision for AI," October 22, 2019, https://hai.stanford.edu/news/we-need-nation-al-vision-ai.

148   *"force multiplier"*: Ibid.

148   *In June 2019*: G20 Ministerial Statement on Trade and Digital Economy, https:// www.mofa.go.jp/files/000486596.pdf#targetText=a)%20AI%20actors%20 should%20respect,and%20internationally%20recognized%20labor%20rights.

148   *experts* and *nonexperts*: For example, the human-centered AI research at Stanford has shown a commitment to humanity ("Stanford University Launches 'Human-Centered' AI Institute Led by John Etchemendy & Fe-Fei Li," Medium, March 14, 2019, https://medium.com/syncedreview/stanford-university-launches

-human-centered-ai-institute-led-by-john-etchemendy-fei-fei-li-4abc5c1ef950). In the U.K., the government-run Centre for Data Ethics and Innovation has demonstrated a similar concern for the broad implications of their research (Centre for Data Ethics and Innovation, retrieved August 29, 2019, https://www.gov.uk/government /organisations/centre-for-data-ethics-and-innovation). Even if individual scientists and leaders in the field are thoughtful, governance on this issue is essential.

Chapter Six – Compromised Truth

151   *The White House had announced*: From "Statement by Press Secretary Sean Spicer," January 21, 2017: "This was the largest audience to ever witness an inauguration—period—both in person and around the globe. . . . These attempts to lessen the enthusiasm of the inauguration are shameful and wrong," https://www.whitehouse .gov/briefings-statements/statement-press-secretary-sean-spicer/.

151   Meet the Press: Chuck Todd's full interview is available on YouTube, "Kellyanne Conway: Presidents 'Aren't Judged by Crowd Size' (Full)," *Meet the Press*, NBC News, https://www.youtube.com/watch?v=MA1vD_L8Mjs.

153   *But my focus here*: My specific purpose in this chapter is to discuss how truth links to ethical decision-making, not to deliver a treatise on truth per se.

153   *"the actual facts"*: *Macmillan English Dictionary*, https://www.macmillandictionary. com/us/dictionary/american/truth. Other definitions include: "II. 5a. True statement; report or account which is in accordance with fact or reality" at "truth, n. and adv. (and int.)," *OED Online*, March 2020, retrieved April 20, 2020, https://www .oed.com/view/Entry/207026; and "the body of real things, events, facts: actuality," *Merriam-Webster*, https://www.merriam-webster.com/dictionary/truth.

153–54 *Everyone is entitled*: The full quote is "Everyone is entitled to his own opinion but not to his own facts." Daniel Patrick Moynihan, *Daniel Patrick Moynihan: A Portrait in Letters of an American Visionary*, edited by Steven R. Weisman (New York: PublicAffairs, 2010), 2.

154   Oxford Dictionaries: Oxford Languages, Word of the Year, 2016, https://languages. oup.com/word-of-the-year/2016/.

154   *increased 2,000 percent:* Alison Flood, "'Post-truth' Named Word of the Year by Oxford Dictionaries," *The Guardian*, November 15, 2016, https://www.theguard ian.com/books/2016/nov/15/post-truth-named-word-of-the-year-by-oxford -dictionaries. Oxford Dictionary president Casper Grathwohl states: "We first saw the frequency really spike this year in June with buzz over the Brexit vote and Donald Trump securing the Republican presidential nomination. Given that usage of the term hasn't shown any signs of slowing down, I wouldn't be surprised if post-truth becomes one of the defining words of our time."

154   *defines "post-truth"*: "post-truth, adj.," *OED Online*, March 2020, www.oed.com /view/Entry/58609044, retrieved April 20, 2020.

154   *The* Oxford *editors said*: Oxford Languages, Word of the Year.

155   *Meitu*: "What is Meitu?" (https://corp.meitu.com/en/about/overview/, retrieved April 20, 2020), states: "Founded in October 2008 with a mission 'to let everyone become beautiful easily,' Meitu is powered by AI and stands as China's leading imaging and video editing social media platform. From its earliest days, Meitu has created a series of software and hardware products with the concept of beauty, or *Mei* (美) in Chinese, at their core." See also "About Meitu," Meitu Global, https:// corp.meitu.com/en/about/overview/, retrieved April 20, 2020.

155   *"beautiful picture"*: Jiayang Fan, "China's Selfie Obsession," *The New Yorker*, December 11, 2017, https://www.newyorker.com/magazine/2017/12/18/chinas-selfie-obsession; Yuan Yang and Gloria Cheung, "Selfie App Meitu Set to Be Valued

at \$5.2bn After IPO," *Financial Times*, December 2, 2016, https://www.ft.com /content/2621cf96-b87f-11e6-ba85-95d1533d9a62; and Jiayang Fan, "China's Selfie Culture: Youth Obsessed with the Power of Appearances," *South China Morning Post*, April 13, 2018, https://www.scmp.com/magazines/post-magazine/long-reads /article/2141257/chinas-selfie-culture-youth-obsessed-power.

155   *"the perfect selfie"*: Meitu Global, retrieved March 15, 2019, https://global.meitu .com.

155   *approximately 282 million*: "Total Monthly Active Users ('MAUs') 282,472," in "Key Operational Data," p. 2, "Annual Results Announcement for the Year Ended December 31, 2019," Meitu, retrieved April 21, 2020, https://corp-public.zone1 .meitudata.com/ARANNENG20200326164738.pdf.

155   *nearly 40 percent*: We came to a figure of 38.5 percent, by referring to the "Total Monthly Active Users ('MAUs'): 282,472," and "MAU Breakdown by Geography: Overseas: 108,841" from "Key Operational Data," p. 2, in "Annual Results Announcement for the Year Ended December 31, 2019," Ibid.

155   *Meitu's foundation for ethics*: Meitu,"Culture and Values," retrieved March 15, 2020, https://corp.meitu.com/en/about/culture/. Meitu Global (https://global.meitu .com/en/company, retrieved April 20, 2020) also states: "Our mission is to create a global community where people from all around the world can explore and discover new ideas related to beauty, and ultimately by using our virtual tools, have more confidence to bring these new ideas into the real world."

156   *Meitu uses algorithms*: Amie Tsang and Emily Feng, "China's Meitu, an Aspirational Beauty App, Goes Public," *New York Times*, December 4, 2016, https://www .nytimes.com/2016/12/14/business/dealbook/meitu-beauty-app-ipo.html.

156   *auto-beautification tools*: Meitu's "BeautyPlus," https://global.meitu.com/en/prod ucts#B+, retrieved May 3, 2020, states: "With its 'one-touch' beautify feature, BeautyPlus users can instantly retouch their photos and video selfies.

156   *data "tells us"*: Fan, "China's Selfie Obsession."

156   *freckles:* Celia Chen, "China's Biggest Selfie App Meitu Turns Its Eye to Social Networking," *South China Morning Post*, April 12, 2018, https://www.scmp.com/tech /article/2141309/chinas-biggest-selfie-app-meitu-turns-its-eye-social-networking.

156   *reflect regionalized notions*: Tsang and Feng, "China's Meitu, an Aspirational Beauty App, Goes Public," write: "Meitu says local teams in different markets are tailoring the software to other standards." They also quote Kai-Fu Lee, a venture capitalist who owns a stake in Meitu, as saying that skin tone is " 'fixed to each country,' . . . 'Is it preferable to have a tan? Some of that is automatic, some within the user's control.' " Fan, in "China's Selfie Obsession," writes: "Earlier this year, there was a spate of outrage on social media after international users pointed out that increasing beauty levels in the app invariably resulted in a lightening of skin color." Finally, Cheng Yu, "Chinese App Is Beautifying the Whole World," *China Daily*, February 22, 2018, writes: "BeautyPlus has location-specific features. In Brazil, for example, a function can darken skin and whiten teeth in an image. 'Our global strategy is to ensure that each of our overseas products is 'hyper-localized' to inspire our users in expressing their beauty,' said Fox Lui, head of Meitu's international business."

156   *"pale skin"*: Tsang and Feng, "China's Meitu, an Aspirational Beauty App, Goes Public."

156   *Meitu's tagline*: Meitu Global, retrieved March 15, 2020, https://global.meitu.com.

156   *unrealistic ideals*: Y. Kelly, A. Zilanawala, C. Booker, & A. Sacker, "Social Media Use and Adolescent Mental Health: Findings From the UK Millennium Cohort Study," *EClinicalMedicine* 6 (January 2019): 59–68, https://www.thelancet.com /journals/eclinm/article/PIIS2589-5370(18)30060-9/fulltext, examined data on 10,904 adolescents in the U.K., and state: "Consistent with other studies we found

an association between social media use and depressive symptoms" (66). They additionally note: "Clearly a large proportion of young people experience dissatisfaction with the way they look and how they feel about their bodies and perhaps a broader societal shift away from the perpetuation of what are often highly distorted images of idealised beauty could help shift these types of negative perceptions" (67). See also "#StatusofMind: Social Media and Young People's Mental Health and Wellbeing," May 2017, Royal Society for Public Health, London, https://www.rsph.org .uk/our-work/campaigns/status-of-mind.html; and Elle Hunt, "Faking It: How Selfie Dysmorphia Is Driving People to Seek Surgery," *The Guardian*, January 23, 2019, https://www.theguardian.com/lifeandstyle/2019/jan/23/faking-it-how-selfie -dysmorphia-is-driving-people-to-seek-surgery.

156 *patients are increasingly asking*: S. Rajanala, M.B.C. Maymone, and N. A. Vashi, "Selfies—Living in the Era of Filtered Photographs," *JAMA Facial Plastic Surgery* 20, no. 6 (2018): 443–44, doi:10.1001/jamafacial.2018.0486, https://jamanetwork .com/journals/jamafacialplasticsurgery/article-abstract/2688763.

156 *"This is an alarming trend"*: Rajanala et al., "Selfies—Living in the Era of Filtered Photographs."

156 *London's Royal Society for Public Health issued*: The authors also noted that social media has been described by young people as more addictive than cigarettes and alcohol. "#StatusofMind: Social Media and Young People's Mental Health and Wellbeing."

156 *The report found that*: Ibid., p. 10.

157 *are increasingly popular*: "Level of Activities on Meitu App Increased Over Tenfold Since Its Revamp," PR Newswire, September 25, 2018, https://www.prnewswire .com/news-releases/level-of-activities-on-meitu-app-increased-over-tenfold-since -its-revamp-300718240.html.

157 *A study commissioned by Meitu*: The study "includes responses from 250 U.S. men and women, ages 18-34 who have used online and mobile dating apps," according to "Surprise! Many Men and Women Retouch Their Dating Profile Photos," Meitu Company News, June 9, 2016, retrieved April 21, 2020, https://corp.meitu.com /en/news/news/21.html.

157 *a 2016 survey*: Conducted by Korean human resources recruiting firm Saramin, the survey was reported by Kelly Kasulis, "South Korea's New 'Blind Hiring' Law Bans Personal Interview Questions," *The World*, July 23, 2019, https://www.pri.org/stories /2019-07-23/south-koreas-new-blind-hiring-law-bans-personal-interview-questions.

157 *One Chinese graduate student told*: Tsang and Feng, "China's Meitu, an Aspirational Beauty App, Goes Public."

158 *Meitu does not*: Meitu's service agreement for BeautyPlus, "5. Your Use of Beauty-Plus," states: "You shall not produce, store or post any following information via BeautyPlus: . . . v. information that violates the terms of this Agreement, laws, regulations, policies, social order and information that disturbs Meitu's normal operation," retrieved April 21, 2020, https://api.meitu.com/agreements/beautyPlus/#/.

158 *"non-commercial"*: "4. Non-commercial Use of BeautyPlus," ibid.

158 *"solely responsible"*: "Your Responsibility for Your User Content," at "8. Content Ownership and License," ibid.

158 *harassment, discrimination*: "5. Your Use of BeautyPlus," ibid.

159 *They advise fashion*: p. 24, "#StatusofMind: Social Media and Young People's Mental Health and Wellbeing."

159 *rising rates of video game addiction*: The rules, announced by China's General Administration of Press and Publication, banned children under eighteen from playing between 10 p.m. and 8 a.m., no more than ninety minutes per day on weekdays, and no more than three hours per day on weekends and holidays. Eric Cheung, "China Fears Young People Are Addicted to Video Games. Now It's Imposing a Curfew,"

CNN, November 6, 2019, https://www.cnn.com/2019/11/06/asia/china-bans
-online-games-minors-intl-hnk/index.html; Anthony Cuthbertson, "China Bans
Children Playing Video Games for More Than 90 Minutes a Day or at Night," *The
Independent*, November 7, 2019, https://www.independent.co.uk/life-style/gadgets
-and-tech/gaming/china-gaming-ban-video-game-addiction-a9188806.html; and
Javier C. Hernández and Albee Zhang, "90 Minutes a Day, Until 10 P.M.: China
Sets Rules for Young Gamers," *New York Times*, November 6, 2019, https://www
.nytimes.com/2019/11/06/business/china-video-game-ban-young.html.

160   *Emile Ratelband*: Daniel Boffey, "Dutch Man, 69, Starts Legal Fight to Identify as
20 Years Younger," *The Guardian*, November 8, 2018, https://www.theguardian
.com/world/2018/nov/08/dutch-man-69-starts-legal-fight-to-identify-as-20-years
-younger.

160   *"change your name"*: His full quote is: "We live in a time when you can change your
name and change your gender. Why can't I decide my own age?" according to
"Emile Ratelband, 69, Told He Cannot Legally Change His Age," BBC News, December 3, 2018, https://www.bbc.com/news/world-europe-46425774; and George
Steer, "Dutch Man, 69, Launches Legal Battle to Lower His Age 20 Years So He
Can Get a Date on Tinder," *Time*, November 9, 2018, https://time.com/5449067
/dutchman-change-age-twenty-years/.

160   *The court wisely disagreed*: The decision by a Dutch court in Arnhem was summarized
in a December 3, 2018, government post, "District Court Refuses to Amend Emil
Ratelband's Date of Birth," and states: "Mr Ratelband is at liberty to feel 20 years
younger than his real age and to act accordingly. But amending his date of birth
would cause 20 years of records to vanish from the register of births, deaths, mar-
riages and registered partnerships. This would have a variety of undesirable legal and
societal implications. The priority must be to ensure that the public registers contain
accurate factual information." (https://www.rechtspraak.nl/Organisatie-en-contact
/Organisatie/Rechtbanken/Rechtbank-Gelderland/Nieuws/Paginas/District
-court-refuses-to-amend-Emil-Ratelbands-date-of-birth.aspx, retrieved April 21, 2020.)

160   *"there are a variety of rights"*: Ibid. The full quote is: "The court did not find any reason in Mr. Ratelband's arguments to create new case law in line with the statutory
provisions on changes to a person's officially registered name or gender. Its main
reason was that, unlike the situation with respect to a change in registered name
or gender, there are a variety of rights and duties . . ." And media accounts, for
example: Camila Domonoske, "Dutch Man Loses Bid to Change His Age, Plans to
Appeal," NPR, December 4, 2018, https://www.npr.org/2018/12/04/673246844
/dutch-man-loses-bid-to-change-his-age-plans-to-appeal.

162   *Picasso's Blue Period*: PabloPicasso.org, 2009, retrieved August 30, 2019, https://
www.pablopicasso.org/blue-period.jsp.

163   *Sir Salman Rushdie*: Author interview with Sir Salman Rushdie, "On Truth,
Beauty, the Ethics Instinct, Universal Humanity and More," The Ethics Incubator,
September 2017, http://ethicsincubator.net/ethics-and-the-arts-interviews/salman
-rushdie-interview.

164   *The Holocaust History Museum*: Yad Vashem: The World Holocaust Remembrance
Center, https://www.yadvashem.org/museum/holocaust-history-museum/galleries
.html.

164   *Martin Roth*: Author interview with Martin Roth, October 7, 2016.

164   *"I have tried to keep memory"*: His full quote is: "That I have tried to keep memory
alive, that I have tried to fight those who would forget. Because if we forget, we
are guilty, we are accomplices." The Elie Wiesel Foundation for Humanity, Nobel
Prize Speech, December 10, 1986, https://eliewieselfoundation.org/elie-wiesel
/nobelprizespeech/.

167   *"In my own effort"*: Her full quote is: "In my own effort to illuminate the character and career of Abraham Lincoln, I have coupled the account of his life with the stories of the remarkable men who were his rivals for the 1860 Republican Presidential nomination—New York senator William H. Seward, Ohio governor Salmon P. Chase, and Missouri's distinguished elder statesman Edward Bates." Doris Kearns Goodwin, *Team of Rivals: The Political Genius of Abraham Lincoln* (New York: Simon & Schuster, 2005), xv.

167   *How inspiring it would be:* My other favorite quote is from Marcel Proust: "The only true voyage, the only bath in the Fountain of Youth, would be not to visit strange lands but to possess other eyes, to see the universe through the eyes of another, of a hundred others, to see the hundred universes that each of them sees, that each of them is." (*The Prisoner*, Volume 5 of *In Search of Lost Time*, 1923).

169   An Inconvenient Truth: Al Gore, *An Inconvenient Truth*, https://www.algore.com /library/an-inconvenient-truth-dvd.

169   *Hans Rosling's*: Hans Rosling, Anna Rosling Rönnlund, and Ola Rosling, *Factfulness: Ten Reasons We're Wrong About the World—and Why Things Are Better Than You Think* (New York: Flatiron Books, 2018).

Chapter Seven – Ethics on the Fly

171   *"ethics on the fly"*: The term "ethics on the fly" was coined by Stephanie Frerich, my editor at Simon & Schuster.

176   *approximately 81 percent of children*: According to a 2010 survey by Research Now, commissioned by internet security Company AVG, which polled 2,200 mothers with children under two from the U.K., Germany, France, Italy, Spain, Canada, the U.S., Australia, New Zealand, and Japan. In the U.S. alone, the figure was 92 percent. "Digital Birth: Welcome to the Online World," *Business Wire*, October 6, 2010, https://www.businesswire.com/news/home/20101006006722/en/Digital-Birth -Online-World. In an April 13, 2020, email exchange with *Sharenthood* author Leah A. Plunkett, a faculty associate at the Berkman Klein Center for Internet & Society at Harvard University and an associate dean & associate professor at the University of New Hampshire School of Law, she pointed to a survey by nonprofits Parent Zone and Nominet ("Share with Care," https://media.nominet.uk/wp -content/uploads/2016/09/Nominet-Share-with-Care-2016-Infographic.pdf), which found that parents post nearly 1,500 photos online by a child's fifth birthday. See also Julie Brown, "'Sharenting': How to Safeguard Your Kids' Personal Information on Social Media," NBC News, September 24, 2019, https://www.nbcnews .com/better/lifestyle/sharenting-how-safeguard-your-kids-personal-information -social-media-ncna1058006; and Mark Milian, "Study: 82 Percent of Kids Under 2 Have an Online Presence," CNN, October 7, 2010, https://www.cnn.com/2010 /TECH/social.media/10/07/baby.pictures/index.html.

176   *"sharenting"*: Leah A. Plunkett, *Sharenthood: Why We Should Think Before We Talk About Our Kids Online* (Cambridge: MIT Press, 2019); and author email with Plunkett, April 13, 2020.

177   *Pew Research finds*: Monica Anderson, "A Majority of Teens Have Experienced Some Form of Cyberbullying," Pew Research Center, September 27, 2018, https:// www.pewresearch.org/internet/2018/09/27/a-majority-of-teens-have-experienced -some-form-of-cyberbullying/.

177   *a gateway for criminals*: "Keeping Children Safe Online," Interpol, retrieved March 26, 2020, https://www.interpol.int/en/Crimes/Crimes-against-children/Keeping- children-safe-online; Press Association, "Social Media–Related Crime Reports Up 780% in Four Years," *The Guardian*, December 27, 2012, https://www.theguardian

.com/media/2012/dec/27/social-media-crime-facebook-twitter; Jane C. Hu, "Insta-gram's 'Digital Kidnappers' Are Stealing Children's Photos and Making Up New Lives," *Quartz*, October 25, 2018, https://qz.com/1434858/digital-kidnapping-is-a-reminder-of-the-dangers-of-social-media/; and Jack Morse, "Think Twice About Posting Photos of Your Kid on Facebook," Mashable, November 21, 2018, https://mashable.com/article/children-facebook-baby-photos-privacy-risk/.

177 *We click "I agree"*: Governments have become more interested in checking their power and influence. In 2018, Mark Zuckerberg was called to testify before a skep-tical Congress regarding data privacy and Russian disinformation on Facebook. During the hearing, Senator Kamala Harris observed: "I'm concerned about how much Facebook values trust and transparency, if we agree that a critical compo-nent of a relationship of trust and transparency is we speak truth and we get to the truth." ("Harris Presses Zuckerberg on Accountability, Transparency Failures," Kamala D. Harris, April 10, 2018, https://www.harris.senate.gov/news/press-releases/harris-presses-zuckerberg-on-accountability-transparency-failures.) Later in the hearing, Zuckerberg admitted: "We now have a lot of work around building trust back." Transcript via *The Washington Post*, April 10, 2018, https://www.washingtonpost.com/news/the-switch/wp/2018/04/10/transcript-of-mark-zuckerbergs-senate-hearing/.

177 *issues of trustworthiness . . . control*: See "Cambridge Analytica and the Future of Data Privacy," Senate Judiciary Committee hearings, May 16, 2018, https://www.judiciary.senate.gov/meetings/cambridge-analytica-and-the-future-of-data-privacy; and "Mass Violence, Extremism, and Digital Responsibility," U.S. Senate Commit-tee on Commerce, Science, & Transportation. September 18, 2019, https://www.commerce.senate.gov/2019/9/mass-violence-extremism-and-digital-responsibility.

178 *Some platforms' terms of service*: For example, "Community Standards" (https://www.facebook.com/communitystandards/), "How Do I Remove a Tag From a Photo or Post I'm Tagged in on Facebook?" (https://www.facebook.com/help/140906109319589), and "Does the Number of Times Something Gets Reported Determine Whether or Not That Content Is Removed?" (https://www.facebook.com/help/408181689281891?helpref=related), Facebook, all retrieved March 26, 2020.

179 *contagion and mutation*: Contagion and mutation connect with informed consent in several ways. First, the consequences of inadequate or absent informed consent spread and mutate. Second, the failure to obtain proper informed consent itself is contagious. The epidemic of parents posting photos of children is also an epidemic of failed informed consent. Third, the normalization of one can reinforce the nor-malization of the other: We start to think that it's just normal to post photos without consent (then it becomes photos of friends, etc.), and also normal not to obtain adequate informed consent for children's photos.

180 *celebrities*: A. Hussain, S. Ali, M. Ahmed, and S. Hussain, "The Anti-vaccination Movement: A Regression in Modern Medicine," *Cureus* 10, no. 7 (July 2018): e2919, https://doi.org/10.7759/cureus.2919, https://www.ncbi.nlm.nih.gov/pmc/articles/PMC6122668/; Timothy Caulfield and Declan Fahy, "Science, Celebri-ties, and Public Engagement," *Issues in Science and Technology* 32, no. 4 (Summer 2016), https://issues.org/perspective-science-celebrities-and-public-engagement/; E. J. Dickson, "A Guide to 17 Anti-Vaccination Celebrities," *Rolling Stone*, June 14, 2019, https://www.rollingstone.com/culture/culture-features/celebrities-anti-vaxxers-jessica-biel-847779/; and Melody Gutierrez and Soumya Karlamangla, "Jes-sica Biel Steps into Vaccine Debate as Other Celebrities Fear the 'Anti-vax' Label," *Los Angeles Times*, June 14, 2019, https://www.latimes.com/politics/la-pol-ca-vaccine-bill-celebrities-jessica-biel-20190613-story.html.

180 *Some parents believe*: C. McKee and K. Bohannon, "Exploring the Reasons Behind

Parental Refusal of Vaccines," *The Journal of Pediatric Pharmacology and Therapeutics* 21, no. 2 (March–April 2016): 104–9, https://doi.org/10.5863/1551-6776-21.2.104.

180   *measles vaccine*: "Measles History," Centers for Disease Control and Prevention, retrieved March 29, 2020, https://www.cdc.gov/measles/about/history.html.

181   *1,282 cases of measles*: "Measles Cases and Outbreaks," Centers for Disease Control and Prevention, retrieved March 29, 2020, https://www.cdc.gov/measles/cases-outbreaks.html.

181   *"the majority of cases"*: Ibid.

181   *complications include*: "Complications of Measles," Centers for Disease Control and Prevention, retrieved March 29, 2020, https://www.cdc.gov/measles/symptoms/complications.html; and "Complications: Measles," National Health Service (UK), retrieved March 29, 2020, https://www.nhs.uk/conditions/measles/complications/.

181   *"highly contagious virus"*: "Transmission of Measles," Centers for Disease Control and Prevention, retrieved April 25, 2020, https://www.cdc.gov/measles/transmission.html.

181   *eliminated in 2000*: "Measles History," Centers for Disease Control and Prevention, retrieved March 29, 2020, https://www.cdc.gov/measles/about/history.html.

181   *A child who has received*: "Vaccine for Measles," Centers for Disease Control and Prevention, retrieved March 29, 2020, https://www.cdc.gov/measles/vaccination.html.

181   *risk of autism:* In 1998, an article in *The Lancet* by Andrew Wakefield and his colleagues suggested a link between the MMR vaccine and autism. A. J. Wakefield, S. H. Murch, A. Anthony, J. Linnell et al., "Ileal-Lymphoid-Nodular Hyperplasia, Non-specific Colitis, and Pervasive Developmental Disorder in Children," *The Lancet* 351 (1998): 637–41. The study was debunked by subsequent scientists (for example, C. Black, J. A. Kaye, H. Jick, "Relation of Childhood Gastrointestinal Disorders to Autism: Nested Case-Control Study Using Data from the UK General Practice Research Database," *BMJ* 325, no. 7361 (August 2002): 419–21, https://www.ncbi.nlm.nih.gov/pmc/articles/PMC119436/), and in 2010, *The Lancet* retracted the paper, noting: "Following the judgment of the UK General Medical Council's Fitness to Practise Panel on January 28, 2010, it has become clear that several elements of the 1998 paper by Wakefield et al. are incorrect, contrary to the findings of an earlier investigation. In particular, the claims in the original paper that children were 'consecutively referred' and that investigations were 'approved' by the local ethics committee have been proven to be false. Therefore we fully retract this paper from the published record." "Retraction—Ileal-Lymphoid-Nodular Hyperplasia, Non-specific Colitis, and Pervasive Developmental Disorder in Children," *The Lancet*, February 6, 2010, https://www.thelancet.com/journals/lancet/article/PIIS0140-6736(10)60175-4/fulltext. See also Vanessa Lam, Steven Teutsch, and Jonathan Fielding, "Refuting a Lie That Won't Die: Taking the Fight for Vaccines Beyond the Doctor's Office," *Health Affairs*, February 28, 2019, https://www.healthaffairs.org/do/10.1377/hblog20190226.742851/full/; and Laura Helft and Emily Willingham, "The Autism-Vaccine Myth," *NOVA*, PBS, September 5, 2014, https://www.pbs.org/wgbh/nova/article/autism-vaccine-myth/, which states: "What the public didn't know in 1998 was that the now-retracted study, which involved just 12 children, would turn out to have some serious flaws—and even to contain apparently falsified data."

181   *In rare cases*: I'm referring to people for whom medical reasons preclude them from receiving the vaccine. See "Who Should Not Get MMR Vaccine?" in "Measles, Mumps, and Rubella (MMR) Vaccination: What Everyone Should Know," Centers for Disease Control and Prevention, retrieved April 25, 2020, https://www.cdc.gov/vaccines/vpd/mmr/public/index.html.

182   *"vaccine hesitancy"*: "Ten Threats to Global Health in 2019," World Health Orga-

nization, Newsroom, retrieved March 20, 2020, https://www.who.int/news-room/feature-stories/ten-threats-to-global-health-in-2019.

182 *well protected against measles*: The vaccine is 97 percent effective at preventing measles if delivered in the recommended double dose; one dose is 93 percent effective, according to "Vaccine for Measles," Centers for Disease Control.

183 *urge legislators*: Indeed, the potential consequences of measles outbreaks are so serious they have already triggered changes in existing vaccination legislation as well as discussions about the introduction of new laws to protect the public. For example, in 2019 New York governor Andrew Cuomo signed legislation that repealed school vaccination exceptions based on religious or personal beliefs. Other states including New Jersey, Vermont, Washington, and Oregon are considering similar legislative changes as of this writing. See Michelle Andrews, "As Measles Outbreak Fades, NY Sets in Motion New Rules on School Vaccinations," *Kaiser Health News*, September 5, 2019, https://khn.org/news/as-measles-outbreak-fades-n-y-sets-in-motion-new-rules-on-school-vaccinations/; and, Salini Mohanty and Dorit Rubinstein Reiss, "Measles Outbreak Prompts States to Consider Stricter Immunization Laws," Health Policy$ense, UPenn Leonard Davis Institute of Health Economics February 13, 2019, https://ldi.upenn.edu/healthpolicysense/measles-outbreak-prompts-states-consider-stricter-immunization-laws.

184 *You are a bystander*: Bystanders can play a crucial role in stemming sexual harassment, in particular. Claire Cain Miller, "Sexual Harassment Training Doesn't Work. But Some Things Do," *New York Times*, December 11, 2017, https://www.nytimes.com/2017/12/11/upshot/sexual-harassment-workplace-prevention-effective.html; and Brigid Schulte, "To Combat Harassment, More Companies Should Try Bystander Training," *Harvard Business Review*, October 31, 2018, https://hbr.org/2018/10/to-combat-harassment-more-companies-should-try-bystander-training.

185 *you see someone hitting a teenager*: See examples in Kwame Anthony Appiah, "Should I Intervene When I See a Parent Mistreating a Child?," The Ethicist, *New York Times*, December 17, 2019, https://www.nytimes.com/2019/12/17/magazine/should-i-intervene-when-i-see-a-parent-mistreating-a-child.html.

187 *millions of people*: According to Global Climate Strike, four million people joined in the marches. Jenny Tuazon, "Over 4 Million Join 2 Days of Global Climate Strike," Global Climate Strike, September 21, 2019, https://globalclimatestrike.net/4-million/; and Somini Sengupta, "Protesting Climate Change, Young People Take to Streets in a Global Strike," *New York Times*, September 20, 2019, https://www.nytimes.com/2019/09/20/climate/global-climate-strike.html.

187 *Global Climate Strike*: Global Climate Strike, retrieved March 21, 2020, https://globalclimatestrike.net.

188 *technology-sector workers*: Tech Workers Coalition, retrieved March 21, 2020, https://techworkerscoalition.org/climate-strike/.

188 *"walk out"*: Ahiza Garcia, "Amazon Workers Walk Out to Protest Climate Change Inaction," CNN Business, September 20, 2019, https://www.cnn.com/2019/09/20/tech/amazon-climate-strike-global-tech/index.html; and @AMZNforClimate Twitter feed, retrieved April 25, 2020, https://twitter.com/AMZNforClimate/status/1174729463344427008.

188 *three thousand Amazon employees*: Ahiza Garcia, "Amazon Workers Walk Out to Protest Climate Change Inaction." For perspective, Amazon had 750,000 employees (full-time and part-time; excluding contractors & temporary personnel) at the end of Q3 2019 (September 30, 2019) and 653,300 employees at the end of the prior quarter (June 30, 2019), according to "Amazon.com Announces Third Quarter Sales Up 24% to $70.0 Billion," Amazon, October 24, 2019, https://ir.aboutamazon.com

/news-release/news-release-details/2019/Amazoncom-Announces-Third-Quarter -Sales-up-24-to-700-Billion/default.aspx, retrieved April 25, 2020.

188 *"We want Amazon"*: Twitter, accessed October 2, 2019, https://twitter.com/AMZN-forClimate/status/1171077286382243840.

188 *CEO Jeff Bezos had responded*: "Amazon Co-founds The Climate Pledge, Setting Goal to Meet the Paris Agreement 10 Years Early," Amazon announcement, https://press.aboutamazon.com/news-releases/news-release-details/amazon-co-founds -climate-pledge-setting-goal-meet-paris; and Alina Selyukh, "Amazon Makes 'Climate Pledge' as Workers Plan Walkout," NPR, September 19, 2019, https://www.npr .org/2019/09/19/762336929/amazon-makes-climate-pledge-as-workers-plan-walkout.

188 *$10 billion*: Bezos Earth Fund, https://www.instagram.com/p/B8rWKFnnQ5c /?hl=en; and Karen Weise, "Jeff Bezos Commits $10 Billion to Address Climate Change," *New York Times*, February 17, 2020, https://www.nytimes.com/2020/02 /17/technology/jeff-bezos-climate-change-earth-fund.html.

188 *oil and gas industry*: David McCabe and Karen Weise, "Amazon Accelerates Efforts to Fight Climate Change," *New York Times*, September 19, 2019, https://www.ny times.com/2019/09/19/technology/amazon-carbon-neutral.html.

188 *Objecting to this decision*: Garcia, "Amazon Workers Walk Out to Protest Climate Change Inaction."

190 *"We're going to work hard"*: McCabe and Weise, "Amazon Accelerates Efforts to Fight Climate Change."

190 *"proves that collective action"*: @AMZNforClimate Twitter feed, retrieved March 21, 2020, https://twitter.com/AMZNforClimate/status/1174729463344427008.

190 *Do you have a choice*: For example, in Microsoft president Brad Smith's book, *Tools and Weapons: The Promise and the Peril of the Digital Age* (New York: Penguin, 2019), 205, he describes how Microsoft offers employees who object to a project, like selling drones to the military, an option to switch projects: "At the same time, we recognized that some of our own employees were uncomfortable working on defense contracts for the US or other military organizations. Some were citizens of other countries, some had different ethical views or were pacifists, and some simply wanted to devote their energy to alternative applications for technology. We respected these views, and we were quick to say that we would work to enable such individuals to work on other projects. Given Microsoft's size and diverse technology portfolio, we felt that we could most likely accommodate those requests." (Kindle version, loc. 3083).

191 *Approximately 147 million*: Or 146.9 million, according to Bret Kinsella, "Amazon Again Topped Q4 Global Smart Speaker Sales Followed by Google and Baidu According to Strategy Analytics. Smart Speaker Shipments Set New Record."

191 *one in four Americans*: "The Smart Audio Report," Edison Research and NPR, January 2020, https://www.nationalpublicmedia.com/insights/reports/smart-audio -report/; and Kourtney Bitterly, "1 in 4 Americans Own a Smart Speaker. What Does That Mean for News?" *New York Times*, August 22, 2019, https://open.nytimes .com/how-might-the-new-york-times-sound-on-smart-speakers-3b59a6a78ae3. Sixty-one percent of these devices are Amazon Echo, according to Bret Kinsella, "U.S. Smart Speaker Ownership Rises 40% in 2018 to 66.4 Million and Amazon Echo Maintains Market Share Lead Says New Report from Voicebot," *Voicebot. ai*, March 7, 2019, https://voicebot.ai/2019/03/07/u-s-smart-speaker-ownership -rises-40-in-2018-to-66-4-million-and-amazon-echo-maintains-market-share-lead -says-new-report-from-voicebot/.

192 *court-ordered warrants*: Brian Schrader, "Alexa, Can You Be Used Against Me in Court?," *LegalTech News*, July 10, 2019, https://www.law.com/legaltechnews/2019 /07/10/alexa-can-you-be-used-against-me-in-court/?slreturn=20200123204854; and Kayla Epstein, "Police Think Amazon's Alexa May Have Information on a

Fatal Stabbing Case," *Washington Post*, November 2, 2019, https://www.washington
post.com/technology/2019/11/02/police-think-amazons-alexa-may-have-inform
ation-fatal-stabbing-case/.

192 *states have laws restricting recording*: Numerous online sources provide some help here
but are not regularly updated and it's advisable to check your own state's laws. For
reference: The Digital Media Law Project of the Berkman Klein Center for Internet
& Society provides a list of state-specific resources that it stopped updating in 2014
(https://www.dmlp.org/legal-guide/state-law-recording); the Reporters Committee
for Freedom of the Press has a 2012 Reporter's Recording Guide (https://www.rcfp
.org/wp-content/uploads/imported/RECORDING.pdf); and Matthiesen, Wickert
& Lehrer, S.C., provide a state-by-state chart, last updated October 2019, https://
www.mwl-law.com/wp-content/uploads/2018/02/RECORDING-CONVERSA
TIONS-CHART.pdf, all retrieved April 25, 2020.

193 *"Amazon processes and retains"*: The full quote is: "You control Alexa with your voice.
Alexa streams audio to the cloud when you interact with Alexa. Amazon processes
and retains your Alexa Interactions, such as your voice inputs, music playlists, and
your Alexa to-do and shopping lists, in the cloud to provide, personalize, and improve our services. Learn more about these voice services including how to delete
voice recordings associated with your account." Alexa Terms of Use Section 1.3,
updated January 11, 2020. Note: Amazon's maximum liability (Section 3.7) is $50,
retrieved April 25, 2020, https://www.amazon.com/gp/help/customer/display
.html?nodeId=201809740.

194 *trigger warning signals*: For instance, 23andMe notes: "The parent or guardian as-
sumes full responsibility for ensuring that the information that he/she provides to
23andMe about his or her child is kept secure and that the information submitted
is accurate." 23andMe, "Full Privacy Statement: 7. Children's Privacy," retrieved
March 26, 2020, https://www.23andme.com/about/privacy/.

Chapter Eight – Resilience and Recovery

197 *On July 17, 2016*: Dr. Séan Cummings, Assistant Coroner for the Coroner Area of
London, "Regulation 28: Report to Prevent Future Deaths," Court and Tribunals Ju-
diciary, October 8, 2018, https://www.judiciary.uk/wp-content/uploads/2018/10
/Natasha-LAPEROUSE-2018-0279.pdf, retrieved April 19, 2020.

197 *South of France*: According to Nadim Ednan-Laperouse (5:57) in his audio interview
with Emily Buchanan, "A Bright Yellow Light," BBC Sounds, December 24, 2019,
https://www.bbc.co.uk/sounds/play/m000cmsf.

197 *ingredients*: Tanya and Nadim describe (1:43) Natasha and the family's being "scru-
pulously aware" and "almost a level of forensic" checking of labels and cautiousness
around allergens in "Our Daughter Died After Eating a Pret A Manger Baguette,"
This Morning with Phillip & Holly, October 1, 2018, YouTube, https://www.youtube
.com/watch?v=hdjLhyDP2Gc.

197 *severe allergies*: Cummings, "Regulation 28: Report to Prevent Future Deaths," and
Haroon Siddique, "Pret A Manger: Coroner in Teen Allergy Inquest Troubled by
Packaging Rules," *The Guardian*, September 26, 2018, https://www.theguardian
.com/society/2018/sep/26/coroner-teen-natasha-ednan-laperouse-allergy-inquest
-concerns-food-pret-a-manger-labelling-rules.

197 *she could safely eat*: Victoria Ward, "Phone Held to the Ear of Girl Who Died
After Eating a Pret A Manger Baguette so Her Mother Could Say Goodbye, Inquest Hears," *The Telegraph*, September 24, 2018, https://www.telegraph.co.uk
/news/2018/09/24/girl-died-eating-pret-manger-baguette-begged-daddy-help
-inquest/; and "Our Daughter Died After Eating a Pret A Manger Baguette."

197   *double-checked the ingredients*: "I looked at it, looked it over and said 'Yep, that's fine for you, absolutely,' " Nadim (2:52) told *This Morning with Phillip & Holly*.

197   *he found none*: "There was nothing . . . nothing visible at all to the eye," Nadim (3:21) told *This Morning with Phillip & Holly*. See also HM Assistant Coroner Dr. Séan Cummings, "The Inquest Touching the Death of Natasha Ednan-Laperouse," Leigh Day, September 28, 2018, https://www.leighday.co.uk/LeighDay/media/LeighDay/documents/Product%20liability/Inquest-Dr-Sean-Cummings-Summing-Up.pdf.

197   *felt an itchy*: At 3:39, *This Morning with Phillip & Holly*; and Haroon Siddique, "Father of Girl Who Died of Allergy on Plane Blames Pret A Manger," *The Guardian*, September 24, 2018, https://www.theguardian.com/society/2018/sep/24/father-of-girl-who-died-of-allergy-on-plane-blames-pret-a-manger.

197   *posted a video*: Brittany Vonow, "Final Moments: Pret A Manger Inquest—Haunting Last Video of Natasha Ednan-Laperouse, 15, Shows Her Moments Before She Died of Allergic Reaction to Sandwich on BA Flight," video, *The Sun*, September 28, 2018, https://www.thesun.co.uk/news/7369132/pret-a-manger-natasha-ednan-laperouse-anaphylactic-shock-ba-flight/.

198   *Approximately twenty-five minutes later*: Cummings, "The Inquest Touching the Death of Natasha Ednan-Laperouse"; and Hilary Clarke, "Pret A Manger Sandwich Labeling Ruled 'Inadequate' After Girl's Death," CNN, September 28, 2018, https://www.cnn.com/2018/09/28/uk/pret-a-manger-food-death-inquest-intl/index.html.

198   *She drank another dose*: Cummings, ibid.; and Siddique, "Father of Girl Who Died of Allergy on Plane Blames Pret A Manger."

198   *"hundreds of jellyfish"*: See father's interview with BBC News, "Pret Allergy Death: Father Had to Ring Wife to Say Daughter Would Die," October 1, 2018, https://www.bbc.com/news/uk-england-london-45703861; and news reports of his statement at inquest, including Ward, "Phone Held to the Ear of Girl Who Died After Eating a Pret A Manger Baguette so Her Mother Could Say Goodbye, Inquest Hears."

198   *Nadim gave Natasha's right thigh*: Nadim describes these events (4:10) in his and Tanya's interview, "Our Daughter Died After Eating a Pret A Manger Baguette."

198   *Nothing changed*: The coroner alerted the Medicines and Healthcare products Regulatory Agency and the manufacturers of EpiPen about this problem. See Cummings, "Regulation 28: Report to Prevent Future Deaths." According to reporting by the BBC, testimony at the inquest revealed that the EpiPens had a 16mm needle "which may be insufficient for adrenalin to reach the muscle" but it was "impossible to tell" if a longer needle would have been better. "Pret Allergy Labelling 'Inadequate,' Baguette Death Inquest Finds," BBC News, September 28, 2018, https://www.bbc.com/news/uk-45679320.

198   *"Daddy, help me"*: Cummings, "The Inquest Touching the Death of Natasha Ednan-Laperouse"; BBC News, "Pret Allergy Labelling 'Inadequate,' Baguette Death Inquest Finds"; and Haroon Siddique, "Pret A Manger: Coroner in Teen Allergy Inquest Troubled by Packaging Rules."

198   *provided her with oxygen*: Cummings, "The Inquest Touching the Death of Natasha Ednan-Laperouse"; BBC News, "Pret Allergy Labelling 'Inadequate'"; and Siddique, "Pret A Manger: Coroner in Teen Allergy Inquest Troubled by Packaging Rules."

198   *A passenger*: Cummings, paragraph 12, "The Inquest Touching the Death of Natasha Ednan-Laperouse"; and Nadim's "A Bright Yellow Light" interview in which he states (11:56) the passenger "had just qualified as a GP the day before. . . . I was so thankful he was there."

198   *Her skin turned blue*: Catherine Wylie, "Teenage Girl Was 'Blue, Not Breathing, Unresponsive' on Flight as She Suffered Fatal Allergic Reaction to Sandwich, Inquest Hears," *Independent.ie*, September 27, 2018, https://www.independent.ie/world

-news/europe/britain/teenage-girl-was-blue-not-breathing-unresponsive-on-flight
-as-she-suffered-fatal-allergic-reaction-to-sandwich-inquest-hears-37362375.html.

198   *too late to make an emergency landing*: Lorna Shaddick, "Pret Incident Was 'Frightening' – BA Crew Manager," SkyNews, September 26, 2018, https://news.sky.com
/story/live-pret-inquest-into-allergy-death-continues-11509075; and BBC News reporter Dan Johnson's minute-by-minute reporting on the testimony, Twitter, September 26, 2018, https://twitter.com/DanJohnsonNews/status/10449187199091
75296, retrieved April 19, 2020.

198   *covering the doors took "priority"*: "Pret Inquest: Flight Crew Did Not Use Defibrillator on Dying Girl," BBC News, September 26, 2018, https://www.bbc.com/news
/uk-england-london-45653749.

198   *Tanya raced*: Tanya describes these moments (5:35) in her and Nadim's interview on
This Morning with Phillip & Holly.

198   *"would not survive"*: Siddique, "Father of Girl Who Died of Allergy on Plane Blames
Pret A Manger"; and Patrick Sawer, " 'My Daughter Was Dying and I Had to
Say Goodbye Over the Phone,' " *The Telegraph*, September 29, 2018, https://www
.telegraph.co.uk/news/2018/09/29/daughter-dying-had-say-goodbye-phone/.

199   *At 7 p.m.*: Tanya and Nadim's interview (6:40), "Our Daughter Died After Eating a
Pret A Manger Baguette."

199   *"Tashi, I love you"*: Jamie Doward, "Pret Allergy Death: Parents Describe Final
Moments with Their Daughter," *The Guardian*, September 29, 2018, https://www
.theguardian.com/society/2018/sep/29/pret-allergy-death-parents-demand-label-
laws; and Sawer, " 'My Daughter Was Dying and I Had to Say Goodbye Over the
Phone.' "

199   *sesame seeds*: Cummings, "Regulation 28: Report to Prevent Future Deaths."

199   *twenty-one other instances*: Caroline Davies, "Pret A Manger 'Had Nine Similar Allergic Reactions in Year Before Girl Died,' " *The Guardian*, September 25, 2018, https://
www.theguardian.com/uk-news/2018/sep/25/pret-a-manger-allergic-reactions
-year-before-natasha-ednan-laperouse-died-inquest-told. Additionally, the mother
of the seventeen-year-old girl contacted Pret's customer service after the incident
to express her concern that the company was only providing allergen information upon request. According to the girl, her mother "expressed her alarm at this
and warned that, in her opinion, other similar adverse events could easily occur."
Jack Hardy, "Pret Did Not Label Baguettes Despite Six Allergic Reaction Cases
in the Year Before Teenager's Death, Inquest Hears," *Independent.ie*, September 25,
2018,   https://www.independent.ie/world-news/europe/britain/pret-did-not-label
-baguettes-despite-six-allergic-reaction-cases-in-the-year-before-teenagers-death
-inquest-hears-37354696.html.

199   *Pret A Manager's director of risk*: According to Davies, "Pret A Manger 'Had Nine
Similar Allergic Reactions in Year Before Girl Died,' " he testified: "We responded
appropriately to each individual complaint at the time." However, in "Regulation 28:
Report to Prevent Future Deaths," Dr. Cummings notes that "[i]n the case of Pret-
a-manger there was no coherent or coordinated system for monitoring customer
allergic reactions despite sales of more than 200 million items. In some cases concerns were notified to Customer Services and in some they were noted to the safety
department. The two did not know what the other was responding to. It was clear
that there was no overarching monitoring system in place." Additionally, reporting
on the inquest by Ceylan Yeginsu, "Pret A Manger Allergy Labeling Ruled 'Inadequate' After Teen's Death," *New York Times*, September 28, 2018, https://www
.nytimes.com/2018/09/28/world/europe/uk-pret-a-manger-allergy-natasha
-ednan-laperouse.html, states: "The chain's director of risk and compliance, Jonathan Perkins, said during the inquest that he accepted that several individuals had

had both negative and tragic experiences consuming some sandwiches, but said that 'thousands of allergy sufferers' had nonetheless been able to shop safely at Pret." And also: "Pret A Manger did not break the law, Mr. Cummings said, but it had not taken allergen monitoring seriously."

199 *"nothing visible at all"*: Nadim's interview (3:21), "Our Daughter Died After Eating a Pret A Manger Baguette."

199 not *legally required*: Although EU countries can choose to adopt their own national policies on the matter, at the time U.K. law did not require comprehensive in-gredient labels on the food itself if it was made on-site. U.K. law 2014 No. 1855, Section 5, http://www.legislation.gov.uk/uksi/2014/1855/pdfs/uksi_20141855_en .pdf; and EU Regulation No. 1169/2011, 2011, Ch. VI, Art. 44(1), https://eur-lex .europa.eu/legal-content/EN/TXT/PDF/?uri=CELEX:02011R1169-20140219& qid=1510149919934&from=EN.

199 *puzzlingly*: Thus, in the case of prepackaged items, the labeling of any allergens used in food or its processing must appear on the package. But in 2016, this "prepacked" food, or "any single item" sold to vendors or consumers in its o-wn packaging, ex-cluded any "foods packed on the sales premises at the consumer's request or pre-packed for direct sale." (EU Regulation No. 1169/2011, 2011, Ch. I, Art. 2e, https:// eur-lex.europa.eu/legal-content/EN/TXT/PDF/?uri=CELEX:02011R1169-2014 0219&qid=1510149919934&from=EN). This meant that food prepared in a large warehouse for a grocery store chain, for example, was subject to different labeling regulations from food made at shops like Pret that make their products on-site.

199 *Pret a Manager may have been operating*: Further, if the goal of the U.K. labeling law is to help consumers make informed food choices, then why make a legal distinc-tion based on where the food is prepared? For consumers worried about allergic reactions, what possible difference could it make where the food is assembled? For example, Chapter II, "General Principles on Food Information," Article 3, "General objectives," section 1, of the law states: "The provision of food information shall pursue a high level of protection of consumers' health and interests by providing a basis for final consumers to make informed choices and to make safe use of food, with particular regard to health, economic, environmental, social and ethical con-siderations," https://eur-lex.europa.eu/legal-content/EN/TXT/PDF/?uri=CEL EX:02011R1169-20140219&qid=1510149919934&from=EN.

200 *store shelves*: Brooke Masters, "Pret's Mishandling of the Allergy Issue Leaves It Vul-nerable," *Financial Times*, October 8, 2018, https://www.ft.com/content/980a2d98 -cae7-11e8-b276-b9069bde0956.

200 *"We believe that this inquest"*: His full quote (:54) was: "Our beloved daughter died in a tragedy that should never have happened. And we believe that this inquest has shown that she died because of inadequate food labeling laws. We are also shocked to learn there have been a number of previous, serious allergic incidents involving sesame seeds at Pret A Manger, before our daughter died. It feels to us that if Pret A Manger were following the law, then the law was playing Russian roulette with our daughter's life." "Natasha Ednan-Laperouse: This Tragedy Shouldn't Have Hap-pened, Says Father," Sky News, video, September 28, 2018, https://news.sky.com /video/square-video-natasha-father-statement-001-mp4-11511127.

200 *public apology*: The statements from Schlee are no longer on Pret's website, but they were reported widely in the press (for example, Matthew Weaver, "Pret A Manger to Bring in Full Labelling After Teenager's Death," *The Guardian*, October 3, 2018, https://www.theguardian.com/uk-news/2018/oct/03/pret-a-manger-to-bring-in -full-labelling-teenagers-death-natasha-ednan-laperouse), and can be accessed in the cached Google page of "Pret's Labelling Commitment," blog by Clive Schlee, Octo-ber 3, 2018, retrieved April 16, 2020.

200   *affixed ingredients labels*: Amie Tsang, "Pret A Manger Starts Labeling Food with Allergens," *New York Times*, October 3, 2018, https://www.nytimes.com/2018/10/03/business/pret-a-manager-allergy-labels.html.

200   *vowed to work*: "Pret's Labelling Commitment"; and Twitter account of Clive Schlee, retrieved March 24, 2020, https://twitter.com/cliveschlee/status/1047407385113976832?lang=en.

200   *"I hope this sets us"*: "Pret's Labelling Commitment."

200   *I wrote to Clive Schlee*: In July 2019, Schlee announced he would step down as CEO in September after sixteen years. Leila Abboud, "Pret A Manger Chief Clive Schlee to Step Down in September," *Financial Times*, July 1, 2019, https://www.ft.com/content/ba5527fa-9bdd-11e9-9c06-a4640c9feebb.

200   *spoke on the phone*: Descriptions about Clive Schlee's decisions and my observations are based on our phone interview on April 10, 2019. He did not respond to email requests to review the passages of the book in which he was mentioned.

202   *Natasha's Law*: "The Food Information (Amendment) (England) Regulations 2019," http://www.legislation.gov.uk/uksi/2019/1218/made, retrieved April 8, 2020; and "FSA Consults on Updated Guidance Following Change to Allergen Labelling Law," Food Standards Agency, January 23, 2020, https://www.food.gov.uk/news-alerts/news/fsa-consults-on-updated-guidance-following-change-to-allergen-labelling-law; and "Gove to Introduce Natasha's Law," Gov.UK, June 25, 2019, https://www.gov.uk/government/news/gove-to-introduce-natashas-law.

202   *Maya Angelou*: Many versions of this quote, some abbreviated, are in circulation. This one is from her official Twitter account, retrieved March 24, 2020, https://twitter.com/drmayaangelou/status/1028663286512930817?.

204   *definitions of resilience*: For ecology definition, "Resilience—rate at which a system returns to a reference state or dynamic after a perturbation," see Section 3, Box 3 "Perturbation-Based Categories," *Stanford Encyclopedia of Philosophy*, https://plato.stanford.edu/entries/ecology, retrieved March 26, 2020/; for the *Oxford English Dictionary*, see "resilience, n." at "II. Figurative uses . . . 5," OED Online, March 2020, www.oed.com/view/Entry/163619, retrieved April 19, 2020.

204   *Judith Rodin*: *The Resilience Dividend: Being Strong in a World Where Things Go Wrong* (New York: PublicAffairs, 2014), 135, "Who will take responsibility for improving readiness in the face of the vulnerabilities? Who should decide which vulnerabilities are most important to address and determine how to do so? Should readiness be an individual responsibility or taken on by a group? Should it be the responsibility of official bodies, such as government agencies, business associations, or health-care institutions, or by neighborhood or community groups?"

204   *its mission*: "About Us," Pret A Manger, September 27, 2015, Wayback Machine, retrieved February 26, 2020, https://web.archive.org/web/20150927175721/http://www.pret.com/en-us/about-pret.

204   *before Natasha's death*: The Pret A Manger "About Us" reads: "No Label Is Good: Fake Prets, petrol stations and high street goliaths provide refuge for the 'long-life sandwich.' How can you tell when a sandwich is a lifer? Easy. English law insists factory-produced long-life sandwiches are plastered with labels containing lots of boring numbers, names, dates and symbols. No label is good. Our food is freshly made and has no labels. Now you know how to spot the difference; boring but important."

205   *The coroner's report*: See paragraph 5(2) of Cummings, "Regulation 28: Report to Prevent Future Deaths."

206   *Manhattan jury found*: Weinstein was convicted on two of five charges; he was acquitted of the others, including first-degree rape and predatory sexual assault. See Manhattan district attorney Cy Vance's "Harvey Weinstein Convicted at Trial," https://www.manhattanda.org/d-a-vance-harvey-weinstein-convicted-at-trial/; and Deanna

Paul, "Harvey Weinstein Convicted of Some Sex Crimes, Acquitted of Others," *Wall Street Journal*, February 24, 2020, https://www.wsj.com/articles/weinstein-convicted -of-third-degree-rape-and-first-degree-criminal-sexual-act-11582562791.

206   *more than ninety women*: Dorothy Wickenden, "Rebecca Solnit on Harvey Weinstein and the Lies That Powerful Men Tell," *The New Yorker*, February 27, 2020, https:// www.newyorker.com/podcast/political-scene/rebecca-solnit-on-harvey-weinstein -and-the-lies-that-powerful-men-tell.

206   *additional criminal charges*: Los Angeles district attorney Jackie Lacey's Twit- ter announcement, March 11, 2019, https://twitter.com/LADAOffice/status /1237789612895899648; and Tom Hals, "Weinstein's Legal Problems Extend Beyond New York Criminal Trial," Reuters, February 19, 2020, https://www .reuters.com/article/us-people-harvey-weinstein-legal/weinsteins-legal-problems -extend-beyond-new-york-criminal-trial-idUSKBN20D1G3.

206   *London and Dublin*: "Harvey Weinstein: Met Police Investigate New Sex Assault Claims," BBC News, October 16, 2017, https://www.bbc.com/news/entertainment -arts-41629689; Conor Lally, "Harvey Weinstein Accused of Dublin Sexual Assault," *Irish Times*, February 5, 2018, https://www.irishtimes.com/news/crime-and-law /harvey-weinstein-accused-of-dublin-sexual-assault-1.3379899; and Shayna Jacobs, "Harvey Weinstein Charged with Multiple Sex Crimes in Los Angeles on the Same Day His Trial Begins in New York," *Washington Post*, January 6, 2020, https://www .washingtonpost.com/national-security/los-angeles-charges-announced-against -harvey-weinstein-as-his-manhattan-trial-begins/2020/01/06/74f3fb20-30b4-11ea -9313-6cba89b1b9fb_story.html.

206   The New Yorker: See the reporting of Ronan Farrow, starting with "From Ag- gressive Overtures to Sexual Assault: Harvey Weinstein's Accusers Tell Their Stories," *The New Yorker*, October 10, 2017, https://www.newyorker.com/news /news-desk/from-aggressive-overtures-to-sexual-assault-harvey-weinsteins-accusers -tell-their-stories.

206   *the* New York Times: See the reporting of Jodi Kantor and Megan Twohey, starting with "Harvey Weinstein Paid Off Sexual Harassment Accusers for Decades," *New York Times*, October 5, 2017, https://www.nytimes.com/2017/10/05/us/harvey -weinstein-harassment-allegations.html.

206   *one in three women*: See p. 1, "Sexual Violence by Any Perpetrator," in S. G. Smith, J. Chen, K. C. Basile, L. K. Gilbert, M. T. Merrick, N. Patel, M. Walling, and A. Jain, "The National Intimate Partner and Sexual Violence Survey (NISVS): 2010– 2012 State Report," 2017, National Center for Injury Prevention and Control, Divi- sion of Violence Prevention, Centers for Disease Control and Prevention, Atlanta, retrieved April 10, 2020, https://www.cdc.gov/violenceprevention/pdf/nisvs -statereportbook.pdf. And worldwide figures at "Violence Against Women," World Health Organization, November 29, 2017, https://www.who.int/en /news-room/fact-sheets/detail/violence-against-women, retrieved March 26, 2020; and "A Staggering One-in-Three Women Experience Physical, Sexual Abuse," UN News, Human Rights section, November 24, 2019, https://news.un.org /en/story/2019/11/1052041.

206   *transgender*: S. E. James, J. L. Herman, S. Rankin, M. Keisling, L. Mottet, and M. Anafi, *The Report of the 2015 U.S. Transgender Survey*, Washington, D.C.: National Center for Transgender Equality, p. 5, https://www.transequality.org/sites/default /files/docs/USTS-Full-Report-FINAL.PDF.

206   *seventy-one additional men*: Sarah Almukhtar, Michael Gold, and Larry Buchanan, "After Weinstein: 71 Men Accused of Sexual Misconduct and Their Fall from Power," *New York Times*, February 8, 2018, https://www.nytimes.com/interactive /2017/11/10/us/men-accused-sexual-misconduct-weinstein.html.

207   *Researchers at Yale*: Roee Levy and Martin Mattsson, "The Effects of Social Move-
      ments: Evidence from #MeToo," December 24, 2019, last revised April 1, 2020,
      available at SSRN, https://ssrn.com/abstract=3496903.

207   *Tarana Burke*: Jodi Kantor, "Weinstein Is Convicted. Where Does #MeToo Go from
      Here?" *New York Times*, February 26, 2020, https://www.nytimes.com/2020/02/26
      /us/harvey-weinstein-metoo-movement-future.html.

207   *"But, I'm innocent"*: Jan Ransom, "Harvey Weinstein Is Found Guilty of Sex Crimes
      in #MeToo Watershed," *New York Times*, February 24, 2020, https://www.nytimes
      .com/2020/02/24/nyregion/harvey-weinstein-trial-rape-verdict.html.

208   *Michael Jackson*: Andrew Dalton, "Lawsuits by Michael Jackson Accusers Likely
      to Be Restored," ABC News, November 18, 2019, https://abcnews.go.com
      /Entertainment/wireStory/lawsuits-michael-jackson-accusers-restored-67119968;
      and Ben Sisario, "What We Know About Michael Jackson's History of Sexual
      Abuse Accusations," *New York Times*, January 31, 2019, https://www.nytimes
      .com/2019/01/31/arts/music/michael-jackson-timeline-sexual-abuse-accusations
      .html; and "Michael Jackson," *FBI Records: The Vault*, https://vault.fbi.gov/Michael
      %20Jackson, retrieved April 16, 2020.

208   *James Watson*: Meilan Solly, "DNA Pioneer James Watson Loses Honorary Titles
      Over Racist Comments," *Smithsonian Magazine*, January 15, 2019, https://www
      .smithsonianmag.com/smart-news/dna-pioneer-james-watson-loses-honorary
      -titles-over-racist-comments-180971266/.

208   *Pablo Picasso*: See Mark Hudson, "Pablo Picasso: Women Are Either Goddesses or
      Doormats," *The Telegraph*, April 8, 2016, https://www.telegraph.co.uk/art/artists
      /pablo-picasso-women-are-either-goddesses-or-doormats/; Alan Riding, "Grandpa
      Picasso: Terribly Famous, Not Terribly Nice," *New York Times*, November 24, 2001,
      https://www.nytimes.com/2001/11/24/books/grandpa-picasso-terribly-famous
      -not-terribly-nice.html; Cody Delistraty, "How Picasso Bled the Women in His
      Life for Art," *The Paris Review*, November 9, 2017, https://www.theparisreview
      .org/blog/2017/11/09/how-picasso-bled-the-women-in-his-life-for-art/; Eudie Pak,
      "How Pablo Picasso's Wives and Mistresses Inspired His Art," June 21, 2019, *Biogra-
      phy*, https://www.biography.com/news/pablo-picasso-wives-mistresses-inspiration;
      and Charles McGrath's *New York Times* June 21, 2012, essay, "Good Art, Bad Peo-
      ple," in which he notes that "Picasso probably takes the prize here: of the seven
      main women in his life, two went mad and two killed themselves," https://www
      .nytimes.com/2012/06/22/opinion/global-agenda-magazine-good-art-bad-people
      .html.

208   *And to great success*: Madeline Berg, "After Expulsion from the Academy, Here Are
      All of Harvey Weinstein's 81 Oscar Wins," *Forbes*, October 13, 2017, https://www
      .forbes.com/sites/maddieberg/2017/10/13/here-are-all-of-harvey-weinsteins
      -oscar-wins/#2ad65955d946.

211   *Universities struggle*: For example, Yale University removed a carving on campus that
      "depicts a Puritan settler holding a musket pointed toward the head of a Native
      American." The piece was made available for study along with written material of
      its historical context. "Disarmament," *Yale Alumni Magazine*, updated August 22,
      2017, https://yalealumnimagazine.com/blog_posts/2695-disarmament. Stanford
      University decided to "rename some, but not all, features on campus named for Fa-
      ther [Junipero] Serra," an 18th-century Roman Catholic missionary, noting that while
      his legacy was "complex," the mission system "inflicted great harm and violence on
      Native Americans." "Frequently Asked Questions on Junipero Serra and Stanford,"
      September 13, 2018, https://news.stanford.edu/2018/09/13/naming-report-faq/.
      One of the Oxford colleges decided not to remove a statue of Cecil Rhodes, a British
      businessman, politician, and imperialist seen by many as the architect of apartheid:

Stephen Castle, "Oxford University Will Keep Statue of Cecil Rhodes," *New York Times*, January 29, 2016, https://www.nytimes.com/2016/01/30/world/europe /oxford-university-oriel-college-cecil-rhodes-statue.html.

211–12 *slave owner or eugenicist*: In 2019, the Eugenics at Stanford History Project formally requested that the school rename Jordan Hall, which honors David Starr Jordan, the founding president of Stanford and a vocal proponent of eugenics. See https://1e033807-0690-4644-9331-5b6e588f7c1e.filesusr.com/ugd/124541_2de 3923f00494368b05cccc68b83817f.pdf.

212 *Georgetown University's fundraising*: Rachel L. Swarns, "Is Georgetown's $400,000 -a-Year Plan to Aid Slave Descendants Enough?," *New York Times*, October 30, 2019, https://www.nytimes.com/2019/10/30/us/georgetown-slavery-reparations.html.

213 *"unintended offensive"*: Peter Lee, corporate vice president, Microsoft Healthcare, "Learning from Tay's Introduction," March 25, 2016, https://blogs.microsoft.com /blog/2016/03/25/learning-tays-introduction/, retrieved April 10, 2020.

214 *what Microsoft had learned*: Ibid.

214 *Justin Trudeau attended*: Trudeau wore brownface and blackface on two different occasions. Anna Purna Kambhampaty, Madeleine Carlisle, and Melissa Chan, "Justin Trudeau Wore Brownface at 2001 'Arabian Nights' Party While He Taught at a Private School," *Time*, September 19, 2019, https://time.com/5680759/justin -trudeau-brownface-photo/.

214 *"I shouldn't have done that"*: See Trudeau's September 18, 2019, statement to reporters at "Trudeau Apology: Brownface Unacceptable and Racist," Associated Press, YouTube, https://www.youtube.com/watch?v=ZkX85WL_tQA, in which he states: "When I was in high school, I dressed up at a talent show and sang 'Day-O' in, with, with makeup on." The next day, during a press conference, he added: "I appreciate calling it makeup but it was blackface and that is just not right" (video at Leyland Cecco, "Trudeau Says He Can't Recall How Many Times He Wore Blackface Makeup," *The Guardian*, September 20, 2019, https://www.theguardian.com /world/2019/sep/19/justin-trudeau-wearing-blackface-details-emerge-third -incident). See also Kambhampaty, Carlisle, and Chan, "Justin Trudeau Wore Brownface at 2001 'Arabian Nights' Party While He Taught at a Private School."

215 *Calhoun College*: As Yale president Peter Salovey said, "The decision to change a college's name is not one we take lightly, but John C. Calhoun's legacy as a white supremacist and a national leader who passionately promoted slavery as a 'positive good' fundamentally conflicts with Yale's mission and values." "Yale Changes Calhoun College's Name to Honor Grace Murray Hopper," *Yale News*, February 11, 2017, https://news.yale.edu/2017/02/11/yale-change-calhoun-college-s-name -honor-grace-murray-hopper-0.

217 *"zero tolerance"*: Susan Liautaud, *Ethics on the Edge* (blog), "Arbitrary Ethics," https:// susanliautaud.com/arbitrary-ethics/.

217 *Disney CEO Robert Iger*: Robert Iger, *The Ride of a Lifetime* (New York: Random House, 2019), 211–13.

SUSAN LIAUTAUD is the founder and managing director of Susan Liautaud & Associates Limited, which advises clients from global corporations to NGOs on complex ethics matters. She teaches cutting-edge ethics courses at Stanford University, serves as Chair of Council at the London School of Economics and Political Science, and is the founder of the nonprofit platform The Ethics Incubator. She also chairs and serves on a number of global nonprofit boards. She divides her time between Palo Alto, California, and London.